Progress to First Certificate

New Edition

SELF-STUDY STUDENT'S BOOK

Leo Jones

Cambridge University Press
Cambridge
New York   Port Chester
Melbourne   Sydney

Published by the Press Syndicate of the University of Cambridge
The Pitt Building, Trumpington Street, Cambridge CB2 1RP
40 West 20th Street, New York, NY 10011, USA
10 Stamford Road, Oakleigh, Melbourne 3166, Australia

© Cambridge University Press 1983, 1990

First published 1983
Fifth printing 1988
Second edition 1990

Printed in Great Britain
by Scotprint Ltd, Musselburgh, Scotland

ISBN 0 521 37958 X Self-study Student's Book
ISBN 0 521 37959 8 Student's Book
ISBN 0 521 37957 1 Teacher's Book
ISBN 0 521 37096 5 Set of 2 Cassettes

Copyright
The law allows a reader to make a single copy of part of a book for purposes of private study. It does not allow the copying of entire books or the making of multiple copies of extracts. Written permission for any such copying must always be obtained from the publisher in advance.

CE

Contents

    Thanks   iv
    Acknowledgements   v
    Welcome!   1
1   **Shopping**   2
2   **Leisure activities**   17
3   **Nature and the environment**   31
4   **Transport and travel**   45
5   **Somewhere to live**   60
6   **Science and technology**   72
7   **Good health!**   85
8   **Holidays**   100
9   **Books and reading**   116
10   **Food and drink**   134
11   **Work and business**   147
12   **In the news**   164
13   **People**   178
14   **The past**   193
    Communication activities   209

    To the self-study student   226
    Notes and answer key for each unit   229

Thanks

No book of this kind can be produced by one person alone and in this case countless people have generously contributed their ideas and advice.

In particular, I'd just like to say how grateful I am to the following friends, colleagues and teachers:
- Jeanne McCarten for guiding the New Edition through from start to finish and for her encouragement, perfectionism and good ideas
- Jill Mountain and Kit Woods for their detailed comments on the first edition and for subsequently reading, evaluating and suggesting improvements to the first draft of this New Edition
- Alison Silver for her editing expertise and sensible suggestions
- Peter Taylor and Studio AVP for their professional skills in producing the recorded material
- Peter Ducker for his meticulous work on the illustrations and design
- Sue Gosling for her help and advice

And thanks to the following teachers whose detailed comments on the first edition and helpful ideas led to many valuable changes in the New Edition:
- Susan Barber, Lake School of English in Oxford
- John Bradbury, FIAC Escola d'idiomes moderns in Sabadell, Catalonia, Spain
- Susan Garvin, British Institute of Florence, Italy
- Roger Johnson and Nick Kenny, British Council in Milan, Italy
- Fern Judet, Swan School in Oxford
- Lynne White, Godmer House School of English in Oxford

And thanks to the following teachers who kindly wrote about their experiences of using the first edition, some of whom gave us their students' feedback:
- H. G. Bernhardt, Tony Buckby and colleagues, J. Carvell, Emily Grammenou, Michael Hadgimichalis, Pearl Herrmann, Jill Jeavons, Katherine Karangianni, Marie Anne Küpper-Compes, Bryan Newman, Cathy Parker and colleagues, Véronique Rouanet, Claire Springett, Andrew Tymn, Robin Visel and J. T. Ward

Finally thanks to the numerous other teachers in many different countries (and their students) who have given us useful informal feedback on the first edition.

Thank you, everyone!

From the first edition

I'd like to express my thanks to Sue Gosling and Christine Cairns for all their encouragement and help during the planning, writing and rewriting of this book. Many thanks also to the teachers who used the pilot edition and made so many useful and perceptive comments. Thanks are due in particular to staff at the following schools and institutes: the British Centre in Venice, the British Institute in Paris, the British School in Florence, the Newnham Language Centre in Cambridge, the Studio School of English in Cambridge and the Université II in Lyons.

Acknowledgements

The author and publishers are grateful to the authors, publishers and others who have given permission for the use of copyright material identified in the text. It has not been possible to identify the sources of all the material used and in such cases the publishers would welcome information from copyright owners.

Dover Publications, Inc. for the pictograms throughout the book from *Handbook of Pictorial Symbols; 3,250 Examples from International Sources* by Rudolf Modley; J. Sainsbury for the pictogram on p. 31; Harrods Ltd for the photograph on p. 3; Stambouli frères s.a. for the advertisement on p. 9; Discoveries for the advertisements (top left, centre, bottom) on p. 11; Première (Issue 2) for the advertisement (top right) on p. 11; *Punch* for the cartoons on pp. 16, 23, 30, 35, 44, 50, 58, 67, 79, 81, 84, 90, 93, 110, 121, 131, 146, 150, 159, 166, 168, 171, 199, 205, 208; *The Illustrated London News* Picture Library for the extract on p. 25; Penguin Books Ltd for the extract on p. 32 from the *Penguin Book of the Natural World*, the extract on pp. 118–9 from *Call for the Dead* by John Le Carré © Victor Gollancz 1961, the cover on p. 125 of *Jupiter's Travels* by Ted Simon © Penguin Books 1980, and the cover on p. 126 of *The Human Factor* by Graham Greene © Penguin Books 1978; *The Guardian* and The Meteorological Office for the chart on p. 38 and the weather summary on p. 213 © The Meteorological Office, based on Crown copyright information; Barnaby's Picture Library for the photograph (top left) on p. 43; Oxfam for the photograph (top right) by Jeremy Hartley on p. 43; Camera Press Ltd for the photograph (bottom right) on p. 43; Venice Simplon – Orient-Express for the map on p. 46; British Airways for the advertisement on p. 53 and the photograph (right) on p. 163; British Railways Board for the map on p. 54; Ordnance Survey and W. Heffer & Sons Ltd for the map on p. 56; *The Observer* for the photographs on p. 61 (top), p. 96 (left) and p. 163 (centre); Greek National Tourist Organisation for the photograph on p. 61 (bottom) by Yannis Scouroyannis; *The Guardian* for the article by David Sharrock on p. 64, the article on p. 73 © Associated Press, the article by Jane McLoughlin on p. 158, the article by Derek Brown on p. 165, the article by Michael White and the map on p. 172 © *The Guardian*; BBC Education for the diagram on p. 77; The Consumers' Association for the article on p. 80; The Health Education Council for the extract on p. 87 and the photograph (right) on p. 96; *The Economist* for the chart on p. 88; *Radio Times* for the extract on p. 94; Kuoni Travel Ltd for the extract on p. 102; *The Daily Telegraph* Colour Library for the photograph (top left) on p. 106; Silk Cut Travel Ltd for the photographs (centre left and right) on p. 106; HF Holidays Ltd for the photographs (top right and bottom left) on p. 106; Yugoslav National Tourist Board for the advertisement (top) on p. 107; Wings Ltd for the extract on p. 109; Longman for the extract on p. 118 from *Call for the Dead* by John Le Carré © Longman Group Ltd; Grafton Books for the cover on p. 123 of *To Be the Best* by

Barbara Taylor Bradford; Grafton Books and Warner Bros Inc. for the cover on p. 125 of *Empire of the Sun* by J. G. Ballard; Michael Joseph Ltd for the cover on p. 123 of *Zoya* by Danielle Steele; Sidgwick & Jackson for the cover on p. 123 of *Savages* by Shirley Conran; Corgi Books for the cover on p. 123 of *Alaska* by James A. Michener; Collins Publishers for the covers of *Glamorous Powers* by Susan Howatch on p. 123 and *Send No More Roses* by Eric Ambler on p. 126; Mills & Boon Ltd and Harlequin Enterprises B.V. for the cover on p. 125 of *Hills of Kalamata* by Anne Hampson; Reinhardt Books for the extract on pp. 127–8 from *The Captain and the Enemy* by Graham Greene © Graham Greene; Jeremy Pembrey for the photographs on pp. 144, 163 (left), 176 (left and right), 220 and 225; Midland Bank PLC for the extract on p. 149 from 'Cheque In'; *Cambridge Evening News* for the photograph (top) on p. 169; *The Guardian* for the photograph (left) on p. 169; S & G Press Agency Ltd for the photograph (centre right) on p. 169; Barnaby's Picture Library for the photograph (bottom right) by Brian L. Arundale on p. 169; Dateline for the extract on pp. 180–2; Curtis Brown Ltd for the extract on pp. 187–8 from *Mr Norris Changes Trains* © 1935 by Christopher Isherwood; Hutchinson Publishing Group Ltd and Random House Inc. for the extract on p. 195 from *Hutchinson History of the World* by J. M. Roberts; Jorvik Viking Centre for the extract on p. 196; Jarrold Colour Publications for the photograph (right) on p. 203; Department of Tourism, York for the photograph (left) on p. 203; Leeds Castle Enterprises Ltd for the extract on p. 207; John Topham Picture Library for the photographs on pp. 213 (centre) and 215 (centre); Benetton and Brigitte Jacquety Ltd for the photograph (top) on p. 215; Spillers Foods for the photograph on p. 219 by Arthur Siddy from Spillers Kattomeat Calendar 1988; Syndication International Ltd for the photograph on p. 223.

Photographs by the author: pp. 43 (bottom left), 69, 106 (bottom right), 213 (top).
Illustrations by Leslie Marshall on p. 26; Trevor Ridley on pp. 28, 191; Clyde Pearson on pp. 135, 204, 205; David Mostyn on pp. 214, 216, 224; Chris Pavely on pp. 218, 220, 225; Thomas Jones on p. 218; Zoë Jones on p. 221.
Artwork by Julie Sailing, Wenham Arts, Joanne Barker, Joanne Currie, Peter Ducker and Hardlines.
Art direction by Peter Ducker MSTD

Welcome!

This book is designed to prepare you progressively for the Cambridge First Certificate in English examination (FCE). The exercises and activities will help you to learn and not just test your knowledge. The nature of the exercises and activities changes gradually through the book until, by the time you reach Unit 14, you'll be answering questions which are just the same as the ones you'll have to answer in the exam itself. Towards the end of the book, the exercises become more like tests with, for example, multiple-choice questions to answer.

To help you to prepare for the FCE exam, the sections in each unit concentrate on different parts of the exam:
▶ Paper 1: Reading Comprehension
    Vocabulary and Reading exercises
▶ Paper 2: Composition
    Composition exercises (towards the end of each unit)
▶ Paper 3: Use of English
    Exercises on Grammar, Word study, Verbs and idioms, Prepositions and Problem solving (directed writing)
▶ Paper 4: Listening Comprehension
    Listening activities, based on the cassettes
▶ Paper 5: Interview
    Communication activities, Pronunciation exercises, Picture conversations and discussion questions

Each unit is based on a different topic and all the exercises and activities in the unit are related to the topic. These topics are the ones that are most likely to come up in the exam – but, perhaps more important, they are topics which will interest you and give you plenty to talk about.

Activities shown with ![] in the main part of the book are Communication Activities, where, if you are working with a partner, you are each given different information that you must communicate to each other. These are printed on pages 209–225. They are 'mixed up' so that your partner can't see your information. If you are working on your own, instructions on how to do the Communication Activities are given in the section **To the self-study student**.

![] indicates that there is recorded material on the cassettes.
★ indicates advice, points to remember or exam tips.

IF YOU ARE WORKING ON YOUR OWN, please see the section **To the self-study student** on pages 226–326, which contains everything you need, including instructions, answers and model compositions, tapescripts, extra ideas and advice.

Good luck during your exam course – enjoy using *Progress to First Certificate*!

1 Shopping

1.1 Shopping habits   *Vocabulary*

A Work in groups or pairs. Ask your partners these questions:
- What kinds of shops are there near your school or college?
- Which ones have you been in?
- Where are the best shops in this town for food, clothes, books, music or shoes?
- What kind of shops do you never or hardly ever go into? Why?
- What kind of shops do you go into at least once a month? Why?
- Which particular shop do you go to most often?

B Find the missing words to complete each sentence. In some cases there are several possible answers. The first one is done for you as an example:

1. In a shop you can use a credit card or charge card, or you can pay in c**ash**.
2. If you're paying by cheque, don't forget to put your s............ at the bottom.
3. Someone who owns a small shop and who serves people in it is called a s............
4. Someone who is employed to serve customers in a shop or store is a s............ a............
5. The salesperson in a shop usually serves the customers from behind a c............
6. Salesperson: 'Can I h............ you?' Customer: 'No, it's all right, thanks. I'm just l............'
7. This real leather handbag was reduced in the summer s............, so I only had to pay £5.95 – it was a real b............!
8. The assistant added up the prices to find the t............ price we had to pay.
9. In case you want to exchange something, remember to keep the r............
10. If the radio goes wrong within twelve months, remember it's still under g............
11. A large store may lose some of its stock as a result of theft or s............
12. If you want something for your headache you can get it at a c............
13. It's unwise to buy new shoes or sandals without first t............ them on.
14. I wanted to buy some walking boots but they hadn't got my s............
15. I've tried on this coat and it doesn't f............ me, it's a bit too
16. I'm going to ask if they have any yellow cotton socks in s............
17. Yellow socks won't m............ your sweater and anyway yellow doesn't s............ you.
18. To find out how to wash a garment, look at the instructions on the l............
19. You can usually get goods cheaper if you buy them in an open-air m............
20. If you have a student identity card, some shops may give you a d............
21. Fruit and vegetables in a supermarket aren't as fresh as at a g............
22. You can spread the payments over twelve months by buying something on h............ p............
23. You can get almost anything you want in a big d............ s............ but some people prefer to buy things by m............ o............
24. If something is too heavy for you to carry home yourself, the shop can d............ it.
25. Personally speaking, I'd say that going shopping is ....

2

C   Work in groups or pairs. Imagine that you have to do some shopping BUT there is no department store or supermarket in the area. What sort of shops can you buy these items in? The first is done for you as an example:

1 *half a dozen bananas and a newspaper*
   Greengrocer's or fruit shop AND a newsagent's or kiosk
2 *a street plan of your town or city and a guidebook about your country*
3 *a litre of milk – and a glass to drink it from*
4 *a kilo of tomatoes – and a knife to cut them with*
5 *some sausages for dinner – and a frying pan to cook them in*
6 *a bottle of white wine – and a corkscrew to open it with*
7 *a personal stereo – and some cassettes to play on it*
8 *a loaf of bread and some butter to spread on it*
9 *a notebook and a pen to write in it with*
10 *a tube of toothpaste and a new toothbrush*
11 *a picture postcard to send to a friend abroad – and a stamp to stick on it*

D   Continue working in groups or pairs. Look at each other's CLOTHES. What are you all wearing at the moment? Make sure you can describe each item of clothing in English and its colour or pattern. What would you be wearing if it was much colder today? What do you wear if you want to look extra smart?

1.2   Enter a different world   *Reading*

A   Harrods is a famous department store in London. Before you read the passage on the next page, look at these statements and see if you can guess which are true (**T**) and which are false (**F**). The first is done as an example:

1 Everyone who visits London goes to Harrods.   *False – but many people do*
2 Harrods is one of the sights of London.
3 Harrods sells five million different products.
4 The only thing you can't buy at Harrods is an elephant.
5 Some of the Queen's food is bought at Harrods.
6 Harrods' new warehouse will be the largest in Europe.

Now read the text to find out if you guessed right.

3

HARRODS LIMITED

Knightsbridge London SW1X 7XL

Telephone 01-730 1234   Telegrams Harrods London Telex   Telex 24319

REGISTERED IN LONDON NO. 30205   REGISTERED OFFICE: 87/135 BROMPTON ROAD LONDON SW1X 7XL

ENTER A DIFFERENT WORLD

Welcome to Harrods – a different world for a million reasons. Harrods is the largest store in Europe with goods displayed in 60 windows and 5½ hectares of selling space. In one year over 14 million purchases are made in the 214 departments where you can buy anything from a pin to an elephant – if you can convince the manager of the Pet Department that you are a suitable elephant owner, that is! It is Harrods' policy to stock a wide and exciting range of merchandise in every department to give the customer a choice of goods which is unique in its variety and which no other store can match: Harrods stocks 100 different whiskies, including 57 single malts, 450 different cheeses, 500 types of shirts and 9,000 ties to go with them, 8,000 dresses and 150 different pianos.

Harrods also offers a number of special services to its customers including a bank, an insurance department, a travel agency, London's last circulating library, a theatre ticket agency and a funeral service. £40 million worth of goods are exported annually from Harrods and the Export Department can deal with any customer purchase or order and will pack and send goods to any address in the world. Recently, for example, six bread rolls were sent to New York, a handkerchief to Los Angeles, a pound of sausages to a yacht anchored in the Mediterranean, a Persian carpet to Iran and a £5,000 chess set to Australia. Harrods has a world-wide reputation for first-class service. It has a staff of 4,000, rising to 6,000 at Christmas time.

Harrods sells 5 million different products, not all of which are actually kept in stock in the store itself. To handle this enormous range, a new computerised warehouse is being built. It will be the largest warehouse in Britain and the second largest in Europe and will deal with a wider range of goods than any other distribution centre in the world. Thanks to its modern technology a customer will be able to order any product (for example, a dining table or a dishwasher) from any assistant in the store. The assistant will be able to check its availability immediately on a computer screen, decide with the customer on a suitable delivery date and time and then pass the order directly to the warehouse through the computer. The time of delivery will be guaranteed to within one hour.

For many of London's visitors Harrods is an important stop on their sightseeing programme. Henry Charles Harrod's first shop was opened in 1849, but the building as it stands today was started in 1901 and it has become one of London's landmarks. It has many items of architectural interest: the plaster ceilings are original, as is the famous Meat Hall with its Victorian wall tiles, and the light fittings on the ground floor date back to the 1930s. A morning spent strolling round Harrods is guaranteed to give any shopper an appetite, and to feed its customers Harrods has six restaurants, ranging from the Circle self-service restaurants offering delicious food at reasonable prices to the famous Harrods Restaurant, where queues form every afternoon for the 'Grand Buffet Tea', which for a fixed price allows you to eat as many cream cakes and gateaux as your greed will allow while waitresses serve you with India or China tea. If you feel like a drink you can choose between the pub atmosphere of the Green Man Tavern and the sophistication of the Cocktail Lounge. Harrods truly is a different world.

B Decide whether the following statements are true (**T**) or false (**F**), according to the passage. Find and underline the words in the text that help you to answer each question.

1 The Pet Department will sell an elephant to any customer who can afford one.
2 Other stores are unable to match Harrods' range of merchandise.
3 There are 500 shirts for sale in Harrods.
4 Harrods stocks 100 different brands of malt whisky.
5 You can borrow books from Harrods.
6 You can arrange for a dead body to be buried by Harrods.
7 A customer once asked to have a handkerchief sent to the USA.
8 Harrods exports over £3 million worth of goods a month.
9 Harrods employs 6,000 regular staff.
10 A greater variety of products will go through the new warehouse than any other in the world.
11 To obtain a product that isn't in the store, a customer has to go to the warehouse.
12 When the new computerised system is operating, any product will be delivered an hour after you have placed the order.
13 The wall tiles in the Meat Hall were made in 1849.
14 The restaurants at Harrods are good but very expensive.
15 You can eat as much as you like at the 'Grand Buffet Tea' for a fixed price.

When you have finished, compare your answers with a partner's. If you disagree about any of the answers, look again at the text to check who was right.

C Work in groups and discuss these questions.

1 What are the **advantages** and **disadvantages** of shopping in a department store? Make a list, considering the following points:
    price   choice   service   quality   convenience
2 What would you personally **never** buy in a department store – and why?
3 What products can you **not** buy in department stores in your town or city? Where would you buy these items instead?

1.3 Present tenses *Grammar*

■ The grammar sections in *Progress to First Certificate* are meant to help you to REVISE grammar points you have probably studied before. The examples and exercises cover the main difficulties that students at your level have with English grammar – but more elementary and more advanced points are not covered.

A These examples show the most common uses of present tenses in English. Fill the gaps with more examples, using your own ideas. The first is done for you as an example:

Permanent or regular actions and situations:
I always have two cups of coffee for breakfast.   PRESENT SIMPLE
Where do you live?   (= What is your permanent address?)
After lunch I sometimes have a cup of black coffee.
I never _never have a cup of black coffee._
Every evening I _have a glass of milk._

Temporary, developing or changing actions and situations:
I'm trying to concentrate, so please don't interrupt.   PRESENT PROGRESSIVE
Where are you living?   (= What is your temporary address?)
At the moment I _am living at my uncles house._
I _am studying on_ a First Certificate course this year.

Actions or situations begun in the past and still true now or continuing now:
Someone has eaten all the cakes.   PRESENT PERFECT SIMPLE
I've never smoked a cigar in my life.
We _have been working for_ hours on this unit so far.

We've been waiting for twenty minutes.   PRESENT PERFECT PROGRESSIVE
What have you been doing since we last met?
I _have been_ English for _nearly a_ years.

■ Remember that FOR is used with a period of time and SINCE is used with a point of time. For example:
for two years   for a long time   for a few minutes   for the last three days
(NOT: since two years ✗)
since 1988   since yesterday   since 5 o'clock   since lunchtime   since April

B Some verbs (STATIVE VERBS) are not normally used in the progressive form, because they usually refer to permanent states or situations.

How much does this cost?   NOT: How much is this costing? ✗
She has owned a car for two years.   NOT: She has been owning a car ... ✗

Write a sentence using each of these stative verbs in NEGATIVE sentences. The first three are done for you as examples:

believe   contain   cost   deserve   fit   know   like   look like   love
matter   owe   realise   remember   seem   smell   suit   understand

I used to believe that shopping was fun, but now I don't believe that any more.
This yogurt doesn't contain any sugar.
A dictionary doesn't cost very much to buy.

C Decide which adverbs from the list below fit into the gaps in these sentences. The first two are done for you as examples:

1 She's looking for a new summer outfit in Harrods ....
2 He .... buys his clothes at Harrods.
3 He goes shopping ....
4 She has been feeling unwell ....

all day 4	always 2	once in a while 4	usually 2
at the moment 1	generally	today 4	frequently 2 3
from time to time	often 2	for a week	now 1
occasionally 3	this morning 1	for a long time 4	since Tuesday 4
sometimes 2	for a long time 4	never	
every week 3	hardly ever 3	rarely	

D Six of these sentences contain errors and two are correct. Find the errors and correct them. The first is done for you as an example:

                   contains
1 This packet ~~is containing~~ 500 grams of coffee.
2 At the moment I read a fascinating book.
3 I'm sometimes buying clothes in the market.
4 I've been waiting for them to arrive since 12 o'clock.
5 My mother prefer to buy fruit in the market.
6 I am waiting since 9 o'clock.
7 This CD is costing £10.99.
8 How are you feeling today? Better I hope!

E Complete the unfinished sentences in this dialogue. The first one is done for you as an example:

Customer: Oh, thanks very much. And I think I'll keep these jeans on now. Do _you mind if I pay by credit cards_ ?
Assistant: Yes, we take all major credit cards.
Customer: Good, here you are.
Assistant: Thanks. Let me just cut off the label ... there we are! And if you could just sign here ...

1.4 I had to go to the shops ...   *Listening*

A Before you hear the recording read these statements through. Then listen to the recording and decide whether they are true (**T**) or false (**F**), according to the conversation. The first is done as an example. Listen to the recording more than once to get all the information, if necessary.

1 Tim is late because he has been shopping. **T**
2 There would be no time for Tim to go shopping in the evening. T
3 Tim didn't use the 'fast' checkout because there was a longer queue there. T
4 Tim enjoys shopping for food. F
5 Ann likes buying presents for people. F
6 Tim likes buying presents for people.
7 Both Tim and Ann like looking for bargains in the sales. F
8 Ann hates shopping at Christmas.
9 Both Tim and Ann like small shops.
10 Tim agrees that supermarket prices are lower.
11 Ann likes mail order shopping.
12 Tim looks forward to automated shopping by computer. F

B Match these products to the containers in which they're sold. How do they fit into this sentence:
  Could you get me a _bottle_ of _milk_, please?

CONTAINERS bottle box can carton jar bar packet tin tube
PRODUCTS   biscuits chocolate Coke honey matches milk
            mineral water peas toothpaste

1.5 Abbreviations and numbers   *Word study*

A Work in pairs. Look at these common abbreviations and write down what each one stands for. The first is done for you as an example:

approx. **approximately**
c/o   intro.   RSVP   care of introduction
cont'd   max.   VAT   continued maximum
GMT   min.   VIP   Greenwich Mean Time minimum
incl.   misc.   vocab. including / inclusive miscellaneously
info.   PTO   Xmas   information please turn over
                                                        christmas

PSVP Please reply to this invitation répondez s'il vous plaît
Very important person a celebrity value added tax vocabulary

8

B Write these numbers out in full. The first is done as an example:

333   three hundred and thirty-three
144   850,000 $\frac{7}{8}$
113   5.75 $1\frac{1}{4} + 2\frac{2}{3} = 3.9167$
227   1,992 $4\frac{3}{4} - 2\frac{1}{2} = 2.25$

When you've finished, compare your answers with a partner.

C 🎧 Listen to the recording and write down the numbers you hear. The first six are telephone numbers, and the rest are different kinds of numbers. The first is done for you as an example:

1 'Five one eight O four double seven'   5180477

When you've finished, compare your answers with a partner. If necessary, listen to the recording again to check your answers.

D 🎬 Work in pairs. One of you should look at Activity 1 (on page 209), the other at Activity 10 (on page 212). You'll each have some names, addresses and phone numbers that you must dictate to your partner. Write down all the information that your partner gives you.

1.6 Advertisements

Speaking and listening

A Look at this advertisement. Imagine that you want to describe it to a friend who hasn't seen it.

- What would you tell them about it?
- What do you find amusing or interesting about the product advertised?

B 🎭 Work in pairs. One of you should look at Activity 13, the other at 20. You'll each see an advertisement that you will have to describe to your partner.

C 📼 You'll hear five authentic radio commercials. Listen to the recording and fill the gaps in these sentences, using the information given.

1 HARRODS is open on August 29th (Bank Holiday Monday) from ...10... a.m. to ...5... p.m.
2 FILIPPO BERIO is a brand of ...olive oil...
   'Filippo Berio olive oils – the natural choice.'
3 HEATBUSTERS can help to make your office ...cold... in ...hot... weather. Heatbusters supply ...portable... air conditioning on hire.
   'Call Freefone Heatbusters – no sweat.'
4 CITRUS SPRING is a sparkling blend of ...spring... water and ...natural orange... juice.
   'Citrus Spring, the ...seriously... fruity drink.'
5 Lucy persuaded Dirk Studebaker to get out of his car by cooking him a meal.
   'I cooked him dinner: frankfurters and ...fries...
   with two ...hamburgers... and for a surprise,
   we had some gammon with a ...pineapple... ring,
   that's what I cooked him.' 'Did you miss ...anything...?' 'Don't think so.'
   'Was the ...ketchup... on the side of his plate?'
   'It was Heinz, it was Heinz on his plate.'
   'Give me more, give me more of that Heinz ketchup taste.
   Eat it all, eat it all, 'cause it's too good to ...waste...
   'Are you seeing Dirk again tonight, Lucy?' 'You betcha !!*'
   'Heinz is the ketchup so ...thick... and so ...smooth...
   Heinz is the ketchup for ...dinner... for two.'

* Yes, definitely!!

When you've finished, compare your answers with a partner. Which of the products would YOU buy and/or not buy?

D Work in groups. Look at some more magazine or newspaper advertisements. IF POSSIBLE, CUT SOME INTERESTING ADVERTISEMENTS OUT OF MAGAZINES AND BRING THEM TO CLASS TO DISCUSS.

- Which is the most attractive and the least attractive? Why?
- Which is the most amusing? Why?
- Which is the most effective and the least effective? Why?

E Describe your favourite AND most hated TV commercials to your partners.

1.7 Which gift? *Problem solving*

The problem-solving sections in *Progress to First Certificate* will help you to deal with the last question in the Use of English paper. In this part of the exam you will have to extract information from a text, advertisement, picture or diagram and then rewrite some of it in your own words.

A Work in small groups. Ask your partners these questions:
- What points do you consider when buying a present for a friend or relation?
- What kind of gifts do you like to receive?

B Read about these products and note down the MAIN ATTRACTION of each one. Which of them (if any) would YOU like to receive as a gift?

Voice Over Could you be a pop star? Like to sing? If so, this is for you. Using this little unit with your personal or home hi-fi you can sing over your favourite tape and record the result at studio quality. The mixer unit includes echo effect, stereo headphones/microphone, a tape of popular backing tracks and a booklet of lyrics. You can sing solo or with a friend. The Voice Over can also be used with any electronic instrument.

£39.95

The Alarm Wallet It looks like a high-quality leather wallet made of soft leather. Inside, there are special pockets for credit cards, loose change, tickets and stamps – as well as two full length pockets for notes.

It would be a shame to lose such an attractive, practical wallet – but you won't, because under the gold-coloured plate on the front is a light-sensitive cell. When you put the wallet into your pocket, slide the plate to the left. If anyone removes the wallet from the darkness of your pocket or handbag (or if it just falls out) a loud electronic alarm will sound. With the Alarm Wallet, you'll never lose your wallet again!

£14.95 (incl. battery)

Shopper Calculator Just what you need for those trips to the supermarket. This handy calculator will add up the prices as you go, so that you'll know how much you have spent before you reach the till. You can also use it to work out whether that large packet is really cheaper than two smaller ones. Complete with trolley attachment and neck cord.

£5.95 (white or black)

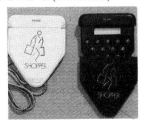

Beach Chair The only companion you need for a day in the sun. Made from strong yellow nylon with a lightweight steel frame, the Beach Chair is easy to carry but has masses of room in its insulated cool bag to hold refreshments, sun-tan oil etc., keeping them cool and out of the heat. There's even space for a magazine or sunshade.

Unfolded, it's a comfortable chair for sunbathing or just relaxing with a good book. Just what you need for holidays or weekends. **£14.95**

C Imagine that your two friends, Chris and Jo, have birthdays very soon:

CHRIS is a student, a person who likes being out of doors, enjoys playing sports and also watching sport on TV. Chris also likes learning languages and enjoys shopping – especially in supermarkets! Next summer Chris hopes to go to the USA to work in a summer vacation camp for children to earn enough money to spend two weeks travelling round the country.

JO is a student who likes reading, going to the cinema and listening to music – and also plays the guitar and likes singing. Jo also enjoys swimming and lives near the sea and in the summer holidays often spends the day at the beach. The other members of Jo's family all work, so Jo is the one who has to do all the shopping for the family.

1 Work in pairs or groups. From the items shown in B, choose a gift for Chris and a gift for Jo. Decide first if they are male or female friends – this isn't clear from their names. If a price seems too high, you could share the cost with your partners. MAKE NOTES of the reasons:
 • why each friend would appreciate the gift you have chosen
 • what uses he or she would find for it
 • AND why the other products would be less suitable.

2 Look at Activity 4, where you will see some model notes.

D Now write two paragraphs, explaining which of the gifts you would buy for Chris and Jo. Here are some structures you could use:

As Jo likes _____, the ideal gift would be ...
Jo enjoys _____ and _____, so ...
_____ would be a suitable gift for Jo because ...

When you've finished, compare your written work with a partner's work. Then look at Activity 27, where you will see two model paragraphs.

1.8 Using prepositions – Revision *Use of English*

about   at   by   down   for   in   of   off
on   out of   over   to   under   up   with

This exercise gives you a chance to TEST YOUR KNOWLEDGE of some prepositions and adverbs that you should already know.
 Fill the gaps in these sentences with a suitable preposition from the list above. The first is done for you as an example:

1 A is ..**for**.. apple.
2 Chris is a very good friend ..of.. mine.
3 We both share a love ..of.. music.
4 It's warm ..for.. the time of year.
5 I've been waiting ..for.. an hour.
6 I'm looking for a book ..about.. animals.
7 Why have you got that funny hat ..on..?

8 Our arrangement for tomorrow is ...off...
9 Hamlet was written ...by... Shakespeare.
10 I've read the works ...of... Shakespeare.
11 We'll discuss this ...at... lunch. over
12 When does the train ...for... London leave?
13 Part-time workers are paid ...by... the hour.
14 When will she be ...out... hospital? of
15 I can't see because the lights are ...off...
16 The shops are closed ...on... Sundays.
17 On Monday I'm taking the day ...off...
18 The bill must be paid ...by on... Monday.
19 When you leave, make sure the gas is ...off...
20 I bought it ...for... £3 in a second-hand shop.
21 I opened the can ...with... a can opener.
22 This pullover is a bargain ...at... £13.99.
23 I was ...about... to go out when the phone rang.
24 Liverpool won ...by... 3 goals ...to... 0.
25 Harrods is a famous store ...in... London.
26 Ships are made ...of... steel.
27 I'm just ...in... to town to do some shopping.
28 Cambridge is 100 km north ...of... London.
29 My brother is very good ...at... maths.
30 Now, I think all our problems are ...over...
31 He gave me a pat ...on... the back.
32 The total cost is ...under... £100. over
33 He was wearing a coat ...with... a torn sleeve.

When you've finished, compare your answers with a partner.

1.9 Buying a camera   *Listening*

A Before you listen to the recording, look at these instructions. From your own knowledge of photography, note down in the gaps any information that you expect will be given. Use a pencil.

ACME INSTAMATIC CAMERA £29.95

SPECIAL OFFER £19.95

INSTRUCTIONS
1 Load film cassette.
2 Set film speed to ...100... or ...400...
3 Press WIND lever till ...'1'... appears in the small ...window...
4 Set focus to symbol of ...face... for close-ups or ...mountain... for landscapes.
5 Press shutter very ...slowly...
  If ...green... light appears, shoot picture.
  If ...red... light appears, switch to ...flash...
6 Wind film on for next shot.

B 🔊 Listen to the recording and fill the gaps in the instructions on the previous page.

When you've finished, compare your answers with a partner. If you had to leave any gaps, or if you disagree about any of the information, listen to the recording again.

C 🏆 The class is divided into an even number of pairs or groups. Half the groups should look at Activity 16, the others at 23. You'll be discussing what advice you'd give to someone on buying something they haven't bought before.

1.10 Starting out... *Composition*

A Even a good composition looks bad if it contains too many spelling mistakes. There are sixteen typical mistakes in these sentences. Find the errors and correct them. The first is done for you as an example:

> *address*
> Please let me know your adress.
> My brother is ninteen years old.
> One day he's hopping to go to Amerika.
> It was a realy wonderfull meal!
> I recieved your letter this morning.
> He want to improve his knoldge of english.
> Concorde flys across the Atlantic in 4 ours.
> Some people find speling especialy dificult.

★ Most spelling errors can be avoided if you use a dictionary to look up any words you're unsure of – and if you check your written work carefully.

B Another problem is punctuation: especially the use of commas and apostrophes. Here is another student's work. Find the punctuation mistakes and correct them. The first is done as an example:

> *London's*
> Harrods is Londons most famous department store, You can buy almost anything there and its one of the Landmark's of London? people come to eat at it's Restaurants and look round its' 214 Departments But not everyone comes to buy many of the people who go there are just having a look at the enormous range of goods on display and at the other customers

C This paragraph has no punctuation at all! Rewrite it, adding any punctuation necessary.

Every Tuesday Friday and Saturday in our part of the city theres an open-air market in the main square which everyone goes to Farmers come in from the countryside to sell their fresh vegetables and fruit Other stalls sell all kinds of things cheese jeans fish and even second-hand furniture Its almost impossible to carry on a conversation above the noise and shouting as customers push their way to the front trying to attract the stall-holders attention and demanding the ripest freshest fruit or the lowest prices

You'll find a corrected version of this paragraph in Activity 37.

D Work in small groups or pairs and discuss these questions:
- What is your favourite shop or store?
- What facts do you know about it?
- What is it like to be there? What impression does a foreigner get?
- What do you like and dislike about it?

E Write two paragraphs about the shop or store you have discussed.
In the first paragraph, describe the shop:
   its location, what it sells, why it's well-known, etc.
In the second paragraph, give your impressions of it:
   what you like and perhaps dislike about it.

1 MAKE NOTES before you start writing.
2 Write the two paragraphs.
3 When you have finished, look through your work and correct any SPELLING or PUNCTUATION mistakes.
4 Show your work to another student and ask for comments. Make any changes you think are necessary before handing your work in to your teacher.
5 Your teacher will mark your work and give you some advice on how your writing could be improved.

1.11 *Look* and *see* — *Verbs and idioms*

A Fill the gaps in these sentences with a suitable verb from the list – in some, more than one verb can be used. The first is done for you as an example:

see   look   watch   notice   recognise   observe   gaze

1 It's quite amusing to **observe** the behaviour of people while they're shopping.
2 We .... them playing football.
3 He .... at her admiringly.
4 I waved at you, but you didn't .... me.
5 I didn't .... you in your new glasses.
6 He tried to get to his seat without being ....
7 I usually .... TV on Fridays.
8 Have you .... that new film yet?
9 I'll .... what I can do to help you.
10 This exercise .... difficult.

B Replace the underlined words with a suitable phrasal verb with LOOK or SEE, using the word on the right. The first two are done as examples:

1 Their aunt <u>cared for</u> them after their mother's death. **looked after**   AFTER
2 They <u>said goodbye</u> to me at the airport. **saw me off**   OFF
3 What are you <u>trying to find</u>?   FOR
4 <u>Be careful</u>! There's a car coming.   OUT
5 All the pupils <u>respect</u> their teacher.   UP TO

6 Leave it to me! I'll <u>take care of</u> all the arrangements.	TO
7 The police are <u>investigating</u> a case of shoplifting.	INTO
8 He said he was innocent but they <u>realised</u> his story <u>was untrue</u>.	THROUGH
9 If you don't know the meaning, <u>find</u> the word in a dictionary.	UP
10 Next time you're in town, why don't you <u>pay us a call</u> and say hello.	IN
11 Before you hand your work in, <u>check</u> it carefully.	THROUGH
12 I'm <u>thinking about</u> my next holiday <u>with pleasure</u>.	FORWARD TO

★ There are four types of phrasal verb. Notice the structures in these examples:

1 LOOK AFTER (= care for) – the same as a verb + preposition
   I looked after someone ✓   I looked after him ✓   He was looked after ✓
   BUT NOT: I looked someone after ✗   I looked him after ✗

2 LOOK OUT (= be careful) – intransitive phrasal verbs (no object)
   You must look out! ✓
   BUT NOT: You were looked out ✗

3 LOOK UP (= find information) – 'separable' phrasal verbs
   I looked up a word ✓   I looked a word up ✓   I looked it up ✓
   The word was looked up ✓
   BUT NOT: I looked up it ✗

4 LOOK UP TO (= respect) – 'inseparable' phrasal verbs
   I look up to someone ✓   I look up to her ✓   She was looked up to by everyone ✓
   BUT NOT: I look someone up to ✗   I look her up to ✗

★ Unfortunately, idiomatic phrasal verbs ARE difficult – the only thing to do is to learn them by heart. Moreover, many phrasal verbs have more than one meaning. In the Verbs and idioms exercises in *Progress to First Certificate* you'll only meet the more common, useful meanings.

'I'll take them!'

2 Leisure activities

2.1 Entertainment and sport   *Vocabulary*

A Work in small groups. Ask your partners these questions:
- What are your hobbies?
- What kinds of entertainment do you enjoy most?
- What kinds of sport do you enjoy playing? And watching?
- If you weren't here in class, what would you like to be doing?

B Find the missing words to fill the gaps in these sentences. The first is done for you as an example:

1. Leisure activities are things you do in your s.pare. time.
2. I've got so much work to do that I don't have much time for r......... *relaxation / recreation*
3. Her hobbies are c......... stamps and t......... photographs. *collecting / taking*
4. A TV show, film or play that makes you laugh is called a c......... *comedy*
5. I sat biting my nails during the film because it was such an exciting th......... *thriller*
6. The story isn't very good – in other words, it has a weak p......... *plot*
7. The person who tells the actors what to do is called the d......... *direction*
8. In a cinema it's cheaper to sit close to the s......... *screen*, but in a theatre it costs more to sit close to the s......... *stage*
9. That film got extremely good r......... in the newspapers. *reviews*
10. The magician asked for two volunteers from the a......... *audience*
11. I like an entertaining show, which is why I enjoy a good m......... *musical*
12. We had a drink during the i......... between the two acts of the play and discussed the p......... *interval / performance*
13. Fewer people go to the cinema but instead they watch films at home on v......... *video*
14. I didn't like the hero or heroine – I preferred the wicked v......... *villain*
15. If you don't like the programme on BBC1, you can switch to another ch......... *channel*
16. I enjoy listening to music on my .... *hifi / stereo / record player*
17. My favourite kinds of music are .... and .... *music*
18. Did you see England play Brazil on TV? It was a very exciting m......... *match*
19. At the end of the game, when the r......... blew his w........., there was loud a......... from the .... *referee / whistle / applause / fans*
20. Liverpool is the football t......... that he s.........
21. The winner of the competition received a silver c......... and a p......... of $300.
22. The result of the game was a d.........: the final s......... was 4 – 4 (four all).
23. Tennis is played on a tennis c......... and golf is played on a golf c.........
24. My favourite sports are .... and ....

⟫→

17

C Work in small groups and find out about each other's favourite summer and winter sports. Using a dictionary, write down the words you need to describe:

- The PLACE each sport is played (in a stadium, on a pitch, in a pool, etc.)
- The EQUIPMENT needed (goals, a racket, skates, etc.)
- The PEOPLE involved in each game (players, referee, linesmen, etc.)
- The system of SCORING (3–nil, 15–love, etc.)

2.2 Fitness or fun? *Reading*

A Before you read this magazine article, look at these questions and see if you can guess the answers. Then find the answers in the text.

1 The most popular sporting activity in Britain is ....
2 More money is spent on .... than any other leisure-related activity.
3 Over the past 15 years 1,500 private .... have been built in Britain.
4 Over the past 15 years 1,500 public .... have been built in Britain.

Fitness *or fun?*

THE BRITISH as a nation do all kinds of things in their spare time: we go shopping or jogging, we play darts or football, we collect records or stamps, we go to church or to the pub. Some of these activities, like visiting relatives or taking driving lessons, may not be fun, but whatever we do, the way we spend our free time is probably providing someone with work. More people work in the sports industry than in the coal industry and the number of employees in restaurants, pubs and shops is rising all the time.

According to a recent survey, the number one leisure expenses are alcohol and smoking: every person in Britain spends £150 a year on beer, £140 on spirits and wine and £110 on cigarettes. Spending on sports is £60 per head and we each spend £20 gambling on sports. Do-it-yourself goods cost each person £50 per year and we each spend £40 on newspapers and magazines and £15 on cassettes, records and CDs. Cinema-going now accounts for only £2.50 per head and many families prefer to sit at home watching the same films on video. We still each spend £25 on our pets, and taking the dog for a walk provides good exercise for the dog and its owner.

In fact, walking is the most popular sport of all: out of a total population of around 55 million people, 9.5 million regularly walk two miles or more. More energetic sports are keep fit, including aerobics and yoga (1.2 million), and football, squash and golf each have 1.2 million regular players. Less actively, 4.7 million play snooker or pool and 1.7 million go fishing.

Watching other people playing is also a popular leisure activity: the favourite sports among TV viewers are horse-racing, football, snooker, cricket and tennis. Although 11 million watched the F.A. Cup Final on TV in May, only 1.3 million regularly go to watch professional and amateur football matches. 'New' TV sports like American football, basketball and even yachting are attracting more and more loyal armchair experts.

The fitness boom of the eighties led to a big rise in the numbers of people participating in sports. To cater for this boom and provide the up-to-date facilities people want, over 1,500 private health and fitness clubs and the same number of public sports and leisure centres have been built during the past fifteen years. These modern centres, with their swimming pools, squash courts, gyms and indoor courts for tennis and other sports are competing with discos, pubs and cinemas as places for people to go to spend their leisure time – and their money. Now practically every town has a leisure pool with a wave machine, water slides and tropical plants. Four million people regularly swim in an indoor pool and now families can spend their holidays at huge indoor water parks, where they can play or relax all day long in warmth and comfort without worrying about the weather outside, though four million do swim in the sea at least once a year. One problem with this is that we may be becoming a nation of splashers not swimmers. The big question fitness experts are asking is: should sport be something you take seriously or should it just be fun?

B Fill the gaps in these charts with information you'll find in the article:

Annual expenditure per head of population:	
Motor vehicles	£180
Beer	£........................
Spirits & wine	£........................
Smoking	£........................
Electricity	£90
Gas	£75
Bread	£75
Sports	£........................
DIY goods	£........................
Newspapers & magazines	£........................
Pets	£........................
Gambling	£........................
Bingo	£5
Cinema	£........................

Number of people who regularly take part in leisure activities: (total population of UK 55 million)	
Walking	....
Snooker & pool	....
Indoor swimming	....
Outdoor swimming	....
Darts	3.8 million
Fishing	....
Going to football matches	1.3 million
Keep fit, aerobics & yoga	....
Football	....
Squash	....
Golf	....

C Work in small groups. Ask your partners these questions:
- What sports and entertainments are most popular in your own country?
- What are the differences between your country and Britain?

2.3 Articles   *Grammar*

A Remember that these common English nouns are 'UNCOUNTABLE':
furniture   information   weather   advice   hair   progress   news
We can't say: *a good news* ✗ or *a furniture* ✗
So we say: *a piece of good news* or *some good news* or *a piece of furniture*

■ Most nouns are 'countable', which means that we can use them in the plural.
We can say: *a car, some cars, many cars*
Some nouns are 'uncountable', which means that they can't be used in the plural.
We can say: *petrol, some petrol, much petrol*, BUT NOT: *a petrol* ✗ or *many petrols* ✗

Other uncountable nouns are: *wine   freedom   safety   water*

19

Which of these nouns are 'countable' and which are 'uncountable' – and which could be either, depending on their meaning?

*bread   butter   food   blood   glass   fire   milk   salt   money   suitcase
luggage   room   accommodation   mathematics   lesson   education   health*

B   Look at these examples and fill the gaps with suitable words. The first is done for you as an example:

THE is used in these cases:
- Referring to things that are UNIQUE:
    I'm worried about the future.   The most popular sport in Britain ......
    The Queen of England ......   **The sea** is too rough to swim in.
    ...... best football team in the world ......   What time does ...... rise?
    (BUT: See the notes on planets, mountains, parks, etc. below.)
- When it's obvious which one you mean:
    We're going to the pub.   I'm taking the dog for a walk.
    How many students are there in ...... ?
    We are taking ...... exam in ......
- When we mean a particular person or thing:
    The actor who played the villain ......
    The big question fitness experts are asking ......
    ...... of the film *Psycho* was Alfred Hitchcock.
- Oceans, seas and rivers:
    the Atlantic, the Aegean, the Thames, ..., ...
- Plural mountain groups, island groups and countries:
    the Andes, the Canary Islands, the Netherlands, ..., ...
- Hotels, cinemas, theatres, museums:
    the Ritz, the Gaumont, the Playhouse, the National Gallery, ..., ...

A or AN is used in these cases:
- Referring to a single thing or person:
    There's a cinema opposite the bank (one of many cinemas in the town).
    It's a difficult exercise.   A leisure pool usually has ......
- A friend of mine ......   She's ...... of Peter's.   (BUT: He's one of my friends.)
- It was quite an interesting story.   She's such ...... person.
- Professions or jobs:
    He's an actor.   She's an engineer.   My father's ......   My mother's ......
- Generalisations:
    An actor performs in front of an audience.   ...... has to be a good leader.

0 – the 'zero article' is used in these cases:
- Generalisations about plural ideas, people or things:
    New cars are expensive.   Bicycles are pollution-free.
    ...... are useful.   ...... are noisy.
- She went to school in England.   You mustn't smoke in class.   We go to church.
- Planets, continents, countries, states:
    Jupiter, Europe, Britain, Holland, California, ..., ...
    (BUT: the Earth, the Sun, the Moon, the Soviet Union, the United Kingdom)
- Languages: English, Dutch, ..., ...
- Mountains and lakes: Mount Fuji, Lake Geneva, ..., ...
- Streets, roads and squares:
    Oxford Street, Fifth Avenue, Trafalgar Square, ..., ..., ...

- Parks, stations and public buildings:
    Central Park, Victoria Station, Gatwick Airport, ..., ..., ...
- Referring to things and ideas that are uncountable:
    shopping, freedom, knowledge, pollution, liberty, democracy, history, music, tennis, stamp-collecting, watching television, swimming

C Each of these sentences contains two (✗✗) or three (✗✗✗) errors. Find the mistakes and correct them. The first is done for you as an example:

1 *I'm attending the class A4, which is preparing for exam in June.* ✗✗
  I'm attending class A4, which is preparing for the exam in June.
2 *I'm looking for an accommodation with a English family.* ✗✗
3 *More women are involved in the politics in Britain than in the other countries.* ✗✗
4 *The most people agree that the women can do the same work as the men.* ✗✗✗
5 *To get to the library, go along the Elizabeth Road and take first right.* ✗✗
6 *The violence is very great problem in the world today.* ✗✗

D Fill the gaps in this story, using *a, an, some, a lot of, lots of* or *the* – or a 'zero article' (∅). The first two are done for you as examples:

Last week I went to ...**an**... exhibition of ...**∅**... paintings at .... Tate Gallery in London. I'm not really .... great art lover but I'd read .... good reviews of .... exhibition and I was keen to see it. When I arrived, there were already .... people waiting outside for .... doors to open. I joined .... queue and in .... end .... doors opened and we went inside to see .... show.

Now, I must be honest and admit that many of .... paintings disappointed me. Although I spent .... time looking carefully at .... each one, I had .... difficulty in understanding what .... artist was getting at. Finally, as I was looking rather stupidly at one of .... paintings and trying to decide if it was .... right way up or not, ... old gentleman came up behind me and started to explain .... whole thing to me. He kindly answered all of .... my questions and we talked for over .... hour. Then he said he had .... appointment and had to go, so we shook hands and said goodbye. I went round .... gallery once more and now I found that all .... paintings seemed really beautiful.

It was only as I was leaving .... gallery that I found out who .... old man was – his self-portrait was on .... posters advertising .... exhibition!

E Write these notes and headlines out in full. More than one version is possible in some cases, and you'll have to change the tenses. The first is done as an example:

1 *Class 4 need information about exam in December.*
  Class 4 need more information about the exam in December.
2 *Please don't send results of exam to address in UK.*
3 *Bring example of good and bad advertisement to class tomorrow.*
4 **President of France and Queen open Channel Tunnel**
5 **GROUP OF TAXI-DRIVERS WIN £1 MILLION IN LOTTERY**
6 **Man finds valuable painting in garden shed**

2.4 What sort of films do you enjoy?

Listening

A 🎧 You'll hear part of a conversation between two friends who are planning to go to the cinema. They're trying to agree what film to go and see.

Mark with a tick (✓) in the appropriate column the films each of them likes, and with a cross (✗) the ones they dislike.

	BOB	SUSAN		BOB	SUSAN
Thrillers	✓		Harrison Ford	✓	✓
Action films	✓		Clint Eastwood	✓	
Horror films	✗		Sylvester Stallone	✓	✗
Love stories	✓		Robert Redford	✓	
Films with subtitles	✓		Eddie Murphy	✓	✓
Comedies	✓				
Cartoons	✓				
Black and white films	✓	✓			

Compare your answers with a partner and, if necessary, listen to the recording again to settle any disagreement.

B 🎧 Now you'll hear the message they heard when they phoned the local multi-screen cinema to find out what was on. Fill the gaps below.

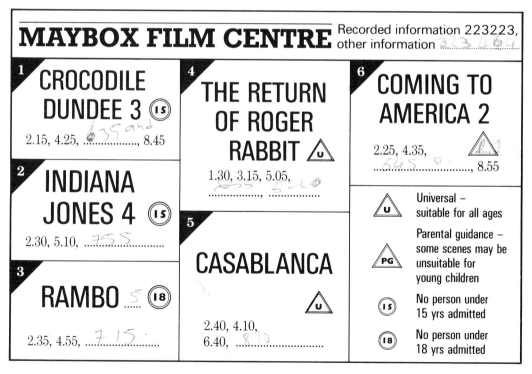

- Which of the films did they decide to go to, do you think?

2.5 Using prefixes
Word study

A Look at these examples and add more of your own, using the root words below with one of the prefixes in this list.

co	co-chairman co-worker
mid	midnight midair midweek
over	overact overpaid overdone
under	undercharged underpaid
re	rebuild reappear redone
self	self-help self-contained
sub	subnormal subway
un	untie undo

afternoon arrange button charge control done driver excited
fold marry morning screw service standard way winter wrap

B Fill the gaps in these sentences, using a prefix with the correct form of the root word on the right. The first is done for you as an example:

1 I was late because I _underestimated_ how much time I'd need. ESTIMATE
2 He wrote the book alone, so he doesn't have a .... AUTHOR
3 Even if you're good at a game, you shouldn't be .... CONFIDENT
4 It is very rude to interrupt someone in .... SENTENCE
5 Many buildings were .... after the earthquake in 1980. BUILD
6 Most people who work feel that they are .... PAY
7 She's having a rest because she has been .... WORK
8 I'd lost my key so I couldn't .... the door when I got home. LOCK
9 We have .... temperatures every night in .... ZERO WINTER
0 People who .... often become .... EAT WEIGHT

2.6 Safety at sea *Listening*

A You'll hear part of a radio broadcast. Before you listen to the recording look at the questions below and try to predict what the answers might be.

B Listen to the recording and answer the questions.
Compare your answers with a partner and, if necessary, listen to the recording again to settle any disagreements.

 The skin diver

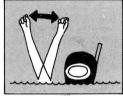  

A B C

 The water skier

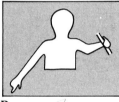  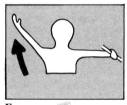 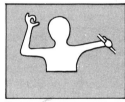

D E F G

1 Match the signals illustrated above to these meanings:
   a) 'I am OK.'
   b) 'I need assistance.'
   c) 'I have a diver down. Keep clear and proceed at slow speed.'
   d) 'Faster!'
   e) 'Slower!'
   f) 'Speed OK.'
   g) 'Back to jetty.'

2 Instead of using the Faster signal, you can ....
3 Instead of using the Slower signal, you can ....
4 Advice to the water skier:
   a) There should be two people in the boat: one to .... and the other to ....
   b) Before starting, your ski-tips must be ....
   c) Give a clear signal to the helmsman of the boat when you are ready to ....
   d) If you are falling forwards you should ....
   e) If you fall sideways, you should ....
   f) If you fall, recover the skis at once because ....

2.7 The Month in View   *Reading/Problem solving*

A Imagine that you are in Britain in November – an ideal month for TV viewing! Which days would you stay at home and watch television if you were interested in the following subjects? The first is done as an example:

1 crime stories   Nov 16
2 France   ....
3 inventions   ....
4 nuclear disarmament   ....
5 painting   ....
6 recent history   ....
7 women in society   ....

DO NOT study the text. Don't use a dictionary to look up unfamiliar words. Just search for the answers to the questions. It is not necessary to understand every word of the article.

THE MONTH IN VIEW

■ Nov 4. **Eureka** (BBC2)
Children's programme in which one of the liveliest of the new television presenters, Jeremy Beadle, tells us who invented what, & how; this week, the ballpoint pen, safety pin, can opener & zipper.

■ Nov 4. **Tom Keating on Painters** (C4)
The master forger of Samuel Palmer's paintings, & much else, tells how he does it. Keating is fascinated by technique. He copies for the joy of it, not in order to mislead, & his descriptions of the Venetians, Constable & Degas are wonderful to hear.

■ Nov 5. **Sorry** (BBC1)
A new series with Ronnie Corbett trying to escape from home.

■ Nov 5. **Ballroom of Romance** (BBC2)
A simple story, beautifully told, about the people at a dance evening in a small Irish village. This kind of gentle story-telling is something that television can do better than any other medium, & *Ballroom* is exceptionally good of its kind; with Cyril Cusack & Brenda Fricker.

■ Nov 5. **The Other 'Arf** (ITV)
The new series starts with Charles Latimer (John Standing) about to leave the Tories & join the SDP. Also with glorious cockney Lorraine Chase & James Villiers.

■ Nov 7. **Nicholas Nickleby** (C4)
The Royal Shakespeare Company production of Dickens's sprawling adventure was one of the theatrical hits of recent years. This four-part, nine-hour TV version, filmed in the theatre, should recapture all the magic of the performances (notably Roger Rees as Nicholas, David Threlfall as Smike & Edward Petherbridge as Newman Noggs) & much of the rapid-fire action as well.

■ Nov 9 **Intensive Care** (BBC1)
A typical Alan Bennett play, keenly observed & extracting humour from situations that, to many people, don't seem funny at all. Alan Bennett, as the remorseful son, sits with his aunt (Thora Hird) in a hospital waiting room, getting to know the staff (including Julie Walters), & other patients.

■ Nov 10. **The Barchester Chronicles** (BBC2)
A welcome seven-part adaptation by Alan Plater of Trollope's story of clerical intrigue & secular romance; the cast has Nigel Hawthorne, Geraldine McEwan, Clive Swift & Susan Hampshire.

■ Nov 10. **Year of the French** (BBC2)
Twice-weekly documentary series showing the lives of 12 French people. Tonight's film is about singer/song-writer Marie-Paule Belle; Friday's programme looks at Bernard Capdérey, a skiing gendarme in the Pyrenees.

■ Nov 11. **Yes, Prime Minister** (BBC2)
Paul Eddington & Nigel Hawthorne return for a third series of this all-too-accurate Whitehall comedy.

■ Nov 12. **Our Winnie** (BBC2)
The first of five shortish plays by Alan Bennett, all on BBC2, to complement his *Play for Today* on BBC1.

■ Nov 16. **The Manhood of Edward Robinson** (ITV)
This engaging story of a spoof burglary is a lovely vignette of Bright Young Things & their parties in the mid 1930s; sadly, it ends Thames's series of Agatha Christie plays.

■ Nov 18. **The Life & Times of Rosie the Riveter** (C4)
A marvellous, if loosely made, film in which US wartime propaganda about the necessity of women working in factories is contrasted with the women's own views. Most wrenching is how at the end of the war the women were summarily sacked & told to go home to look after the men.

■ Nov 23. **The Bomb** (ITV)
John Pilger, one of TV's (& Fleet Street's) most aggressive investigators, shows how western governments & the media are trying to accustom us to the idea of a limited nuclear war.

■ Nov 26. **The Sixties** (C4)
The best-loved decade since the war? The last of the good times or the beginning of the crack up? This six-part series remembers the Beatles (via an interview with their generous press agent, Derek Taylor), explains why the BMC Mini never made money, & offers an analysis of the economic problems & the emergence of political radicalism.

■ Nov 30. **Stuntman Challenge** (ITV)
Film stuntmen challenge each other to a series of stunts & tricks; an odd mix of bravery & lunacy.

B Decide which of the following statements are true (**T**) or false (**F**), according to the text. Find the relevant programme and check the information given – you don't need to understand every word. The first is done for you as an example:

1 The presenter of *Eureka* is a well-known old inventor. **F**
2 Tom Keating is famous for his own style of painting.
3 *Sorry* is about a criminal in prison.
4 *Ballroom of Romance* is a story about people in Ireland.
5 Each episode of *Nicholas Nickleby* lasts over two hours.
6 *Intensive Care* is a tragic play about people in hospital.
7 *The Barchester Chronicles* is a serial based on a story by Trollope.
8 *Year of the French* can be seen once a fortnight.
9 *Yes, Prime Minister* is a popular funny programme.
10 According to John Pilger in *The Bomb*, some governments want us to agree that nuclear weapons can be used in a small war.

C Work in small groups. Out of all the programmes listed, which would you like to see? Which would you definitely NOT watch? Note down your reasons.

If there are no programmes that interest you among those listed, discuss what's *really* on TV (or at the cinema) this week.

★ In the Directed Writing section of the Use of English paper you'll have to write 3–4 paragraphs based on an information-gathering task. These problem-solving sections will help you to develop your paragraph-writing skills.

D Write two paragraphs:
1 Explain which of the programmes listed in The Month in View (or TV programmes or films that are really on this week) you would like to see and give your reasons.
2 Explain which of the programmes (or films) you would NOT like to see.

Show your completed paragraphs to a partner and ask for his or her comments.

2.8 Position and direction   *Prepositions*

A Take a pen or pencil and use it to DEMONSTRATE the meaning of these prepositions and prepositional phrases:

above
behind
underneath
on top of
in the top left-hand corner of
at the back of
beside
in the middle of
on the left/right of

at the bottom of
between
next to
on the other side of

at the top of
opposite
on the edge of
in the bottom right-hand corner of

B Look at this rectangle and add the letters B to F in the places described. The first (B) is done for you as an example:

1 B is half-way between A and the right-hand edge of the rectangle.
2 C is half-way between A and B.
3 D is about 1 centimetre above C.
4 E is underneath B.
5 F is in the top left-hand corner of the rectangle.

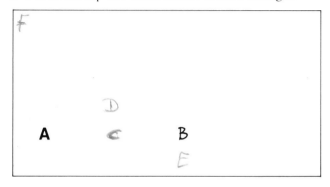

C Work in pairs. One of you should tell the other where to put letters G to K, the other should tell the other where to put letters L to P.

D Work in pairs. One of you should look at Activity 32, the other at 40. You'll each have to explain to your partner the 'route' your partner's pencil should take between, past, above and below the letters and numbers in this grid to draw the picture in your activity. Begin like this: 'First of all draw a round spot beside the top right-hand part of R. Now draw another spot just above and to the left of S. OK? Now start drawing a line from ...'

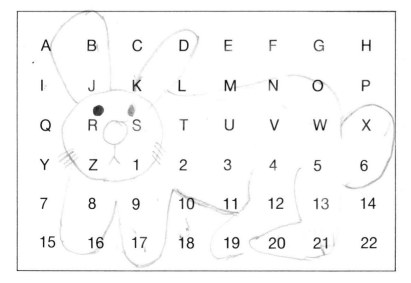

2.9 The jogger's wallet — *Listening*

Before you listen to the recording, look at these pictures and see if you can guess what happened to the man in the story.

🎧 Listen to the story and number the pictures to show the correct order.

2.10 Telling a story — *Communication activity*

A Work in groups. Discuss these questions:
- What kinds of stories do you enjoy listening to or reading?
- Why are some people better at telling stories than others?
- Which of these things should a storyteller do?
  – get the events in the right sequence
  – add personal feelings and reactions
  – add dialogue
  – think of your audience: put yourself in their shoes

B Look again at the pictures illustrating 'The jogger's wallet' story above. As a class, decide how you would tell the story as if it had happened to a friend of a friend of yours. (The same kind of event could have happened in a train, bus or lift, so you might decide to change the setting.)

Here are some questions that a listener or reader might ask:

> What happened before that? What happened next?
> What did you/he/she do after that? How did you/she/he feel?
> What did you/she/he say? Why did she/he/you do that?

C Work in groups of three. Student A should look at Activity 17, student B at 24 and C at 46. You'll each see some scenes from a film and will have to work out the story of that film.

2.11 Writing a narrative *Composition*

One of the topics in the Composition Paper of the exam is a narrative-writing question. When writing a narrative, you should consider how the reader will react to your story – will he or she be bored or interested?

A Work in small groups. Look at this narrative and decide together:
1. What is wrong with the way it's written (the style)?
2. How can it be improved? What could be ADDED or CHANGED to make it more interesting to the reader? The first improvement is made for you as an example.

I'll never forget the night... *We were on our way home after a marvellous evening out with some friends.*
I'll never forget the night our car broke down. We were 9.5 km from home and we had to walk there. It was 12.45 and it started to rain. We arrived home at 02.05. The door of our house was locked because we had left the front door key in the car. We broke a window but a policeman came and we had to explain the situation to him. We went to bed at 3 o'clock.

Look at Activity 9, where you will see an improved version of the story.

B Now decide how this narrative could be improved. What could be ADDED or CHANGED to make it more interesting to the reader?

CASABLANCA, starring Humphrey Bogart and Ingrid Bergman

An American (Rick) owned a night club in Casablanca (Morocco) in the war. A girl (Ilsa) came there with her husband (Victor Laszlo). Rick and Ilsa had been in love in Paris before the war. Laszlo was in danger and had to escape to Lisbon (by plane) but he had no visa. Rick sold his club and bought two visas on the black market. In the end Laszlo and Ilsa flew off to freedom. Rick and the chief of police (Renault) stayed at the airport. The End.

Look at Activity 3, where you will see an improved version of the story.

C Write a composition on one of these topics:
1 Tell the story of a film you remember well.
2 Write a story about your own or someone else's experiences beginning:
    'I'll never forget the night ...' or 'I'll never forget the day ...'
  or 'This may sound incredible but it really happened: ...'

D Before handing your story in to be corrected, show it to one or two other students and ask for their comments.
* How could your stories be improved?
* Which of your partners' ideas could you use in your own written work?

2.12 *Make* and *do*   *Verbs and idioms*

A Decide which of the endings below go with these beginnings:

Bill made ...
Shirley did ...

...Shirley laugh   ...Bill a favour   ...the washing-up   ...his/her duty
...a cake   ...a noise   ...a mistake   ...an arrangement   ...the shopping
...a comment   ...a decision   ...an exercise   ...his/her homework
...a good job   ...badly in the test   ...a good impression   ...me an offer
...a promise   ...a statement   ...her/his best   ...very well   ...nothing at all

B Fill the gaps with suitable forms of the phrasal verbs below:

do
1 Phew, I'm ever so thirsty, I could .... a drink.
2 They've just finished .... their flat and it looks really nice now.
3 She was very angry because her rival had .... her .... of the reward.
4 He had to .... sugar in his coffee, because he was on a diet.
make
5 I can't quite .... if that's your sister or you in this photo.
6 As you've arrived late, you'll have to .... the time you've lost.
7 We were .... the station when the thunderstorm broke.
8 Is this the truth or are you .... it .... ?
9 A dog picked up my sandwich in its mouth and .... it.

do someone out of   do up   do with   do without
make for   make off with   make out   make up
make up for

3 Nature and the environment

3.1 Plants and animals   *Vocabulary*

A Add THREE more items to each list. Use a dictionary if necessary. The first is done for you as an example:

1. Cereals: oats, rye, **maize, barley, wheat**
2. Fruit: grape, pear, peach, apple, orange, watermelon
3. Vegetables: spinach, radish, carrot, lettuce, tomato, ___
4. Trees: pine, olive, oak, ___
5. Flowers: rose, daisy, carnation, tulip, daffodil, chrysanthemum
6. Wild animals (mammals): rabbit, tiger, whale, elephant, giraffe, rat
7. Domestic animals: turkey, camel, goat, cow, chicken, chip
8. Pets: parrot, goldfish, cat, dog, hamster
9. Birds: sparrow, eagle, pigeon, owl, vulture, blackbird
10. Young animals: puppy, calf, chick, kitten, piglet, duckling
11. Reptiles: lizard, alligator, crocodile, snake, salamander
12. Insects: butterfly, wasp, ant, beetle, earwig, mosquito, bee
13. Fish: salmon, shark, trout, herring, cod
14. Other sea creatures: oyster, octopus, crab, mussels, starfish, dolphin

B Find the missing words to fill the gaps in these sentences. The first one is done for you as an example:

1. Less than 2% of the British labour force is employed on farms in **agriculture**.
2. In the autumn, at h_arvest_ time, the c_rop_s in the fields have to be gathered in and the fruit in the orchards has to be p_icked_.
3. In the Alps, cows are kept indoors in winter and spend the summer in the m_ountains_.
4. The sport that involves chasing or shooting animals is called h_unting_.
5. P_ollution_ is caused when waste products or p_oisons_ contaminate the environment.
6. According to the weather f_orecast_, there will be sunny i_ntervals_ this morning.
7. In the early morning there may be thick f_og_ and motorists should drive slowly.
8. We couldn't see very far from the top of the hill because it was slightly m_isty_.
9. During the night t_emperature_ will fall below freezing and there will be a f_rost_.
10. During the s_torm_ many trees were blown down.
11. Although it was really boiling in the sun, there was a light b_reeze_ from the sea, which made it feel quite pleasant in the s_hade_.
12. Although the storm passed us by, we could hear the th_under_ and see the l_ightning_ in the distance.
13. It's not going to rain all day, it's just a sh_ower_. We'll soon be able to go out.
14. The s_cenery_ in the north of the country is spectacular with deep v_alleys_ and high snow-capped peaks, but the c_limate_ tends to be cool and wet.
15. The west c_oast_ of the country has high c_liffs_ as well as sandy beaches.

31

3.2 The balance of nature   *Reading*

A Work in small groups. Before you read the passage, ask your partners these questions:
- What kinds of animals would be found in a wood or forest in your country?
- What kinds of plants would be found there?

B Read the passage through to find out what it's about. DO NOT use a dictionary.

All the different plants and animals in a natural community are in a state of balance. This balance is achieved by the plants and animals interacting with each other and with their non-living surroundings. An example of a natural community is a woodland, and a woodland is usually dominated by a particular species of plant, such as the oak tree in an oak wood. The oak tree in this example is therefore called the dominant species but there are also many other types of plants, from brambles, bushes and small trees to mosses, lichens and algae growing on tree trunks and rocks.

The plants of a community are the producers: they use carbon dioxide, oxygen, water and nitrogen to build up their tissues using energy in the form of sunlight. The plant tissues form food for the plant-eating animals (herbivores) which are in turn eaten by the flesh-eating animals (carnivores). Thus plants produce the basic food supply for all the animals of a community. The animals themselves are the consumers, and are either herbivores or carnivores.

Examples of herbivores in a woodland community are rabbits, deer, mice and snails, and insects such as aphids and caterpillars. The herbivores are sometimes eaten by the carnivores. Woodland carnivores are of all sizes, from insects such as beetles and lacewings to animals such as owls, shrews and foxes. Some carnivores feed on herbivores, some feed on the smaller carnivores, while some feed on both: a tawny owl will eat beetles and shrews as well as voles and mice. These food relationships between the different members of the community are known as food chains or food webs. All food chains start with plants. The links of the chain are formed by the herbivores that eat the plants and the carnivores that feed on the herbivores. There are more organisms at the base of a food chain than at the top; for example, there are many more green plants than carnivores in a community.

Another important section of the community is made up of the decomposers. They include the bacteria and fungi that live in the soil and feed on dead animals and plants. By doing this they break down the tissues of the dead organisms and release mineral salts into the soil.

C It would be hard to make sense of the passage without knowing the words in the following list:
1 Find the words in the passage and underline them.
2 Read the sentences before and after each word.
3 Match the words to their definitions below:

natural community (line 1)   species (line 5)   links (line 26)
woodland (line 4)   tissues (line 11)   organisms (line 28)
dominated (line 5)   flesh (line 14)   decomposers (line 32)

a) area covered with growing trees
b) have the most important position
c) living things
d) meat
e) material making up a living thing
f) one ring in a chain
g) organisms that feed on dead tissues
h) type of plant or animal
i) plants and animals living in one place

D These words in the passage are less important and it's only necessary to know what KINDS of things they are.
  Match the words to their approximate meanings below.

oak (line 5)   trunk (line 9)   lacewing (line 20)
bramble (line 8)   snail (line 18)   shrew (line 21)
moss (line 8)   aphid (line 18)   vole (line 23)
lichen (line 8)   caterpillar (line 18)   fungi (line 32)
algae (line 9)

a kind of insect   a kind of large plant
a kind of simple plant   a kind of small animal
a kind of tree   part of a tree

E Decide whether the following statements are true (**T**) or false (**F**), according to the text.

1 All the animals in a wood depend on plants for their food supply.
2 All the plants in a wood are eaten by animals.
3 Some animals eat other animals.
4 Plants depend on the sun to grow.
5 Plants depend on the gases in the atmosphere to grow.
6 Not every food chain starts with plants.
7 The consumers are at the base of a food chain.
8 Some animals eat plant-eating animals and also flesh-eating animals.

F Work in small groups. Ask your partners these questions:
• How does man interfere with the balance of nature?
• What might the consequences of this be?

★ Although it's rarely necessary to understand every single word in a reading passage, some of the unfamiliar words may be KEY WORDS that you must know to understand the meaning of the passage. You can often work out the meaning of such words from their CONTEXT. This is often much easier and quicker to do than using a dictionary, or even asking your teacher.

3.3 The past — *Grammar*

A Study these examples. Fill the gaps with suitable words, using the correct form of the word on the right. The first is done as an example:

The SIMPLE PAST is the tense most commonly used to refer to events that happened in the past:

The Second World War started in 1939.
I *went* to the cinema last week. — GO
I *saw* a film about animals on TV last Wednesday evening. — SEE
In 1988 I *spent* my summer holidays in *Paris*. — SPEND

The PAST PROGRESSIVE is used to refer to simultaneous events or activities that continued or were interrupted:

We were lying in the sun while she was revising for her exam.
At 7.45 last night it was still raining.
We *were playing* cards when the light went out. — PLAY
As the sun *was shining* we decided to go for a drive. — SHINE
While you *were waiting* the bus, we walked all the way here. — WAIT

USED TO emphasises that the activity no longer takes place:

He used to smoke twenty cigarettes a day (but not now).
Before the war, more people *used to work* on the land. — WORK
When I was a child, we *used to have* a dog. — HAVE

The PAST PERFECT is normally used to emphasise that one past event happened before another:

Before we got our cat, we had never had a pet in our family.
It rained all day but I *had forgotten* to pack an umbrella. — FORGET
After I *had read* the book, I made some notes on it. — READ
They were still friends even though they *had been* apart for ten years. — BE

The PRESENT PERFECT is only used to refer to the past:
− when no definite time in the past is given or known, or
− when the activity began in the past and has not yet finished.
It is often used with:
just   already   never   yet

He has seen that film three times.   Have you done your homework?
I have never seen a lion in the wild.
We *have* already *studied the first* two units in this book. — STUDY
She *has made* five phone calls since lunchtime. — MAKE
Have you *ever visited* Britain? — VISIT

■ Remember that the PRESENT PERFECT is NOT used to refer to a definite time in the past and is NOT normally used after *When...?*
It is not used with:
last week, in July, on Wednesday, yesterday, a few minutes ago, etc.

I saw that film last week. ✓   NOT: I have seen that film last week. ✗
We did this exercise on Monday. ✓   NOT: We have done this exercise on Monday. ✗
When did you go there? ✓   NOT: When have you gone there? ✗

B Find and correct the mistakes in these sentences. The first is done for you as an example:

The weather ~~were~~ lovely yesterday. **was**
I have gone to the zoo last weekend.
When have you left school?
Where you went on holiday last year?
She has been born in 1975.
Our family is used to live in a smaller flat when I am younger.
Our broken window wasn't mended yet.
The rain started during they played tennis.

C Finish the incomplete sentences in such a way that each one means the same as the complete sentence before it. The first is done for you as an example:

1 We had a snack and then we had a look round the shops.
   After we **had had a snack, we had a look round the shops.**
2 The farmer started his tractor and began to plough the field.
   When
3 The rain began to fall during my walk in the country.
   While
4 We had lunch and then went for a walk by the river.
   After we
5 They don't have a dog any more.
   They used
6 I went to the zoo last year and that is where I saw a real tiger for the first time.
   Before I

D Work in pairs. One of you should look at Activity 18, the other at 42. You'll each have a short story to tell, using past tenses.
1 Read the story through to yourself.
2 Make a few notes to help you remember the main points.
3 Tell the story to your partner – as if it really happened to some friends of a friend. Turn the book over while you're telling the story. Don't read it aloud.

'There's a furry thing in here eating cheese. I understand that's your department.'

3.4 The earth at risk
Listening

A You'll hear an interview with a film-maker who has made a series of TV documentaries about the harm being done to the Earth.

Look at the questions below with a partner. Which of them can you answer before you hear the interview?

B Listen to the recording and fill the gaps in these sentences.

1. In Africa, the Sahara Desert is **expanding** as people cut down trees for .... and their .... animals eat all the available plants.
2. In the USA intensive agriculture requires a plentiful supply of .... for crops to grow.
3. Growing crops stabilise ....; without them it just blows away.
4. American farmers grow huge quantities of extra ...., ... and soya beans that feed the world.
5. In South America (as in Central Africa and Southern Asia) .... are being cut down at an alarming rate.
6. Forests are cut down so that people can support themselves by growing .... or to create ranches where cattle can be raised for export to .... or .... as tinned meat.
7. The problem is that the soil is so .... that only a couple of harvests are possible before this very thin soil becomes ....
8. Huge numbers of trees are being cut down for export as hardwood to Japan, Europe, and .... to make luxury ....
9. Tropical forests contain .... , which we can use for ....
10. Destroying forests affects the climate of the whole ....
11. Floods in Bangladesh happen because forests in .... and .... have been cut down. Trees would hold .... in their roots.
12. There are three suggested solutions:
    1. National governments have to consider the results of their policies in .... or .... years and all the countries in the world have to work together on an .... basis.
    2. The population has to be .... in some way.
    3. We in the West should use .... instead of tropical ....

Paper for books and newspapers normally comes from 'tree farms', where new trees are planted to replace the trees that have been cut down. Softwood for furniture and building is produced in the same way.

3.5 Using negative prefixes *Word study*

A Look at these examples and fill each gap with more examples, using the root words below with one of the negative prefixes in this list.

un	unkind untidy	unhappy unfriendly unlucky unable unknown unwise
in	indirect indecent	inaccurate inconvenient inaccessible invisible
il	illegal illegible illiterate	illegible
ir	irregular irrelevant	
im	immature impossible immoral	impatient impersonal improbable
dis	disagree dissatisfied	dislike disobey disapprove
mis	misunderstand misbehave	mispronounce misspell

accurate approve comfortable convenient expected familiar known
like lucky obey patient personal popular probable pronounce
spell tolerant visible

B Fill the gaps in these sentences, using a negative prefix with the correct form of the root word on the right. The first is done for you as an example:

1 Don't depend on him, he's a very __unreliable__ person.   RELY
2 Don't be so __im__, we've only been waiting a few minutes.   PATIENT
3 7.30 a.m. on a Saturday is a rather __in__ time for an appointment.   CONVENIENT
4 Please don't be so __un__, I can't do all the work by myself.   REASON
5 There are always mistakes because the firm is so __in__.   EFFICIENT
6 Sorry about the mistake, I __mis__ the instructions you gave me.   UNDERSTAND
7 They've __mis__ my name on this form – the first letter is L not R.   SPELL
8 After I had got to know him better, I __dis__ him intensely.   LIKE

3.6 What's the weather going to be like? *Problem solving*

Work in pairs or small groups for these activities. Imagine three friends of yours are travelling to different parts of the world.

A 🎧 Listen to three recorded messages from your friends. Note down the places each of them will be this week and their contact phone number in each city.

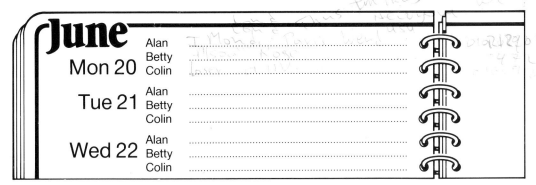

- What temperatures and weather would these places have in June?

B Look at the weather forecast for this week.

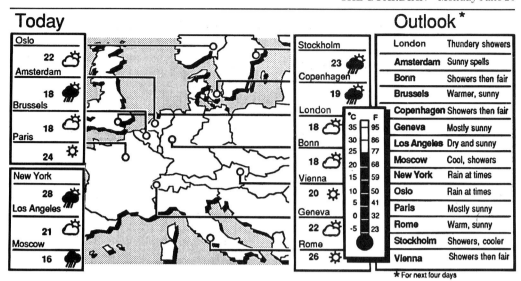

THE GUARDIAN   Monday June 20

- Note down the weather that Alan, Betty and Colin can expect on each day, according to the forecast.
- What clothes should they each pack, do you think?

C Now look at Activity 15, where you will find out if the forecast for the middle of the week was correct or not.
- Which place had the worst weather?
- Which friend was most unlucky with the weather?

D Read this postcard from Alan and then write two more postcards from Betty and Colin in a similar style, describing the weather in each place.

New York, Wednesday evening, 22 June

Dear Eddie,
It's really boiling here in New York: today has been really hot and sunny with a high of 36°! I was expecting that there would be some rain, but it was sunny at lunchtime when I went for a walk in Central Park. Paris on Tuesday was sunny too, but not as hot as here. London was warmer than I had expected but there was some rain in the afternoon.
See you on Saturday. What's the weather been like where you are?

Best wishes,
Alan

3.7 Compound prepositions — Use of English

Fill the gaps in these sentences with suitable phrases from the list below.
The first is done for you as an example:

1 The flight was cancelled **owing to** the fog.
2 We had wonderful weather every day .... Sunday.
3 Pollution can only be prevented .... international laws.
4 I love all animals .... dogs.
5 Tropical forests are being destroyed .... the demand for hardwood for furniture.
6 .... the weather forecast, it's going to snow.
7 Just a minute, I'll go .... you and hold the door open.
8 Hello. I'm phoning .... Mr Brown. He asked me to give you a message.
9 People should protect trees .... cutting them down.
10 They have two cats .... four pet rabbits.
11 .... pets, I don't think that people should keep them in small apartments.
12 .... conservation, I believe that the government should impose controls.

according to   ahead of   apart from   as for   as regards   by means of
due to   except for   in addition to/as well as   instead of   on behalf of
owing to ✓

3.8 The Greenhouse Effect — Reading

A Fill the gaps in this diagram with information from the passage:

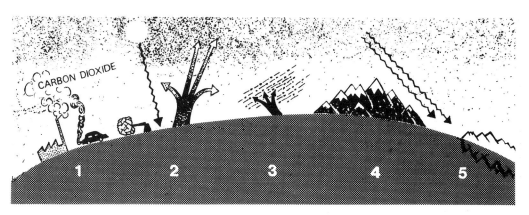

1 The burning of .... (coal, oil and natural gas) and the destruction of .... increase CO_2 in the ....
2 The surface of the Earth radiates .... Some of this escapes into ...., but the rest is .... by the CO_2. The temperature rises.
3 The rise in temperature increases the amount of water .... in the air and this .... more of the Earth's heat.
4 At the poles, snow and ice melt as the .... temperature rises. Because the exposed surface doesn't .... the heat so well, it absorbs more sunlight and more .... is melted.
5 As the oceans .... more heat, they increase the .... effect. The oceans .... and rise as more snow and ice melt.

39

THE GREENHOUSE EFFECT

In the 1960s Professor Bert Bolin predicted that the 'greenhouse effect', caused by an increase in the amount of carbon dioxide (CO_2) in the atmosphere, would lead to important changes in the Earth's climate. At the time his predictions were regarded as science fiction. But it is now generally agreed that the amount of carbon dioxide in the atmosphere will double from 0.03% to 0.06% in the next 50 years and that temperatures worldwide will rise by 2° Celsius.

Although a temperature rise of 2° may not seem significant, the local effects may be much greater: in polar regions a rise of 10° by 2025 is expected and in Northern Europe a rise of 4°. Indeed the first effects will be felt before the end of the century – perhaps they are already being felt . . .

But how does the 'greenhouse effect' operate and why should such a tiny proportion of CO_2 have such a harmful effect? When living creatures breathe out or when things are burned, CO_2 enters the atmosphere. Until recently all of this was absorbed by plants, which converted it back into oxygen.

However, the balance of nature has been disturbed. In power stations, in factories and in our cars, we are burning more and more fossil fuels (coal, oil and natural gas) and this produces huge quantities of CO_2 – 18 billion tons of it enter the atmosphere every year. Added to this, the destruction of forests means that less CO_2 can be converted into oxygen by plants. So, the amount of CO_2 in the atmosphere is increasing every year.

As sunlight enters the Earth's atmosphere, the surface of the Earth is warmed. Some of this heat escapes back into space, but the rest is trapped by CO_2, which acts like the glass in a greenhouse, allowing sunshine and heat to pass in but not out again. Consequently the temperature rises.

As the temperature rises, the amount of water vapour in the air will increase and this too will absorb more of the Earth's heat. The oceans too will become warmer and store more heat, so that they increase the warming effect.

According to Dr Syukuro Manabe of Princeton University, the polar icecaps will start to melt and the oceans will expand as more snow and ice melt. Because the exposed ground, formerly covered in snow, won't reflect the heat so well it will absorb more sunlight and this will lead to even more snow melting.

It is predicted that the level of the sea will have risen by ½ to 1½ metres by 2050 and this will affect many low-lying areas of the world – millions of people today live less than one metre above sea level.

Some areas may actually benefit: the higher temperatures may allow a longer growing season, for example. For Northern Europeans, the extra warmth may be welcome – but there is also likely to be increased rainfall.

But many areas may suffer: the southern states of the USA can expect hotter summers and less rainfall, leading to worse conditions for agriculture, and the Mediterranean region will probably be much drier and hotter than now.

The experts agree that the 'greenhouse effect' will bring significant changes to the Earth's climate. The inhabitants of this planet will have to get used to living in a hotter world.

B Decide whether the following statements are true (**T**) or false (**F**), according to the text.
1 Professor Bolin's predictions were not taken seriously at first.
2 Only a small proportion of the atmosphere consists of carbon dioxide.
3 No changes in climate will become noticeable for 50 years or more.
4 The rise in temperature will probably be 2° in every part of the world.
5 In the north of Europe, temperatures are likely to rise less than in polar regions.
6 CO_2 is produced naturally when we breathe or burn things.
7 CO_2 is converted naturally into oxygen by plants and trees.
8 Increased temperatures will also affect the amount of rainfall.
9 Countries like Greece and Italy are likely to have more rain.
10 Some parts of the world may become cooler as a result of the 'greenhouse effect'.

3.9 Making notes *Composition*

The most important key to writing better compositions is deciding what to write before you put pen to paper – by making notes. Notes help you to:
– organise your thoughts before you begin writing
– remember your ideas after you've started writing a composition.

A There are several styles of making notes. Which of these examples do you prefer?

1 RECYCLING
   1 Advantages:
     (a) saving energy
     (b) less need to burn fossil fuels
     (c) reusing resources
   2 Examples:
     (a) paper – save energy + save trees (but much paper produced on tree farms in places like Canada and Finland)
     (b) bottles – save energy by making new bottles out of old ones, but better to reuse bottles; reusable glass bottles better than throw-away plastic
     (c) aluminium cans – aluminium can be recycled, less need to mine
     (d) steel – save energy
   3 Drawbacks:
     (a) may be expensive
     (b) may require high technology

2
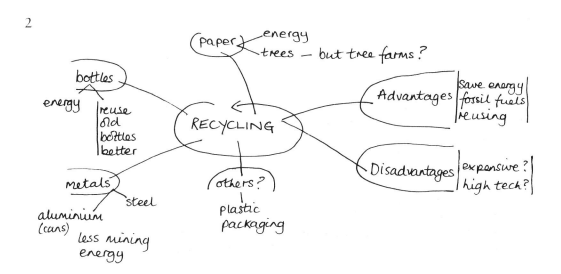

3   paper – save energy, save trees
    bottles – save energy by making new bottles out of old ones,
        but even more saved by reusing bottles
    cans – aluminium can be recycled, less need to mine
    steel – save energy
    energy saving / reusing resources
    expensive / high tech ?

B Work in pairs. Make your own notes, summarising your own views
FOR and AGAINST one of these questions:
1 Save the whales
2 Stop scientific experiments on animals
3 Close all zoos

C Write two paragraphs of about 100 words each, giving reasons why
you agree with and disagree with the question.
   Check your completed work through and correct any errors in spelling
or grammar.

3.10   For or against?   *Listening*

A   You'll hear three topics being discussed. Take notes (in your
own notebook) on the points the speakers make. The first is started for
you as an example here:

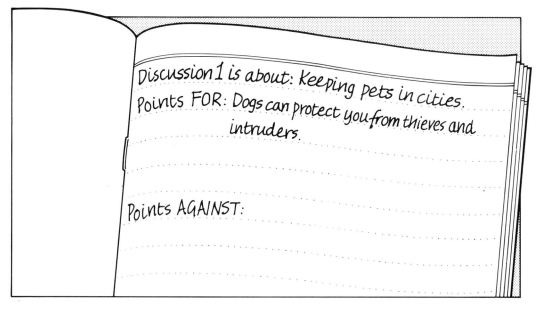

Discussion 1 is about: Keeping pets in cities.
Points FOR: Dogs can protect you from thieves and intruders.

Points AGAINST:

B Work in small groups. Find out your partners' views on the topics
that were discussed.

3.11 How sweet !?
Picture conversation

A Work in pairs. Look at the pictures and write down THREE or FOUR questions that you can ask another pair about each one, or about any related discussion points. Try to think of questions that will lead to INTERESTING, LONG ANSWERS – not just Yes or No.

B Join another pair and ask them your questions. If you get a very short answer, encourage them to say more by prompting them, like this:
- What do you mean exactly?
- Can you give an example?
- I don't quite follow you.
- That's interesting.
- I see, is that what you both think?

C Work in pairs. One of you should look at Activity 34, the other at 44. You'll each have a different picture. Ask your partner these questions:
- What does your photograph show?
- What do you like and dislike about it?
- What kind of pets did your family have when you were younger?
- How would you feel if you were the person in the picture?

43

3.12 Get — Verbs and idioms

A Fill each gap with a suitable phrase from the list below.

1 I'm trying to .... my cold.
2 I hope you soon ....
3 I .... after working all night.
4 She .... because her work was unsatisfactory.
5 We ought to go home, it's ....
6 He didn't laugh because he didn't ....
7 I need plenty of time to .... before I go out.
8 I .... after the party.
9 I was so excited that I couldn't ....
10 If you can't do it yourself, you'll have to .... for you.

get better   get ready   get rid of   get someone else to do it   get the joke
get to sleep   get dark   get a headache   get home late   get the sack

B Fill the gaps in these sentences using the phrasal verbs given below.
The first is done for you as an example:

1 Please ..**get on with**.. your work, I didn't mean to interrupt you.
2 She doesn't .... her younger brother, they're always quarrelling.
3 I hope I'll be able to .... answering the letters this evening.
4 They managed to .... doing the work by pretending to be busy.
5 I tried to .... the point .... to him but he didn't seem to see what I was ....
6 This dull weather is so depressing – it's .... me ....
7 However difficult a problem is, there's usually a way to .... it.
8 You don't need two hot meals a day. I'm sure you can .... on one.
9 .... the bus when you get to the railway station.
10 How are you .... with this exercise?
11 I've tried ringing her several times but I haven't been able to ....
12 They decided to .... later in the week for an informal meeting.

get across   get around/round   get at   get by   get down   get off
get on   get on with ✓   get on with   get out of   get round to
get through   get together

'As you can see, we're very humane in the way we test cosmetics on animals.'

4 Transport and travel

4.1 On the move *Vocabulary*

A Fill the gaps in these sentences with suitable words. The first is done for you as an example:

1 We got on the bus and the c_onductor_ came along to collect our f_are_s.
2 Some cities have buses, trolley-buses and also t_ram_s.
3 By 1993, there won't just be ferries across the English Channel but also a t_unnel_.
4 If you're travelling you can get a single or a r_eturn_ ticket.
5 Pedestrians are supposed to walk on the p_avement_ – sidewalk American
6 We were pleased to find there was a f_ootpath_ so we had a beautiful walk along the cliff top.
7 The lower tax on unleaded p_etrol_ is not going to affect many m_otorists_.
8 If you're sitting in the front seat of a car, you're supposed to wear a s_eat belt_.
9 Before you get in the car, put your luggage in the b_oot_.
10 Chris started the engine, looked in the m_irror_ and drove _off_.
11 There was something wrong with the e_ngine_ of the car so I looked under the b_onnet_.
12 In Britain you have to give w_ay_ to traffic from the right on a r_oundabout_.
13 If you're going to turn left at the traffic l_ights_, get into the left-hand l_ane_.
14 On a narrow road it's almost impossible to overtake a car that's towing a c_aravan_.
15 Take the first left, then the second right and then go s_traight_ on.
16 We drove round the town centre for half an hour looking for a parking s_pace_.
17 Jo hates being a passenger in a car because she gets c_ar s_ick.
18 The driver swerved to avoid hitting the dog but he crashed into a road s_ign_.
19 In Britain, drivers usually stop if you're waiting to cross at a p_edestrian c_rossing. pedestrian
20 When someone is leaving you can say to them, 'Have a nice t_rip_', 'Have a good j_ourney_' or 'Have a safe j_ourney_!'

B In these sentences, choose the best of the alternatives given to fill the gaps.

1 The quickest way to get from London to the north of England is to take the M1 _motorway_.
   by-pass   highway   main road   main street   motorway   ring road
2 It's quicker to cross London by _tube_ than to drive across.
   bus   car   foot   metro   subway   tube
3 It's generally cheaper to travel a long distance by _coach_ than to take the train.
   coach   hearse   limousine   plane   pullman   taxi
4 Go straight down the hill and take the third _turning_ on the left. You can't miss it.
   bend   branch   corner   crossroads   junction   roundabout   turning
5 If you want to stop the car, what you have to do is put your foot on the _brakes_.
   accelerator   brake   break   choke   clutch   handbrake   gas

45

C These nouns are all used in connection with travel, to describe different kinds of JOURNEYS. Match each word to its definition on the right. One is done as an example:

cruise — a short pleasure trip with a group
trip — visiting different places, often with a guide
tour — a short journey or a journey made on business
flight — by ship between two ports
crossing — visiting different places by ship
voyage — by air
excursion — a short pleasure trip
outing — a long distance by ship

★ Remember that the noun *travel* is uncountable and only used as a general term. People say 'Travel broadens the mind' but NOT 'Did you have a good travel?'

D Work in small groups. Ask your partners these questions:
- How do you usually travel to work or school? Why?
- If you have to go to an island, how do you like to travel? Why?
- If you're going away for the weekend, how do you prefer to travel?
- If you have to travel abroad, how do you usually travel?
- When was the last time you ...
  went by train took a taxi flew sailed on a car-ferry rode a bike

4.2 The Orient-Express   *Reading*

A Read through the text fairly quickly. Indicate with an arrow (↓) on the map where the following meals are eaten during a journey on the Orient-Express:

Lunch (day 1)   Dinner   Breakfast   Lunch (day 2)

46

DEPARTURE INTO LEGEND

The 'Orient-Express' was originally conceived by two men, Georges Nagelmackers and George Mortimer Pullman, and built to standards of outrageous luxury late last century and early this. Many carriages were lost during the war. The remainder gradually fell into disuse and finally, in 1977, the service was discontinued.

The present owners began buying one carriage here, another there and restoring them in a way that has not so much become a legend as recreated one.

Today's passenger's first sight of the train is of the magnificent English 'Pullman' cars waiting grandly at London's Victoria Station for their prompt departure.

Days of Days
Just as you may take any sector of the London-Venice route, so you may, of course, fly in to Venice and take the train in a northerly direction home. The route is exactly the same and in both directions we coincide lunch in all its splendour with the Alpine panoramas in all theirs.

But let us suppose that you are journeying from London south to Venice. Your lunch, as you diddly-dum (and you really do) through the ever-pleasing countryside of Kent, will be a taste of things to come. Exquisite food flawlessly served in surroundings of magnificent opulence.

At Folkestone you will slip aboard the ferry, special accommodation reserved and refreshments available, to bid the white cliffs farewell and savour the prospect of the Continental sector.

At Boulogne the stewards are on the platform to welcome you aboard. Courteous and professional to a fault, they love the train and show it in everything they do.

In your cabin, a private day room till its nightly transformation into a bedroom, you will be greeted by your luggage, yet more dazzling marquetry and period brass fitments that will fascinate you. Unpack. Try the gadgets so carefully demonstrated by your steward. Pen a line home on the cards or writing paper provided. Plot your route on the map.

Because now you are well and truly on your journey.

If you are travelling only to Paris your dinner sitting will be the early one.

But early or late, it will be dinner worth calling dinner — and worth dressing for. Course after tantalising course cooked to perfection by superb French chefs, accompanied by famous wines and formally served in restaurant cars each differently appointed but equally devastating in its Twenties opulence.

Yet not even with the brandy is your evening over. For as you retrace your footsteps live piano music lures you to the Bar-Salon.

A Night to Remember
And so, with your cabin miraculously transformed, top sheet turned down and reading lamp left thoughtfully aglow, to bed.

As the train pauses at daybreak your steward will tiptoe past your cabin to pick up the morning papers and fresh croissants.

Continental breakfast, served in your cabin at the time you arranged, sees you stopping at Zürich before the real ascent begins.

Up and up you climb, the views ever grander as you head for the dizzying Arlberg Pass and its $6\frac{1}{2}$ miles of amazing tunnel, then a brief stop at St Anton before lunch.

Lunch, as we promised is a scenic one. Towering forests, and peaks you have to crane to see, alternate with pretty waterfalls and rushing streams to take your breath away.

Innsbruck, 'Roof Garden of Europe' is yet to come, the colossal Brenner Pass where Austria joins Italy, and then the grand descent through the Dolomites to Verona and across the Venetian Plain to the most romantic city in the world.

Venice the Unforgettable
Few would dispute that the train journey is a difficult act to follow.

Even fewer, however, would dispute that if one city can follow it at all, it is certainly Venice.

Over 200 palazzi line the Grand Canal. 400 picturesque bridges link island to island in a web of secluded squares, narrow streets and tiny gardens.

Venice is a splendid prelude or a grand finale to the world's most romantic adventure.

From Venice you can now travel on to Istanbul, the train's original destination, by sea. Board the mv 'Orient-Express' for a week-long cruise back to Venice calling at Piraeus for Athens and the Parthenon, Istanbul, Kusadasi for Ephesus, Patmos and finally Katakolon for Olympia.

B Decide whether the following statements are true (**T**) or false (**F**), according to the text. Refer back to the text whenever necessary.

1 The Orient-Express has been running continuously for 100 years. F
2 You can fly from London to Venice and then return on the Orient-Express. T
3 Lunch is taken on board the ferry between England and France. F
4 At Boulogne you will be greeted in your cabin by your steward. F
5 From Boulogne you travel in a private cabin. T
6 Your cabin on the train is converted into a sleeping compartment by night. T
7 After dinner you can dance to the music of a band in the Bar-Salon. F
8 In the morning, breakfast is served in the restaurant car. F
9 After Innsbruck, the train takes you on to Verona and Venice. T
10 From Venice you can sail to Piraeus and Istanbul. T

C Now underline FIVE phrases used in the passage that help to create an impression of luxury, elegance, wonder and excitement (for example: *built to standards of outrageous luxury*).

D Work in small groups. Describe to your partners a journey you regularly make (e.g. to work, to school, to a holiday destination, etc.). Try to make it sound as attractive, exciting and interesting as possible!

4.3 Revision of modal verbs *Grammar*

A These examples revise the main uses of modal verbs, most of which you should be familiar with. The forms given on the right are the past tense forms. Fill the gaps with suitable words, using your own ideas.

Ability: can / is able to   was able to / managed to
Inability: can't / be unable to / not be able to   couldn't / wasn't able to
Questions about ability: Can he?   Was he able to?

Alex can't swim. Tony can speak Spanish very well.
Anne was able to do the research, but she couldn't write the report.
I know you're a good swimmer, but how well .... on your back?
I .... find my pen anywhere – .... you help me to .... it?
I .... unable .... finish all my work yesterday, but I hope .... it tomorrow.

Possibility: can/may/might/could   may have/could have/might have
Certainty (or near certainty): must   must have
Impossibility: can't/couldn't   can't have/couldn't have
Questions about possibility: Could/Might it ...?

It could/may/might rain later.
We may not be able to get on the bus – it may be full up.
If his name's Spiros, he can't be Italian, he must be Greek.
Your bus .... been two hours late, surely?
.... difficult to get a seat at such short notice?
Jane is always so careful, she .... forgotten to check the timetable – the train .... been delayed.

Permission: can/may   was allowed to
Refusing permission: can't/musn't   couldn't
Questions about permission: Can/Could/May we ...?
   You can/may make notes during the talk if you like.
   Can/Could/May I finish off this work tomorrow?
   We were allowed to visit the church after the service was over.
   You .... when you're in a non-smoking seat.
   You .... a calculator in the maths test because it was against the rules.

Obligation or responsibility:
   must/have to/have got to/should/ought to   had to/should have
Lack of obligation or responsibility:
   don't have to/needn't   needn't have
Obligation or responsibility NOT to do something:
   can't/mustn't/shouldn't/oughtn't to   wasn't allowed to/shouldn't have
Questions about obligation or responsibility:
   Must/Have we got to/Do we have to/Should/Ought we to/Do we need to?
   Do I have to hand the work in tomorrow?
   You don't have to/needn't book in advance if you're going by rail.
   You must/should arrive at 4.30 if you want to get a good seat on the train.
   You .... on the bus unless all the seats are occupied.
   In the exam .... in pen or are we allowed to use pencils?
   You .... so much time listening to music when you .... working.

■ One of the more difficult aspects of the use of modal verbs is that some different forms have different implications. Look at these examples:
   I should have checked my ticket implies that I didn't check it.
   I had to check my ticket implies that I did check it.
   You shouldn't have used a dictionary implies that you did use one.
   We weren't allowed to use dictionaries implies that we didn't use them.
   He needn't have said that implies that he said it even though it was unnecessary to.

B   Find the errors in these sentences and correct them:

1 You needn't to worry about meeting me at the station, I'll get a taxi.
2 Do I ought to phone the airport to find out if there might be any delays?
3 Did you able to find the papers you lost?
4 I couldn't have to show my passport to get a rail ticket.
5 I could buy my ticket after queueing for five minutes.
6 You mustn't write anything down unless you want to.
7 I checked the timetable so I can't to be wrong about the departure time!
8 You don't spend as much time as you must on your homework.
9 May you tell me where I can catch a bus to the railway station?

C Change these sentences so that their meaning remains the same, using a modal verb.

1 In Japan you aren't supposed to eat food as you walk down the street. You ...
2 It was a mistake for me to spend so much money on records. I shouldn't ...
3 Is it necessary for me to pay for my ticket now? Do ...?
4 Please tell me how much luggage I am allowed to take on the plane. Can ...?
5 It isn't possible that her car has broken down again. Her car ...
6 If you have a reserved seat it isn't necessary to stand on the train. You ...
7 I'm sure that you made a mistake when you added up the total. You ...
8 Can you manage to get to the airport at 6.30 a.m.? Will ...?
9 Why did you travel first class? It wasn't necessary, you know. You ...
10 The ticket inspector didn't let us go onto the platform. We ...

D In this short story, all the auxiliaries (will, did, do, have, etc.) and modal verbs are missing. Fill the gaps using the words listed below. Some of them are needed more than once.

1 _Have_ you ever driven a van? I 2 _did_ once. It 3 _was_ just after I left college and I 4 _had_ got myself a temporary job as a delivery man. When I accepted the job I thought I 5 _would_ have to sit beside a driver, chat to him and help him to carry things from the van to the houses, but no, I 6 _was_ on my own and I 7 _had_ to drive the van and carry everything by myself. It 8 _might_ have been very strenuous but after no more than a week I 9 _had_ got used to it and I 10 _was_ able to relax and enjoy the driving. But I 11 _must_ say that I 12 _was_ very glad when I 13 _had_ finished after six weeks. It 14 _would_ have been rather boring in the long run. I 15 _can_ imagine that someone who 16 _has_ to do that kind of job permanently 17 _oughtn't_ mind getting held up in traffic hold-ups as much as I 18 _must_, but something really 19 _could_ to be done to improve road conditions: it 20 _can_ be so frustrating having to spend half your working life sitting in traffic jams. If you 21 _could_ read a book or something it 22 _wouldn't_ be too bad, but of course that 23 _is_ impossible. All you 24 _can_ do is listen to the radio and smoke too much!

can could did do does had has have is might must ought was would

'It's for you.'

50

4.4 Getting the message   *Listening*

A Before you hear the recordings, study the maps and the questions below.

🔊 Now listen to a loudspeaker announcement being made at Southampton railway station. Note down your answers to the questions.

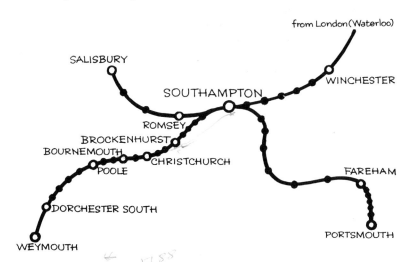

1. Which platform would you go to for a connecting train to ...
   a) Lyndhurst Road   b) Portsmouth   c) Romsey
2. Should you get on the train now if you want to go to ...
   a) Poole   b) Dorchester South   c) Christchurch
3. What should you do if you want to go to ...
   a) Parkstone   b) New Milton   c) Millbrook

B 🔊 Listen to a recorded telephone report on road conditions. Put a cross (✗) at the four places on the map that drivers should AVOID on Saturday afternoon.

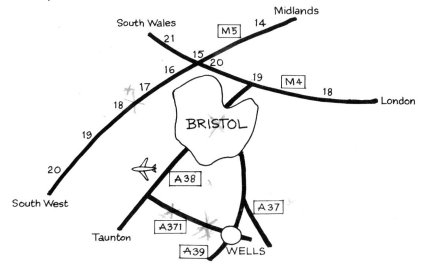

4.5 Using suffixes: Adjectives
Word study

A Look at these examples and fill the gaps with more examples, using the root words below + one of the suffixes in this list.

- -al   regional national *musical, professional, traditional*
- -ical biological geographical *alphabetical, grammatical, mathematical*
- -able acceptable reliable *breakable, enjoyable, obtainable*
- -ful   careful fearful *hopeful, painful, colourful, restful, thoughtful, successful*
- -less painless thoughtless *careless, fearless, restless, useless*
- -ish   childish whitish *foolish, greyish, oldish, smallish, tallish, youngish*
- -y   hairy woolly *bumpy, draughty, noisy, rainy, sleepy, smelly, sunny*

alphabet break bump care colour comfort draught enjoy
fear fool grammar grey hope mathematics music noise
obtain old pain profession rain rest sleep small smell
success sun tall thought tradition use wash young

★ Remember that these words end in -IBLE not -able:
(in)credible (in)edible (in)flexible (im)possible (ir)responsible
(in)visible eligible horrible indelible negligible terrible

B Fill the gaps in these sentences, using a suffix with the correct form of the root word on the right. The first is done for you as an example:

1. It was very ___careless___ of you to break that coffee cup. CARE*less*
2. Thank you for your postcard, it was very _____ of you to send it. THOUGHT*ful*
3. She's quite _____: she plays the flute and the piano. MUSIC*al*
4. It was rather _____ of him to cry when he did badly in the test. CHILD*ish*
5. We started our trip on a beautiful _____ morning. SUN*ny*
6. I enjoyed the book very much because it was so _____ READ*able*
7. His _____ knowledge is very poor – he thinks Paris is in Italy. GEOGRAPHY*cal*
8. Her hair is _____, not bright red. RED*ish*
9. A very old car is usually an un_____ car. RELY *iable*
10. I'll always remember that journey – it was an un_____ experience. *un*FORGET*table*

4.6 *Come* and *go*
Verbs and idioms

A Fill the gaps in these sentences with a suitable form of:
bring carry come deliver fetch go take

1. Will you be able to __come__ and see us next weekend?
2. Will you be able to __go__ and see them in London?
3. I'm certainly going to __take__ a swimsuit with me when I go to the coast.
4. __Come__ round to my house tonight and __bring__ a friend with you, if you like.
5. It was very kind of you to __carry__ my suitcase for me.
6. The goods were __delivered__ to the factory in a van.
7. I'm just going to my room to __fetch__ my glasses – I'll be back in a minute.

52

B Replace the underlined words with a phrasal verb with COME or GO.

1 While I was going through my drawers I found these old love letters.   ACROSS
2 We were faced with several problems.   UP AGAINST
3 I don't understand how these difficulties happened.   ABOUT
4 You shouldn't wear those red socks, they don't match your grey suit.   WITH
5 The beach is washed clean by the sea when the tide rises and you can
   see the rocks sticking out of the water when the tide falls.   IN   OUT
6 Bob has been Mary's boyfriend for a year.   OUT WITH
7 The date on this yogurt is May 1: it must have gone bad by now.   OFF
8 A bomb has exploded and several people have been hurt.   OFF
9 She left at 7 a.m. and we never saw her again.   OFF
10 He entered the competition and won a Caribbean cruise.   IN FOR
11 Hurry up! We have to be at the station in half an hour.   ON
12 Before we continue, let's examine the correct answers to this exercise.   ON   OVER

4.7 Avoid the queues   *Reading and discussion*

A Look at the advertisement and then answer these questions:

1 How many Qs are missing in the advertisement?
2 Which flights depart from Terminal 4 at Heathrow?
3 Why does Terminal 4 seem so calm?
4 What features make Terminal 4 so convenient for motorists?
5 Where do British Airways domestic flights depart from?
6 How can British Airways passengers get from Terminal 1 to Terminal 4?

uiet,
uick,
tran uil.

(You'll miss the Q's when you fly through Terminal 4.)

Right on cue, Terminal 4 at Heathrow opened on April 12th.

If you're flying with British Airways to Paris or Amsterdam, or any intercontinental destination, you'll find it quite different from other terminals.

First there's the sheer size of the place: 64 Check-In desks mean less congestion, and less queueing.

This unique quality of calm continues all the way through to boarding.

Avoiding lifts, stairs and escalators you can quickly wheel your trolley direct from car to plane.

There's easy access by road, parking for 3,200 cars, a brand new Underground station and our own fast, frequent bus service from Terminal 1 for passengers connecting from domestic flights.

In fact everything's organised to help you fly through Terminal 4 in double-quick time.

Any questions?

BRITISH AIRWAYS
The world's favourite airline

B Work in small groups. Find out about your partners' experiences of airports and long distance travel by land, sea and air. Ask these questions:
- What do you like and dislike about airports and flying?
    If you've flown, tell us about your most recent experience.
    Describe the last time you saw someone off or met someone at an airport.
- What do you enjoy and hate about travelling by sea?
    Have you ever been on a ferry? Tell us about it.
- What are the advantages and disadvantages of travelling by car?
- What do you like and dislike about travelling by coach or train?
- What was the most UNUSUAL journey you've ever experienced?
- What was the WORST journey by land, sea or air you've ever experienced?

4.8 InterCity services *Problem solving*

A Work in pairs. Imagine that three friends of yours (Alain, Bobby and Conny) are in Britain for the first time. Each of them has to make a different journey.

Using the map and timetables decide what advice you'd give them:
- What trains should they catch?
- When will they arrive at their final destination?
- How long will the journey take?
- What should they do if there is a slight delay and they miss the first train?

(They should allow at least 40 minutes to travel between London stations by Underground, preferably longer.)

MAKE NOTES on the times and routes you have chosen.

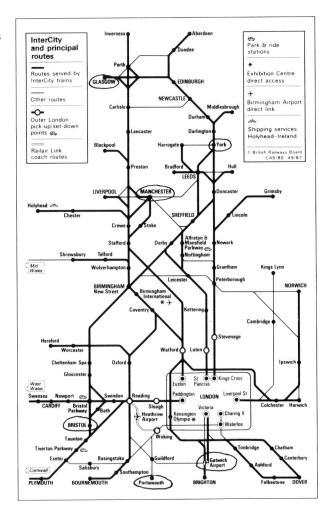

ALAIN is arriving by ferry at Portsmouth at 07.30. He has to get to Glasgow as soon as possible. There is a free bus from the Ferry Port to Portsmouth Station (journey time 15 mins). How can he get to Glasgow and when will he arrive there?

Portsmouth – London						
Portsmouth	0755	0855	0955	1055	1155	1255
London Waterloo	0919	1019	1120	1218	1322	1418

London – Scotland					
London Euston	1030	—	—	1300	1400
London Kings Cross	—	1100	1135	—	—
Glasgow Central	1544	—	—	1830	2009
Edinburgh	—	1556	1652	—	—
Glasgow Queen Street	—	1718*	1821*	—	—

*change at Edinburgh

✈ **London Heathrow – Glasgow**

London Heathrow*	0715	0815	then flights every hour until	2015
Glasgow Airport†	0825	0925		2125

*Underground from Central London to Heathrow – journey time 55 minutes
†Express coach from Airport to Glasgow City Centre every 30 minutes – journey time 20 minutes

BOBBY is flying in to London, Gatwick from Dallas, Texas at 09.55. How can he get to Manchester and when will he arrive there?

Gatwick Airport – The Northwest (direct trains)			
Gatwick Airport	1017	1347	1857
Clapham Junction	1049	1419	1939
Kensington Olympia	1057	1427	1953
Manchester Piccadilly	1405	1805	0010

Gatwick Express: London – Gatwick Airport					
Gatwick Airport	0620	0635	0650	then trains every	2250
London Victoria	0650	0705	0720	15 minutes until	2320

London – Manchester						
London Euston	1020	1150	1250	1420	1520	1600	1700
Manchester Piccadilly	1258	1436	1525	1659	1805	1833	1936

CONNY has been staying in Bristol for a few weeks and on Monday she has an interview in York. The interview is at 12.30.

Bristol – London						
Bristol Temple Meads	0620	0700	0740	0813	0925	1008
Bath Spa	0632	0712	—	0825	0937	1047
London Paddington	0801	0839	0906	0940	1058	1213

London – York							
London Kings Cross	0900	0935	1000	1025	1100	1135	1200
York	1110	1154	1211	1224	1307	1354	1401

Bristol – Midlands – The North				
Bristol Temple Meads	0617	0848	0959	1135
Birmingham New Street	0755	1029	1129	1256
York	1046	1325*	1338	1513

*change at Leeds

B Now look at Activity 12 for some more information about Alain, Bobby and Conny and discuss this with your partner. Make notes on your decisions.

C Using the notes you have made, write three postcards or short letters – one to each friend. Include the advice you would give if they start their journeys on time AND the advice you'd give if they are delayed (as explained in Activity 12). Here are some expressions you can use:

> *When you get to ..., you should ...*
> *If you miss the connection in ..., you should ...*
> *If all goes well, you'll arrive in ... at ...*
> *The best train to take is the ...*
> *If you're late, you should ...*
> *Have a good journey!*

4.9 How do I get there?

Listening

A 🖭 You'll hear a telephone conversation. The man wants to get from Trumpington Street (marked with a ✱ on the map) to an office in St Mary's Street (marked with another ✱). Unfortunately, because of the one-way system he can't just drive straight there, so he phones the office for directions.

Mark the route he has to take with arrows (→→) on the map.

★ Warning: At one point his route takes him off the edge of the map!

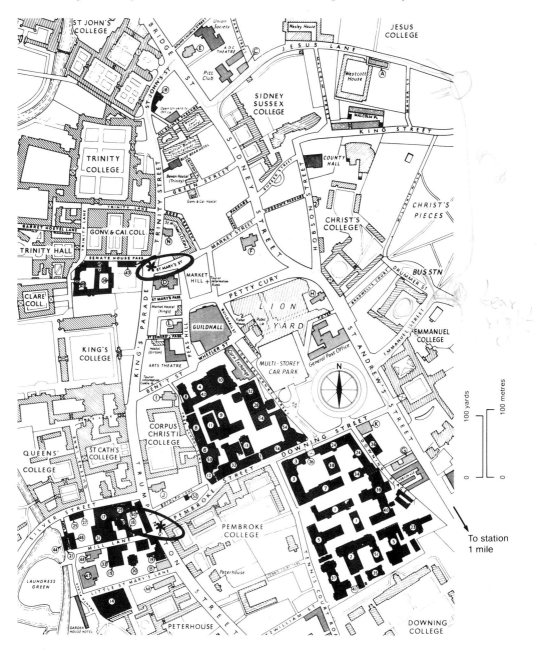

B Work in pairs. Using the map of Cambridge, take it in turns to tell each other how to get on foot:
- from St Mary's Street to the Bus Station
- from the Bus Station to Bridge Street
- from Bridge Street to St Mary's Street
- from St Mary's Street to the station

Here are some useful expressions:

> *Excuse me. Could you tell me how to get to …?*
>
> *Go straight on until you get to the … and then cross the road.*
> *Bear right at the junction and the … is about 5 minutes' walk.*
> *Go past the … and take the first turning on the left.*
> *You'll see the … on your right. You can't miss it.*

4.10 Layout of letters, directions   *Composition*

A In the two letters which follow, Jan is writing to a friend from abroad who is coming to stay for a few days and needs to be told how to get from the airport to 12A Pine Road.

Work in pairs or small groups:
- Which letter do you prefer?
- Looking at both letters, decide which parts of each are more helpful and which parts are less helpful.

> 12A Pine Road
> Greenwood GD12 5OK
>
> 6th June 19--
>
> Dear Alex,
>   I'm afraid I won't be able to meet you when you arrive at the airport as I'll be at work. Unfortunately, there's no easy way of getting here apart from taking a taxi, which would be very expensive.
>   So, if you haven't got too much luggage, I'd suggest taking the underground. You'll have to change twice to get to the nearest station (GREENWOOD). When you come out of the station, turn left and walk along the main road past Sainsburys supermarket and take the first left (South Road). Pine Road is on the right and 12A is on the first floor. My mother will be there to welcome you!
>   But if you don't mind a slower journey there is a direct bus (No. 108) which will take you all the way from the airport - there's a stop opposite Greenwood Station. Ask the driver to tell you when to get off.
>   Looking forward to seeing you on Friday evening.
>   Jan
>
> P.S. If you get lost or if you're delayed, phone me at work (071 4418 extension 679).

12A Pine Road
Greenwood GD12 5OK

6 June 19--

Dear Alex,

Sorry I won't be able to meet you. Here's a quick note on how to get here from the airport. There are three alternatives:

1/ TAXI: This would be very expensive, so unless you have a lot of luggage not advisable.
2/ BUS: There is a direct bus (number 108), which is cheap, but slow. Ask the driver to tell you when he gets to Greenwood Station.
3/ UNDERGROUND: This is quick but you'd have to change twice, which could be tricky if you have loads of luggage.
Looking forward to seeing you.

Jan

P.S. I enclose a map to help you find your way to our flat in Greenwood.

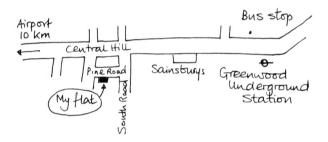

B How do you get from the airport (or main station) in YOUR city or town to YOUR home?

1 Write an informal letter to a friend who has never visited your country before, giving advice on how to get to your home when he or she arrives.
2 Make notes before you start.
3 Check your completed letter through afterwards and correct any mistakes you notice.
4 Show your completed letter to another student and ask for comments.

'Excuse me, those seats are taken.'

4.11 Using prepositions – 1 — *Use of English*

This is the first of three exercises on prepositions used after certain verbs, adjectives and nouns.

Fill the gaps with a suitable preposition from the list below:

1. Everyone **admires** him __for__ his wisdom and common sense.
2. I **agree** __with__ you __about__ the need to improve public transport services.
3. Dick **apologised** __for__ not sending us a thank you letter.
4. I don't **approve** __of__ travelling first class on trains or planes.
5. We all started to **argue** __with__ him __about__ his political ideas.
6. I **believe** __in__ government support for public transport services.
7. Everyone can **benefit** __from__ a better road system.
8. You can't **blame** me __for__ your own mistakes.
9. Peter's always **boasting** __about__ his own achievements.
10. Would you like to **borrow** a pen __from__ me?
11. Max is **capable** __of__ doing much better work than this.
12. We would like to **congratulate** you __on__ getting engaged.
13. Water **consists** __of__ hydrogen and oxygen.
14. The salesman tried to **convince** me __of__ the advantages of buying the car.
15. There is no simple **cure** __for__ hay fever.

about for from in of on with

4.12 Transport in the future — *Communication activity*

What changes will there be to transport systems in the future?

1. Work alone. Begin by making a few notes on this subject.
2. 🎭 Work in groups of three. One of you should look at Activity 2, another at 8 and the other at 28. You'll each have different ideas to consider about transport in the future. Study the notes for a few moments.
3. Ask your partners for their views on transport in the future. DON'T read word-for-word from the notes.

Here are some useful expressions:

> I'm quite sure that in the future ...   It seems to me that ...
> Perhaps one day in the future we'll ...   Do you think that ... ?
> I don't agree that ...   Why do you think that ... ?

5 Somewhere to live

5.1 Make yourself at home! *Vocabulary*

A Work in small groups. Ask your partners these questions:
- In your own home, where do you work or study? How is this room furnished?
- When you're working, do you need complete silence or is it easy to concentrate?

B Fill the gaps in these sentences with suitable words:

1 If I could build my own house I'd make sure it had an a...tic.
2 Our n.e.i....s are always complaining about the noise we make.
3 My friends live in a small terr... house in a street where all the houses look alike.
4 The block of flats she lives in has five s.tore...s and she lives on the top f.loor.
5 In the city centre, inexpensive a........ is hard to find because it is scarce.
6 Many new estates are being built on the o........s of the city and in the s........s.
7 I'd love to m........ to the country and live in an old ....
8 If someone borrows money to buy their home, they have to repay the m........
9 If someone else owns your house or flat, you have to pay r........ to a l........
10 Modern flats often don't have enough .... to store things in.
11 Books are usually kept in a b........ or on s........s.
12 Even though their house has c........ h........ there is a fireplace in the l........
13 In a bedroom, clothes are kept in a ....
14 The most important thing about a house or flat is that it should be ....

C Choose the best alternative to fill the gaps in these sentences:

1 Some houses have a basement room where things are stored called a(n) ....
   attic   cave   cellar   grave   loft
2 Some rooms don't have curtains at the windows, they have .... instead.
   blinds   carpets   glass   stores   wallpaper
3 We haven't got a garage, so we leave our car outside the house in the ....
   drive   garden   parking   patio   pavement   porch
4 He keeps all his tools and do-it-yourself equipment in a .... in the back garden.
   barn   bungalow   hut   shack   shed   stable
5 In your own garden, you can sunbathe on the .... in the summer.
   field   flowerbed   lawn   meadow   pasture

D Work in small groups. Draw a floor plan of your own homes.
- Explain to your partners what FURNITURE and equipment is in each room.
- Find out about your partners' homes and the area or district they live in.
- How are your homes different from each other's?
- If they had the choice, where would your partners most like to live?

5.2 Different places   *Listening and speaking*

A Listen to the conversation and answer these questions:

1 Where exactly does Charles live?
2 Where exactly does Ruth live?
3 What does Ruth like about where she lives?
4 What does Charles like about where he lives?
5 What does Charles dislike about it?
6 What does Ruth dislike about it?
7 Where would Charles prefer to live?
8 Where would Ruth prefer to live?

B Work in groups. Ask your partners these questions about the photographs:
- What would it be like to live in each place? (Or what is it like to live there?)
- What would be the attractions of living there?
- What would be the disadvantages of living there?
- If you had to choose between the two, which would you prefer and why?
- How is the place you live in different from these places? How is it similar?

5.3 The future *Grammar*

A The examples below show the ways in which we can refer to the future. Fill the gaps with suitable words, using your own ideas.

PREDICTIONS + GENERAL FUTURE: *will/will be doing/will have done*

In the future the Earth will be hotter.   I expect it will rain tomorrow.
By the end of this year I'll have taken my exam.
While I'm studying, my younger sister will be enjoying herself.
I'm sure the weather .... towards the end of the week.
She is very clever, so I expect that she .... her exams next summer.
If you don't hurry up, the bus .... before we get to the bus stop!

- Remember that *will* and *'ll* are NOT normally used in a clause following a time conjunction: *when if until before after while by the time*
If you do your work tonight, you'll be able to go out tomorrow.
We'll tidy up our rooms before she arrives.
After he has done the housework, he'll have to start cooking the dinner.
If you ...., you'll find it easier to remember the new words.
When my friend ...., I'll tell her all about my plans.
By the time our guests ...., all the food will have been eaten.

The short form *'ll* is normally only used after pronouns:
I'll do it.   It'll rain tomorrow.
But in writing, or for emphasis, the full form is often used:
I will do it.   It will rain tomorrow.

FUTURE EVENTS that we can 'see coming': *going to*

One day there's going to be a terrible accident on that road.
My wife's going to have a baby.
Look out! That dog is going to bite you!
Look at those black clouds – it is going to .... soon.

INTENTIONS and PLANS: *going to*

I'm going to leave now.   We're going to visit Spain next year.
I .... the work later, when I've got more time.
Your room is in a terrible mess – when .... ?

ARRANGEMENTS: PRESENT CONTINUOUS

I'm seeing the dentist at 2.30.   I'm meeting my friend this afternoon.
I can't meet you this evening because ....
Mr and Mrs Jones .... to dinner tomorrow.

FIXED EVENTS on a timetable or calendar: PRESENT SIMPLE

The exam takes place on June 13th and 14th. (= it's in the calendar)
The plane from London .... at 9.30.
Tomorrow, according to my diary, the sun .... at 5.09.

- *Going to* can be used instead of *will* or a present tense. In conversation, *going to* is more common than *will*, but in writing *will* is more often used. A rule of thumb for conversation is: 'If in doubt, use *going to*' – except if you're making a promise, offer or suggestion (when *going to* may sound like a threat).

PROMISES, SUGGESTIONS and OFFERS: *will*

I'll pay for lunch if you help me with my work.   I'll help you tomorrow.
Give me your suitcase and .... in the boot of the car for you.
I .... the money you lent me next Friday.

■ Normally, in modern English, *shall* is only used when making suggestions:
   Shall I help you? ✓   NOT: Will I help you? ✗
   Shall we take a break now? ✓   NOT: Will we take a break now? ✗
and NOT in these cases:
   He shan't arrive on time. ✗   They shall be late. ✗
   He won't arrive on time. ✓   They'll (will) be late. ✓

B Find the errors in these sentences and correct them.

1 If the telephone will ring, I'll answer it.
2 After the floor will have been cleaned, I'll polish the furniture.
3 This evening I tidy my room.
4 By the time you get home we will finish dinner.
5 We'll be waiting for you when your plane is going to land at the airport.
6 Elizabeth has a baby next month.
7 The new by-pass shall be finished in the spring.
8 You won't be able to unlock the door if you won't remember your key.

C Rewrite this 'telegram' as an informal letter – add any necessary grammatical words but NO extra information. Each line of the 'telegram' should become a complete sentence, as the examples show.

Dear Jan,
1 WE NOT SEE / YOU / SUCH A LONG TIME.
   We haven't seen you for such a long time.
2 OUR LATEST NEWS BE / NEXT WEEK / WE MOVE HOUSE!
   Our latest news is that ...
3 NEW FLAT BE / OUTSKIRTS / CITY.
4 FLAT NOT BE LARGER / BUT WE BE ABLE GROW / VEGETABLES / GARDEN.
5 WE HOPE / NO PROBLEMS / NOISY AND NOSY NEIGHBOURS AS / NOW.
6 WE BE GLAD / ESCAPE / NOISE AND TRAFFIC / CITY CENTRE.
7 MY JOURNEY TO WORK TAKE LONGER / BUT / ENJOY / FRESH AIR AND PRIVACY.
8 WE / TAKE / DOG / WALK / ACROSS FIELDS EVERY EVENING.
9 SUNDAY 14TH / WE HAVE / FLAT-WARMING PARTY.
10 YOU BE ABLE / COME?
11 WE LOOK FORWARD / SEE YOU / ANY TIME AFTER 7 P.M.
   Best wishes from Terry and Jo
12 P.S. YOU NOT FIND / NEW FLAT / WITHOUT DIRECTIONS.
13 IF YOU PHONE ME / I TELL YOU / HOW / GET THERE.

5.4 A nice place to live

Reading

A Decide which of these statements are true (**T**) or false (**F**), according to the newspaper article.

1 Swansea was the second politest place in the country.
2 The British Polite Society tested Norwich by visiting the city.
3 The British Polite Society's secretary has not personally visited Norwich yet.
4 The healthiest town in Britain is now Shrewsbury.
5 The rudest place in Britain is not named by Mr Gregory.
6 The British Polite Society has received complaints about doctors.
7 Both bar staff and bar customers are rude to each other.
8 According to Julian Roux there is one place nicer than Norwich.
9 In 1988 Norwich was named the most pleasant place in Europe.
10 Norwich's public relations officer says nowhere is as nice as Norwich.

Norwich is pleased to pull off a nice one

David Sharrock

IF you're reading this in Norwich, the chances are that you got out of bed on the right side this morning, that the newsagent smiled and said thank you as he took your money, that your bus queue is orderly and well-behaved, and that all is peace and harmony.

That's because the British Polite Society has just named the good people of Norwich as the "courteous community of the year".

The society's secretary, the Reverend Ian Gregory, said Norwich received the most recommendations from members this year, beating Swansea, Northampton and Portsmouth, and squeezing Alresford, Hampshire, into second place.

Polite Society agents tested the city's reputation, and returned with nothing but praise for the manners of its hoteliers, shopkeepers and publicans.

"We found Norwich to be a city with a smile," says Mr Gregory, who will visit the town for the first time this week. "Last year Shrewsbury won the award, and I hear they've just been placed top of a list for healthy living."

Could he name the rudest place in Britain? "No, we don't do that sort of thing," recalling the commitment to good manners. What about a clue, then? "Well, we did have a problem with doctors' receptionists about six months ago, and we get a lot of complaints about bar staff. But then, we also get complaints from bar staff about the customers."

None of this, needless to say, concerns Norwich. Julian Roux, landlord of the Louis Marchesi pub, swears he knows not a single unpleasant person, and rates only Lowestoft, his birthplace, as a nicer place. "The people here are very relaxed, which a Londoner would probably mistake for stupidity. If you played poker here, you'd discover we can be very cunning."

Probably none of this will come as a surprise to the citizens because in 1986 the EEC decided that Norwich possessed the most pleasant environment in Europe.

It fell to Norwich council's public relations officer, Mr Tim Anderson, to offer the only consolation non-Norwich residents can expect. "We're reasonably nice to each other, but I'm sure that many other towns are equally as nice." Now isn't that nice of him to say so?

B Find the word or phrase in each paragraph of the passage that means the same as these words and phrases. There are nine paragraphs: the numbers show which paragraph you should look at. The first is done for you as an example:

1 were in a good mood – *got out of bed on the right side*
2 polite   5 prize   8 people
3 pushing   6 behaviour   9 comfort or reassurance
4 representatives   7 of course

C Work in small groups. Ask each other these questions:
- How polite are people in different parts of your own country?
- Which place would win the 'most courteous community' award in your country?
- Which nation would win the 'most courteous nation award'?
- Why are people sometimes rude or unpleasant to each other?
- What kind of behaviour would you describe as 'nice' and 'polite'?

5.5 High-rise buildings *Listening*

A You'll hear a radio programme in which an expert is being interviewed about skyscrapers and high-rise apartment blocks. Make notes in the spaces below:

NOTES

Where and when was the first skyscraper built?
....
Why was it built? 1 ....
                   2 ....
                   3 ....
Where is the world's tallest apartment block?
....
Where is the tallest in the UK?
....
How do people who live in tower blocks feel?
....
What kind of flats are vandalised?
....
How can vandalism be prevented?
   1 ....
   2 ....
   3 ....
   4 ....

B Work in small groups. Find out about your partners' experiences of living in high-rise flats. Is vandalism a problem in their area or their city?

5.6 Using prepositions – 2   *Use of English*

Fill the gaps in these sentences with a suitable preposition:

1. How are we going to **deal** _with_ this problem?
2. There's no such thing as a perfect home – it all **depends** .... the individual.
3. Bill was **engaged** _to_ Liz for two years and then got **married** _to_ Jane!
4. I'll never **forgive** Bill _for_ the way he treated his fiancée.
5. Our new sofa was uncomfortable so we **exchanged** it _for_ a different one.
6. I said I could move the furniture by myself, but she **insisted** _on_ helping me.
7. I hope that our plans don't **interfere** _with_ your own arrangements.
8. Helen, I'd like to **introduce** you _to_ George, our next-door neighbour.
9. George is **involved** _in_ politics: he's our local councillor.
10. Now that George has been elected we all **hope** _for_ better things in the future.
11. Are you **interested** _in_ local politics, by any chance?
12. Many residents don't have much **confidence** _in_ our new mayor.
13. Some of the tenants are angry about the **lack** _of_ car parking spaces in the area.
14. She's **longing** _for_ the day when they can move out of the city.

5.7 Spelling and pronunciation: Vowels   *Word study*

A   One of the main difficulties of English spelling is that some words are spelt differently and have different meanings but are pronounced the same. Can you think of words pronounced the same as each of these, but spelt differently?

guessed _guest_   brake _break_   whole _hole_   steel _steal_   threw _through_

B   Work in small groups. Add the words on the next page to the appropriate lists below, according to their pronunciation. The first is done for you as an example:

æ	bad	damage	**scandal marry**	
e	bed	pleasure	leisure	lent/leant
aɪ	bite	height	guide	eye/I
ɑː	calm	heart		
ɔː	bored/board	warm	caught/court	
ɜː	bird	worm		
aʊ	now	crowd		
ɔɪ	boy	point		
eə	there/their	scarce	where/wear	
ɪə	here/hear	steer		
eɪ	make	sale/sail	break/brake	
əʊ	note	joke	whole/hole	
iː	sheep	piece/peace		
ɪ	ship	sink	mystery	

ɒ	pot	what	yacht			
uː	boot	truly	threw/through			
ʊ	put	should	wood/would			
ʌ	cut	worry	money			

plough allowed/aloud • not/knot knowledge quality wander
• ceiling/sealing seize/seas weak/week receive meat/meet
seen/scene • cleared atmosphere sincere • wore/war
shore/sure source/sauce walk warn/worn raw/roar • cushion
butcher pull push • scandal marry • destroy employer •
bury/berry weather/whether guessed/guest merry check/cheque •
stares/stairs fare/fair pair/pear • guilty business witch/which
mist/missed • paint wait/weight male/mail waste/waist •
turn work • soup blue/blew root/route new/knew •
folk soap nose/knows • laugh castle half guard • blood
tongue country one/won thorough wonder • climb it/climate
right/write by/buy/'bye

★ Note that in American English and in regional accents of British
English, several of these 'rules' of pronunciation and spelling don't apply.
For example, *caught* and *court* are pronounced differently in many accents.

C Find the THREE spelling mistakes in each of these sentences and
correct them:

1 I am quite shore that this weak is going too be wonderful.
2 We are truely sorry that you had to weight so long four the delivery.
3 He has dredful manners — he paws tomato source on all his food.
4 They couldn't get thier new armchare threw the door.
5 Witch of these too alternatives is the write one?
6 He lent the ladder agenst the wall and climed onto the roof.
7 The cieling and walls of this room need peinting ergently.

D Now listen to the tape and write down the missing word in
each of these sentences. The first is done for you as an example:

1 I'm afraid that I might ...**break**... this glass.
2 What's the matter with him I ....?
3 They .... across the park hand in hand.
4 What is the .... of this wall?
5 In some cities, apartment blocks have ....
6 I don't really have any .... of this subject.
7 I find that .... to work keeps me fit.
8 It's no fun if you're .... in a downpour.
9 I'll pay for any .... I have caused.
10 Let me know when you .... the package.

5.8 Finding a flat
Listening and problem solving

Imagine that Jill and John are two English friends of yours who are looking for a flat to live in when they get married in the spring. They have been looking at flats in Greenwood, where Jill works. John works in the city, about half an hour by train from Greenwood station.

A First look at these advertisements for three flats they have decided are worth viewing.
- Which of these properties would YOU prefer?
- What is not mentioned in the ads that you would only find out by viewing them?

B 🎧 You'll hear Jill and John discussing the three flats after viewing them.
- Listen to their discussion and MAKE NOTES on the pros and cons of each flat.
- Which of the three did they like best of all, do you think? Did they both agree on this?

C Write three paragraphs, describing your friends' feelings about each of the flats they viewed, beginning as follows:
Jill and John might have chosen 7B Windsor Avenue because ...
They might have decided against 44C Sandringham Gardens because ...
They might have rejected 13A Balmoral Way because ...

D Work in small groups. Design your own ideal home. Draw a simple plan and make a list of the features you would have.
When you're ready, describe your dream house to the rest of the class.

5.9 Welcome to G__! *Reading*

A Read the passage through and then answer the questions on the next page.

G __ is a delightfully unspoilt village surrounded by fields and woods at the mouth of a river. Yet it's only a short bus ride from the old city of H __ with its factories, industry and heavy traffic.

The countryside around the village is incredibly green, with fertile fields, olive groves and eucalyptus and cypress trees. Through the village flows a wide, clear river, along the banks of which are moored a fleet of fishing boats. Upstream the river is broader and shallower and is the home of a multitude of birds and other wildlife. Along the banks of the river you can glimpse wild duck peeping shyly from the undergrowth.

If you're a nature-lover the walk through the countryside to Lake K __ is wonderful and as it takes less than an hour is well worth the effort. This big inland lake which is fed by the melting winter snow off the mountains is lovely for swimming. The fishing is said to be excellent too, though I've no personal experience of this.

In the centre of G __ is the village square. Like many of the 'roads' in G __, the square is unpaved but rock hard from centuries of foot traffic. Dominating the square are a couple of silver-barked eucalyptus trees which in the spring are alive with nesting birds. Between the trees are a statue and a fountain. Around the square are a few inexpensive restaurants, a couple of bars and some little shops. Right in the middle of the square, in the way of what little traffic there is, is a small kiosk run by an old lady, who sells everything from razor blades to chewing gum. Locals and visitors alike sit for hours over a drink in one of the bars, watching nothing much happen.

From the village square a dirt track

leads you down through eucalyptus trees to the beach in a few minutes. This is a magnificent stretch of pale yellow sand, overlooked by bamboos and a few trees, which stretches away to the horizon. There's just one bar on the beach which serves light lunches and drinks.

The local people are farmers or fishermen, though more and more are now building extra rooms on their property, which they let to visitors in the summer. However, so far there are no large hotels and the village has avoided the effects of mass tourism and kept its character and charm.

If you're looking for peace and quiet and a lovely rural environment, then G __ is the place to escape to – before everyone else discovers it!

Welcome to G __!

1 From G__ to the nearest town it is ...
   a long way   not far ✓
2 At its mouth the river is ...
   shallow ✓   deep
3 From G__, Lake K__ is ...
   under an hour's walk ✓   over an hour's walk
4 G__'s village square is ...
   lively   sleepy ✓
5 From the village square to the beach is ...
   a short walk ✓   a long walk
6 For their income the local people ...
   depend on tourism   don't depend on tourism ✓
7 As more visitors come to G__, they have ...
   changed its atmosphere   not changed its atmosphere ✓
8 The writer refers to the village as 'G__' because he or she ...
   wants to keep it a secret ✓   doesn't remember its name

B Work in small groups. Ask your partners these questions:
- Would you like to live in a place like G__?
- What are the advantages and disadvantages of living in a village like G__?
- What are the benefits and drawbacks of living in a large city?
- If you could choose, would you rather live in a city or in the country? Why?

5.10 Starting and ending well   *Composition*

A good piece of writing requires:
- an INTRODUCTION that will catch the reader's attention
  and
- an ENDING that will leave the reader satisfied.

The first and the last sentence are particularly important.

A Which of these sentences could be used in place of the opening sentence of the description of G__ in 5.9:
   'G__ is a delightfully unspoilt village surrounded by fields and woods at the mouth of a river.'

1 ... is a village I know very well.
2 One of the most interesting developments of recent years is ...
3 The village of ... is set on a scenic river mouth.
4 The other day, I was talking with some friends about ...
5 I'll never forget the day that I first went to ...
6 One thing we tend to take for granted nowadays is ...
7 Recently everyone has been talking about ...
8 ... is a subject that is on everyone's mind these days.
9 I'm going to tell you something about a place I know, called ...
10 I'd just like to say a few words about ...

B Which of these sentences could be used instead of the closing sentence:

'Welcome to G__!'

1 Looking forward to seeing you in ... before too long.
2 You can imagine how we felt!
3 You can catch a bus back to the city from the village square.
4 So that's about all there is to say about it.
5 One thing is certain: a solution must be found before it is too late.
6 You'll find that ... is surprisingly easy to make and delicious too!
7 So, goodbye from ...!
8 It is quite different from other places you may have visited.
9 So I hope you'll be able to come with me to ... soon.
10 I can't think of anything else to write.

C Work in pairs. Look back through all the previous reading passages in Units 1 to 5 and pick your two favourite opening sentences and your two favourite closing sentences.

Look at your own recent compositions. Can you or your partner improve on the opening and closing sentences you wrote?

D Write a description of:
the district, town or village you live in OR your own home.
Imagine that you're writing to a foreign friend and you want to persuade him or her to come and visit you.
- MAKE NOTES before you start writing and decide what your opening and closing sentences will be.
- Check your work through afterwards.

5.11 Grammar revision

This exercise revises some of the grammar points that you have studied in the first five units. In the exam, you'll have to do an exercise very like this one.

Finish each incomplete sentence in such a way that it means the same as the complete sentence before it. The first is done for you as an example:

1 We have known each other since 1987. We first ...
   We first met in 1987.
2 We lived in the country during my childhood. When ...
3 We moved into this district eight years ago. We have ...
4 The chairs and tables have to be moved from this room. The furniture ...
5 We'll redecorate our flat after our summer holiday. After we ...
6 I'm sure that someone forgot to lock the door. Someone must ...
7 We finished spring-cleaning and then went out for a meal. After we ...
8 During our meal, we discussed what to do at the weekend. While ...
9 This room has been painted since the last time I was here. You hadn't ...
10 It wasn't a good idea to paint the walls pink. You ...

6 Science and technology

6.1 Talking about science   *Vocabulary*

A Work in small groups. Ask your partners these questions:
- What aspects of science or technology have a direct effect on your life?
- What is the purpose of scientific research?
- What is the purpose of studying the stars and other planets?
- Is it worth spending huge amounts of money on space travel and exploration?

B Fill the gaps in these sentences with suitable words.

1. A single __molecule__ of water (H_2O) consists of two a__toms__s of hydrogen and one of oxygen.
2. The most common e__lement__ in the air we breathe is nitrogen (N).
3. Salt (sodium chloride – NaCl) is a c__ompound__ of sodium and chlorine.
4. Plutonium and uranium are r__adioactive__ substances used in nuclear power stations.
5. The three main branches of science are: ch__emistry__ (the study of the elements that make up the universe), ph__ysics__ (the study of matter and natural forces) and b__iology__ (the study of living things).
6. Einstein's famous f__ormula__ $E = mc^2$ (where E = energy, m = mass and c = the speed of light), is part of his theory of relativity.
7. Scientists can find out if a theory is true by carrying out e__xperiments__s.
8. An experimental scientist does much of his or her work in a l__aboratory__.
9. The inventor made a working model of his invention in his w__orkshop__ and then invited the press to watch a d__emonstration__.
10. An idea may sound as if it works in theory, but it may not work in p__ractice__.
11. In mathematics, a theorem (e.g. 'the sum of the angles in any triangle is 180°') is a concept or idea that can be p__roved__ by logical reasoning.
12. Technology is the activity of using scientific knowledge for p__ractical__ purposes.
13. An expert method or skill used in doing something (e.g. playing a musical instrument or taking exams) is called a te__chnique__.
14. Computers, radios and TV are all el__ectronic__ equipment.
15. A computer and the equipment used with it are known as the h__ard__ware and the programs that tell it what to do are known as s__oft__ware.
16. The data (information) produced on a computer is stored on a d__isc / tape__.
17. To find out how something works and how to operate it you must read the i__nstructions__.
18. Some video recorders have a remote control: you just have to press a i__nstruct__ to pause or to rewind the tape.
19. You can a__djust__ the volume on the TV by turning this knob.
20. Any complicated piece of equipment needs to be s__erviced__ regularly, otherwise it may b__reak down__ unexpectedly at any time and it may be expensive to have it r__epaired__.
21. In a modern car factory, some of the work is done by r__obot__s, not people.

22 Two of the *components* of a car are the tyres and the engine.
23 Some common tools used by a *carpenter* are a hammer, a saw and a *drill*.
24 To make a piece of furniture you need some wood, *screw* and some *nails*.
25 If you're not sure what something is called you can call it a watchamacallit or a thingumajig or a whatnot or a *divice*.

C Work in small groups. Think of some gadgets or equipment that you use at home or at work (e.g. bicycle, hairdryer, electric shaver, cassette player, etc.). Without getting too technical (and without opening them up to find out what's inside!), list the important controls, parts and components. Use a dictionary if necessary. Tell the other groups what you have found out.

6.2 For a pint, just add water *Reading*

A Before you read the article, find out if anyone in the class knows how beer is brewed – what are the ingredients and how do they become beer?

B Read the newspaper article and answer the questions on the next page.

For a pint, just add water

STRASBOURG: Fischer, the third largest brewery in France, has developed a new product that it hopes will put some life back into the beer market – a beer concentrate.

The thick brown liquid is the latest product to emerge from Fischer's laboratory. When mixed with six parts of carbonated water, the reconstituted beer is indistinguishable from the real stuff even to experts, the brewery's president Mr Michel Debus said.

Mr Debus said it took 30 years to develop a method of removing water from beer without sacrificing its original flavour or fragrance.

Fischer uses a new process called "inverted osmosis". The beer is forced at high pressure through a molecular sieve which separates water and alcohol from the brew.

A similar process is used in some Arab countries to desalinate seawater. Fischer has patented the process but has added a secret technique to preserve the beer's taste.

Beer concentrate, Mr Debus said, "is the dream of brewers all over the world." In the beer brewing business, he said, increasing capacity meant building new, costly breweries. With the concentrate, "one plant can supply bottlers anywhere on earth."

Fischer has sent samples of the concentrate to dozens of countries, offering an impressive variety of flavours, sweet for the United States, bitter for Japan, non-alcoholic for Muslim countries.

The initial response, Mr Debus said, was very encouraging. Fischer hopes to sign its first big contract in September for the distribution of reconstituted beer in Japan, and is negotiating deals with West German and Swiss firms.

Mr Debus said Fischer is likely to do most business with countries in the Far East and North Africa where brewing beer is either not well established or impractical. He wants to break into the US market with the non-alcoholic version, to be called Energy.

The concentrate, Mr Debus said, will be sold only to bottling companies, not directly to consumers, and bottlers will be required to use water specified by Fischer but may add alcohol and choose the trade name.

Fischer hopes to corner 2 per cent of the 26 billion gallon world beer market.

1 This article is about ...
   a) a new kind of beer that contains no alcohol
   b) a new kind of beer that is more tasty than traditional beers
   c) a new liquid that can be mixed with water to make beer
2 According to Mr Debus ...
   a) Only the most expert tasters can tell that the concentrate is not real beer.
   b) No one can taste the difference between the concentrate and real beer.
   c) The average consumer cannot taste the difference.
3 The process used by Fischer is similar to ...
   a) freezing   b) removing salt from seawater   c) filtering coffee
4 The advantage of the new process is that beer ...
   a) will be cheaper
   b) can be bottled more cheaply
   c) will be more tasty all over the world
5 Mr Debus thinks the most promising market will be ...
   a) the USA   b) Europe   c) Asia and North Africa
6 Fischer will supply ...
   a) one flavour   b) a wide range of flavours   c) three flavours
7 Mr Debus hopes to sell the product in America as ...
   a) a drink for active people
   b) an old-fashioned European beer
   c) a non-alcoholic drink
8 The new product will be on sale to consumers ...
   a) as a concentrate
   b) under the 'Fischer' brand name
   c) under various brand names

6.3 Using the passive   *Grammar*

A Study these rules and examples of the main uses of the passive.

The passive is used when the person responsible for an action is not known or is not important:
   The beer **is forced** at high pressure through a sieve.
   A similar process **is used** in some Arab countries.
   I **was given** a watch for my birthday.
   These problems **will have to be solved** before we can go ahead.

The passive is also used when we want to avoid mentioning the person responsible for an action:
   You **were asked** to arrive at 8 a.m.   (less 'personal' than: I asked you to arrive.)
   This composition **must be handed in** next Monday.

By **is often used with the passive to show who was responsible for an action:**
   Penicillin **was discovered by** Alexander Fleming.
   The first landing on the moon **was made** in 1969 **by** the Americans.
   The research **is being done by** a team of European scientists.

■ Often there is no great difference in meaning between a passive and an active sentence when the person who performed the action is unimportant. The passive can be used to give variety to the style of a passage, as in these examples:

Seventeen muscles **are used** when you smile but 43 **are used** when you frown.
You use seventeen muscles when you smile but you use 43 when you frown.
Fischer has sent samples to dozens of countries.
Samples **have been sent** to dozens of countries.
The committee will announce the names of the Nobel Prize winners in May.
The names of the Nobel Prize winners **will be announced** in May.

(But NOT: I'll meet you tomorrow. / You will be met tomorrow.)

B Fill the gaps in this table, which shows the basic structures used in the passive. The first two are done for you as examples:

ACTIVE		PASSIVE
They often do it.	→	It is often done.
They are doing it now.	→	It is being done now.
They did it yesterday.	→	It was done yesterday.
They were doing it last week.	→	It was been done last week.
They have already done it.	→	It has already been done.
They will soon do it.	→	It will soon be done.
They will soon have done it.	→	It will soon have been done it.
They had done it earlier.	→	It had been done earlier.
They have to do it at once.	→	It has to be done at once.
They may not have done it yet.	→	It may not have been done yet.

C Finish the incomplete sentences in such a way that each one means the same as the complete sentence before it.

1 Fischer has patented the process. — The process ...
2 Fischer will only sell the concentrate to bottling companies. — The concentrate ...
3 Fischer will require bottlers to use water that Fischer specifies. — Bottlers ...
4 The bottlers can choose the trade name. — The trade name ...
5 You can only see these particles through a microscope. — These particles ...
6 Charles Townes produced the first laser in 1960. — The first ...
7 People are using computers in all kinds of work. — Computers ...
8 You have to keep dangerous chemicals in a safe place. — Dangerous ...
9 You shouldn't have left the laboratory unlocked. — The laboratory ...
10 We are unlikely to discover intelligent life on other planets. — Intelligent life ...

D Work in small groups. Can you decide which of these inventions or discoveries were made in which year?
Write a sentence beginning with *If* ... about each of them. One is done for you as an example below.

bicycle computer jet engine laser margarine printing press Scotch tape telephone television thermometer
1455 1593 1840 1869 1876 1926 1930 1937 1943 1960 1971

'I think the thermometer was invented in 1593.'
If the thermometer hadn't been invented, we wouldn't be able to measure temperature.

6.4 Serendipity   *Listening*

serendipity /serəndɪpəti/ is the natural talent that some people have for finding interesting or valuable things by chance.

A You'll hear part of a broadcast about some important discoveries which happened by accident. Answer the multiple-choice questions below.

1 Penicillin was discovered when Alexander Fleming found some mould growing on a laboratory dish he had left ...
   a) beside the window   b) in a dark corner   c) above the window
2 Antibiotic drugs based on penicillin have helped to ...
   a) cure every disease   b) stop bacteria spreading
   c) reduce the number of deaths from disease
3 Radar is now used ...
   a) by military scientists   b) by motorists   c) by ships and aircraft
4 Radar was discovered while scientists were looking for a new ...
   a) form of radio communication   b) type of weapon
   c) way of increasing safety at sea
5 Teflon was discovered while chemists were doing research on ...
   a) cooling systems   b) plastic   c) poisonous gases
6 Teflon is now used in ...
   a) computers   b) refrigerators   c) spacecraft
7 Artificial sweeteners were discovered when scientists ...
   a) tasted a substance they had produced in the laboratory
   b) were doing experiments with sweet substances
   c) were looking for patterns in substances
8 Chewing gum was discovered while scientists were doing research into ...
   a) artificial sweeteners   b) materials to use instead of rubber
   c) trees in Mexico
9 'Post-It Notes' were invented after a researcher discovered a substance that ...
   a) could be used instead of sticky tape   b) would stick for ever
   c) wouldn't stick properly
10 The 'useless' adhesive ...
    a) left a mark on some surfaces   b) became less sticky after a while
    c) could be easily removed later
11 On Sundays the 3M researcher ...
    a) did research into adhesives   b) sang in a church   c) wrote songs
12 'Post-it Notes' are now used ...
    a) by choirs in churches   b) to leave messages for people
    c) to send messages by mail

B Work in small groups. Find out your partners' views on luck by asking these questions:
- Do you believe in good luck and bad luck?
- What part has 'good luck' played in your life?
- What lucky accidents have happened to you?
- Are some people born lucky and others born unlucky?

6.5 Helping people to understand

Pronunciation

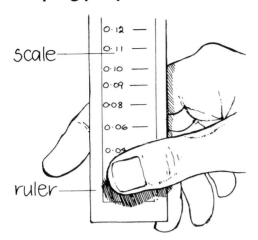

A The passage below describes a simple experiment that you can carry out with different people to test the speed of their reactions. Read the passage before you listen to the recording.

A SIMPLE REACTION TIMER

Quick reactions are important if you're an airline pilot, a motorist, or even a cyclist – and of course in sports, fast reactions are especially valuable. This simple but effective Reaction Timer makes use of the principle that, if we ignore the effects of air resistance, all objects fall with the same acceleration.

Equipment required:
a 30 cm ruler, sticky tape, paper, scissors and a pen.

Procedure:
1. Cut out a piece of paper the same size as this page.
2. You will see along the side of the page a scale with divisions marked on it. Each division shows a time interval. These represent fractions of a second.
3. Copy the scale carefully onto the side of the piece of paper you have cut out and then tightly wrap it round the ruler so that the scale is visible. The bottom end of the scale should be at the bottom end of the ruler. Fix it securely with sticky tape.
4. While you hold the ruler at the point marked 'HOLD HERE', get the person to place his or her thumb and forefinger on either side of the zero line on the scale. Tell them to catch the ruler as soon as it begins to fall. If they grip the ruler *before* it begins to fall, this result is not counted.
5. Without letting the person know when you are about to drop it, release the ruler. The time that it took the person to react is shown in seconds on the scale at the point they caught it.
6. Repeat the experiment several times with each person and record the results in a chart.

B Listen to the first part of the recording. You'll hear the first paragraph read aloud. Why is this reading difficult to understand?

C 🔊 Now you'll hear a better version of the instructions. As you listen, mark the PAUSES that the reader makes, using a vertical line (|), on the passage on the previous page. The first paragraph is done as an example:

Quick reactions are important if you're an airline pilot, | a motorist, or even a cyclist | – and of course in sports, | fast reactions are especially valuable. | This simple but effective Reaction Timer | makes use of the principle that, | if we ignore the effects of air resistance, | all objects fall with the same acceleration. |

D 🔊 Now listen to the recording again. This time, mark the syllables that are STRESSED in each sentence in the text. Again, the first paragraph is done for you as an example:

Quíck reáctions are impórtant íf you're an aírline pílot, a mótorist, or éven a cýclist – ánd of cóurse in spórts, fást reactions are espécially váluable. Thís símple but efféctive Reáction Tímer makes úse of the príncple that, íf we ignóre the effécts of aír resístance, áll óbjects fáll with the sáme accelerátion.

When you have finished, compare your version with a partner and then look at the completed version in Activity 11.

E Now read the passage aloud yourself. If you're working with a partner, take it in turns to read alternate paragraphs and comment on each other's reading.
- Did you find it easy to understand your partner?
- How could he or she read more clearly?

6.6 Reaction times   *Directed writing*

A Work in small groups. Imagine that you have carried out the Reaction Timer experiment (in 6.5) with the other members of your group. You have recorded the results in this table:

RESULTS OF OUR GROUP AFTER 6 ATTEMPTS

Try no.	1st	2nd	3rd	4th	5th	6th	Average (mean)	
Hand:	RIGHT	LEFT	RIGHT	LEFT	RIGHT	LEFT	RIGHT	LEFT
ANNE	0.14	0.19	0.15	0.20	0.13	0.20	0.14	0.20
BILL	0.19	0.20	0.18	0.10	0.18	0.09	0.18	0.13
CHRIS	0.11	0.11	0.12	missed	0.12	0.10	0.12	0.10
ME	missed	0.19	0.17	0.04	0.16	0.13	0.16	0.12

Which person had the fastest and slowest reactions?
- taking each one's average (mean) score
- taking only their best efforts
- taking only their worst efforts

B Write three paragraphs:

1 Imagine that you carried out the Reaction Timer experiment and summarise the PROCEDURE (see 6.5), beginning like this:
   'An experiment was carried out in which ...'

2 Imagine that you carried out the experiment and describe the RESULTS (see A above), beginning like this:
   'We found that ...'

3 Explain how you would feel if you really had to carry out the experiment, beginning like this:
   'I think carrying out the experiment would ...'
   OR, if you really have carried out the experiment:
   'We thought that the experiment was ...'

6.7 Using prepositions – 3   *Use of English*

Fill the gaps in these sentences with suitable prepositions.

1. Sarah **quarrelled** .... Louise .... the **preparations** .... the party.
2. Eric **reminds** me .... Paul McCartney, but they aren't **related** .... each other.
3. You can never **rely** .... Anna to **provide** you .... information.
4. The staff are **responsible** .... their boss .... the decisions they make.
5. You can only **succeed** .... passing an exam if you **revise** carefully .... it.
6. I've got plenty of sandwiches, would you like to **share** them .... me?
7. The police suspected that the goods had been **stolen** .... the shop, but the receipt proved that they had been **paid** ....
8. Kate is **suffering** .... a bad cold and she wants you to **sympathise** .... her.
9. At the end of the party, we **thanked** our host and hostess .... inviting us.
10. I'm **tired** .... waiting .... Jim to arrive. I **object** .... his unpunctuality.
11. On behalf of the students and staff, I'd like to **welcome** you .... our school.
12. Helen **worked** .... ACME plc for a year and then she **resigned** .... the job.

6.8 Chips with everything
Reading

A This article comes from a consumer magazine. When you've read it, answer the questions on the next page.

WHAT DOES THE CHIP MEAN FOR YOU?

Massive and unreliable, the first computers of thirty years ago are as dead as the dinosaur. Today, computers which are 30,000 times smaller and 10,000 times cheaper can beat them hollow. High-speed, low-cost computing power has begun to convert science fiction into reality.

In this report, we use the words **chip** or **microchip** when we're referring to the chips themselves. Where we're dealing with the wider subject of chips in use – eg in computers, communication systems, and the like – we use the words **microelectronics**, or **micros**, for short.

A LOOK TO THE FUTURE

What will the world of the future be like? Here are some ideas to consider:

● **a divided society?** The coming of the micro will benefit many people: others may be left behind. People at risk are those who can't afford to use new technology, or who can't understand it. Something can be done for both groups –public viewdata terminals can give free access to information, and new machines (including computers) can be made easy to use, provided time, money and care is spent in programming them.

● **variety or uniformity?** Will we be surrounded by an enormous variety of products? Or will the result of micros be cheap uniformity? Either of these is possible. The main factor is the cost of writing programs. If the cost remains high, products will have to be made in large quantities – in order to spread the cost. To get variety, programming costs need to come down. There are signs that this may happen: some manufacturers are now using relatively unsophisticated chips, which can be cheaply programmed for simple functions.

● **goodbye humans?** If people work at home and do their banking and shopping at home, the result could be an inward-looking and immobile society, as families retreat into a private world of video games and computer holograms. On the other hand, people seem to need human contact, and to enjoy the social aspects of office life and escaping from their homes.

● **beyond the human brain.** A simple electronic calculator goes far beyond the human brain in speed and accuracy – but only in a very closely defined field. In the future, computers will surpass humans in more and more ways. It's predicted by some people (and hotly disputed by others) that the intellectual capabilities of the human brain will be overtaken in the early years of the next century. When (or if) this happens, we will no longer be the most intelligent entities on the planet. No-one knows how we would cope with this wounding loss of status.

CONCLUSIONS

The microchip revolution is based on size and cost. Microchips give us cheap computing power in a tiny space. As the cost of microchips continues to fall, it becomes economically worthwhile to use them in more and more ways.

We have to accept the microchip, or face the alternative of opting out of the free world market.

Accepting the microchip brings benefits and problems. The benefits include greater efficiency in finding and using information; the possibility of higher living standards through increased productivity; greater control over pollution and the use of natural resources; help for the sick and the disabled; and a whole range of 'smart' machines to inform, entertain and serve us.

We can guard against some of the problems. We can, for example, be alive to the danger of the misuse of information held on computer files.

There is the problem of alienation: people who cannot find a place in the technological world of the future. To guard against this problem, we need education and training schemes, and machines which are easy to use. Finally, there's the problem of people whose skills are made redundant by machines. Again, there's a need for education and retraining. The wealth needed to pay for schemes like these is more likely to appear if we use the microchip.

1 In the article the word 'micros' refers to ...
   a) all kinds of computers   b) microchips   c) microchips and their uses
2 The new machines will be easier to use ...
   a) because we will all be familiar with them
   b) only if the programs are user-friendly
   c) because the programs will be user-friendly
3 All products are likely to become very similar to each other unless ...
   a) production costs fall
   b) programming costs fall   c) the public demands variety
4 Microchips are not used everywhere at present because they are still too ...
   a) complicated   b) expensive   c) small   d) specialised
5 According to the article, the average person ...
   a) likes going to work
   b) dislikes going to work   c) enjoys working at home
6 A computer that is more intelligent than a person will be developed after 2000 ...
   a) according to all the experts
   b) according to some of the experts   c) according to the article
7 Retraining people who lose their jobs because of computers will be ...
   a) cheap   b) easy   c) expensive   d) impossible
8 On the whole, the article suggests that ...
   a) there are more problems than benefits
   b) there are fewer problems than benefits   c) the problems match the benefits

B Find words in the text that have the following meanings. The numbers show which paragraph you should look at. The first is done as an example:

very large (1) *massive*

change (1)   do better than (7)
bring advantages for (4)   painful (7)
in danger (4)   not taking part in (9)
lack of differences (5)   intelligent (10)
simple (5)   feeling of not belonging (12)

C Work in small groups. Ask your partners these questions:
- Which parts of the article do you agree with and which do you disagree with?
- What do you see as the main benefits of computers?
- What are the main disadvantages of computers and electronic equipment?
- Do you enjoy using a computer – or do you find it unpleasant or difficult?
- What have you used a computer for? What will you use one for in the future?
- To what extent are computers over- or underused nowadays in your country?

'When we split up, James got the hardware and I got the software.'

6.9 I'd better explain how it works
Listening

🔊 Listen to the instructions that Annie is being given. Decide which of these photos show the 'right way' to load and operate the dishwasher.

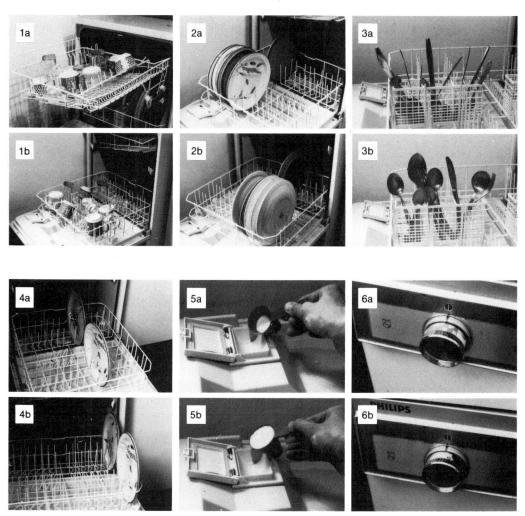

6.10 How does it work?
Communication activity

📺 The class is divided into an even number of pairs.

Half the pairs should look at Activity 39, the other half at 47.

Study the explanations there. Later you'll have to explain to another pair how soap or a cassette works.

6.11 Explaining a process *Composition*

★ Normally, you write things so that someone else can read them – so try to imagine how your reader will react. Put yourself in your reader's place as you write.

You can assume that the 'general reader' (or the average examiner!) knows something about the subjects you know about – but he or she may not be an expert. Bear this in mind as you look at the extracts below.

A Decide what is 'GOOD' and 'BAD' about these paragraphs:

> Soap is made up of molecules. Each one has a tail and this sticks to the dirt and it pulls away from the cloth, making the cloth clean.

> The cassette consists of a plastic case, containing the recording tape. The two halves of the case are sometimes screwed together but may also be glued permanently together. The tape travels between the spools across tiny rollers and behind a small opening. When the recorder is going, the tape leaves the first spool and is wound onto the second. As it travels behind the opening in the case the tape head pushes against the tape, so that it remains in contact as it winds past it.

B Write an explanation of how another everyday process works – for example, a telephone, an LP record or compact disc, a microwave oven, etc.

(If you are not a technically-minded person, you may prefer to describe one of the processes shown in Activity 39 or 47 – but the information contained within the diagrams must be given in words.)

First of all, make notes of the main points you want to make in the composition. If possible, discuss your notes with another student before you start writing.

★ When you check your work afterwards, look systematically for mistakes you may have made in each of these areas:

Spelling
   What was the affect of this? ✗
Prepositions
   I'm interested for science. ✗
Verb forms and endings
   I was gave it. ✗   *If I would be rich...* ✗   *She live in London.* ✗
Articles
   I'm interested in the science. ✗

6.12 *Keep* and *take*   *Verbs and idioms*

A Which of the endings below go with these beginnings:

Kim and Chris took ...
Chris and Kim kept ...

some photographs   calm   a holiday together   a long time
house for their father   control of the situation   quiet   action
no notice of each other   their tempers   the engine to pieces   care of the children
their hands in their pockets   listening   an eye on each other

B Fill the gaps in these sentences with suitable verbs from the list below:

keep
1 You're doing very well. Try to _____ the good work!
2 Don't give up. You've got to _____ your work until you've finished.
3 I advise you to _____ that machine, it's dangerous.
4 One member of the audience _____ snoring throughout the lecture.
5 Zoë is such a fast runner that I couldn't _____ her.

take
6 The magician's trick _____ everyone in the audience.
7 You need to keep fit. Why don't you _____ jogging?
8 Our new boss was so pleasant that everyone _____ her at once.
9 If you ask David for help, he always wants to _____ completely.
10 We had to check in at 3 a.m., but the plane didn't _____ till 7.
11 I find that my work _____ so much of my time that I don't have any free time.
12 There was simply too much information, I couldn't _____ it all _____.
13 If you _____ 6 _____ 21, the answer is 15.
14 His grandfather and father were lazy too. I think he _____ both of them!

keep away from   keep on   keep on with   keep up   keep up with
take after   take away from   take in   take in   take off   take over
take to   take up   take up

'No, no – that's E as in Einstein,
M as in Manhattan, C as in cataclysm …'

7 Good health!

7.1 In sickness and in health
Vocabulary

A Fill the gaps with suitable words.

1. If you want to find out someone's temperature, use a ....thermometer....
2. Please don't cough all over everyone! Don't forget that a cold is ....contagious....
   As it is a virus, there is no ....cure.... for it.
3. I hurt my wrist yesterday playing football and today it's ....bruised....
4. I had to wait three-quarters of an hour in the doctor's ....surgery....
5. I went to the doctor about my insomnia and she prescribed some ....medicine....
6. The main symptom of hay fever is that you keep ....sneezing....
7. It was quite a bad cut and it was bleeding a lot, so I put on a ....plaster....
8. I think he's broken his leg! Quick, someone call an ....ambulance....
9. If someone is seriously ill they may need to go to hospital to have an ....operation....
10. I hate going to the dentist – I've got to have two ....fillings.... done.
11. If you want to stay fit, don't eat too much and take plenty of ....exercise....
12. Her mother sent her to bed because she had a ....fever....
13. He was ten kilos overweight and was advised to go on a ....diet....
14. You've eaten too much, that's why you have a pain in your ....stomach....
15. Oh dear, I feel awful. I think I'm going to ....faint....

B Choose the best alternative to fill each of the gaps in the next five sentences.

1. If you want antibiotics, you'll have to ask the doctor for a ....prescription....
   medicine   note   prescription   receipt   recipe
2. She was in terrible pain, so the nurse gave her a(n) ....injection....
   injection   scratch   stab   vaccine   wound
3. If you've got measles, your skin is covered in ....spots....
   blots   dots   freckles   spots   stains
4. Why not take up tennis? It'll help you to keep fit and it's a great ....game....
   amusement   game   match   play   tournament
5. He didn't feel like going to the party because he had a terrible ....headache....
   disease   headache   homesickness   infection   nostalgia

C In the last five sentences THREE of the alternatives are correct and TWO of them are wrong. Choose the three best alternatives for each.

1. If you've got a bad cold, it's no wonder you're feeling ....
   off your food   on form   out of order   out of sorts   under the weather
2. I walked into a door yesterday, which is why I have a .... on my forehead.
   black eye   bruise   bump   cut   hurt

3 You're less likely to become ill if you are ....
   hygienic   physically fit   living a healthy life   in good shape   running
4 Doctors say that smoking and drinking can both .... your health.
   affect   damage   improve   ruin   wound
5 As I haven't had anything to eat today, I'm feeling a bit ....
   dizzy   faint   funny   silly   unconscious

D   Work in pairs. Draw a rough sketch of the human body at the centre of a blank page and label the parts, starting at the toes or at the fingers. Use a dictionary if necessary.

When you've finished, compare your labelled body with another pair's.

- What can go wrong with each part? Write sentences like this:
  HEAD – She's got a headache.
  WRIST – He's sprained his wrist.

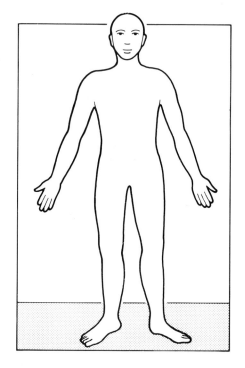

7.2   What to do about flu   *Reading*

A   Read these sentences. Which do you think are true (**T**) or false (**F**)?
Then read the leaflet on the next page and find out if you were right, according to the text.

1 One symptom of flu is an aching back.
2 Antibiotics can help you to get better from flu.
3 Flu always lasts several days.
4 It's advisable to drink two to three litres of liquid a day.
5 If you have flu, it's essential to eat three times a day.
6 Flu is not a serious illness for anyone.
7 Flu is infectious – other people can catch it from you.
8 People are more likely to catch flu in a crowded place.
9 Elderly people should tell their doctor if they think they've got flu.
10 If you have flu badly, you should lie in a darkened room.
11 Doctors, nurses and policemen are always vaccinated against flu.
12 One vaccination gives several years' protection against flu.
13 The worst time of year for flu is the autumn.
14 Wash up very thoroughly if someone in your family has flu.
15 You should call the doctor if your flu goes on for longer than a week.

You've got your own defence system – here's how to make it work.

You're feeling rotten – weak, shivery, with an aching head, back and limbs. Your temperature's up over 38°C (100°F). Probably you're sweating a lot, you've lost your appetite and you feel sick. You've got flu.

So what do you do?

There's no quick cure. Flu – influenza – is caused by a virus. And viruses can't be killed with antibiotics. Only the body's own defence system can get rid of them.
So for most of us there's no point in seeing the doctor when we've got flu. But while a bout of flu lasts, which may be anything from 24 hours to several days,

here's what you should do.

Stay indoors, keep warm, and keep away from other people as much as possible so you don't pass on the infection.

Have plenty of cool drinks – water, fruit drinks, milky drinks. About 2-3 litres a day.

If you feel shivery or feverish, with a temperature over 38°C (100°F) or aches or pains, try taking soluble aspirin every 4 hours during the day. And rest in bed if you can.

Try to have 3 light meals a day. But don't force yourself to eat if you've lost your appetite.

But if you are elderly and in poor health, or if you suffer from a severe chest condition like bronchitis or asthma, then flu can become a more serious illness.
So remember:
* When there's flu about, try to avoid crowded places and keep away from anyone who's got flu.
* If you think you've caught flu, get in touch with your doctor. Then he can at least keep an eye on you.
* In the autumn, ask your doctor if he thinks you should be vaccinated against flu.

FLU VACCINATION Flu vaccine is usually only given to people who are especially at risk because of their health and to people who cannot miss work, like nurses, doctors, firemen or policemen. These people may be offered flu vaccination once a year, generally in the autumn before winter epidemics. But even vaccination cannot give complete protection against flu.

REMEMBER Keep flu to yourself. Stay away from other people. Make sure handkerchiefs and also plates, knives, forks etc., are always well washed.
Look after yourself by resting in bed and having lots of cool drinks.
There's no need for the doctor unless the flu persists for more than a few days or gets suddenly worse.

B Work in pairs. Imagine that a friend of yours is unwell and may have flu.
- Write down five questions you would ask to find out if he or she has flu.
- What advice would you give, once you're sure he or she has flu?

Role-play the conversation, with one of you playing the role of sick friend. Look at these expressions before you begin.

> If I were you, I'd ...   The best thing to do is to ...
> I think you should ...   It's best to ...
> You ought to ...

C Now imagine that your friend hasn't got flu, just a BAD COLD. What advice would you give him or her?
Role-play the conversation. This time the *other* person is the sick friend.

7.3 Comparing and contrasting   *Grammar*

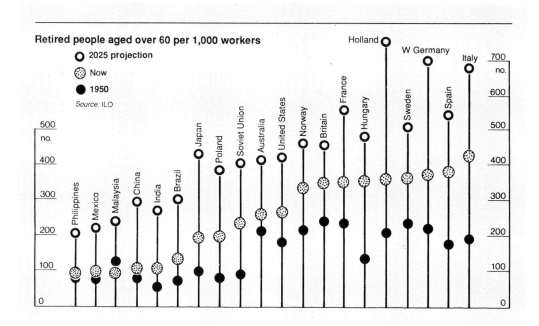

A These examples show the principal uses of comparatives and superlatives. Notice how similar ideas can be expressed in different ways.

People in Italy live **longer than** anywhere else in the world.
= There are **more** retired people in Italy **than** anywhere else in the world.
= Italy has **the oldest** population in the world.
Far more people live to retirement age in Britain **than** in the Philippines.
= **Not as many** people live to retirement age in the Philippines.
There are **about the same** number of old people in Australia **as** in the USA.
= The number of old people in Australia is **similar to** the number in the USA.
There are **not as many** old people in Mexico **as** in Japan.
= There are **fewer** old people in Mexico **than** in Japan.
The population of France is **less young than** the population of Brazil.
= The population of Brazil is **not as old as** the population of France.
There are about **twice as many** retired people in the USA **as** in Brazil.
= There are about **half as many** retired people in Brazil **as** in the USA.
Spain has **the second oldest** population.
Throughout the world, people live **much longer** nowadays **than** they used to.
The number of old people in China is **nothing like as** high **as** in Sweden.

B Referring to the statistics in the table, write five sentences comparing 1950 with the present day AND five sentences comparing 2025 with the present day.

C Find and correct the errors in these sentences. One of them has *no* errors.

1 Hot, wet weather has a much worse effect on people's health than cool, dry weather.
2 July in Cairo is far more dryer as Athens.
3 The daytime temperature in Tokyo in July is the same than New York.
4 There are much differences between the weather in Cairo and Tokyo.
5 The weather in Athens in July is more warmer than London.
6 New York is more cold in winter as London.

World Weather Guide

	Average temperature: JULY		JANUARY		Average number of rainy days: JULY	JANUARY
	day	night	day	night		
Athens	33°	23°	13°	6°	2	16
Buenos Aires	14°	6°	29°	17°	7	8
Cairo	36°	21°	18°	8°	0	1
London	22°	14°	6°	2°	12	15
New York	28°	19°	3°	−4°	12	12
Tokyo	28°	21°	8°	−2°	10	5

D Rewrite each sentence starting with the words on the right, so that its meaning remains the same.

1 Cairo is much hotter than London in July. — London isn't ...
2 There are fewer rainy days in Buenos Aires than in New York. — There aren't ...
3 There is less rain in Tokyo than in Athens in January. — More rain ...
4 In July New York is warmer than Buenos Aires, but wetter. — Buenos Aires ...
5 The amount of rainfall is similar in London and New York. — About the same ...
6 Summer nights in Cairo are much warmer than in London. — In London ...
7 A broken leg is more serious than a sprained wrist. — A sprained wrist ...
8 No one can imagine a more frightening illness than AIDS. — AIDS is ...
9 Flu is a more serious illness than a cold. — A cold is less ...
10 Fewer people die from flu than 50 years ago. — Not as ...

E Work in small groups. What are the SIMILARITIES and DIFFERENCES between your country and Britain and/or the USA? Consider the following aspects:

size   population   climate   scenery
health care   music   entertainment   TV and radio
family life   science   technology   transport
food and eating habits: breakfast, lunch, dinner, snacks
drinks: hot drinks, non-alcoholic, alcoholic
attitudes to health: illness, drugs, a healthy diet, keeping fit, etc.

Make notes of the most interesting points that are made. Write ten sentences about the major differences between life in the two countries you've discussed.

7.4 Sleep and dreams *Listening*

A Before you listen to the recording, look at the statements below. Which do you think are true (**T**) or false (**F**)?
  Then listen to the interview and find out if you were right.

1 Our brains require deep sleep, not REM (rapid eye movement) sleep, to restore them. T
2 Dreams occur when you are about to wake up. F
3 Dreams occur during REM sleep. T
4 Dreams only last a few seconds: they happen much more quickly than in real life. F
5 Dreams can help sleepers to solve problems in their waking lives. T
6 In dreams of falling or being chased, the dreamer is not usually hurt or caught. T
7 There are some people who never have dreams. F
8 Most people require eight hours' sleep a night. F
9 Many successful people need only a few hours' sleep a night. T
10 Talking in your sleep only occurs during dreaming sleep. F
11 People who take a midday sleep (a siesta) need more hours' sleep in 24 hours. F
12 A very short sleep (a nap) has no physical benefits. T

B Work in groups. Carry out some 'research' by asking each other these questions:

- How much sleep do you need?
- How do you feel if you have less sleep than normal?
- Are you a light sleeper? What kinds of things wake you up?
- Do you ever suffer from insomnia? What do you do to help you to get to sleep?
- Do you find it easy to go to sleep?
- Do you remember your dreams? Tell us about one of them.
- Have you ever dreamt about anyone in the class?

Report to the rest of the class about your 'research'. Do your findings confirm or contradict the research of the doctor you heard in the recording?

'If diseases were easier to pronounce, Mrs Jarvis, everyone would have them.'

7.5 Using suffixes: Actions and people   *Word study*

A Look at these examples of verbs. Add more of your own, using the root words below with one of the suffixes in this list.

-ise/-ize modernise sterilise
-en   widen strengthen harden lengthen
-ify   classify clarify

central flat individual less loose pure sharp simple soft
summary symbol tight

★ Notice that these verbs don't have a suffix:
  ↑ raise lift   ↓ lower drop
    heat warm melt   cool chill freeze
    cure heal

B In these examples of personal nouns, the stressed syllables are shown with accents: emplóyer, employée, etc. Add more examples, using the root words below.

-er   emplóyer (= someone who employs) ríder advíser
-ee   employée (= someone who is employed) trainée addressée
-or   invéntor condúctor
-ant partícipant ímmigrant sérvant
-ist chémist biólogist mótorist

art assist broadcast clean cycle direct inhabit inspect instruct
manage science sing ski teach type visit

★ Notice that these words all end in **-ent**:
absent ancient efficient correspondent confident convenient
efficient evident independent frequent resident patient student
violent

C Fill the gaps in these sentences, using the correct form of the root words:

1 If someone faints you should .... their clothing, not .... it.   LOOSE TIGHT
2 The .... needed an .... to help with the experiment.   SCIENCE ASSIST
3 After the road had been .... every .... drove faster.   WIDE MOTOR
4 A good .... pays all his .... well.   EMPLOY EMPLOY
5 The knife may need .... before it is used.   SHARP
6 Milk can be .... by .... it to boiling point.   STERILE HOT
7 A motorbike .... can go much faster than a ....   RIDE CYCLE
8 The city has over a million ....   INHABIT

91

7.6 Welcome to the health farm! *Listening*

A 🎧 You'll hear some newly arrived guests being welcomed to a 'health farm' (a centre where people go to lose weight and become fit). Decide which of these statements are true (**T**) or false (**F**).

1. Guests are not allowed to leave the premises.
2. If you don't lose weight your diet will change.
3. Sports and exercise are optional.
4. The only social activity is a cross-country treasure hunt.
5. Visitors are only permitted before 11 p.m.
6. Breakfast is served at 7.15 a.m.
7. Guests on the intensive one-week course don't get breakfast.
8. Cakes are only served on Sundays.
9. Incoming mail for the guests is opened in case it contains food.
10. Guests with problems are dealt with by Mr O'Hara.

B Work in small groups. Ask your partners these questions:
- What is your reaction to the idea of a 'health farm'? What kind of people pay to starve?
- Have you ever gone on a diet? Describe the experience.
- What do you think are the best ways for an overweight and unfit person to lose weight and to become fit?
- Are spas or health resorts common in your country? What kind of people go to them?

7.7 Suppleness, strength and stamina *Problem solving*

A Work in pairs. Read the information below and decide which of the sports described would be most suitable for your partner to take up – and which would be least suitable.

Activity	Suppleness rating	Strength rating	Stamina rating
Cycling (hard)	☆☆	☆☆☆	☆☆☆☆
Dancing	☆☆☆☆	☆	☆☆☆
Football	☆☆☆	☆☆☆	☆☆☆
Golf	☆☆	☆	☆
Gymnastics	☆☆☆☆	☆☆☆	☆☆
Jogging	☆☆	☆☆	☆☆☆☆
Swimming (hard)	☆☆☆☆	☆☆☆☆	☆☆☆☆
Tennis	☆☆☆	☆☆	☆☆
Weight lifting	☆	☆☆☆☆	☆
Yoga	☆☆☆☆	☆	☆

☆ SUPPLENESS is flexibility: being able to move your neck, spine and body easily. The more supple you are, the less likely you are to suffer from stiffness and aches.

☆ STRENGTH is muscle power: being able to lift things and do heavy work. Strong stomach muscles help you take the strain when lifting heavy objects and keep a slim waistline.
☆ STAMINA is endurance: being able to keep going longer without gasping for breath. With stamina you have a slower, more powerful heartbeat.

B Now look at these profiles and decide which of the activities you would recommend to each person.
Make notes of the REASONS for your recommendations.

ANNA is 15 years old. She lives in the city centre but is not allowed to go out on her own in the nearby park. She plays the piano and likes classical music, but not pop. She usually gets out of breath when climbing stairs. She needs to take more exercise. What do you recommend?

RICHARD is 35 years old and slightly overweight. He lives 3 km from the city centre where he runs his own computer business. He always drives to work. He often suffers from stiffness. As he is very busy he hasn't got much free time, so he can't take up anything too time-consuming. What should he do?

ERIC is 55 years old. He is the manager of a seaside hotel, but he can't swim. He used to play football but gave it up 15 years ago. What do you recommend?

C Write three paragraphs (about 50 words each), explaining what advice you would give to each person, beginning as follows:

'My advice to Anna is ...'
'If Richard wants to keep fit ...'
'The best thing for Eric to do would be ...'

AND write a fourth paragraph about yourself:
'What I do / should do to keep fit is ...'

★ In this part of the exam you'll often have to continue a sentence by using a particular structure: you may have to use conditionals or passives, for example. But once the first sentence is completed, you may be able to steer the paragraph back to easier structures!

7.8 A pain in the neck

Reading

A Work in small groups. Before you read the article, ask your partners these questions:
- What is stress? What are its symptoms?
- How does it affect you or people like you?

TAKING THE STRAIN

Monday 11.40 BBC1

Every year, one person in six resorts to tranquillisers. In BBC1's series, Noel Edmonds investigates healthier ways of coping with stress. For the next five weeks, **Robert Eagle** offers practical advice on the problem

A pain in the neck

PEOPLE USUALLY think of 'stress' as something the world inflicts on them. Worry and hassle are blamed for all kinds of ailments, from asthma to headaches, from high blood pressure to stomach ulcers. And we often blame other people for making us feel bad: when we call someone a 'pain in the neck', we are describing the physical and psychological effect they have on us.

But although it is tempting to regard stress as some nasty germ attacking us from outside, the truth is that we are largely responsible for what stress does to our bodies. Once we make ourselves aware of how our bodies respond to worry, fear, anger and fatigue (all of which are forms of stress), we can start learning to relax.

Pains in the neck are a very common stress complaint. Some people get a pain in the neck from driving, others from working at an office desk. I suffer from a complaint I call 'typewriter neck', which tends to strike when I am hunched over my typewriter worrying about an approaching deadline. (Arthritis or bone injuries might also give you a pain in the neck, of course, but I suspect that these are a much less common cause than muscular tension.)

It would be easy to blame these pains on 'bad posture'. Hunching your shoulders up to your ears is certainly not a relaxing way of sitting.

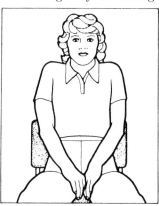

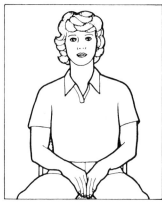

But we should first think about why we adopt this posture. In fact, it is an instinctive way of reacting to a situation which alarms or worries us. It is a defensive stance – and many people find that they tend to make their hands into a fist or grip their steering wheel or the arms of a chair at the same time.

Because it is instinctive, we are often not aware that we are doing it and wonder why we get a pain in the neck. If you find yourself doing it, there are two kinds of relaxation exercise which may help you overcome the habit. You can either exaggerate it: deliberately raise your shoulders as high as they will go, hold the position for a few seconds, then drop your shoulders, and feel the difference. Alternatively, you can exercise the muscles which pull your shoulders in the opposite direction: balance your head on the top of your neck so that it is not dragging your shoulders forward, then draw your shoulders down towards your feet. Stop and feel the difference.

If you are a fist-clencher, try similar routines with your hands. Clench them very tightly, then let go. Or stretch and splay your fingers and thumbs, then stop and feel the difference as they rest on your thighs.

Though simple, these exercises should help you regain control of these parts of your body. ●

Taking the Strain by Robert Eagle (BBC Publications) is available from bookshops.

B When you've read the article, choose the best alternative to complete each of these sentences:

1 People suffer from stress because ...
   a) modern life is full of worries   c) they don't know how to relax
   b) other people inflict it on them   d) they have no time to relax
2 The writer gets a pain in the neck when he ...
   a) is driving   c) is stuck in a traffic jam
   b) is in a hurry to finish some work   d) meets annoying people
3 People who sit like the woman in the top picture ...
   a) deny that they do it   c) don't realise how they're sitting
   b) do it deliberately   d) find it helps them to sit like that
4 The writer describes altogether ...
   a) one exercise   b) two exercises   c) three exercises   d) four exercises
5 The idea of the exercises recommended by the writer is to help you to ...
   a) become a relaxed person   c) know what your muscles are doing
   b) feel different   d) relax for a short while

C Work in pairs. Help each other to try doing the exercises recommended by the writer. Which seemed the most difficult and the most pleasant?

D Work in small groups. Ask your partners these questions:
- Do you agree with the ideas expressed in the article?
- What kinds of things cause stress (e.g. living in a city, driving, etc.)?
- How can people reduce or cope with stress or worry (e.g. screaming, yoga, etc.)?

7.9 At ...   *Prepositional phrases*

Fill the gaps in these sentences with a suitable phrase from the list below:

1 I thought .... that I had flu, but then I realised it was only a cold.
2 There were .... 500 people in the crowd, probably more.
3 Sorry to keep you waiting, I've finished .... !
4 .... it looked like a new car, and I didn't realise it was second-hand.
5 A successful business sells its products .... and not ....
6 For five years the two countries were .... but now they are ....
7 The receptionist only allows one patient to see the doctor ....
8 You can't lose weight just by taking exercise, ... I don't think so.
9 When you receive the report, please pass it on to me ....
10 The twins always speak .... as each other.

at first   at first sight   at last   at least   at a loss   at once   at peace   at a profit
at any rate   at a time   at the same time   at war

7.10 Staying healthy *Picture conversation*

★ The Interview Paper of the exam includes a 'Picture Conversation'. The purpose of this exercise is to give you a topic to talk about – not to force you to describe every detail of the picture at great length.

A Work in pairs. Write down SIX questions that you can ask another pair about these photos. Questions like these are NOT suitable:
  Is the woman running?   What kind of packet is this?
because they'll only lead to very short answers, like these:
  Yes.   A cigarette packet.

B Now join another pair and ask them your questions. Don't interrupt, but encourage them to say as much as they like in answer to your questions – even if they seem to be going off the subject.

7.11 Doctor's orders   *Listening*

A You'll hear a doctor giving some advice to one of her patients, a Mr Brown. Before you listen to the recording, can you guess which of these foods are less healthy, and perhaps likely to be forbidden?

```
Fresh fish ✓          Bread ✗             Apples            Grapes
Canned fish           Margarine           Bananas           Carrots
Fish and chips        Butter (unsalted) ✓ Potatoes          Crisps ✗
Fresh meat ✓          Tomato ketchup      Sausages          Hamburgers ✗
Salt                  Coffee              Tea               Beer
```

B 🔊 Listen to the recording and mark with a tick (✓) the foods Mr Brown can eat and with a cross (✗) the foods that he is not permitted to eat.

C Compare your ticks and crosses with a partner. Can you work out what is wrong with Mr Brown and how this diet will help him?

D Complete the unfinished sentences in this dialogue. The first one is done as an example. You'll have to use your imagination to finish it!

Patient: Good morning, doctor.
Doctor: Hallo, Mr Jones, what **seems to be the trouble** ?
Patient: Well, I keep getting these headaches.
Doctor: When _____
Patient: After I get home from work usually.
Doctor: What _____
Patient: I usually take a couple of aspirins and that seems to do the trick.
Doctor: How long _____
Patient: For the past two or three months.
Doctor: Why _____
Patient: Well, it didn't really seem bad enough to be worth troubling you about.
Doctor: Have _____ than usual?
Patient: Yes, I suppose so. Since my assistant was made redundant I've been doing his work as well as mine.
Doctor: Have _____
Patient: Yes, but he says that if I can't do the work, I'll lose my job too.
Doctor: What _____
Patient: Can you give me a certificate so that I can be off work for a week – then my boss will have to do my work for a week and he'll see how overworked I am.
Doctor: Would _____
Patient: Oh yes, *two* weeks would be even better.
Doctor: _____
Patient: Thank you very much.
Doctor: _____
Patient: All right, doctor.

7.12 What would you say?   *Composition*

A In the exam you'll have to write two compositions of 120 to 180 words. Look at the last two or three compositions you've written and count the number of words in them to give you an idea of how much space your own writing takes up. (Count the number of words in 5 or 10 lines and then work out the total, rather than counting every single word!) For the composition exercise in this and in later units, try to keep to about 150 words each time.

★ In the exam don't waste time by counting the *exact* total number of words you have used. If you write too much or too little, this will count against you – so you should get used to writing 150-word compositions!

B One of the writing tasks you may choose to do in the exam is to write down what you would say in a particular situation.
Do you remember Dr Lawrence's speech in 7.6? This is how it began:

> Good afternoon, everybody. I'm Dr Jane Lawrence, the administrator and medical officer. I hope you're all going to be very happy here. I must explain first that you've got to participate in all the activities we offer and no absences from the premises will be permitted. Every morning everybody has to weigh in and your progress will be monitored. Your diets are adjusted according to the progress you make – that is, how much weight you lose. Now first of all, I'd like to introduce Mr O'Hara, the sports organiser ...

and this is how it ended:

> ... Let me wish you a pleasant stay here with us and if you have any questions about the course you are on, please come and see me in my office.

C Work in pairs. Imagine that you are organising a weekly keep-fit course – less strict than Dr Lawrence's! What would you need to tell the course members at the start of the first session? Look at the information about suppleness, strength and stamina in 7.7 for some ideas.
Make notes on the points you would make – and decide which are the most important ones.

Here are some useful expressions you could include in your speech:

> *Ladies and gentlemen, ...*
> *Could I have your attention for a moment?*
> *I'd just like to say a few words about ...*
> *Does anyone have any questions?*
> *Thank you very much and enjoy the ...*

D Write the welcome speech. It should be about 150 words long.

E When you have written your speech, show it to a partner (or perhaps read it out as if you were really making the speech). Ask for comments.

7.13 Put   *Verbs and idioms*

Fill the gaps in these sentences, using the phrasal verbs listed below.

1. It's getting dark, could you ___put___ the light ___on___ please?
2. If you want to stay with us, we can ___put___ you ___up___ in our spare room.
3. I'm trying to concentrate but if you keep whistling you'll ___put___ me ___off___.
4. Don't forget to ___put___ the lights ___off___ when you leave the room.
5. I'm afraid we'll have to ___put___ our meeting ___off___ till next month.
6. Since I last stayed at this hotel, they have ___put___ their prices ___up___.
7. He has ___put___ ___on___ a lot of weight since I last saw him.
8. You'll remember the words if you ___put___ them ___down___ in your notebook.
9. If you've finished with the book, would you mind ___put___ it ___back___ on the shelf?
10. I ___put___ the aspirins ___away___ somewhere safe, but now I can't remember where.
11. At the start of Summer Time we ___put___ the clocks ___forward___ and at the end we ___put___ them ___out___.
12. Mr Green is on the line, shall I ___put___ him ___through___ or ask him to ring back?
13. If you've got a cold, you've just got to ___put___ ___up___ ___with___ it.
14. They had planned to go out but they were ___put___ ___off___ by the bad weather.

put away   put back   put back   put down   put forward   put off   put off   put off
put on   put on   put out/off   put through   put up   put up   put up with

7.14 Fill the gaps   *Exam practice*

Fill the gaps in this newspaper article with suitable prepositions.

HAY FEVER HITS OPERA
The star 1 ___of___ the largest scale opera performance ever staged 2 ___in___ Britain pulled out 3 ___of___ its opening night 4 ___on___ Sunday. Verdi's Aïda is being performed 5 ___at___ London's Earl's Court Arena 6 ___with___ a cast of 600 singers, dancers and actors. American soprano Grace Bumbry 7 ___in___ the title role was suffering 8 ___from___ hay fever, but had promised to be 'all right on the night even if my nose drips like the Nile'. Half-way 9 ___through___ the performance she was unable to continue and was replaced 10 ___in___ mid-performance 11 ___by___ Russian soprano Ghena Dimitrova who was sitting 12 ___in___ the audience watching the show. She was taken 13 ___to___ a dressing room where she put on Ms Bumbry's costume and was made up. She was ready to go 14 ___on___ the stage 15 ___after___ a longer-than-usual interval.

Tuesday's performance 16 ___in___ the presence 17 ___of___ the Prince and Princess of Wales will go ahead 18 ___without___ Ms Bumbry – her role will be taken 19 ___by___ Martina Arroyo 20 ___from___ Italy.

'I'm writing an opera about hay fever.'

8 Holidays

8.1 Getting away from it all *Vocabulary*

A Work in small groups. Ask your partners these questions:
- Where did you spend your holidays last year and the year before?
- What did you enjoy and not enjoy about these holidays?
- What kind of holidays did you have when you were much younger?
- What kind of holidays would you like to have in the future?

B These questions are similar to the ones you'll have to answer in the first part of the Reading Comprehension paper of the exam. Choose the best alternative to complete each sentence. Be careful because some of the alternatives are only slightly wrong!

1 Read all the .... carefully before you decide where to go on holiday.
   brochures   handouts   tickets   prospectuses
2 I'd like to book a room with a(n) .... of the sea.
   outlook   scenery   sight   view
3 And, if possible, I'd like a room with its own ....
   balcony   box   gallery   porch
4 When I'm on holiday, I enjoy ....
   getting sunburnt   getting sunstroke   having a sunbathe   sunbathing
5 The cheapest way to go is to take a charter ....
   crossing   flight   fly   travel
6 I always get nervous on a plane before it ....
   lifts off   lifts up   takes off   takes up
7 And I'm even more worried when it's about to ....
   anchor   fall   ground   land
8 The most popular destinations for .... holidays are Spain, Italy and Greece.
   charter   package   packed   packet
9 When you're abroad, it's useful to be able to speak the language ....
   currently   flowingly   fluently   hesitantly
10 If you can't speak the language it's a good idea to take a(n) .... with you.
   guide book   interpreter   language guide   phrase book
11 If you don't know the language, you may have to use .... language.
   hand   gesture   sign   signal
12 When you're staying at a popular resort, there are plenty of .... to go on.
   excursions   expeditions   pilgrimages   sightseeings
13 One day when I'm rich and famous, I'm going to go on a round-the-world ....
   cruise   sail   travel   trip
14 We brought home a beautiful pottery vase as a .... of our holiday.
   memorial   reminder   souvenir   trophy

100

15 I wanted to book my summer holiday, so I went to my local travel ....
    agency   bureau   office   service
16 I don't speak Greek very well, but I can make myself ....
    comprehended   heard   listened to   understood
17 We spent a fortnight in the mountains at a winter sports ....
    marina   resort   spa   youth hostel
18 On a winter sports holiday you need warm clothes to .... you from the cold.
    defend   hide   protect   shelter
19 The main attraction of the town is its long sandy ....
    beach   coast   seaside   shore
20 You can save money by choosing a .... holiday.
    do-it-yourself   self-catering   self-study   survival

★ Check through the wrong answers: there's useful vocabulary among them.

C In these questions there are THREE correct answers and TWO wrong ones.
(These aren't exam-style questions, but they'll help you widen your vocabulary.)

1 In the summer, this little mountain village is full of ....
   beachcombers   day-trippers   globetrotters   holiday-makers   sightseers
2 We stayed in a charming little guest house where we paid £25 a night for ....
   bed and breakfast   breakfast and bed   full board   half board   a pension
3 Some people like to be .... when they're on holiday.
   active   busy   energetic   strenuous   tiring
4 Others prefer a .... holiday.
   dull   lazy   relaxing   restful   tedious
5 Most people like to have a .... of things to do when they're away from home.
   confusion   choice   muddle   range   variety

D Work in small groups. Find out about each other's experiences of the items in this list. Which would you enjoy and which would you *not* enjoy? Give your reasons. Perhaps give each one a mark from 1 to 10 according to how you feel.

ACCOMMODATION: camping   caravan   villa   apartment
five-star hotel   small hotel   guest house   staying with relations
farmhouse
PLACES: seaside   mountains   countryside   city   at home
ACTIVITIES: studying a language   sunbathing   working (a holiday job)
mountaineering   walking   sightseeing   cycling   winter sports
water sports   other sports   doing nothing   eating and drinking   + ...

E Make a list of the countries that surround your own country AND the countries that most visitors from abroad come from. Here are some examples:

COUNTRY	NATIONALITY	A PERSON	THE PEOPLE	LANGUAGE(S)
France	French	a Frenchman/woman	The French	French
Greece	Greek	a Greek	The Greeks	Greek
England	British/English	an Englishman/woman	The English	English
Scotland	British/Scottish	a Scot	The Scots	English

8.2 Brazilian Contrasts

Reading

Copacabana Beach

Brazilian Contrasts
Rio de Janeiro: 5 nights
Brasilia: 1 night
Salvador: 3 nights
Sao Paulo: 1 night
Iguacu: 2 nights
plus extension weeks in Rio

Day 1 Wed/London/Rio
Evening departure from Heathrow by scheduled service of Varig Brazilian Airlines to Rio.

Day 2 Thu Rio
Early morning arrival in Rio and transfer to your hotel. In the afternoon an optional tour of the city including cable-car ride up Sugar Loaf mountain, one of this exciting city's most famous landmarks.

Day 3 Fri/Rio/Brasilia
Afternoon departure to Brasilia. This futuristic city was purpose built to become Brazil's new capital in 1960 and its unusual architecture and design sets it apart from all others.

Day 4 Sat Brasilia/Salvador
Late afternoon flight to Salvador. Contrast the unusual designs of Brasilia, with the colour and tradition of Salvador, one of Brazil's oldest cities.

Day 5 Sun and Day 6 Mon Salvador
Two full days to explore this intriguing old city. Rickety old buildings interspersed by narrow, cobbled streets wind up and down the hills on which Salvador was built, providing a fascinating glimpse of the taste and atmosphere of old Brazil.

Day 7 Tue Salvador/Sao Paulo
Early morning departure for Sao Paulo. A million new citizens are added every year to this vibrant city, a plane lands every minute, a new building goes up every hour and there are more daily newspapers, radio and TV stations than any other city in the world.

Day 8 Wed Sao Paulo/Iguacu
Morning flight to Iguacu. The distant roar of the Falls increases to a deafening crescendo as you approach, announcing your arrival at one of the natural wonders of the world.

Day 9 Thu Iguacu
Full day at leisure to explore this incredible natural phenomenon. Niagara and Victoria Falls pale into insignificance as 275 separate cataracts and falls empty a million gallons of water every second into the foaming Parana river.

Day 10 Fri Iguacu/Rio
An afternoon flight to Rio and transfer to the Continental hotel which is located just 50 yards from Avenida Atlantica and legendary Copacabana Beach.

Day 11 Sat to Day 13 Mon Rio
Three full days at leisure in this exciting city. Visit the statue of Christ the Redeemer on top of Corcovado and enjoy one of the most famous views in the world. In the evening, take the optional Carioca night tour; see the city lights, enjoy dinner at a speciality churrascaria restaurant and then finally on to a samba show, where you'll see some of those fabulous carnival costumes.

Day 14 Tue Rio/London
Final day at leisure before an evening departure by scheduled Varig flight to Heathrow, arriving in the UK early on Wednesday afternoon. Alternatively, why not extend your stay in Rio and return one week later.

LUXOR CONTINENTAL, RIO

Facts: Rooms: 290 Type of building: high rise. Lifts: four.

Location: Some 50 yards from the Avenida Atlantica and legendary Copacabana Beach, surrounded by cafes, shops, bars, night clubs and the exciting Samba shows.

Facilities: Restaurant, bar and small lounge.

Accommodation: Rooms vary in size and location but all have modern furnishings, central air conditioning, telephone, colour TV, radio, fridge, mini-bar and bathroom with shower only.

Entertainment: It's all around you, so go outside your hotel and discover the night life of the world's most exciting city.

Opinion: An efficiently run hotel. Combining modern accommodation and friendly service with a superb location near Copacabana Beach – excellent value for money.

Rio Carnival

Savour the most famous Carnival in the world by staying in Rio between 04 and 07 February when the main parades and festivities take place. For carnival supplements see price box below.

A In which places, according to the text, could you find the following?

the atmosphere of old Brazil
historic buildings
a rapidly growing city
a statue of Christ
one of the world's most famous views

a cable car ride
unusual architecture
a samba show
a magnificent waterfall
wonderful costumes

B Now answer these more detailed questions:

1 Would your flight from London be a charter flight?
2 What time of day would you arrive in Rio on your first day?
3 What are the two optional tours of Rio that you could go on?
4 What is the capital city of Brazil?
5 What are the streets of Salvador like?
6 How quickly is the population of São Paulo growing?
7 How would you know that you were approaching Iguaçu Falls?
8 What time of day would you leave Rio on your last day?
9 When is Carnival in Rio?
10 Would the holiday cost the same if you went during Carnival?

Underline the phrases in the text that led you to choose the answers (for example, <u>Early morning arrival</u>).

C Now find the answers to these questions about the hotel in Rio. Again underline the phrases in the text that provide the answers.

1 What is the name of the hotel?
2 Is it a large hotel?
3 Is the hotel on the beach?
4 Would you get a good view from your hotel room?
5 Would your room have a bath?
6 Is it an old-fashioned hotel?

D Work in small groups. Ask your partners these questions:
- What would you enjoy most if you went on the Brazilian Contrasts holiday?
- What might be the disadvantages or difficulties you might face in some of the places mentioned (e.g. insects, heat, expense, etc.)?
- What difficulties have you (or friends or relations of yours) suffered abroad? And on holidays closer to home?

8.3 *If* sentences   *Grammar*

A *If* sentences are used to describe or imagine the consequences of events. Study these examples and fill the gaps:

TYPE 1 [*If* + present, followed by *will*] **is used to imagine the consequences of events that are likely to happen:**
If our flight lands on time, we'll arrive in time for lunch.
If you book your summer holiday in December, you'll get a discount.
If you ___want___ to go to the USA, you ___will need___ a visa.

103

TYPE 2 [*If* + past, followed by *would*] **is used to imagine the consequences of events that are very unlikely to happen or events that cannot possibly happen:**

What would you do if you could go anywhere in the world?
If I was (*or* were) English, I wouldn't need to take this exam.
If I had enough money, I'd go to Brazil.
If you ...had... £1,000 to spend, where would you go on holiday?

In some situations, either Type 2 or Type 1 may be used:

I would go to the USA if I had enough money. (... but I haven't got enough)
I'll go to the USA if I manage to save up enough money. (*more optimistic*)
If I ...want... abroad next summer, I ...will... a new passport.

TYPE 3 [*If* + past perfect, followed by *would have*] **is used to imagine the consequences of events that happened or began to happen in the past:**

If I'd known about the delay, I wouldn't have got to the airport early.
If there hadn't been a mix-up with our booking, we'd have had a room with a view.
If you ...had... me to confirm the booking, I .... you a letter.

We can also 'mix' Types 2 and 3 in the same sentence:

If the weather had been better we would go back there again next year.
If I'd been (had been) born in 1975, I'd be .... today.

- Remember that 'd is the short form of *had* and *would*:
  If he'd (he had) reminded me I'd have (I would have) arrived on time.

Rewrite each of these sentences with their full forms:

1 They'd have written back by now if they'd received my letter.
2 It'd be better if we travelled light.
3 Who'd have known that it'd be such awful weather in September?
4 I'd have sent you a postcard if I'd remembered your address.

- Notice the difference in meaning between *if* and the words underlined here:
  I'll be in England <u>when</u> the spring comes.
  – *but notice we'd say* ... <u>if</u> the weather gets better.
  I'll be arriving on Sunday, <u>unless</u> I inform you otherwise. (= if I don't inform you)
  I'll wait here at the airport <u>until</u> she arrives.
  I'll take an overnight bag <u>in case</u> I have to stay the night.

B Find and correct the errors in these sentences. Two of them contain no errors.

1 If I would have known, I could have helped you.
2 If it's my birthday tomorrow, I'll invite my friends out for a meal.
3 If I were rich, I would buy a villa in the Caribbean.
4 If the weather had been better, we had gone to the beach yesterday.
5 If you will need any help, please let me know.

6 We'll enjoy our holiday unless it rains all the time.
7 If I hadn't just been on holiday, I would have had more money now.
8 Where you would go if you can go anywhere in the world?

C Finish the incomplete sentences in such a way that each one means the same as the complete sentence before it. The first is done for you as an example:

1 My family own a holiday flat and that's why we always go to the same place.
   If _my family didn't own a holiday flat, we wouldn't always go to the same place._
2 Go to Britain and you'll be able to speak English all day long.
   If _you go to britain you will able English_
3 You'll get sunburnt by sunbathing all day long.
   If _____
4 I can't go on holiday because I've got a holiday job this summer.
   If _____
5 You won't find any accommodation if you don't book it in advance.
   Unless _you book it in advance_
6 I didn't enjoy my holiday there and so I'm not going back.
   If _I had enjoyed I would back_
7 I couldn't get in touch because you didn't tell me where you were staying.
   If _you had told me where I could have_
8 The evenings may be cool, so pack a jumper to wear after dark.
   take a jumper in case _____
9 Why don't you come on holiday with us – you'll enjoy it.
   If _you come with us you will enjoy_

D Work in pairs. Suppose you had three weeks' holiday starting tomorrow, and £500 each to spend ...
• Where would you go?
• How would you travel?
• What would you do?
When you've decided what you'd do, compare your ideas with another pair.

> *If we went to .... we could ...*
> *You'd enjoy it in .... because ...*
> *I think it would be much better to ...*

E Work in groups of three. Student A should look at Activity 19, student B at 33 and C at 43. You'll each see a different advertisement. Try to persuade your partners how lovely the idea described in your activity **would be**.

8.4 Getting away from it all? *Picture conversation*

A Work in pairs. Ask each other these questions about each picture:
- What does the picture show? What part of the world is it?
- What would it be like to be there on holiday?
- What would you be able to do if you were there on holiday?
- What kind of people take their holidays there?
- In what ways are your own holidays different from the ones shown?
- Which of the places would you most like to be in? Why?

B Bring a few of your own holiday photos to class and tell everyone about them!

C Work in pairs. Ask your partner these questions about the advertisements:
- What would you enjoy about Yugoslavia and Cyprus?
- What kinds of things that *you* enjoy on holiday don't seem to be available in Yugoslavia or Cyprus?
- Which of the advertisements do you prefer and why?

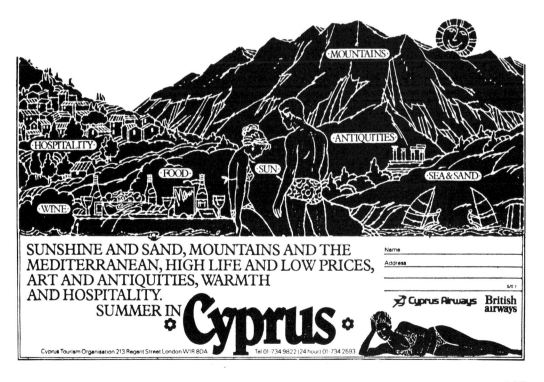

8.5 Island-hopping   *Listening*

A 🎧 You'll hear a travel agent giving some advice to a customer. As you listen, make brief notes on the attractions and drawbacks of the places mentioned.

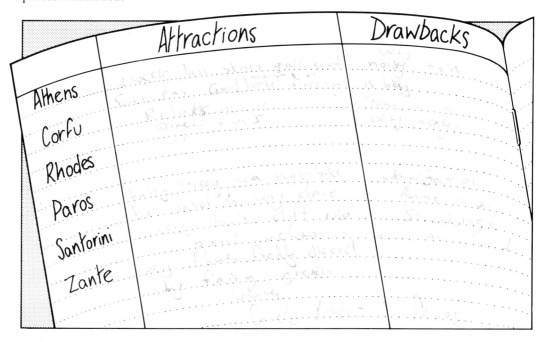

B Work in pairs. Imagine that someone wants to visit *your* country or region for a holiday. What are its attractions and drawbacks? Make a short list.

Role-play a conversation between a travel agent and a customer and discuss your own country or region.

8.6 Three more islands! *Problem solving*

A Work in pairs. Decide which of the islands you would like to visit in August, in April or in October. Why?

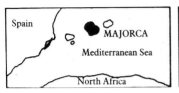
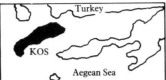
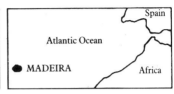

MAJORCA

Majorca, largest of the Balearic Islands, lies off the south-eastern coast of Spain. Its wealth of scenery, fine beaches and nightlife have made it one of the most popular holiday areas in the world.

The scenery of this Mediterranean island is particularly beautiful. The majestic mountain ranges of the north contrast with the windmill-dotted plains of the south. Hidden among the folds of the hills are small farming communities which the twentieth century seems almost to have passed by. Yet, on the island's south coast are extensive holiday resorts with many modern hotels, bars, restaurants and two good golf courses.

Contrary to popular belief, not everywhere on Majorca is modern and sophisticated. Wide, tree-lined promenades contrast oddly with dusty cart-tracks. Luxury hotels rub shoulders with modest pensions. You can choose between elegant nightclubs and restaurants or simple bodegas where you'll find fishermen at the neighbouring tables. Majorca caters for all tastes and all budgets.

KOS

Kos is a genuinely unspoilt Paradise of long, white beaches, and almost continual sunshine. It was here that Hippocrates, the father of Greek medicine, founded the first ever School of Medicine – and, centuries later, it is still as peaceful, as relaxing, and as regenerative.

It is a large island, which means that it's easy for you to set off and find yourself a secluded spot to soak up the sun. The almost endless beaches guarantee that you won't suffer from the sort of over-crowding that can ruin a beach holiday.

But, as well as the beaches, Kos offers a great deal to tempt the holiday-maker. The main town of Kos itself is an intriguing blend of narrow back-streets and open, tree-filled squares – with open-air cafés.

The nightlife is excellent, with a wide choice of discos and nightclubs, as sophisticated as you could wish, while the local tavernas provide an ethnic alternative.

It's easy to hire a bicycle, so that you can explore this island fully. A trip through some of the ancient villages will be unforgettable.

MADEIRA

The peaceful island of Madeira, for many years a favourite with British travellers, lies far out in the Atlantic off the north-west coast of Africa. It is a green, fertile island of volcanic origin, with a ridge of great mountains, rising to over 6,000 feet high, running east to west.

Great ravines run down from the mountains and picturesque little fishing villages are usually found where they reach the sea. Miles of levades, old artificial water-courses, carry water from the wild, rugged interior to the closely-settled coastlands where every available patch of land is under cultivation.

The influence of the Gulf Stream gives Madeira a lovely climate. Exotic plants flower throughout the year. Bananas and sugar-cane flourish. And the grapes which produce the world-famous Madeira wine ripen gently in the warm sun.

Miles of unfrequented roads, lined with shrubs and trees, wind through Madeira's varied landscapes on their way to unspoiled fishing villages and to hamlets in the hills. The drive across the island to Porto Moniz on the north coast and to Santana, with its delightful little thatched cottages, is a memorable one. And for those of you interested in walking, Madeira's fantastic scenery is ideally seen on foot.

Close to Funchal, at Cabo Girao, is the world's second-highest sea-cliff and nearby is the fishing village of Camara de Lobos where Winston Churchill loved to paint. At the village of Camacha you will find the centre of the wickerwork industry and throughout the island you will often see women making fine embroidery outside their neat cottages.

YOUR HOLIDAY WEATHER

	Average daytime temperatures				*Average hours of sunshine daily*			
	London	Majorca	Kos	Madeira	London	Majorca	Kos	Madeira
April	13°	19°	20°	19°	5	7	8	8
May	17°	21°	24°	20°	6	9	9	7
June	19°	25°	28°	22°	7	10	11	7
July	21°	29°	30°	23°	6	11	11	8
August	20°	29°	30°	24°	6	11	12	8
September	18°	26°	26°	24°	5	8	11	7
October	13°	22°	23°	23°	3	6	8	7
November	9°	18°	18°	21°	2	5	4	6

B Work in small groups. Choose one of these roles. If there are four of you, the fourth person can give advice to all three people.

GERRY: You can only go away during the school holidays. You'd like to find peace and quiet on an unspoilt island.

KIM: You love walking and wild flowers. You want to go on holiday in the autumn (September or October) to somewhere warm and sunny.

SANDY: You want to go away in the spring (April or May). You like to be active and enjoy scenery, nightlife and hot weather.

Role-play a conversation between the three friends, and discuss your holiday plans.

C Write four paragraphs, beginning as follows:

'I'd advise Gerry to ...'
'If I were Kim I'd ...'
'My advice to Sandy would be to ...'
'If I could go to one of the islands ...'

8.7 By ... *Prepositional phrases*

Fill the gaps in these sentences with suitable phrases from the list below:

1 The Mediterranean is *by far* the most popular holiday area in Europe.
2 I know them both *sight* but I don't know either of them *by name*.
3 You can cross the Atlantic quickly *by plane* or more slowly *by ship*.
4 The only way to remember the words is to learn them *by heart*.
5 I didn't tread on your foot on purpose, it happened *by accident*.
6 It takes several days to cross Europe *by car* and even longer *by train*.
7 The weather is very hot *by day* but it may be quite cool *by night*.
8 The thunderstorm took us *by surprise* and we all got wet.
9 We didn't arrange to meet on the beach – we ran into each other *by chance*.
10 'Could you fill in this registration form?' 'Yes, *by all means*.'
11 Oh, dear, I've put down my old address on the form *by mistake*.
12 There's no need to send the letter *by post*, I can deliver it myself *by hand*.
13 It's very hard to put sun-cream on your back if you're *by yourself*.

by accident   by all means   by car
by chance   by day   by far   by hand
by heart   by mistake   by name
by night   by plane   by post   by ship
by sight   by surprise   by train
by yourself

'Why is it we *never* go on migration?'

8.8 An excursion programme   *Listening*

A 🔊 Imagine that you are in a hotel in Edinburgh having breakfast on the first day of your holiday in Scotland. You'll hear the tour leader announcing some changes to the excursion programme.
  Make any necessary alterations to the times and places shown on the programme, according to what the tour leader tells you.

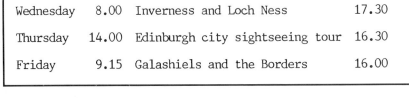

	Depart		Return
Sunday			
Monday	9.00	Braemar Castle and Aberdeen	17.30
Tuesday	8.30	Glencoe and Fort William	17.30
Wednesday	8.00	Inverness and Loch Ness	17.30
Thursday	14.00	Edinburgh city sightseeing tour	16.30
Friday	9.15	Galashiels and the Borders	16.00

B Work in pairs. If you had to organise a one-day excursion by coach around your own area, what places would you visit? Make brief notes.
• Join another pair and describe your excursion to them.

8.9 Spelling and pronunciation: Consonants   *Word study*

A The consonant sounds of English can often be spelt in several ways. Look at these examples first:

p   p ↔ pp
stop   stopped   supposed
b   b ↔ bb
bubble   beach
t   t ↔ tt
bottle   little   capital
d   d ↔ dd
paddle   handled   muddy
k   k ↔ c ↔ cc ↔ ck ↔ qu ↔ ch
climate   accommodation   king
quantity   chemist   lucky
g   g ↔ gg
guard   struggle
dʒ   j ↔ g
jet   germ   jumping
tʃ   ch ↔ ti ↔ tu
church   question   nature

l   l ↔ ll
skilful   silly
n   n ↔ nn
run   running   banana
m   m ↔ mm
image   monument
r   r ↔ rr
wrist   rescue
s   z   s ↔ z ↔ ss
circle   stone   police   zero
ʃ   ʒ   sh ↔ s ↔ ti ↔ c
shirt   sure   leisure   competition   ocean
f   f ↔ ff ↔ ph ↔ gh
affair   photograph   afraid
apostrophe   enough
v   v
vacation

θ ð th	j y ↔ u
thing this truth clothes	yacht union Europe

w w ↔ u ↔ o
weather/whether quite
once wheel/we'll

B 🔊 Listen to the tape and add the words you hear to the appropriate lists above. You'll find the correct spellings in Activity 25.

C Some consonants are written but not pronounced. Here are some examples of these 'silent letters'. Think of more examples to add to these lists.

gh: sigh light caught fought
b: lamb bomb climb combing
t: castle Christmas listen
k: knife knee
l: half walk could
r: beard word *(in some British accents only)*
h: honest hourly

D 👥 Work in pairs. One of you should look at Activity 5, the other at 22. You'll each have some more words to dictate to your partner.

8.10 Writing letters   *Composition*

A In real life, you probably only write letters to people you know to tell them things they don't know. In the exam, you may choose to write a letter to an imaginary person. Here are two typical exam questions:

1 Imagine that you are on holiday, having a wonderful time. Write a letter to the friend who was unable to come with you.

2 Write a letter to a hotel reserving accommodation for your family and yourself. Find out the price you will have to pay and request special arrangements for one member of your family who is a vegetarian.

And here are two students' compositions, both of which contain faults in content and style. What improvements could be made to them both? Add your improvements and corrections to the content and the style.

Villa Don Carlos
Marbella, Spain

August 30th

Dear John,
It is nice here in Spain. The sun is shining and the weather is good. The food is nice, for example yesterday we had a good meal. And the people are friendly, for example the other day we met a man who was very nice.
There are a lot of nice places to visit. On Sunday for example, we went to a town which was very old and interesting.

It's a pity we haven't got a car because the buses are slow. On the other hand it would take a long time to drive here from England because it is a long way. You can hire cars here.

It's a pity you couldn't come with us – perhaps next year. It's lovely here and we like it here.

love,
Jenny and Bill x

London, April 1st

Dear Hotel Romantica,

I want to reserve a room for me and my family for a week from July 7th. We want nice rooms and we want to see the sea from them. How much will they cost? Can you send me a brochure?

My father-in-law is a vegetarian. Is that all right for you? He has a small dog. Do you mind?

See you in July.
Let me know if everything is O.K.
Best wishes,
Alan Green

P.S. Mr Brown told me you weren't a bad hotel. Do you remember him?

B Now look at Activity 41, where you will see better versions of the two compositions. What improvements have been made?

★ If you choose to write a letter in the examination, make sure the style you use is appropriate. A formal letter is laid out differently from a personal letter – as the examples in Activity 41 show.

C Now write your own composition (about 150 words, *not* including the address, date, etc.), choosing from these topics:

1 Write a letter to an English friend from your favourite holiday place. Tell your friend about some of the things you have done during your holiday so far and what else you're going to do.
2 Write a letter on behalf of your family to a hotel to reserve accommodation. Include some special requirements and questions.
3 Write a letter to a tour company complaining about the hotel they sent you to.

MAKE NOTES before you start. If possible, discuss your notes with a partner.

D When you have completed your composition CHECK IT THROUGH and correct any mistakes you have made before handing it in.

Show your letter to a partner and ask for comments on the content, style, grammar and spelling.

8.11 Duty-free goods
Listening

🔊 You'll hear part of a radio programme in which information is being given about duty-free goods. Fill in the missing details below.

1 Add the prices of duty-free goods to this chart. The first two are done as examples:

```
Airports                    Airlines

Amsterdam                   British Airways  £10.50
Athens                      Air France
Gatwick         £10         Alitalia
Heathrow                    Iberia
Madrid                      JAL
Manchester                  KLM
New York                    Olympic
Paris                       Swissair
Rome                        Varig
Tokyo
Zurich
```

2 The problem with buying duty-free goods on a plane is that ....
3 Abroad, locally-produced wines and spirits are often cheaper if you buy them in ....
4 A bottle of the local drink is a nicer .... than a bottle of whisky.
5 Before making a duty-free purchase, ask yourself two questions:
   • Do I .... ?
   • Is it .... ?
6 'Duty-free prices' are often .... than prices in a .... shop.

8.12 *Break, bring, call, cut*
Verbs and idioms

A Which of the endings below go with these beginnings?

Kit broke ...   **Lee called** ...
Chris brought ...   **Sandy cut** ...

a doctor   a piece of paper   a window   Jan's heart   Lee to the party
the book to Sandy   the dog Rover   the grass   the ice   the news to us
to see Sandy   himself/herself

B Fill the gaps with a suitable form of the phrasal verbs opposite:

break
1 We had to interrupt our journey because the car had ....
2 He .... in mid-sentence to go and see who was at the door.
3 The children were all happy when their school .... for the holidays.
bring
4 Can you explain what .... these problems?
5 They were .... by their grandmother after their mother died.
6 My glasses are upstairs, could you .... them .... for me, please?
7 When you've finished with the books, please .... them ....

114

call

8 Not enough people booked for the excursion, so it has been ....
9 If you're ever in the area, do .... and see me.
10 They were engaged for six months but they decided to .... it ....
11 I'll .... you at 7.30 – will you be ready?
12 I'm very busy at the moment, could you .... me .... later, please?

cut

13 I can't give up smoking altogether but I'm trying to ....
14 Do you need a pair of scissors to .... the coupon?
15 During the strike all electricity supplies were ....

break down   break off   break up
bring about   bring back   bring down   bring up
call back   call in   call for   call off   call off
cut down   cut off   cut out

8.13   Fill the gaps   *Use of English*

A   What words are missing in each of these sentences?

1 If you have flu you often have a .... headache.
2 I spent a sleepless .... worrying about my problems.
3 It's safest to .... the street at a pedestrian crossing.
4 We .... arrived after a long journey.
5 .... beach holiday is .... most boring kind of holiday I can imagine.

★ When you're doing this kind of exercise and you're not sure what word fits best, try to decide if the missing word is an adjective (as 1 above), a noun (as 2 above), a verb (as 3), an adverb (as 4) or an article (as 5).

B   Fill each gap in this story with one word only. The first is done as an example:

We were late as 1 *usual*. Michael had insisted on doing his packing by 2 ...., and when he discovered that he couldn't manage he'd asked me for help at the last 3 .... So now we had an hour to get to the 4 .... Luckily, there wasn't much traffic on the 5 .... and we were able to get there just in 6 .... We checked in and went straight to the departure 7 .... to wait for our 8 .... to be called. We waited and waited but no announcement was 9 .... We asked at the information 10 .... and the girl there told us that the plane hadn't even arrived yet. In the 11 .... there was another announcement telling us that passengers waiting for Flight LJ 108 could collect a 12 .... meal voucher and that the plane hadn't left Spain because of 13 .... problems. We thought that meant that it wasn't safe for the plane to 14 .... We waited again for 15 .... until late evening when we were asked to report to the 16 .... desk again. They told us we would be spending the 17 .... in a hotel at the airline's 18 ....

The next morning after a sleepless 19 .... because of all the planes taking off and landing, we reported back to the airport. Guess what had 20 .... while we were 21 ....! Our plane had arrived and taken off again leaving us 22 .... All the other 23 .... had been woken up in the night to catch the plane, but for some 24 .... or other we had been forgotten. You can imagine how we felt!

9 Books and reading

9.1 A good read   *Vocabulary*

A Work in small groups. Ask your partners these questions:
- What was the last book you read (in your own language)?
- What was it about? What was it like? Would you recommend it?
- How long do you spend reading books, magazines or newspapers per week?
- Which British and American authors can you name?
- What is your favourite kind of book?

B Fill the gaps in these sentences with suitable words:

1 You can borrow books from a .... or buy them from a ....
2 A writer can also be called an ....
3 I can't afford to buy the book in hardback, so I'll wait till it comes out in ....
4 I can't remember the .... of the book, but I know it had a yellow ....
5 A book that tells somebody's life story is called a ....

C Choose the best alternative to complete each sentence.

1 *Oliver Twist* is a classic work of English ....
 editions   letters   literature   non-fiction
2 The plot of the novel was exciting, but I didn't find the .... very interesting.
 characters   figures   people   persons
3 Poetry is written in ....
 lines   paragraphs   prose   verse
4 In a poem or a song, the last word in a line often .... with the next.
 matches   rhymes   rhythms   suits
5 You can find out the titles of the units in this book by looking at the ....
 appendix   glossary   supplement   table of contents
6 If you need to find some information in a non-fiction book, look it up in the ....
 atlas   catalogue   diary   index
7 Most novels are divided into several ....
 chapters   units   passages   sections
8 Cambridge University Press is the .... of the book you're reading.
 author   editor   printer   publisher
9 A great novel has a good plot and a ....
 communication   meaning   message   significance
10 The book was marvellously .... and it was a joy to read.
 stylistic   tedious   well-written   wonderful
11 Ernest Hemingway is one of my .... American writers.
 best   favourite   ideal   most popular

12 The thriller was so exciting that I couldn't ....
    drop it   pick it up   put it down   read it
13 I'm not enjoying this book because I haven't been able to .... it yet.
    begin   complete   finish   get into
14 Even the .... characters in the book are really interesting.
    less   minor   small   tiny
15 I'd like to .... that book when you've read it.
    borrow   hire   lend   loan

D In these sentences THREE alternatives are correct and TWO are wrong:

1 The .... character in the book is called Oliver.
    central   main   principal   principle   top
2 I enjoy her books because her style is so very ....
    dull   entertaining   readable   tedious   true-to-life
3 I found that the characters in the story were very ....
    amusing   believable   informative   likeable   thrilling
4 There were so many twists in the plot that I didn't really think it was ....
    accurate   convincing   correct   realistic   true-to-life
5 She doesn't read any fiction because she prefers reading ....
    about real life   non-fiction   science fiction   short stories   textbooks
6 I can't .... books like those – they just send me to sleep.
    appreciate   bear   carry   stand   suffer

E Work in small groups. Ask your partners these questions:
- Who are the most famous writers in your country's literature?
- Who are the most popular writers in your country today?
- Imagine that you are recommending one of their books to a foreign person – what would you tell them about the book and its author?

★ Each year FCE candidates are given a choice of three optional 'prescribed books' to read. If you read one of these you can, if you wish, answer a question on it in the Composition paper and also discuss it in the Interview. Your teacher can tell you more about this, if he or she hasn't already done so.

9.2 Call for the Dead   *Reading*

A Read the two extracts on the next page, which come from two versions of the same novel: a 'simplified edition' and the original edition of *Call for the Dead* by John Le Carré.

Work in small groups. Ask your partners these questions:
- Which version of the story do you prefer?
- What are the advantages and disadvantages of each version?
- What is added and left out in the simplified version?
- Why do people read simplified editions of famous books?

A

He felt safe and warm in the taxi, safe because everything around him seemed unreal. Why was London the only capital in the world that lost its personality at night?

The taxi turned into Cambridge Circus and Smiley sat up suddenly, remembering the reason for the phone call. He could remember every word of the conversation – a skill he had learned years before.

"Smiley. Maston speaking. You interviewed Samuel Arthur Fennan at the Foreign Office on Monday, am I right?"

"Yes . . . yes, I did."

"What was the case?"

"An anonymous letter accusing him of joining the Communist Party while he was a student at Oxford. An ordinary interview, approved by the Director of Security."

(Fennan *can't* have complained, thought Smiley. He knew I'd clear him of the accusation.)

"Were you unfriendly at all? Would he feel that you were attacking him, Smiley? Tell me that."

(Fennan must have complained to the whole Government for Maston to sound so frightened.)

"No. We liked one another, I think. As a matter of fact, I told him not to worry. He was clearly anxious."

"*What* did you tell him?"

"I said that I had no powers and nor had my department, but I could see no reason why we should trouble him further. That's absolutely all."

(He'll never forgive me for making him so dependent on my answers.)

"He says you accused him of disloyalty, that his career at the Foreign Office is in ruins, that people have been paid to give false information against him."

"He must have gone completely mad – he knows he's cleared. What else does he want?"

"Nothing. He's dead. Killed himself at 10.30 this evening. Left a letter to the Foreign Secretary. There's going to be an inquiry."

B

He felt safe in the taxi. Safe and warm. The warmth was contraband, smuggled from his bed and hoarded against the wet January night. Safe because unreal: it was his ghost that ranged the London streets and took note of their unhappy pleasure-seekers, scuttling under commissionaires' umbrellas. It was his ghost, he decided, which had climbed from the well of sleep and stopped the telephone shrieking on the bedside table . . . Oxford Street . . . why was London the only capital in the world that lost its personality at night? Smiley, as he pulled his coat more closely about him, could think of nowhere, from Los Angeles to Berne, which so readily gave up its daily struggle for identity.

The cab turned into Cambridge Circus, and Smiley sat up with a jolt. He remembered why the Duty Officer had rung, and the memory woke him brutally from his dreams. The conversation came back to him word for word – a feat of recollection long ago achieved.

'Duty Officer speaking, Smiley. I have the Adviser on the line . . .'

'Smiley; Maston speaking. You interviewed Samuel Arthur Fennan at the Foreign Office on Monday, am I right?'

'Yes . . . yes I did.'

'What was the case?'

'Anonymous letter alleging Party membership at Oxford. Routine interview, authorized by the Director of Security.'

(Fennan *can't* have complained, thought Smiley; he knew I'd clear him. There was nothing irregular, nothing.)

'Did you go for him at all? Was it hostile, Smiley, tell me that?'

(Lord, he does sound frightened. Fennan must have put the whole Cabinet on to us.)

'No. It was a particularly friendly interview; we liked one another, I think. As a matter of fact I exceeded my brief in a way.'

'How, Smiley, how?'

'Well, I more or less told him not to worry.'

'You *what?*'

'I told him not to worry; he was obviously in a bit of a state, and so I told him.'

'*What* did you tell him?'

'I said I had no powers and nor had the Service; but I could see no reason why we should bother him further.'

'Is that all?'

Smiley paused for a second; he had never known Maston like this, never known him so dependent.

'Yes, that's all. Absolutely all.' (He'll never forgive me for this. So much for the studied calm, the cream shirts and silver ties, the smart luncheons with ministers.)

'He says you cast doubts on his loyalty, that his career in the F.O. is ruined, that he is the victim of paid informers.'

'He said *what?* He must have gone stark mad. He knows he's cleared. What else does he want?'

'Nothing. He's dead. Killed himself at 10.30 this evening. Left a letter to the Foreign Secretary. The police rang one of his secretaries and got permission to open the letter. Then they told us. There's going to be an inquiry.'

B Note down your answers to these questions, showing whether you found the answers in version A, version B or in both. The first is done as an example:

1 What time of year did the taxi ride take place? January – B
2 Why was Smiley taking this taxi ride?
3 Why was he able to remember the whole of the phone call?
4 Why had Smiley talked to Fennan on Monday?
5 Was the conversation with Fennan friendly or unfriendly?
6 Why did Smiley tell Fennan not to worry?
7 According to Smiley, was Fennan's Foreign Office career ruined?
8 How did Fennan die?

C Work in small groups. Ask your partners these questions:
- How do you decide whether to read a particular book – a friend's recommendation, reading the first page, reading reviews, or what?
- Why do you read or *not* read:
  Spy stories, thrillers, detective stories, poetry, romantic novels, history books, biographies, science fiction, classic works of literature, etc.?
- Do you now want to read more of *Call for the Dead*? Why/Why not?

★ Once you have read a simplified version of a story, it might be worth rereading it in the original version – if you enjoyed it.

9.3 Joining sentences *Grammar*

A IDENTIFYING RELATIVE CLAUSES identify which person or thing is meant. Notice the lack of commas:

Fennan is the man **who** has killed himself at the beginning of the story.
London was the only capital in the world **that** lost its personality at night.
... it was his ghost **which** had climbed from the well of sleep.
One writer **whose** books I always enjoy is Graham Greene.
I liked the part of the story **where** the car broke down.

When it's the subject of the relative clause, the relative pronoun (who, that, which, etc.) can be omitted:

... a skill he had learned years before.
The person I liked best in the story was the father.
Call for the Dead is a book I'm sure you'll enjoy.

- Notice that *whom* is uncommon in informal writing and in conversation.

Instead of: we'd normally say:
The person to whom you spoke was ... The person you spoke to was ...
The people with whom I am working ... The people I'm working with ...
The man from whom I received the letter ... The man I got the letter from ...

B NON-IDENTIFYING RELATIVE CLAUSES give extra information.
They are often used to join sentences and are more common in writing than in speech. *That* is not used in these clauses. Notice the use of commas. Fill the gaps in the last three examples.

Smiley , **who** is the main character in the book , is an ordinary sort of man.
Jupiter's Travels , **which** is about a motorcycle journey , is a fascinating story.
Hamlet , ... is a famous play by Shakespeare , is a tragedy.
Hamlet's father , ... dies before the play begins , appears to Hamlet as a ghost.
Hamlet's mother , ... husband has died , married her husband's brother.

C Join these pairs of sentences, beginning with the words on the right.
The first is done for you as an example:

1 The detective knew all the answers. He solved the mystery. The detective ...
   The detective who solved the mystery knew all the answers.
   OR The detective who knew all the answers solved the mystery.
2 New York is a wonderful city. I'd love to visit it one day. New York ...
3 Ms Fortune was a writer. Her body was found in the cellar. Ms Fortune ...
4 I met an old friend. He told me all about a book he'd just read. I met ...
5 A car was stolen. It was found at the airport. The car ...
6 Science fiction books are about the future and space travel. Some people love them, others hate them. Science ...
7 You recommended that book to me. It was very good. The book ...
8 A simplified edition is easier to read than the original. It's shorter. A simplified ...

D Look at these examples of CONJUNCTIONS and PREPOSITIONS used to join sentences:

TIME **conjunctions:** and   before   after   while   as
REASON, CAUSE or CONSEQUENCE **conjunctions:**
  and   because   as   so that   so ... that   such a(n) ... that
CONTRAST **conjunctions:**   but   although   even though

> I took some books with me **so that** I would have something to do on the beach.
> I read the book **while** I was on holiday.
> The book was **so** exciting **that** I couldn't put it down.
> It was **such a** good book **that** I stayed up all night reading it.
> **Even though** I tried very hard, I didn't manage to finish the book.

TIME **prepositions:**   before   after   during
REASON, CAUSE or CONSEQUENCE **prepositions:**   because of   due to
CONTRAST **prepositions:**   in spite of   despite

> It was impossible to concentrate **because of** the noise of the traffic outside.
> I read the book **during** my holiday.
> **In spite of** my efforts I wasn't able to finish the book.

To show PURPOSE, an infinitive clause can also be used:
> I used a dictionary **to** / **in order to** / **so as to** look up any unfamiliar words.

We can also join two sentences using these conjunctions:
TIME: Then,   Afterwards,   Beforehand,   Meanwhile,
REASON, CAUSE or CONSEQUENCE: Consequently,   Therefore,   That's why ...
CONTRAST: However,   Nevertheless,

> I tried to finish the book. **However,** I didn't manage to.
> We all read the book. **Afterwards,** we discussed it.
> It's a wonderful book. **That's why** I recommended it to you.

E Rewrite these sentences so that they still mean the same, beginning with the words on the right.

1. The difficulties were enormous but she managed to escape.   In spite of …
2. It is a wonderful story and I'd recommend it to anyone.   It is such …
3. I phoned my friends. I wanted them to know when I'd be arriving   As …
4. I was sitting in bed reading. Meanwhile, my friends were dancing.   While …
5. The book is over 500 pages long. Nevertheless, I'm going to try to read it before next week.   Although …
6. I'm going to read the book first. Then I'll go and see the film.   Before …
7. The heroine escaped from the villain. Then she rescued the hero.   After …
8. I read a lot of books while I was on holiday in the summer.   During …

F Fill the gaps in this story with suitable words. Most of the missing words, but not all, are relative pronouns and conjunctions.

The Captain and the Enemy is a novel *1* .... was written by Graham Greene in 1988. It is a story *2* .... a boy, Victor Baxter, *3* .... father (*4* .... he calls 'The Devil') loses him in a game of backgammon to a man *5* .... is only known as the Captain. The Captain, *6* .... real name is never revealed, appears to be some sort *7* .... criminal. *8* .... the boy has been taken away from his boarding school, he is brought *9* .... by a woman called Lisa, *10* .... is the Captain's mistress. From time to *11* .... the Captain returns *12* .... visit them, *13* .... for months on end they are alone together. *14* .... this time a close relationship develops *15* .... them, and Lisa treats Victor as if he is her son. Eventually, the Captain goes to live in Panama, *16* .... tells them that they cannot join him there *17* .... he has made enough money. *18* .... he is eighteen, Victor leaves Lisa and gets his own flat, but *19* .... her death in a road accident he flies to Panama *20* .... meet the Captain …

9.4 Reading habits   *Listening*

A Before you hear the recording, look at the questions and see if you can guess what some of the answers are.

🔲 Listen to the recording and fill the gaps with information from the broadcast:

1. According to recent research .... % of American adolescents can't read a printed page unless they have an accompanying background of ....
2. The main advantages of printed books over cassettes and computers are that they are relatively .... and very ....
3. To use a book the only equipment you need is a ....
4. Many people only buy .... book(s) a year, which they read in the ...., on the .... and on the ....
5. Books by .... are selling more copies every year.
6. Five best-selling books are mentioned in the broadcast. Match the plots (A to E) to the titles opposite:

122

A   Five pampered rich women, the wives of powerful mining executives who are battling for control of an international company, travel with their husbands on business to Australia: afterwards they visit a nearby tropical island.

While their husbands visit a copper mine, the women explore the beautiful coast by luxury yacht. On the return trip the yacht breaks down and the women are forced to finish the journey on foot.

As they near the hotel their trip becomes a nightmare when they see their husbands murdered in cold blood by terrorists . . .

B   *One woman's odyssey through a century of turmoil . . .*
St Petersburg: one famous night of violence in the October Revolution shatters the dreams of young Countess Ossupov forever.

Paris: under the shadow of the Great War, émigrés struggle for survival as taxi drivers, seamstresses and ballet dancers. The Countess flees there in poverty . . . and leaves in glory.

America: a glittering world of fast cars and furs in the Roaring Twenties; a world of comfort that would come crashing down without warning.

C   This thrilling new novel is a story of man against the elements, struggling to survive, growing with the land, shaping it, spoiling it, and above all falling under its spell. It is a tale of explorers, Russian and American, fighting their way through this ice-bound world, contesting the colonisation of an increasingly precious territory.

Ranging from pre-history to the present day, this is a classic novel, huge in scope, as vast as the land so richly described – a truly panoramic novel.

D   Jon Darrow, a man with psychic powers, is a man who has played many parts: a shady faith-healer, a naval chaplain, a passionate husband, an awkward father, an Anglo-Catholic monk.

In 1940 Darrow returns to the world he once renounced, but faced with many unforeseen temptations he fails to control his psychic powers. Corruption lies in wait for him, and threatens not only his future as a priest but his happiness with Anne, the young woman he has come to love.

E   Set in Yorkshire, Australia, Hong Kong and America, this remarkable novel continues the story of an unorthodox and fascinating family. As the spirit of Emma Harte lives on in her granddaughter, Paula O'Neill, an engrossing drama is played out in the glamorous arena of the wealthy and privileged, in a cut-throat world of jealousy and treachery.

Paula must act with daring and courage to preserve her formidable grandmother's glittering empire from unscrupulous enemies – so that Emma's precious dream lives on for the next generation . . .

B   Work in small groups. Find out your partners' opinions on these questions:
- Will new technology replace printed books, magazines and newspapers?
- In the future, will students use computers instead of textbooks?

9.5 Using suffixes: Abstract nouns *Word study*

A Nouns from verbs
Add more examples, using the root words below with these suffixes:

- **-ation*** pronunciation qualification
- **-ion** prediction description depression
- **-ment** arrangement replacement
- **-al** arrival refusal
- **-ance** performance appearance

accept approve assist associate astonish connect demonstrate
disappear embarrass encourage improve object propose reflect
remove starve survive translate

B Nouns from adjectives and nouns
Look at these examples and add more of your own, using the root words below with one of these suffixes. Use a dictionary to check your spelling, if necessary.

- **-ness** kindness friendliness
- **-ce** violence permanence
- **-ity*** ability possibility
- **-y** honesty frequency
- **-ship** friendship relationship
- **-hood** childhood fatherhood

accurate available blind careless cheerful confident efficient
fluent intelligent leader member mother owner parent
patient photograph probable real sad selfish shy silent
sportsman suitable weak

* Notice where the stress falls in these verbs and nouns:
démonstrate demonstrátion quálify qualificátion
áble abílity póssible possibílity réal reálity

Notice the following associated adjectives and nouns:
anxious ↔ anxiety strong ↔ strength delighted ↔ delight
wise ↔ wisdom bored ↔ boredom proud ↔ pride
hungry ↔ hunger thirsty ↔ thirst

C
Fill the gaps in these sentences, using a prefix with the correct form of the root word on the right. The first is done for you as an example:

1 The book describes the ......**relationship**...... between a mother and her son. RELATION
2 I've read *War and Peace* – but only in .... TRANSLATE
3 There was too much .... in the story. VIOLENT
4 The main .... of the book was the predictable ending. WEAK
5 There's a lovely .... of the author's early .... DESCRIBE CHILD
6 You can't help admiring him for his .... and .... KIND HONEST

9.6 Holiday reading *Problem solving*

A Work in small groups. Which of these books would you choose to read on holiday? Give your reasons.

HILLS OF KALAMATA

It was more or less unwittingly that Sarah Gilmore got herself involved in a plot to kidnap the Greek Charon Drakos – but unfortunately for Sarah he turned the tables and kidnapped her instead. So there she was, borne off to Charon's grim fortress-like home in the most remote, primitive part of Greece, forced into marriage with him. 'Whether you like my kisses or not you're going to have to accept them!' he assured her grimly – and how could Sarah escape him? And yet, when the chance came, she found she did not want to . . .

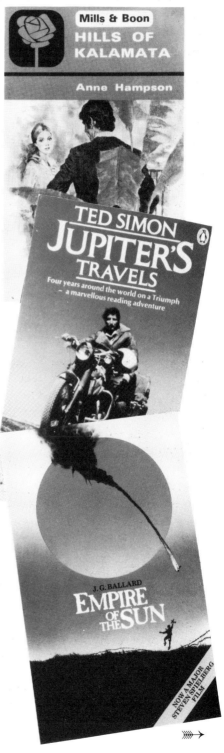

Like Marco Polo or Clare Francis, Ted Simon made a journey that millions dream of. He rode 63,000 miles, four years and fifty-four countries round the world. Spinning through the Sudanese desert, into prison in Brazil, into the Californian commune; through war, revolutions, disasters; into depths of fear, heights of euphoria and a fleeting love affair . . . Riding the tightrope across vast continents, meeting their peoples, he is seen as a spy, as a glamorous, astonishing stranger and as a deity. And for Ted Simon, Magellan on a motorbike, it became a journey to the centre of his soul.

HE IS SEPARATED FROM HIS PARENTS IN A WORLD AT WAR. TO SURVIVE, HE MUST FIND A STRENGTH GREATER THAN ALL THE EVENTS THAT SURROUND HIM . . .

In EMPIRE OF THE SUN J. G. Ballard has produced a mesmerizing, hypnotically compelling novel of war, of starvation and survival, of internment camps and death marches, which blends searing honesty with an almost hallucinatory vision of a world thrown utterly out of joint. Rooted as it is in the author's own disturbing experience of war in our time, it is one of a handful of novels by which the Twentieth Century will be not only remembered but judged.

'A book of quite astonishing authority and power, one of the very best novels of recent years'
PAUL BAILEY THE STANDARD

'As fine a novel as he has ever written' –
Observer

A leak is traced to a small sub-section of SIS, sparking off the inevitable security checks, tensions and suspicions. The sort of atmosphere, perhaps, where mistakes could be made?

For Maurice Castle – dull, but brilliant with files – it is time to retire to live peacefully with his African wife, Sarah.

To the lonely, isolated, neurotic world of the Secret Service Graham Greene brings his brilliance and perception, laying bare the secret motivations that impel us all.

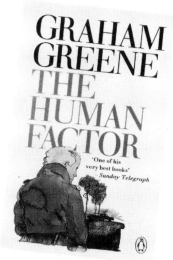

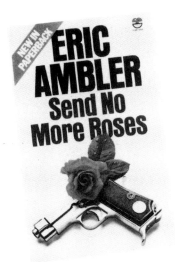

The Able Criminal . . . does not get caught – he is not even suspected.

But Professor Krom thinks he has cornered one. Paul Firman, alias Oberholzer, is suitably rich, undeniably shady and obviously frightened of his academic persecutor. He agrees to an interview in his secluded villa on the French Riviera.

He also plans a few surprises. Or were they laid on by his master, the really able criminal?

B The following people took one of the books on holiday with them, but each regretted their choice. Why did they NOT enjoy their books and which book(s) might have suited them better?

ANNA is 13. She chose *Jupiter's Travels* to take with her to read during her holiday at the seaside with her parents.

BOB is 25 and works as a car mechanic. He chose *The Human Factor* to read during his walking holiday.

COLIN is 19 and is studying English literature. He chose *Send No More Roses* to read on the train while he was travelling round Europe.

and YOU took *Hills of Kalamata* with you on YOUR last summer holiday.

C Write four paragraphs beginning as follows:

'Anna may be rather too young ...'
'*The Human Factor* sounds as if ...'
'Colin's choice of holiday reading was unfortunate because ...'
'I'm sorry I took *Hills of Kalamata* with me because ...'

9.7 In ...   *Prepositional phrases*

Fill the gaps in these sentences with suitable phrases from the list below.

1 They get on well with each other because they have so much ....
2 The main character knew she was .... and she managed to escape.
3 She must have been .... because she rushed past me without saying hello.
4 This book contains 224 pages ....
5 .... I like spy stories but I didn't enjoy that particular one.
6 Graham Greene's novels are all good, but I like *The Captain and the Enemy* ....
7 He didn't want anyone else to know, so he told them ....
8 The hero had spent all his money and was ....
9 Let me know if you're .... and I'll see if I can help you at all.
10 He seems charming ...., but .... he's aggressive and disagreeable.
11 If someone says, 'I agree with you ....' it means, ..., that they don't really agree.
12 At the end of the story the heroine was .... because her husband was ....

in a hurry   in a way   in all   in common   in danger   in debt
in difficulties   in general   in other words   in particular   in prison
in private   in public   in secret   in tears

9.8 The Captain and the Enemy   *Reading*

A Read this passage and then answer the exam-style questions. Be careful because some of the wrong alternatives are only slightly wrong!

1

I am now in my twenty-second year and yet the only birthday which I can clearly distinguish among all the rest is my twelfth, for it was on that damp and misty day in September I met the Captain for the first time. I can still remember the wetness of the gravel under my gym shoes and how the blown leaves made the courtyard slippery as I ran recklessly to escape from my enemies between one class and the next. I slithered and came to an abrupt halt while my pursuers went whistling away, because there in the middle of the courtyard stood our formidable headmaster talking to a tall man in a bowler hat, a rare sight already at that date, so that he looked a little like an actor in costume – an impression not so far wrong, for I never saw him in a bowler hat again. He carried a walking-stick over his shoulder at the slope like a soldier with a rifle. I had no idea who he might be, nor, of course, did I know how he had won me the previous night, or so he was to claim, in a backgammon game with my father.

I slid so far that I landed on my knees at the two men's feet, and when I picked myself up the headmaster was glaring at me from under his heavy eyebrows. I heard him say, 'I *think* this is the one you want – Baxter Three. Are you Baxter Three?'

'Yes, sir,' I said.

The man, whom I would never come to know by any more permanent name than the Captain, said, 'What does Three indicate?'

'He is the youngest of three Baxters,' the headmaster said, 'but not one of them is related by blood.'

'That puts me in a bit of a quandary,' the Captain said. 'For which of them is the Baxter I want? The Christian name, unlikely as it may sound, is Victor. Victor Baxter – the names don't pair very well.'

'We have little occasion here for Christian names. Are you called Victor Baxter?' the headmaster inquired of me sharply.

'Yes, sir,' I said after some hesitation, for I was reluctant to admit to a name which I had tried unsuccessfully to conceal from my fellows. I knew very well that Victor for some obscure reason was one of the unacceptable names, like Vincent or Marmaduke.

'Well then, I suppose that this is the Baxter you want, sir. Your face needs washing, boy.'

The stern morality of the school prevented me from telling the headmaster that it had been quite clean until my enemies had splashed it with ink. I saw the Captain regarding me with brown, friendly and what I came to learn later from hearsay, unreliable eyes. He had such deep black hair that it might well have been dyed and a long thin nose which reminded me of a pair of scissors left partly ajar, as though his nose was preparing to trim the military moustache just below it. I thought that he winked at me, but I could hardly believe it. In my experience grown-ups did not wink, except at each other.

(from *The Captain and the Enemy* by Graham Greene)

1 How old was Victor (the narrator) when he first met the Captain?
   a) 11   b) 12   c) 21   d) 22
2 How old is Victor at the time of writing?
   a) 11   b) 12   c) 21   d) 22
3 Victor is called Baxter Three because ...
   a) he has two elder brothers in the school
   b) he has two younger brothers in the school
   c) there are two older boys called Baxter in the school
   d) there are two younger boys called Baxter in the school
4 Victor was running fast because ...
   a) he was playing with some other boys   c) other boys were chasing him
   b) he wanted to meet the Captain   d) the headmaster had called him
5 The Captain said later that Victor's father had ...
   a) asked the Captain to look after Victor
   b) given Victor to him
   c) lost Victor to him in a gambling game
   d) sold Victor to him
6 Victor's fellow pupils ...
   a) did not know his first name   c) liked the name Victor
   b) knew his first name   d) were keen to find out his first name
7 Victor's face was dirty because ...
   a) he had had an accident with some ink   c) he was a careless boy
   b) he hadn't washed that morning   d) the other boys had made it dirty
8 The adults that Victor knew all seemed to him to be ...
   a) kind and generous   c) strict and severe
   b) humorous and friendly   d) unhappy and bad-tempered

Check your answers and, if you made any mistakes, make sure you understand WHY you were wrong. Did any of the questions seem 'unfair' to you?

B Find words or phrases in the passage that mean the same as these words or phrases. Don't use a dictionary – try to work out the meanings from the context. The first is done for you as an example:

1 stones   gravel
2 sports shoes
3 not worrying about the danger
4 slid
5 sudden
6 not knowing what to do
7 unwilling
8 keep secret
9 hard to understand
10 according to what other people said
11 half open
12 cut

C Work in groups. Ask your partners these questions:
- What kind of person does Victor seem to be?
- What would it be like to be a boy like Victor in a tough boarding school?
- What are your views on boarding schools?
- What are your views on single-sex schools, as opposed to coeducational ones?

9.9 Talking about books   *Listening and speaking*

A 🔊 You'll hear a number of people talking about books they have recently read. As you listen to the recording for the first time, match the titles of the books to their authors.

Title	Author
A Taste for Death	Maya Angelou
Boy	Margaret Atwood
Catch 22	Roald Dahl
Cider with Rosie	Joseph Heller
I Know Why the Caged Bird Sings	P. D. James
Surfacing	Laurie Lee

B 🔊 Now listen to the recording again and decide which of these statements are true (**T**) or false (**F**):

1 **David** enjoys thrillers.
2 *A Taste for Death* is about two famous men who are found dead in a church.
3 He liked *A Taste for Death* because it was very amusing.
4 **Jocelyn** enjoys thrillers.
5 The author of *Surfacing* comes from Canada.
6 She enjoyed *Surfacing* because it was more than just funny.
7 **Ken** enjoys books about travel.
8 *Cider with Rosie* is about a period that now seems very long ago.
9 He found some of the descriptions rather dull.
10 **Jill** enjoys reading about people's lives.
11 She enjoyed the simple style of *I Know Why the Caged Bird Sings*.
12 **Blain** likes books that make him laugh.
13 He enjoys *Catch 22* because it is about the author's childhood.
14 **Judy** only likes books that are exciting.
15 She enjoyed the simple style of *Boy*.
16 Some parts of *Boy* are terrifying.

C Complete the unfinished sentences in this dialogue with questions that fit the answers that are given. The first is done for you as an example:

YOU: What *kinds of books do you enjoy reading* ?
Friend: Books that are easy to read and exciting.
YOU: Who _____ ?
Friend: Oh, John Le Carré, Len Deighton — writers like that.
YOU: Do _____ ?
Friend: No, not only spy stories. I do read other kinds of books too.
YOU: And what _____ ?
Friend: At the moment? Well, I'm on the very last chapter of a book by J. G. Ballard.
YOU: What _____ ?
Friend: 'Empire of the Sun'.
YOU: What _____ ?
Friend: It's about a boy who is separated from his parents during the war.

YOU:	Where _____ ?
Friend:	In Shanghai.
YOU:	What _____ ?
Friend:	He learns how to survive in spite of all the suffering and starvation.
YOU:	Is _____ ? It sounds as if it is.
Friend:	Yes, parts of it are depressing and even horrifying, I suppose.
YOU:	Then what _____ ?
Friend:	Well, it's very exciting and it's really well-written too.
YOU:	Would _____ ?
Friend:	Yes, I certainly would. I think you'd enjoy it.
YOU:	Will _____ ?
Friend:	Yes, sure. I'll try to remember to bring it along tomorrow.

D Work in small groups. Find out the same information from your partners, perhaps using the dialogue in C.

E Work in small groups. Here are some 'typical questions' you may be asked about the PRESCRIBED BOOK you're studying if it's a work of fiction or a play. Ask each other the questions.
(If you are not studying a prescribed book, leave out this section.)

- What ideas or 'message' is the writer communicating to the reader?
- Who is the most interesting or attractive character in the story? Why?
- Describe the main character in the story.
- Describe one of the minor characters and what happens to him or her in the story.
- Tell the story of the book as if you were one of the characters.
- Describe one of the minor characters and the part he or she plays in the story.
- What have you found especially interesting about the book?
- What makes the book 'different' from other books you have read?
- Why would you (not) recommend it to a friend who is not taking the exam?
- Did you enjoy the book? Why/Why not?

If your prescribed book is non-fiction, what kinds of questions are you likely to be asked about it?

9.10 Writing about a book *Composition*

★ In the exam, you'll have to write two compositions in 1½ hours – that's 45 minutes per composition, including making notes and checking afterwards. From now on, whenever you write a composition, time yourself. Try to finish every composition within 45 minutes (including planning and checking time).

★ In the exam, you'll need to use your time as efficiently as possible. It may be best to make notes on BOTH compositions at the beginning, in case you run out of ideas later. Use a system and routine for making notes and for checking your work that best suits your way of working.

A A 150-word composition, like any piece of extended writing, needs to be divided into PARAGRAPHS. Work in pairs.

1. Look again at the text in 9.8 (*The Captain and the Enemy*) and decide WHY the writer chose to start each new paragraph in the place he did.
   If the first paragraph were split into two, where could it be broken?
2. Now look again at the two versions in 9.2. Why does each new paragraph start at the place it does?
3. Look at some of the reading passages from previous units – why does each paragraph start at the place it does?
4. Look at two of your own previous compositions. Are they divided into paragraphs in a suitable way? Ask your partner to comment on them too.

★ In the exam, if you leave three or four blank lines between each paragraph, there will be room to add an extra sentence later. If your paragraphs are all squashed up together, you won't be able to do this.

B Write 120 to 180 words in answer to ONE of these questions, some of which you may have already discussed in 9.9 E. If your prescribed book is non-fiction, choose between questions 1 and 7. If you aren't studying a prescribed book, answer question 8.

1. What lesson or message does the story have for us?
2. Who is the most interesting or attractive character in the story? Why?
3. Describe the main character in the story.
4. Describe one of the minor characters and what happens to him or her in the story.
5. Tell the story of the book from the point of view of one of the minor characters.
6. Describe the setting or background of the story.
7. What have you found especially interesting about the book?
8. Imagine that you're recommending a book you've read to an English-speaking friend. Write a letter explaining what it's about and why your friend will enjoy it.

Time yourself. Make notes before you start and check your work afterwards.

★ In the exam, you may decide to answer one question on your prescribed book (if you've read one) OR to answer two of the general questions. This will depend on whether the Prescribed Book question you get in the exam is easy or not – this question is always optional.

9.11 You know that book I borrowed ... *Listening*

A 🔊 Listen to the conversation and fill the gaps with the missing information – there's no need to write the *exact* words the speakers use.

1 Jean says Peter borrowed the book ..**two months**.. ago.
2 Peter says he borrowed it .... ago.
3 Peter says he left the book in the .... and it got wet in the rain.
4 Peter admits that he dried the book out on a ....
5 Jean thinks he must have dropped it in the ....
6 Jean points out that the book is now ....
7 Peter offers to ....
8 She accuses him of always losing things and ....
9 The last time he borrowed her bike, he ....
10 She says that in future ....

B Work in small groups. Discuss these questions with your partners:
- Have you ever been involved in a similar situation?
- How would you have reacted if Peter had damaged your book?
- Imagine that you have borrowed something valuable from a friend and lost it. You know it can't be replaced. What would you do? How would you break the news?

9.12 *Fall* and *hold* *Verbs and idioms*

Fill the gaps with suitable forms of the phrasal verbs below:

fall
1 In a romantic novel the heroine always .... the handsome hero.
2 She .... him because he was very rude to her.
3 As he wasn't looking where he was going, he tripped and ....
4 I eventually persuaded everyone to .... my proposals.
5 Unfortunately, our plans to spend the weekend away have ....
hold
6 The robbers .... the security van and got away with £200,000.
7 I tried to get the book from him, but he was .... it so hard that I couldn't get it out of his hand.
8 If you could just .... a minute, I'll try to find the information you require.
9 All the traffic was .... because a lorry had overturned on the motorway.
10 As the explorers had eaten all their food, they had to .... until further supplies arrived.

fall for   fall in with   fall out with   fall over   fall through
hold on   hold on to   hold out   hold up   hold up

10 Food and drink

10.1 Talking about food
Vocabulary

A Work in small groups. Ask your partners these questions:
- What's your favourite dessert?
- What do you normally drink with a meal?
- What did you have for breakfast this morning?
- What did you have for dinner last night?
- What is the worst thing AND the most delicious thing you've ever eaten?

B Fill the gaps with suitable words or phrases – in some cases there are several possibilities.

1 They love eating at home because they are both fantastic ....
2 Carrots can be steamed and they can also be eaten ....
3 You can save yourself a lot of work in the kitchen if you have a(n) ....
4 Before the onions are fried, they should be finely ....
5 While the sauce is cooking, it should be .... from time to time.
6 Food can be cooked in many ways: bread and cakes are .... in an oven, vegetables can be .... or .... and meat can be .... or ....
7 My sister doesn't eat meat because she's a ....
8 The best way to boil water to make tea is in a ....
9 Before eating an apple some people use a knife to .... it.
10 Mix the flour, eggs and milk together in a large ....
11 Pour the mixture into a baking tin and put it in a preheated ....
12 Most people can't drink pure lemon juice because it's too ....
13 The problem with cooking for a lot of people is the .... afterwards.
14 My favourite sorts of meat are .... and ....
15 We can only recognise four tastes: sweet, ..., ... and ....

C Choose the best alternative to complete each sentence:

1 I don't really like eating a curry which is very ....
   hot   peppery   sharp   spiced   warm
2 Roast beef is one of my favourite ....
   bowls   courses   dishes   plates   sauces
3 That was absolutely delicious, can you give me the ....?
   formula   instructions   prescription   receipt   recipe
4 Would you like your steak well-done, medium or ....?
   bloody   blue   rare   raw   red
5 A lot of food you buy nowadays contains all sorts of artificial ....
   additions   additives   extras   spices   supplements

134

6 Waiter, could I see the ...., please?
   card of wines   list of wines   wine card   wine list   wine menu
7 The reason why he always eats so much is simply that he's very ....
   eager   greedy   hungry   peckish   starving
8 She liked the dessert so much that she asked for a second ....
   dish   go   helping   plate   serving
9 If you're on a diet there are some foods you have to ....
   avoid   deny   escape   lack   stop
10 You forgot to put the milk in the fridge and it has ....
   gone back   gone down   gone in   gone off   gone out

D Work in pairs. Make three lists:

10 KINDS OF FRUIT   and   10 KINDS OF VEGETABLES   and   10 DRINKS

Compare your lists with another pair's lists.
Which of the fruit, vegetables and drinks in your lists do you LOVE or HATE?

10.2 Eating out   *Reading*

A Before you read the passage on the next page, look at these questions.
What do you EXPECT the answers to be, from your own experience of eating out?

When you're eating out why should you ...
 1 bother to ring up to cancel a booking?
 2 ring up if you're going to arrive late?
 3 inform the restaurant beforehand if you're bringing a young child with you?
 4 read the menu outside before you go in?
 5 spend plenty of time studying the menu at your table?
 6 ask the staff questions about the dishes on the menu?
 7 worry about your fellow diners?
 8 criticise the way the meal was prepared, if it was poor?
 9 give the waiter a tip even if you had a bad meal?
10 tell your friends about your eating experiences?

B Read the magazine article and find the answers that the *Good Food Guide* gives to the questions above. Are they the same as your answers?

C Work in small groups. Ask your partners these questions:
• How do the *Good Food Guide*'s recommendations differ from your own ideas?
• Which of them would you NOT follow at a restaurant in your own country?
• Which of the recommendations do you try to follow when eating out? Why?
• What advice would you give a foreign visitor about eating out in your country?
• How do you attract a waiter's attention in your country?
• What are 'polite table manners' in your country? Is it bad manners to eat chicken with your fingers, put your elbows on the table, etc.?

Eating out —
Some rules for diners

If you don't very often eat out in a restaurant, you may need some advice — as the latest issue of the *Good Food Guide* points out. Several rules for people eating out are given, some of which seem perhaps to favour restaurant staff more than they are likely to help diners! For example the *Guide* tells its readers to be sure to phone up and cancel any booking they make which they can't keep. The restaurant may otherwise be holding a table and turning away customers at its busiest time. Apparently this is a legal requirement, though how anyone could trace a Mr Smith or a Ms Jones who didn't turn up with a party of six is anyone's guess. The *Guide* also advises you to ring up if you're going to be delayed by more than a quarter of an hour; if you don't, your table may be given to someone else and it's only polite, according to the *Guide*.

Another rule they give is to let the restaurant know in advance if a member of your party has any special needs. So if you're eating with a small child, a very old person, a disabled person, a vegetarian or a Moslem let the restaurant know at least a day ahead so that you can all be sure of having better food and a happy time. A good restaurant owner will be only too happy to look after his guests' individual requirements.

Before you go inside the restaurant, make sure you spend some time reading the menu outside quite carefully. Try to notice what the prices include and what they don't include. In particular look for any mention of cover charges, service charge and VAT. You might be in for a nasty shock when the bill comes if you haven't budgeted for these 'extras' and not all the menus you're shown at table mention these items. Once inside and seated comfortably at a table that suits you (and if you want a table by the window or in a quiet corner, do say so when you book) look at the menu carefully and insist that you're allowed enough time to decide at leisure what to order and to discuss with your companions what you're each going to have. There's nothing worse than being rushed into making a choice you'll regret later. By the way, don't be afraid to order two different dishes and to swop with a companion half-way through.

Another rule is to ask the staff questions: how is this dish cooked? what goes with what? what's that rather tasty looking dish the people at the next table are having? and so on. The *Guide* stresses that the people at the next table deserve consideration, too. If you want to smoke, you should ask them if they mind. This is more than just a polite formality since many people do object to breathing in other people's cigarette or, worse, cigar smoke while they're trying to appreciate good food.

While you're eating, someone will probably ask you 'Everything all right?' and probably expect the answer 'Fine, lovely!' but experienced diners should treat this as a serious enquiry and be prepared to offer compliments, criticisms (or both) honestly. Don't take any notice of companions who urge you not to 'make a fuss'. The trouble is, however, that you're usually asked this question when you have a mouth full of food, which makes it difficult to do more than nod and go 'Mmm'.

Finally, at the end of the meal, when you've been given the bill and are ready to pay you should thank the staff. Giving the waiter a big tip is no substitute for a warm thank you and a smile — if you've been served professionally and cheerfully you should reward the waiter with both gratitude and money! And if the food was poor, don't blame the waiter (it probably wasn't his fault — he wasn't the one who cooked the food) and don't refuse to give him a tip, either. In this case ask to see the manager and tell him you didn't really enjoy the meal and make sure you explain why.

By following these rules and guidelines, says the *Good Food Guide*, you can help yourself and others to enjoy better food. And if you do have a really good meal locally, tell your friends about it and encourage them to go to the same place. If you have a disastrous one, tell them about that too. After all, a good restaurant deserves to do good business and a bad one shouldn't be in business at all, perhaps.

(The Good Food Guide is published annually by the Consumers' Association)

10.3 -ing and to —   *Grammar*

A Study these examples and fill the gaps with your own ideas:

–ing as the subject of a sentence:
Preparing a meal every day is hard work.   Eating out can be expensive.
.... abroad is interesting.   .... after a meal is boring.

–ing after prepositions:
Is anyone interested in joining me for a drink after work?
I'm looking forward to .... to Spain on holiday.
I can't get used to .... tea without milk.
I had an upset stomach after ....

Verbs + –ing:
can't help   enjoy   finish   dislike   avoid   give up   go on
don't mind   practise   delay
   I've finished preparing the salad.
   I avoid .... in expensive hotels.
   I couldn't help .... when he fell over.
   I'm trying to give up smoking.
   I dislike .... after a meal.
   I always enjoy .... new dishes.

Verbs + to —:
learn   manage   mean   choose   decide   forget   can't afford
help   pretend   need   didn't mean   expect   hope   offer   refuse
want   agree   promise   I'd like   recommend   encourage   train   try
teach   allow
   I'd like you to give me a hand with the washing-up.
   They promised to invite me to lunch.
   I can't afford .... at the Ritz.
   We managed .... a table by the window.
   He didn't mean to spill the soup.
   We decided .... a drink in the pub.
   He tried .... the lid.

Verbs + –ing OR + to — with no difference in meaning:
begin   start   continue   intend   hate   like   love   prefer   propose
   She began to eat/eating her meal.
   I don't like .... alone in restaurants.
   After the meal we continued ....
   I love to eat/eating Chinese food.
   Which dessert do you intend ....?
   I .... black coffee.

Verbs + –ing OR + to — with a difference in meaning:
stop -ing and *stop to —*
   Please stop making that noise, it's driving me mad! (= don't continue ...)
   Their mother told them to stop ....
   We stopped to get some petrol and have some lunch. (= stop in order to ...)
   I was half-way through my meal but I had to stop .... the phone.

137

remember to — and *remember -ing*
   Did you remember to buy the lettuce for dinner? (= not forget ...)
   I don't remember you asking me to buy a lettuce. (= have a clear memory of ...)
   You should have remembered .... Jill an invitation to the party.
   I remember .... the letter yesterday evening after work.

to — after adjectives:
pleased glad surprised disappointed relieved shocked etc.
interesting kind hard essential difficult easy etc.
   I was pleased to receive your invitation.   It was kind of you to invite me.
   I was glad .... my old school friends again after so many years.
   We were surprised .... a bill for £45.
   It's easier .... from here to the centre by bus than .... by car.

too ... to — AND **... enough to —**
   We arrived early enough to get a seat.   My coffee is too hot to drink.
   The tray was too heavy for me ....   Boiled eggs are easy enough ....

B Rewrite these sentences, using the words on the right.

1 I'll be happy when I can see my friends on Friday.   I'm looking forward ...
2 If you want a table for ten you must phone the
   restaurant.   It's essential ...
3 I don't normally eat at restaurants.   I'm not used ...
4 You could sit by the window or outside on the terrace.   Would you prefer ...
5 They went on smoking all through the meal.   They didn't stop ...
6 I forgot to bring my wallet with me, have you got
   yours?   I didn't remember ...
7 Boiling an egg is not difficult.   It's ...
8 I'm very thirsty, could you get me some water, please?   I'd like you ...
9 Expensive restaurants are out of my price range.   I can't afford ...
10 You could share my pizza, if you like.   I don't mind you ...

C Make all the changes and additions necessary to produce sentences
that together make a complete story. You may have to do an exercise like
this in the Use of English paper. The first is done for you as an example:

   Dear Martin,
1 Last Sunday we go out / the country / visit my grandparents.
   Last Sunday we went out into the country to visit my grandparents.
2 I always look forward / go / see them and enjoy spend / day with them.
3 My grandmother like / grow all / own vegetables.
4 She never prepare / meal without / use fresh vegetables and / refuse / use any
   ingredients / have artificial additives.
5 When we arrive / we decide / go for / short walk before / sit down / lunch.
6 I love / walk in / country, even though I dislike / walk when I be in the city.
7 When we get back, / table be laid in / garden for lunch and we all begin / eat and talk
   and we go on / eat and drink all afternoon!
8 I be not used / eat a lot, / but everything be so delicious / I just can not stop / eat!
9 I manage / eat / great deal more than I intend / eat.
10 When we all finish / eat, we sit round / table and go on / talk / till it get dark.
   We all had a marvellous day,
                              Best wishes, George

10.4 A memorable meal
Listening

A 🔊 You'll hear six people describing a meal they remember. Decide whether these statements are true (**T**) or false (**F**).

1. Last Boxing Day **Judy** had invited all her family to dinner. T
2. Her sister's children behaved very badly. F
3. **Anne** was in the West Indies visiting some friends. T
4. She arrived early in the morning. F
5. The meal consisted of wonderful tropical fruit. F
6. **Blain** was on holiday in Crete and loved the food. F
7. When he returned to Britain he went straight to McDonald's. T
8. While in Greece, **Jill** and her friends ate in the same restaurant every day. T
9. The owner of the restaurant gave them wine instead of ordering a taxi. T
10. They only had to pay for the wine, not the food. F
11. **Ishia**'s meal in Italy consisted of twelve courses. F
12. About half the courses were some kind of pasta. T
13. **Coralyn** had invited four people to lunch at her flat. T
14. The vegetarian couple fortunately had a sense of humour. F
15. Her boyfriend saved the day by cooking everyone an omelette. F

B Work in small groups. Ask your partners to recall a particular meal they once had. It may be the food, the place or the situation they remember.

10.5 *On* ... and *out of* ...
Prepositional phrases

Fill the gaps in these sentences with suitable phrases from the list below.

1. It's important to arrive *on time* if you're meeting someone *on business*.
2. The lift is .... so we'll have to use the stairs. *out of order*
3. When we're *on holiday* we always like to eat .... if the weather's nice. *vacation*
4. Surely you don't want to sit .... – why don't you join us? *on your own*
5. There was nothing to pay because Harry, the owner, said their meal was *on the house*.
6. Don't get angry, I didn't break the plate *on purpose*.
7. Last year's diary is no use because it is *out of date*.
8. We're not ...., so I'll ring you from a public phone. *on the telephone*
9. Frozen food is certainly convenient but, ..., fresh food tastes much better. *on the other hand*
10. He lost his job last year and he's been .... ever since. *out of work*
11. The frying pan is on the top shelf, it's *out of reach*.
12. I couldn't get any mustard – it was .... at my local shop. *out of stock*
13. A policeman shouldn't join you for a drink if he's *on duty*.
14. .... I must say that I prefer eating at home to eating out. *on the whole*

on business   on duty   on purpose   on the other hand
on the house   on the telephone   on the whole   on holiday/vacation
on time   on your own   out of date   out of doors   out of order
out of reach   out of stock   out of work

10.6 The humble spud
Reading

A Before reading the passage, work in small groups. Ask your partners these questions:
- Do you like potatoes or not? Why?
- How many different ways can potatoes be cooked or served?

The humble spud

Potatoes have been a staple food of the Old World for so long that it's easy to forget that they originated in the New World. The first ones came to England from Chile in 1586 and the new vegetable soon became popular and in parts of Europe replaced bread as the staple diet of the poor. The original potatoes were misshapen and full of large deep eyes, unlike modern varieties which have been bred to be disease-free, smooth-skinned and free from deep eyes. Potatoes tend to be either floury or waxy in texture, the former being good for boiling whilst the latter are best for frying or eating cold. You can't do better than to grow your own, which is easier than you may think — you can even grow them in large flower pots on a balcony. If you buy potatoes in a greengrocer's, however, make sure you look for them with plenty of damp soil on them because they're likely to be fresher than the ones that have been around long enough to have been washed, graded and bagged in polythene! Flavour and nutrition are better retained if the potatoes are cleaned and then boiled in their skins, rather than peeled before boiling. New potatoes taste great, steamed and unpeeled with butter and salt. The four easy recipes that follow are for six people (or four hungry ones!).

Grilled potatoes
Boil or steam 1 kilo medium sized potatoes in their skins, drain and peel them while still warm. Cut each potato lengthways and brush with melted butter. Then put under a hot grill until golden brown. Serve with salt and freshly ground black pepper.

Potato salad
1 kilo medium sized waxy potatoes
2 tablespoons chopped chives, onion or parsley
mayonnaise or yoghurt dressing
Boil the potatoes in their skins and then peel and slice while still warm. Add the chives, onion or parsley to the dressing and coat the potato slices evenly. Leave to cool in the refrigerator before serving.

Potatoes with sesame seeds
1 kilo potatoes
6 tablespoons vegetable oil
2 tablespoons sesame seeds
about ¼ teaspoon cayenne pepper or chilli powder
1 teaspoon salt
juice of half a lemon
Boil or steam the potatoes in their skins, drain and peel. Cut into 2cm cubes and allow to cool. Heat the oil in a frying pan and when hot, throw in the sesame seeds. When they start to pop, add the potatoes and fry for 5 minutes, stirring all the time. Then add the cayenne pepper, salt and lemon juice and continue frying till crisp and brown.

Potatoes in their jackets
6 large potatoes
250ml sour cream
3 tablespoons chopped chives
oil
Preheat oven to 200°C. Wash the potatoes and rub them all over with the oil. Bake for 1 to 1½ hours, or until tender. (They'll cook faster if you put a skewer through each potato beforehand.) When cooked through, cut each potato in half lengthways and sprinkle salt and pepper on top, then let everyone spoon on the sour cream and sprinkle the chives on top.

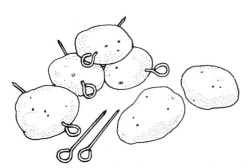

B Choose the best alternative to complete each sentence.
1 The first potatoes .... modern ones.
   a) didn't taste as good as
   b) weren't as smooth as ✓
   c) were more healthy than
   d) were smaller than
2 According to the passage, the best potatoes for eating cold are ...
   a) floury ones
   b) small ones
   c) large ones
   d) waxy ones ✓
3 According to the passage, the best potatoes are ...
   a) bought locally
   b) grown in flower pots
   c) home-grown ✓
   d) grown locally
4 It's best to buy ...
   a) clean potatoes
   b) potatoes in plastic bags
   c) dirty potatoes ✓
   d) small potatoes
5 New potatoes are delicious ...
   a) ✓ cooked and eaten in their skins
   b) eaten raw
   c) cooked in their skins and then peeled
   d) peeled and then cooked

C When should you ...
1 peel the potatoes to make 'Grilled potatoes'?
2 cut the potatoes to make 'Potato salad'?
3 remove 'Potatoes with sesame seeds' from the pan?
4 put the potatoes in the oven to make 'Potatoes in their jackets'?
5 take the 'Potatoes in their jackets' out of the oven?
6 put the sour cream on the 'Potatoes in their jackets'?

D Work in small groups. Ask your partners these questions:
• What do people eat as basic foods in your country?
• How do cooks in your country make basic foods like rice more interesting?

10.7 In a restaurant *Listening and Interview exercise*

A Before you hear the recording, look at the questions below. Which of them can you already answer, from your own knowledge of international food?
  Now listen to the recording and fill the gaps:
1 Before the meal, Philip has a gin and tonic to drink and Anne has sparkling water.
2 A Greek salad is made of cucumber, tomatoes, olives and cheese.
3 *Wiener Schnitzel* is a thin piece of veal coated in egg and breadcrumbs, fried in oil.
4 A Spanish omelette is made of eggs, chorizo and potatoes, onions.
5 *Lasagne al forno* is thin layers of pasta and meat sauce with a béchamel sauce, baked in the oven with cheese on top.
6 *Moules marinière* are mussels cooked in wine with onions and a little cream. You can have it as a starter or as a main course.
7 *Rösti* is grated potatoes, bacon and onions fried together. You can have it with two fried eggs on top as a main course.
8 Anne orders moules as a starter and sheve as a main course with a green salad.
9 Philip orders ???? as a starter and lasagne as a main course.
10 With the meal, Anne has fresh orange juice to drink and Philip has half a bottle of house red wine.

B Work in groups of three. Imagine that you are sitting together in a restaurant looking at this menu – the problem is that you don't understand some of the dishes. For more information, student A should look at Activity 7, student B at 35 and C at 48.

> Could you tell me what ... is?
> I'm not sure what ... is.   I'd like to know what ... is.
> Could I have ... to start with and ... to follow, please?

LEO'S RESTAURANT

MENU
£11.99 for three courses, including VAT and service

STARTERS
Avocado with prawns
Home-made paté
Melon and orange salad

MAIN COURSES
Lancashire Hotpot with seasonal vegetables
Steak and kidney pie with new potatoes and vegetables
Cottage pie with seasonal vegetables
Chicken Madras with rice
Chicken Maryland with French fries
Nut and mushroom roast with brown rice
Omelette, plain or with your choice of filling

DESSERTS
Pancakes served with lemon juice and brown sugar
Sherry trifle with whipped cream
Blackberry fool
Bread and butter pudding
Chocolate mousse

All our dishes are prepared in our own kitchens, using the freshest ingredients.
ENJOY YOUR MEAL !

10.8 Compound words   *Word study*

A Compound adjectives and compound nouns are formed from two parts. The best way to learn these words is to make a note of them when you read them or hear them. Usually, the meaning of a compound word can be worked out from the meanings of the words it is made from:

She is a kind-hearted person	(= she has a kind heart)
He is left-handed	(= he writes with his left hand)
A blue-eyed, red-haired boy	(= a boy with blue eyes and red hair)
This is my second-best suit	(= not my very best suit)
He uses a food processor	(= a kitchen machine that processes food)
I asked to see the wine list	(= the list of wines served in the restaurant)
She needs a tin opener	(= a gadget to open tins with)

Write down more examples of compound adjectives and nouns.

B Look at these examples and fill the gaps, using the words listed below.

first	first cousin	first-class	
high	high-speed	high-pressure	
home	home-made		
middle	middle-class	middle name	
second	second-class	second course	
self	self-control	self-defence	
well	well-done	well-informed	

-aged -best -class -discipline -grown -hand -known -level
-off -produced -respect -service -sized
floor name course cousin

★ Compound adjectives are usually (but not always) written with a hyphen, while compound nouns usually have no hyphen – but see section D below.

C Combine the words in these two lists to make compound nouns. These are compound nouns that are normally written as TWO WORDS, with no hyphens. The first two are: *air travel* and *cake tin*.

air cake coffee exercise food instant intelligence railway
recipe restaurant salad savings sports story tea television
tennis tomato wholemeal yogurt

account bag beans book book bread carton coffee court
dressing ground owner processor set soup station telling
test tin travel

D Combine the words in these two lists to make compound nouns. These are compound nouns that are normally written as ONE WORD, with no hyphens. The first two are: *airport* and *boyfriend*.

air boy bread chair dish head house play post sea tax
tea tooth tooth tooth

ache ache brush crumbs food friend ground keeping man
man paste payer port pot washer

★ Remember that a tea cup is a cup used for tea (perhaps empty), while a cup of tea is a cup full of tea. So a soup bowl and a bowl of soup are also different!

E Fill the blanks in these sentences with a word that combines with the one given to make a suitable compound word.

1. We've got a new high-............ microwave oven.
2. I'm afraid I've chipped one of your coffee ....
3. Could you buy me a tube of tooth............ at the supermarket?
4. He ate so much that he's got a stomach............ now.
5. My aunt's daughter is my first ....
6. I'd like my steak well-............, please.
7. Have you met Richard's new girl............?
8. We always eat home-............ vegetables in the summer.
9. Some people prefer old-............ cooking to modern fast foods.
10. Could I have some salad .... to put on my salad, please?

10.9 A nice cake
Listening

A Before you hear the recording, look at the ingredients and list of instructions below. The instructions are in the wrong order: can you decide what might be the correct order? The first is done as an example:

RICH DUNDEE CAKE
220g flour
1½ teaspoons of mixed spice
(ground cinammon, nutmeg, cloves)
150g butter
150g sugar
3 eggs
300g mixed dried fruit
(raisins, currants, sultanas)
50g glace cherries
1 tablespoon of sherry
1 tablespoon of rum
50g ground almonds
50g split almonds

    A Remove cake from tin.
    B Test after 2 hours with knitting needle.
    C Beat eggs and add to creamed butter and sugar.
    D Arrange split almonds on top.
    E Add remaining ingredients.
    F Fold in flour and mixed spice.
1 **G** Measure out all ingredients.
    H Allow to cool completely before cutting.
    I Cook in preheated oven (160°C) for 2½ hours.
    J If ready, remove from oven and allow to cool for 15 mins.
    K Grease a medium-size cake tin.
    L Pour mixture into cake tin.
    M Cream butter and sugar in large mixing bowl until light and fluffy.

B Listen to the recording and rearrange the instructions in the correct order. Compare your answers with a partner and, if necessary, listen again to settle any disagreements.

C The class is divided into an even number of pairs. Half the pairs should look at Activity 6, the other half at 29. You'll see some instructions on how to make two refreshing non-alcoholic drinks.

10.10 Revision exercise
Grammar

Rewrite each sentence using the words on the right:

1 Someone is preparing a meal for us now. — A meal ...
2 I've laid the table, so you can sit down now. — As the table ...
3 Brown bread is supposed to be better for you than white. — White bread ...
4 The worst meal I've ever had was at my brother's flat. — I've never ...
5 You've arrived too early, that's why the meal isn't ready. — If ...
6 We'll get there early so that we'll be able to get a table. — If ...
7 As there was no coffee left, we had to have tea. — If there ...
8 I love chocolates but I'm on a diet – still, I'll just have one. — Although ...
9 There was a power cut while we were having dinner. — During ...
10 They'll arrive soon. I'll make some tea then. — When ...

10.11 How to make a national dish *Composition*

When you're writing a composition, it's important to consider WHO is supposed to be your reader. In the exam, your real reader will be the examiner, but if the question says:
  'Write a letter to a stranger ...' or 'Write what you would say to a child ...' or 'Write instructions for a friend ...'
— you'll need to suit your style of writing to the imaginary reader.

A Look at these extracts. Who do you imagine is the reader or listener in each case?

1 Now, then. Let's suppose you want to make some old-fashioned lemonade. Well, it's quite easy really, but you might need a little bit of help with boiling the water. You need to make sure you've got four nice juicy lemons and some sugar, all right?

2 This is a favourite drink in our family and it's easy to prepare. All you need is four lemons and some sugar. All right? Well, first of all you have to peel the lemons, but very thinly so that you remove only the rind – that's the outside part of the peel, not the white part. OK, everyone? Good. Then you have to ...

3 You ought to try making your own lemonade, you know. It's ever so easy – anyone can do it! And it's much better for you than fizzy lemonade – and cheaper too. All you need is a few lemons and some sugar. Really, that's all, plus some water. Shall I tell you how to make it?

4 To make old-fashioned lemonade you need four lemons and 500 grams of sugar. The process is extremely straightforward and I'll explain it to you briefly ...

5 Unlike the commercial fizzy lemonade that is available in cans or bottles, home-made lemonade is pure, tasty and free from artificial additives. It contains only lemons and sugar and is simple to prepare. It is also considerably cheaper than commercial lemonade ...

6 ... Peel the lemons thinly, removing only the rind, and squeeze the juice into a large bowl. Add the sugar ...

B Work in pairs. Imagine that a foreign friend has asked you for the recipe of a typical NATIONAL DISH that is a speciality of your country (or region), which he or she can prepare easily. Decide on a suitable national dish. What ingredients are needed and are they obtainable abroad, do you think? How is it made, step by step? Why have you chosen this particular dish? Use a dictionary, if necessary. Make notes.

C Write a letter to an English-speaking friend who has asked you for the recipe of a national dish from your country or region. Explain why you have chosen this dish and how the dish can be prepared.
  Show your completed composition to another student and ask for comments.

10.12 Leave, let, pull and run — Verbs and idioms

A Fill the gaps with suitable forms of LEAVE, LET, PULL or RUN:

1 Could you ..... let ..... her know the news?
2 I'm not serious, I'm just ..... pulling ..... your leg.
3 Don't push the door, ... pull ..... it to open it.
4 I asked him to ..... leave ..... me alone.
5 Let's ..... leave ..... the washing-up till tomorrow.
6 They ..... let ..... the flat for £200 a month.
7 When does the London train ..... leave ..... ?
8 She ..... runs ..... five kilometres before breakfast.
9 She was ..... left ..... £2,000 in her aunt's will.
10 I'm just going to ..... run ..... a bath.
11 The police ..... let ..... him go after questioning him.
12 My uncle ..... runs ..... a restaurant in the old city.

B Fill the gaps with suitable forms of the phrasal verbs below.

leave + let
1 It's a very exclusive restaurant, they won't .... anyone .... wearing jeans.
2 I'm sorry that I .... you .... by arriving so late.
3 If you can't answer a question, don't .... it .... – guess the answer.
4 It's very dangerous to .... fireworks .... indoors.

pull
5 You can't get on or off a bus when it .... at traffic lights.
6 If you've got toothache, you may have to have that tooth ....
7 It's a shame that all the old buildings have been ..... pulled down ..... .

run
8 He braked suddenly to avoid .... a dog but he lost control and .... a tree.
9 You won't believe this: the pub has .... beer.
10 We were walking past the farm when a large black dog started to .... us.
11 I .... an old school friend of mine the other day.
12 Mrs Brown has .... her best friend's husband.

leave out   let down   let in   let off
pull down   pull out   pull up
run after   run away with   run into   run into   run out of   run over

'Don't go to any trouble on my account. I'll just have what everybody else is having.'

11 Work and business

11.1 Earning a living   *Vocabulary*

A Work in small groups. Ask your partners these questions:
- What do you do / plan to do for a living?
- What do the other members of your family do for a living?
- If you could choose any job in the world, what would it be? Why?

B Choose the best alternative to fill each gap. As in the exam, there are four alternatives to choose between.

1 He has all the right .... for the job.
  certificates   degrees   diplomas   qualifications
2 She's looking for a better position with another ....
  association   firm   house   society
3 A doctor is a member of a respected ....
  occupation   profession   trade   work
4 It's wise to think about choosing a .... before leaving school.
  business   career   living   profession
5 If you want a job you have to .... for one.
  applicate   apply   ask   request
6 You'll probably have to .... an application form.
  fill down   fill in   fill on   fill through
7 And you'll need to give the names of two or three ....
  hostages   judges   referees   umpires
8 All the members of our .... are expected to work hard.
  personal   personnel   staff   gang
9 If you're a(n) .... you have to do what your boss tells you.
  director   employee   employer   manager
10 You can earn more money by working ....
  extraordinary hours   overhours   overtime   supplementary hours
11 It's difficult these days for a young person to find a well-paid .... job.
  eternal   permanent   reliable   stable
12 She was .... after three years with the company.
  advanced   elevated   promoted   raised
13 An apprentice is required to do several years' ....
  coaching   education   formation   training
14 In Britain, people are usually unwilling to tell other people how much they ....
  deserve   earn   gain   obtain
15 A retired person is paid a ....
  grant   pension   rent   scholarship
16 According to everyone in the ...., she is a very good boss.
  apartment   compartment   department   employment

147

17 Some of my work is quite interesting, but a lot of it is just ....
   habit   practice   routine   tradition
18 If you are paid monthly, rather than weekly, you receive ....
   revenue   a reward   a salary   wages
19 The purpose of running a business is to make a ....
   contribution   money   profit   service
20 The .... were delivered to the warehouse by lorry.
   data   goods   material   stuff

C In these questions THREE of the alternatives are correct and TWO are wrong.

1 Ford is a multi-national corporation that .... motor vehicles.
   constructs   fabricates   makes   manufactures   produces
2 He was .... because he was an unreliable and lazy worker.
   dismissed   dispatched   fired   released   sacked
3 When the factory closed down, 500 people ....
   became unoccupied   became unemployed   lost employment   lost their jobs   were made redundant
4 A good worker is usually someone with the right kind of ....
   experience   experiences   experiment   personality   qualifications
5 Business letters are produced on a ....
   computer   printer   typist   typewriter   word processor

D Work in small groups. Ask your partners these questions:
- People who work often say that students have an easy time. Do you agree?
- What is the most difficult job you can imagine?
- What is the most unpleasant job you can imagine? And the most pleasant?

11.2 How to create a good impression ...   *Reading*

A Imagine that a young friend is about to attend his or her first job interview. Before you read the passage, decide which of these pieces of advice are DOs and which are DON'TS.

1 Find out as much information as you can about the job and the company.
2 Arrive early for the interview.
3 Make a list of reasons why you are suitable for the job.
4 Have something to eat before you go to the interview.
5 Go to the toilet before the interview.
6 Have a drink before the interview.
7 Take all your certificates and letters of recommendation with you.
8 Admit your ignorance if you don't know about the technical aspects of the job.
9 Show your best side only.
10 Shake hands with the interviewer.
11 Tell the interviewer about your shortcomings.
12 Ask about the pay you'll get if you're successful.

Then read the passage to see if your ideas are the same as the writer's.

YOUR FIRST INTERVIEW

With unemployment so high, and often scores of applicants chasing every job, you have to count yourself lucky to be called for an interview. If it's your first, you're bound to be nervous. (In fact if you're not nervous maybe your attitude is wrong!) But don't let the jitters side-track you from the main issue - which is getting this job. The only way you can do that is by creating a good impression on the person who is interviewing you. Here's how:

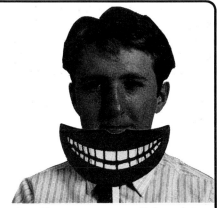

DO

Find out as much as you can about the job beforehand. Ask the job centre or employment agency for as much information as possible.

Jot down your qualifications and experience and think about how they relate to the job. Why should the employer employ you and not somebody else?

Choose your interview clothing with care; no one is going to employ you if you look as though you've wandered out of a disco. Whether you like it or not, appearance counts.

Make sure you know where the interview office is and how to get there. Be on time, or better, a few minutes early.

Bring a pen; you will probably be asked to fill in an application form. Answer all the questions as best you can. And write neatly. The interviewer will be looking at the application during the interview; he or she must be able to read it.

Have a light meal to eat, and go to the toilet. If you don't, you may well be thinking about your inside during the interview.

DON'T

Ever walk into the interview chewing gum, sucking on a sweet or smoking.

Forget to bring with you any school certificates, samples of your work or letters of recommendation from your teachers or anyone else you might have worked part-time for.

Have a drink beforehand to give you courage.

The interview

The interview is designed to find out more about you and to see if you are suitable for the job. The interviewer will do this by asking you questions. The way you answer will show what kind of person you are and if your education, skills and experience match what they're looking for.

DO

Make a real effort to answer every question the interviewer asks. Be clear and concise. Never answer 'Yes' or 'No' or shrug.

Admit it if you do not know something about the more technical aspects of the job. Stress that you are willing to learn.

Show some enthusiasm when the job is explained to you. Concentrate on what the interviewer is saying, and if he or she asks if you have any questions, have at least one ready to show that you're interested and have done your homework.

Sell yourself. This doesn't mean exaggerating (you'll just get caught out) or making your experience or interests seem unimportant (if you sell yourself short no one will employ you).

Ask questions at the close of the interview. For instance, about the pay, hours, holidays, or if there is a training programme.

DON'T

Forget to shake hands with the interviewer. Smoke or sit down until you are invited to.

Give the interviewer a hard time by giggling, yawning, rambling on unnecessarily or appearing cocky or argumentative.

Ever stress poor aspects of yourself, like your problem of getting up in the morning. Always show your best side: especially your keenness to work and your sense of responsibility.

After the interview

Think about how you presented yourself: could you have done better? If so, and if you do not get the job, you can be better prepared when you are next called for an interview. Good luck!

B Find these words and phrases in the passage and work out their meanings from their **context** – don't use a dictionary. The first is done as an example:

1 scores of (line 1)
   a) a few   b) hardly any   c) a large number of ✓
2 chasing (line 2)
   a) escaping from   b) running after   c) applying for
3 count yourself (line 2)
   a) congratulate yourself for being   c) consider yourself to be
   b) feel proud that you are
4 the jitters (line 6)
   a) over-confidence   b) nervousness   c) lack of experience
5 side-track (line 6)
   a) distract   b) emphasise   c) interest
6 issue (line 7)
   a) argument   b) purpose   c) difficulty
7 Jot down (line 15)
   a) mention   b) type   c) note down
8 done your homework (line 62)
   a) practised being interviewed   b) worked hard at school
   c) found out as much information as possible about the company
9 get caught out (line 65)
   a) be found to be lying   c) be wasting your time
   b) be in danger
10 sell yourself short (line 67)
    a) are too nervous   b) are too modest   c) don't talk enough
11 giggling (line 74)
    a) arguing   b) coughing   c) laughing in a silly way
12 rambling on (line 75)
    a) talking for too long   b) going for a walk   c) hesitating
13 cocky (line 76)
    a) nervous   b) proud   c) over-confident

Now use a dictionary to look up the ones you couldn't guess from the context.

C Work in small groups. Ask your partners these questions:
- Which of the advice given in the passage would hold good for an FCE interview?
- How important/unimportant are job interviews in your country?
- Which of the advice given did you find most useful and least useful? Why?

'I'm basically a problem solver – as long as the problems are simple.'

11.3 Reported speech *Grammar*

A Reporting Statements

Look at these examples and fill the gaps. Imagine that your friend Helen was talking to you the other day and you want to tell someone else what she told you.

1. Helen said, "I'm looking for a new job."
   → Helen said that she was looking for a new job.
2. "I want a job that pays well."
   → She told me that she wanted a job that paid well.
3. "I haven't found a job that suits me yet."
   → She said that _____
4. "I'll telephone them and I'll ask them to send me an application form."
   → She told me _____
5. "I didn't get that job I applied for."
   → I found out _____
6. "I did very badly at the interview."
   → She admitted _____

These verbs are often used to report statements:
*add   admit   announce   answer   complain   explain   find out
inform someone   let someone know   reply   report   say   shout   state
suggest   tell someone   whisper*

- If the information is still relevant or true, the tense often isn't changed:
  My boss didn't let me know whether **I'm going to** get a pay rise next year.
  He told us that Jupiter **is** the largest planet.

B Reporting Orders, Promises, Offers, Requests and Advice

Look at these examples and fill the gaps. Imagine that your friend Michael was talking to you about applying for a job when you last met him.

1. I said to Michael, "Apply right away if you want to get the job."
   → I told Michael to apply right away if he wanted to get the job.
2. "You'd better write them a letter."
   → I advised him to write them a letter.
3. "Would you mind typing this letter out for me, please?"
   → He wanted me _____
4. "I'll do it on my word processor if you like."
   → I offered _____
5. "You must send it by first-class post."
   → I reminded him _____
6. "You will make a photocopy of it for me, won't you? All right?"
   → He persuaded _____

These verbs are often used to report orders, promises, offers, requests and advice:
*advise   encourage   invite   offer   order   persuade   promise
recommend   remind   threaten   want   warn*

C Reporting Questions

Look at these examples and fill the gaps. Imagine that you were talking to your friend Irene last month about an interview she was soon going to have.

1. I said to Irene, "What time do you have to be at the interview?"
   → I asked Irene what time she had to be at the interview.
2. "Have you had many interviews before?"
   → I wanted to know if she had had many interviews before.
3. "Is this your first interview?"
   → I asked her if it _was her first interview._
4. "What is the most important thing to remember at an interview?"
   → She asked me what the _most important thing to remember at an interview._
5. "What are you going to wear for the interview?"
   → I wanted to know _what she was going to wear for the interview._
6. "How do you think you'll feel before the interview?"
   → I wondered _how she would feel before the interview._
7. When I saw Irene after the interview, I asked, "Did you get the job?"
   → I asked her if _she had got the job when I saw Irene after the interview._
8. "Yes." "Why don't you look pleased, then?"
   → I tried to find out _why do you look unhappy?_
9. "Because it's not really the kind of work I want to do."
   → She said she was disappointed because _it wasn't really the kind of work she wanted to do._

These verbs can be used to report questions:
ask   wonder   want to know   inquire   try to find out

- Remember that when you're reporting times and places, these words usually (but not always) have to be changed:
   here→there   now→then   this→the   tomorrow→the next day
   yesterday→the day before   this week→that week
   last week→the week before
e.g. "Phone them tomorrow." → She told me to phone them the next day.

- Remember that the actual words used can be omitted in reported speech:
   "I wonder if you'd mind helping me?"→She asked me to help her.
   "Why don't we have lunch together?"→He invited me to have lunch with him.

D   Rewrite these sentences, starting with the words on the right:

1. "I'm not enjoying my work," he said.   He said that ...
2. "I didn't remember to post this letter last night," he said.   He told me ...
3. "I want you to get here early tomorrow."   She said ...
4. "Have you already phoned our clients or will you do it later?"   She asked ...
5. "Don't forget to order the supplies I need," she said.   She reminded ...
6. "When will the delivery van arrive?" he asked.   He wanted to know ...
7. "Don't you think it would be a good idea if we phoned them?"   She persuaded ...
8. "I think I'd better tell you that it was my fault."   He admitted ...
9. "If you don't all stop laughing, I'll scream."   She threatened ...
10. "I'll make that phone call first thing tomorrow."   He promised ...

11.4 Four candidates
Listening

A Work in small groups. Ask your partners what qualities and skills are required to be a good ...
  manager   shop assistant   secretary   factory worker   waiter/waitress

B 🔊 Listen to the conversation. Two colleagues are discussing the four candidates short-listed for a job in their department. Make notes as you listen.

	GOOD POINTS	BAD POINTS
Mr Anderson		
Miss Ballantyne		
Mr Collins		
Miss Davis		

C Work in pairs. Compare your notes and, if necessary, listen to the conversation again. Ask your partner these questions:
- Which of the candidates did get the job? Give your reasons.
- What was the job they were being interviewed for, do you think?

11.5 Fill the gaps
Use of English

Fill each gap in this story with ONE word only:

One of 1 _the_ most enjoyable jobs I've 2 _ever_ done was when I 3 _was_ a student. When you 4 _hear_ what it was you may be a 5 _little_ shocked, but 6 _although_ I know it sounds unpleasant I can assure you that it was 7 _a_ fact delightful. Believe it or 8 _not_, I was a grave-digger for a 9 _dry_ summer. It was one of 10 _the_ hot, dry summers which made the 11 _soil_ as hard as rock and it needed a great deal of 12 _effort_ to dig the graves. Now, a grave-digger doesn't have 13 _nothing_ to do with dead bodies. All he has to do is dig two-metre deep holes and fill them in 14 _again_ when the coffin has been put in. As I 15 _said_, it was a marvellous summer and I'm glad to say 16 _that_ I didn't have to work on my 17 _own_. I had a workmate who had been digging graves 18 _since_ 1950. In 19 _spite_ of his depressing trade he was a cheerful character, always laughing and 20 _making_ jokes. He used to tell me 21 _all_ about his experiences and I 22 _listened_ to him for hours on end. Mind you, we had to work quite 23 _hard_ and usually there were two or three graves to dig every day. By the 24 _time_ I had to go 25 _back_ to college I was fitter, browner and in some 26 _ways_ a wiser person.

★ In the exam there will be twenty gaps to fill. Make sure you read the whole story through BEFORE you start adding words. If you're unsure, leave a blank and come back to the exercise later.

11.6 Situations vacant   *Problem solving*

INN ON THE PARK
requires
ROOM SERVICE ORDER TAKER

Previous experience would be an advantage, but the successful applicant will have a pleasant telephone manner and a good knowledge of food and beverage. Good salary, 40-hour week.
For further details
please phone 01-499 2252.

ATTENTION!
Men, Women and Students

If you are new to London, temporarily discontinuing your education, recently discharged from the Services or for any reason seeking temporary or career work, consider this unique opportunity in our Publishing Sales Field Department.

You CAN EARN £250 PER WEEK

based on your productivity, commission plus incentives. The men and women we are looking for may be tired of typing, folding papers, warehouse jobs and working for a limited income.

Work with young people. Rapid advancement possible. If you are 18 or over and will be available to start work immediately, call Mr Allison, 606 1419 between 9 a.m. – 5 p.m.

TWO YEARS AGO I WAS BROKE

Now I drive an Aston Martin, live in a 5-bedroom house, take my holidays abroad and earn a five-figure income. I need 2 ambitious people to share in my success, aged 22-40. Ring now, Terry Bilham, on 404 4522 or 404 0113.

01-408 2080
Personnel

The 4-star luxury Selfridge Hotel is currently seeking an experienced

DAY TELEPHONIST
(M/F)

Hours 7.30 am to 3 pm and 3 pm to 10 pm on a 5-day week rota. Knowledge of PABX3 switchboard is essential plus previous experience in a similar quality operation. Excellent salary, meals on duty plus benefits associated with a large hotel company.

**A member of
Thistle Hotel Group.**
Interested applicants should telephone Personnel on the above number.

SECRETARY/ RECEPTIONIST WANTED

for language school. Essentials: fast typing, friendly calm personality, working knowledge of German or Greek. Will be in close contact with clients.
Tel. 489 8071 – ref. PDQ

STEWARDESSES

Adventure, travel, excitement aboard 41ft luxury charter and pleasure sailboat located in Miami cruising the Bahamas and Florida Keys, equipped for diving, live aboard, will train.

Salary plus travel expenses.

Send photo and resume to: T.W. Charters, Pier 3, Slip 9, Box L, Dinner Key Marina, Miami, Florida 33133, USA.

PART-TIME. If you are aged between 18-30, have a sparkling personality, intelligence, energy, and own a car, an interesting job awaits you on Sundays throughout the season. You can earn £100 plus for approx. 7 hours' work. No selling involved. Training given. – Tel. for interview B'mth 21362 Sunday 2 pm – 5.30 pm and 7 pm – 10 pm.

PART-TIME bar staff required. Please apply to – Personnel.

A Look at the advertisements above and choose four jobs, one for each of the people who describe themselves below. Decide on the advantages and disadvantages of each of the jobs you have chosen.

ANNE: 'I'm 29 next birthday and I've been looking at the job ads in the evening paper lately. Alan and I are really short of cash these days and I'd like to get out of the house and earn a bit of money if I can. The trouble is that I can't leave the kids alone when Alan's at work – Alison's only $2\frac{1}{2}$ after all – but at weekends when Alan's at home, I could do something. I could use the car at weekends, too.'

BOB: 'I'm 21 now and I've just left college. Unfortunately, I kept getting these headaches in my final year and I couldn't concentrate on my studies, so I failed the exams. The problem now is how to earn a bit of money and decide what to do with my life. I still feel awfully mixed-up. I don't think I ought to make any hasty decisions about a career at this stage. I'd like a job I can do fairly mechanically while I look around for something more rewarding and try to sort myself out.'

CHERRY: 'I'm 23 now and I've done all sorts of secretarial work, you know, apart from the obvious shorthand and typing, I've used word processors and worked the switchboard and done reception work. My last-but-one job was good because there was such a variety of work to do. But then I left them for a much better paid job in another firm and then two months later they went bankrupt! So now here I am looking for something which is going to be interesting and where I can use all of the skills I've learned.'

DORIS: 'Unlike the others, I've still got a job but I'm getting more and more bored with it. I'm 24 now and I mainly do clerical work, filing, sorting out documents, answering the phone, you know, stuff like that. I can't type and I did quite badly at school – I'm not stupid, mind you, it's just that I got bored with what we did there. I want to find a job that'll give me a chance to do something more exciting. I've got no ties or responsibilities, so I could go anywhere.'

B Write four paragraphs (about 50 words each) about each job you have selected, beginning as follows:

'The best job for Anne ...'
'Bob would ...'
'Cherry might ...'
'Doris should ...'

11.7 Word stress + Joining up words *Pronunciation*

A It's important to stress the right part of a word. Mark the stressed syllables in these words and read the examples aloud. The first three are done as examples:

	Verbs and -ing forms	*Nouns and adjectives*
conduct*	I was condúcted round the museum.	I disapprove of their bad cónduct.
contract*	Metal contrácts when it gets cooler.	They signed the cóntract.
export	We expórted the goods to the USA.	Tourism is an invisible éxport.
import	These bananas are imported.	Imports have risen this month.
insult	He insulted me.	That was a terrible insult.
object*	I object to being insulted.	Unidentified Flying Object
perfect	They perfected a new method.	Your work is not quite perfect.
permit	Smoking is not permitted.	You need a permit to fish in the river.
progress	His work is progressing well.	Progress to First Certificate
protest	They protested about the situation.	They held a protest meeting.
record	Listen to the recording.	Have you heard their new record?
suspect	He is suspected of the crime.	He is the main suspect.

* In these cases, the meanings are different.

B   When a word has more than two syllables, it's sometimes difficult to remember where the main stress is placed – especially when there is a similar word in your own language.

Look at these words and **mark** the main stressed **syl**lable in each one like this:
em**plóy**   em**plóy**er   em**plóy**ment   employ**ée**   ap**plý**   appli**cá**tion

employ   employer   employee   employment   apply   application
advertising   advertisement   attraction   certificate   comfortable
communication   deputy   desert   dessert   desirable   details
development   experience   girlfriend   himself   information   intelligence
machine   permanent   photograph   photography   qualification   receptionist
reservation   secretarial   secretary   telephone   telephonist   temporary
themselves   toothache   vegetable   yourself

C   Generally speaking, grammatical words (modal verbs, articles, prepositions, etc.) are not stressed in a sentence. Content words (nouns, adjectives, verbs and adverbs) are stressed. Listen to these examples and mark the stréssed sýllables:

1 Stress is just as important in a conversation as when you're reading something aloud.
2 Knowledge of at least one foreign language is required in this job.
3 The unemployment figures are higher again this month, it says in the paper.
4 I heard on the news that exports are up again this year.
5 Male secretaries were replaced by women in the First World War.
6 Find out as much as possible about the job beforehand.
7 Show some enthusiasm when the job is explained to you.
8 No one is going to employ you if you look as if you've wandered out of a disco.
9 The way you answer will show what kind of person you are and if your education, skills and experience match what they're looking for.
10 It takes most people a long time to perfect their pronunciation in English.

D   If you're quoting a sentence from a letter or book, it's important to read in such a way that people can understand you easily.

It   is   very   hard   to   understand   someone   if   they   pause   between   each   of   the   words   in   a   sentence.
Normally, the words in a sentence are 'joined up', like this:
The words in a sentence are joined up when the last sound in a word is a consonant and the first sound in the next word is a vowel.

1 Mark the places in the sentences in C above where the words are joined up, when spoken.
2 Listen to the recording again and compare your marks with the voices on the tape.
3 Work in pairs. Take it in turns to read each of the sentences aloud.

E   Look again at the passage about interviews in 11.2 and find:
- the most useful piece of advice given
- the least useful piece of advice given
- the most obvious piece of advice, that everyone already knows

Mark where the words in the sentences you have chosen are joined up and then read them aloud.

11.8 First jobs   *Listening*

A You'll hear four people describing the first jobs they had. Decide which of the alternatives best completes each sentence.

1 **Jill** first worked in a design studio as ...
   a) a clerk   b) a designer   c) a secretary   d) a typist
2 She left the job ...
   a) when her boss returned from holiday   c) after she had returned from holiday
   b) while her boss was on holiday   d) after she had taken a day off
3 Some weeks later, when her boss wrote her a letter, ...
   a) she didn't return to the studio   c) the horrible woman had been sacked
   b) she returned to the studio   d) the horrible woman was on holiday
4 **David** enjoyed himself in the library by ...
   a) giving people the wrong books
   b) guessing what books people were going to borrow
   c) hiding books
   d) putting books on the wrong shelves
5 **Richard** found that the other postmen in Berlin used to ...
   a) arrive early for work   c) take his mail
   b) help him   d) think he was strange
6 His journey to work took about ...
   a) 30 minutes   b) one hour   c) 90 minutes   d) five hours
7 Compared with an English postman's work, the work of a German postman seemed to be more ...
   a) enjoyable   b) exciting   c) responsible   d) tiring
8 If **Jocelyn** didn't sell any encyclopedias, she ...
   a) didn't earn any money   c) earned just enough to live on
   b) didn't earn enough to live on   d) earned very little
9 She found that the key to success in the job was ...
   a) having a sense of humour   c) talking about encyclopedias
   b) not being shy   d) talking to people
10 She earned enough to ...
   a) buy a car   c) pay for her education
   b) pay for a holiday   d) support her family

B If anyone in your class has worked (even only holiday work) get them to describe their first job. Ask them questions like these:
- What did you have to do?
- What was enjoyable/dull about the work?
- How hard did you have to work?

★ In the exam, some of the listening comprehension questions may be very difficult. Remember that you don't have to get ALL the answers right in order to pass, just most of them. As you'll hear each recording twice, you'll always get a second chance to try to answer the difficult questions.

11.9 The secretary *Reading*

WORKFACE

Jane McLoughlin

IN OLDEN DAYS, when a glimpse of stocking was looked upon as something far too shocking to distract the serious work of an office, secretaries were men.

Then came the first World War and the male secretaries were replaced by women. A man's secretary became his personal servant, charged with remembering his wife's birthday and buying her presents; taking his suits to the dry-cleaners; telling lies on the telephone to keep people he did not wish to speak to at bay; and, of course, typing and filing and taking shorthand.

Now all this may be changing again. The microchip and high technology is sweeping the British office, taking with it much of the routine clerical work that secretaries did.

"Once office technology takes over generally, the status of the job will rise again because it will involve only the high-powered work — and then men will want to do it again."

That was said by one of the executives (male) of one of the biggest secretarial agencies in this country. What he has predicted is already under way in the US. One girl described to me a recent temporary job placing men in secretarial jobs in San Francisco, she noted that all the men she dealt with appeared to be gay so possibly that is just a new twist to the old story.

Over here, though, there are men coming onto the job market as secretaries. Classically, girls have learned shorthand and typing and gone into a company to seek their fortune from the bottom — and that's what happened to John Bowman. Although he joined a national grocery chain as secretary to its first woman senior manager, he has since been promoted to an administration job.

"I filled in the application form and said I could do audio / typing, and in fact I was the only applicant. The girls were reluctant to work for this young, glamorous new woman with all this power in the firm.

"I did typing at school, and then a commercial course. I just thought it would be useful finding a job. I never got any funny treatment from the girls, though I admit I've never met another male secretary. But then I joined the Post Office as a clerk and fiddled with the typewriter, and wrote letters, and thought that after all secretaries were getting a good £1,000 a year more than clerks like me. There was a shortage at that time, you see.

"It was simpler working for a woman than for a man. I found she made decisions, she told everybody what she thought, and there was none of that male bitchiness, or that stuff 'ring this number for me dear,' which men go in for.

"Don't forget, we were a team — that's how I feel about it — not boss and servant but two people doing different things for the same purpose."

Once high technology has made the job of secretary less routine, will there be a male takeover? Men should beware of thinking that they can walk right into the better jobs. There are a lot of women secretaries who will do the job as well as they — not just because they can buy negligees for the boss's wife, but because they are as efficient and well-trained to cope with word processors and computers, and men.

A Decide which alternative best completes each sentence, according to the text.

1 Before 1914 female secretaries were rare because they ...
   a) were less efficient than men
   b) wore stockings
   c) were not as serious as men
   d) would have disturbed the other office workers

2 A female secretary has been expected, besides other duties, to ...
   a) be her boss's memory   c) clean her boss's clothes
   b) do everything her boss asked her to   d) telephone her boss's wife

3 Secretaries, until recently, had to do a lot of work now done by …
  a) machines   b) servants   c) other staff   d) wives
4 A secretary in the future will …
  a) be better paid   c) have higher status
  b) have less work to do   d) have more work to do
5 John Bowman is now a …
  a) junior manager   c) male secretary
  b) member of the administrative staff   d) senior manager
6 He was given his first job as a secretary because …
  a) he had the best qualifications   c) he wanted to work for a woman
  b) he was lucky   d) no one else applied
7 He did a commercial course because he …
  a) couldn't think of anything else to do
  b) thought it would help him to find a job
  c) had done typing at school
  d) wanted to become a secretary
8 When he was a post office clerk, secretaries were better paid because …
  a) not many were looking for jobs   c) they had greater responsibility
  b) they were better trained   d) they worked longer hours
9 He found that working for a female boss was less …
  a) boring   b) easy   c) complicated   d) frustrating
10 The writer believes that before long …
  a) men and women will be secretaries
  b) men will take over women's jobs as secretaries
  c) men will be better with machines
  d) women will operate most office machines

B Work in small groups. Ask your partners these questions:
- Is your job (or the job you plan to do when you finish studying) often done by someone of the opposite sex? Can it be done just as well by men and by women?
- In your country, which of these jobs are normally done only by men or women:
    secretary, clerk, shop assistant, bus driver, train driver, airline pilot, taxi driver, ship's captain, building worker, doctor, schoolteacher, receptionist, politician?
- Would you rather work for a female boss or a male boss? Give your reasons.

11.10 A typical working day *Listening*

A 🔊 Listen to the recording and try to guess the speakers' jobs.

B 🔊 Listen to the recording again and decide which of these statements about Albert Wilson's work are true (**T**) or false (**F**):

1 He always has to get up at 4 a.m.
2 The work he does makes him feel tired.
3 He spends all his working life below ground.
4 The work is unhealthy because it strains the nerves.
5 He really enjoys his work.
6 He is able to talk to his workmates after every journey.
7 He thinks he is well paid.
8 He prefers working on the evening shift.
9 He gets one day off per week.
10 The members of his family don't have to pay for transport in London.

C 🔊 Decide which of these statements about Gordon Spencer's work are true (**T**) or false (**F**):

1 He works at home.
2 No one can disturb him when he's working.
3 He begins each day by typing notes.
4 He never leaves work unfinished until the next day.
5 He only stops working to have lunch.
6 He goes to work by bicycle.
7 As soon as he arrives home, he has a meal.
8 It takes seven weeks to write a book.
9 He writes one book a year.
10 He travels round the world mainly for pleasure.

11.11 Writing a formal letter *Composition*

A It's important, when writing a composition, to include only ideas and information that are relevant – if you're writing a composition about 'my ideal job', there's no point in writing about all the jobs you would *hate* to do!

Work in pairs. Imagine that you or a friend wants to apply for this job:
• What kind of information would be RELEVANT in your letter?
• What kind of information would be IRRELEVANT?

PART-TIME IMPORT/EXPORT CLERK
We are looking for an intelligent, self-confident young person who is fluent in at least one foreign language. The work involves answering correspondence, using a typewriter or word processor, and dealing on the phone with clients abroad. The working week will be 20 hours per week Monday-Friday, mornings or afternoons only.
A good salary will be paid to a suitable applicant.

Apply in writing to Ms Brown, ACME Enterprises, 13 Armada Way, Brookfield BF2 7LJ.

B Look at these two letters. What important information is missing from each of them? Which of them do you prefer and why?

```
                                c/o Mrs Grey
                                15 Green Road
                                Brookfield
                                (Tel. 345678)

                                1 April 199#
Dear Sir,
    After reading your advertisement in the Evening
Chronicle, I wonder if I might be suitable for the part-
time post advertised. I am a Greek national, and I am
studying in England for a year. My typing is quite good
and I enjoy dealing with people.
    Please let me know if you think I may be suitable for
the post. I can come for an interview at any time
convenient for you.
    Yours sincerely,
```

```
                                c/o Mrs Green
                                51 Grey Road
Ms Brown                        Brookfield BF8 9DN
ACME Enterprises
13 Armada Way
Brookfield BF2 7LJ

Dear Ms Brown,
    I am interested in applying for the post of Part-time
Import/Export Clerk.
    I am 20 years of age and in my third year studying business
administration at Brookfield Polytechnic. As my lectures
take place only in the mornings and evenings I would be
available to work in the afternoons from about 1.30 or 2 p.m.
    I speak and write fluent Italian and some German, as
well as English. I have had some experience of office
work in my own country. I am available for interview any
afternoon and would be pleased to discuss my suitability
for the post on the telephone.
    I look forward to hearing from you.
    Yours sincerely,
```

★ In the exam you'll have to write two compositions in 90 minutes – that's 45 minutes per composition INCLUDING time for planning, making notes and checking your work through afterwards.

C Time how long it takes you to write this composition:

Write a letter of 120–180 words applying for the job advertised on the next page. (Make sure your letter is laid out in the appropriate style with your address at the top, today's date in the right place, etc. These words shouldn't be counted as part of the composition.)

Remember to make notes before you start.
Check your work through afterwards and correct any mistakes you notice in SPELLING and GRAMMAR.

> **TEMPORARY HOTEL RECEPTIONIST**
> Pleasant medium-size hotel in the heart of Cambridge seeks young person with pleasant personality to assist in reception office.
> Previous experience an advantage but not essential. Knowledge of at least one foreign language required. Good pay for someone who can work sensibly and cheerfully in our team. Apply in writing to
> **College Hotel, King's Parade, Cambridge.**

★ If you took longer than 45 minutes, you'll need to improve your speed. If you only took 25–30 minutes, you may not be spending enough time planning beforehand or checking afterwards.

★ In the exam, if you write too many words the examiner will only look closely at the first 180 words of your composition. Although you may get some credit for relevant material at the end of the composition, it's not worth the risk.

11.12 *Set, stand* and *turn* — *Verbs and idioms*

A Fill the gaps with suitable forms of SET, STAND or TURN.

1. The house _____ on a hill.
2. The weather _____ cloudy.
3. Our agreement still _____.
4. She _____ a good chance in the exam.
5. What time does the sun _____ ?
6. He _____ his back on her.
7. Can you _____ on your head?
8. The novel is _____ in New York.
9. I can't _____ the way he laughs.
10. Please _____ the table for dinner.
11. She _____ the page.
12. I _____ my alarm clock for 6 a.m.
13. Go straight on and then _____ left.
14. The milk _____ sour.

B Fill the gaps with suitable forms of the phrasal verbs below:

set
1. As they had a long way to go, they _____ early in the morning.
2. An organisation was _____ to help unemployed people and their families.
3. The union rule book _____ the rules all members must follow.

stand
4. While the boss is away, her assistant is _____ her.
5. I will not _____ such terrible behaviour.
6. I'm not afraid to _____ the boss if I know I'm right.
7. What's the name of the man who _____ President in the USA in 1988 and lost?
8. A good friend will _____ you in good times and bad.
9. Everyone _____ while the national anthem was played.

turn
10. There's no need to make an appointment, you can _____ at any time.
11. If you _____ the next page, you'll see exercise 12.1.
12. He was happy in his work and _____ the offer of promotion.

set off/set out   set out   set up
stand by   stand for   stand for   stand in for   stand up   stand up to
turn down   turn over   turn up

11.13 Different kinds of jobs *Interview exercises*

★ In the Interview in the exam, the activities you'll have to do (Talking about pictures, Discussion/Communication activity, etc.) will all be based on a single topic. If you're lucky, this topic will be one that you've discussed in *Progress to First Certificate* – but not necessarily.

A Work in pairs or small groups. Ask your partners these questions about the photos:
- What kind of work does each of these people do?
- What sort of people are they?
- What does each one do on a 'typical working day'?
- Which of their jobs would you most like to do AND least like to do? Why?
- What kind of work do you do? OR would you like to do one day?

Can you think of any other questions you could ask them?

★ Remember that the purpose of the questions in this exercise is to encourage you to speak and express your ideas – NOT to test your knowledge of specialist vocabulary to describe all the objects in the picture.

B Work in groups of three. Ask your partners these questions:
- Which of these occupations are well paid and badly paid?
- Which should be paid most?
- What would be the attractions of the jobs?
- What would be the drawbacks of the jobs?

AUTHOR   CARPENTER   GOVERNMENT MINISTER
NURSE   POSTMAN/WOMAN   SALES REPRESENTATIVE
SECRETARY   SHOP ASSISTANT   TAXI DRIVER

For more information, student A can look Activity 26, student B at 30 and C at 45.

12 In the news

12.1 The press, politics and crime   *Vocabulary*

A Work in small groups. Ask your partners these questions:
- Where do *you* find out about the news: local newspaper, TV or radio?
- Do you find the news depressing, interesting, annoying or amusing?

B Choose the best alternative to complete each sentence.

1 I read an interesting .... in the paper the other day.
   article   information   news   reporting
2 I've only had time to read the .... in this morning's paper.
   columns   headings   headlines   sections
3 A newspaper's opinions are given in its ....
   cartoons   editorial   reports   titles
4 The person who reads the news on TV is called a(n) ....
   announcer   commentator   journalist   newsreader
5 The terrorists who hijacked the plane last night are still holding ten ....
   casualties   hostages   pedestrians   victims
6 I read in the newspaper that there has just been a .... in Transylvania.
   revelation   revolting   revolution   revolver
7 Over a thousand people are believed to have died in the ....
   bomb   earthquake   earthwork   explode
8 Only a small number of countries possess nuclear ...., thank goodness.
   ammunition   equipment   guns   weapons
9 Does that newspaper .... the government or oppose it?
   advantage   assist   encourage   support
10 In a .... everyone over a certain age is allowed to vote.
    democracy   dictatorship   nation   state
11 In some countries it is compulsory to vote in a(n) ....
    choice   constituency   election   selection
12 In the USA the most important person in the .... is the President.
    bureaucracy   civil service   government   state
13 In Britain the leader of the majority party in Parliament is the ....
    Chancellor   President   Prime Minister   Sovereign
14 The police have .... the man who is suspected of committing the murder.
    arrested   captivated   imprisoned   punished
15 Over £2 million was .... in the robbery.
    ceased   liberated   robbed   stolen
16 The arrested criminal admitted nothing and said that he wanted to see his ....
    accountant   advocate   lawyer   supervisor
17 The burglar was sentenced to 20 years in ....
    dock   goal   jail   trial

18 He was found .... of the crime and fined £500.
    convicted   guilty   innocent   responsible
19 In a British law court a case is heard by a judge and a .... of twelve people.
    cabinet   committee   jury   panel
20 He's a .... and so he always votes for the Labour Party.
    conservative   liberal   socialist   socialite

C Work in small groups. Ask your partners these questions:
- What have been the main national and international news stories during the past week? How many can you remember?
- What is the most awful thing that has happened in the last week?
- What is the most amusing thing that has happened in the last week?

12.2 The robber gendarme   *Reading*

A Work in pairs. Before you read this article, look at the headline. What do you think the story is going to be about?

Bingo brings down the robber gendarme

Derek Brown in Brussels

DAVID Saucez's bank robbing was as bad as his bingo. Desperate to pay off his gambling debts, he held up his local bank, and made off with around £2,000 before turning up for work – as a member of the Belgian gendarmerie.

It was the easiest arrest his colleagues could have possibly expected. For Saucez not only used his service pistol in the hold-up, but also made his get-away in his own easily recognised family car.

The car's number was taken by the manager of the Sud Belge bank in the Brussels suburb of Schaerbeek. He witnessed the hold-up, but was unnoticed by Saucez.

The unhappy gendarme told colleagues who arrested him that he had run up a debt of 60,000 Belgian francs (around £800), playing bingo. He was also paying off a home loan, and his wife – who works in another bank – did not know of his gambling.

Saucez, described as a "model gendarme" with six years' service, said he considered robbing the same bank the week before. His nerve failed at the last moment, and he ended up asking for advice on a loan.

On Monday this week he returned to the same bank, and the same temptation. This time it was too much.

He told arresting officers: "I had no intention of committing a hold-up. I left the barracks to go to the bank and request a delay in repaying my loans. It was on the way there that I decided to take action."

He was well equipped for the job, if not the getaway. Producing his service pistol, he demanded and got the money and then made off in his distinctive red Vauxhall.

He was already late for duty, but paused on the way to pay off 20,000 francs of his debt. By that time the net was inevitably closing in.

The gendarmerie, having answered the manager's alarm call too late to catch the robber red-handed, at least had the information to catch him red-vehicled.

They traced the car number to Saucez, alerted his unit in Brussels, which said he had been on duty but was now absent. A few minutes later he turned up complete with the hold-up weapon, the getaway car, and the remainder of the loot in his pocket.

B Here are the main events in the story. Rearrange them into the correct sequence and number them 1–9. The first is done as an example:

Alarm raised by manager   Arrested   Decided to rob bank
Found himself in debt   Paid part of his debts   Played bingo 1
Reported for duty   Robbed bank   Was afraid to rob bank

C Decide which of the alternatives best completes each sentence:

1 David Saucez's wife works …
   a) as a policewoman   c) in the bank he robbed
   b) as a security guard   d) in another bank
2 David Saucez's wife …
   a) disapproved of his gambling
   b) tried to help him to give up gambling
   c) was unaware that he was so heavily in debt
   d) was worried about his debts
3 David Saucez used …
   a) a borrowed car   c) a red car
   b) a car with false number plates   d) a stolen car
4 The previous week, David Saucez had planned to rob the bank, but …
   a) asked them to lend him some money
   b) asked them what he should do about borrowing money
   c) paid some money into his account there
   d) didn't dare to go inside
5 The police knew about the robbery because …
   a) David Saucez admitted his guilt
   b) David Saucez had parked his car outside the bank
   c) David Saucez was unlucky
   d) the bank manager made an alarm call
6 David Saucez arrived late for duty because he …
   a) stopped to pay back some of the money he owed
   b) was afraid to report for duty
   c) was going to rob the bank
   d) was trying to escape

D Work in small groups. Ask your partners these questions:
• If you had been David Saucez, what would you have done differently?
• If you had been his wife, what would you have done?
• If you were in debt, how could you avoid getting involved in crime?

'You won't get away with this!'

12.3 Word order   *Grammar*

A   Adverbs
Look at these examples, showing where the adverbs are normally placed in the sentence:

Before	*Mid*	*After*
Recently he was arrested.	He was recently arrested.	He was arrested recently.
Unexpectedly, he was arrested.	He was unexpectedly arrested.	He was arrested unexpectedly.
—	He was never arrested.	—
Certainly he was arrested.	He was certainly arrested.	—
Yesterday he was arrested.	—	He was arrested yesterday.
—	—	He was arrested by the police.

B   Notice the following points:
- We DON'T normally say or write:
   By the police he was arrested. ✗   Never he was arrested. ✗
 but we CAN say or write:
   He certainly was arrested.   He never was arrested.   He recently was arrested.

- Notice where these adverbs are placed when there is a modal verb in the sentence:
   He will certainly be arrested.   He will never be arrested.
   NOT: He will be certainly arrested. ✗   He will be never arrested. ✗

- Normally, an adverb is not placed between a verb and a direct object:
   I like very much tennis. ✗   or   He drove very fast the car. ✗

C   Decide where each of the adverbs below can be placed in these sentences:

   They   didn't   arrive on time   .
   She   was   able to finish her meal   .
   We   knew   that the work   would   be very difficult

almost   always   hardly ever   just   nearly   never   rarely   seldom

as usual   certainly   definitely   frequently   maybe   normally
obviously   often   one day   on Friday   perhaps   possibly   probably
really   still   usually   yesterday

D   Place the adverbs in suitable positions in these sentences:

1 She worked to finish the essay.   hard
2 You read about my country in the newspapers.   hardly ever
3 It was a hard task that took a long time to finish.   unexpectedly
4 He walked into the room and clapped his hands.   slowly
5 They did the work on their own.   very well

⟫→

167

6 There is not much news in the paper.   normally   on Saturday
7 We will hear the election results on TV.   definitely   on Sunday
8 We listen to the evening news on the radio.   always   during dinner

E IT and THERE used at the beginning of a sentence

Look at these examples and fill the gaps. Notice the word order:

2,000 people were in the crowd.	→	There were 2,000 people in the crowd.
Everyone applauded at the end.	→	There was _____
John told me the news.	→	It was John who told me the news.
I didn't break the window.	→	It wasn't me who _____
The other person is to blame.	→	It's the other person who is to blame.
The tall man started the fight.	→	It was _____
Hearing only bad news is depressing.	→	It's depressing to hear only bad news.
Good news is also interesting to read.	→	It's also _____
They believe he will win the election.	→	It is believed that he will win the election.
People say that crime is increasing.	→	It is said _____

F Rewrite these sentences, using the words on the right.

1 Rewriting sentences is not as easy as it looks.   It isn't ...
2 The election was won by the right-wing party.   It was ...
3 Thank you for helping me.   It was kind ...
4 You needn't read the paper unless you want to.   There's no ...
5 The policies of the two parties are very similar.   There isn't ...
6 Unexpectedly, the left-wing candidate was elected.   It was ...
7 Unfortunately, no one survived the air disaster.   There were ...
8 George Bush was elected President in 1988.   It was ...
9 100 people have been killed, according to reports.   It is believed ...
10 The weather is probably not going to change.   There will ...

'Yes, but is there any news of the iceberg?'

12.4 What happened? *Composition*

As the Composition paper is the one that causes most candidates most difficulties, there are two composition sections in this unit.

A Work in pairs.
1 Look at these photographs and decide what's happening in each one. What happened before and what is likely to happen next?
2 Work out a story which includes at least THREE of these events within the same story. The people involved could include yourselves and/or friends of yours.

B In 45 minutes, without using a dictionary, write the story in 120–180 words.
- Make notes before you start.
- Check your work and correct any mistakes in spelling and grammar. (Remember to check verb forms and endings, prepositions and articles.)

★ In the exam, the examiner will be looking at:
how well you have communicated, how accurate your writing is, and the variety of structures and vocabulary you have used.

But remember that short sentences and simple vocabulary may be more effective than wrongly-used complicated sentences or misused 'advanced' vocabulary – it may be better to keep your sentences short.

12.5 Better safe than sorry! *Listening*

A You'll hear part of a talk about crime prevention. Choose the correct alternatives and fill the gaps, according to the information given in the talk.

1 According to the speaker, ... of crimes are against property, not against people.
   80%   85%   90%   95%
2 A recent survey showed that .... of homes do not have window locks.
   6%   16%   60%   66%
3 .... of all burglars get in through windows.
   one third   one half   two thirds   three quarters
4 To increase the security of your home, you should make sure that ...
   a) you have .... on all windows.
   b) there is a lock on the .... that can only be opened and closed with a ....
   c) you have a .... on the front door.
   d) your property is ....
5 In Britain over .... cars are broken into or stolen each year.
   ½ million   1 million   1½ million   5 million
6 According to the speaker, if you regularly park your car in a city street, there is a .... chance it will be stolen or broken into.
   4%   20%   25%   40%
7 When you leave your car you should always ...
   a) lock all the .... and the ....
   b) take your .... with you or lock them in the ....
   c) close the .... completely.
   d) make sure you park in a .... street at night.
8 When you leave your bicycle don't use a combination lock because ...
   a) you may ....
   b) and it only takes a thief .... minutes to open one.

B Work in small groups. Ask your partners these questions:
- What advice do you think the speaker gave the audience on personal safety?
- Suppose you wanted to reassure an old lady who is afraid of being attacked when she goes out. What advice would you give her?
- What are the commonest crimes that are committed in your city: theft, robbery, murder, mugging, shop-lifting, etc.?
- Which crimes are on the increase?

12.6 Opposites *Word study*

A First, some revision. Write down the opposites of these words. The first two are done as examples:

accurate ↔ *inaccurate*   painful ↔ *painless*

accurate painful agree approve comfortable harmless honest
kind legal lucky polite regular relevant safe willing

B Now write down the opposites of these words. The first two are done as examples:

difficult ↔ *easy*   bright ↔ *dull*

difficult bright arrogant beautiful cheap cruel defeat fail
follow freeze hate ill lose noisy rude stale tight wide awake

C The opposites of some of these words are formed by adding a suffix or prefix, while others are different words. In some cases there may be more than one possibility. Look at the examples first:

ashamed ↔ *proud*   like ↔ *dislike, hate*

ashamed like cooked dangerous different fiction hollow
mature necessary oppose personal pleasant polite rough true
visible winner wrong

★ When you're writing a composition and you can't think of the right word to express your idea, try thinking of the OPPOSITE – it may help you to remember the right word. If not, leave a gap in your composition and come back to it later.

'Look, I'd sit down if I were you. Have you got a drink? Now, it's nothing to worry about, really it isn't ...'

12.7 Hurricane Gilbert   *Reading*

A Read the newspaper article and answer the questions on the next page.

Texas prepares for the worst

Michael White in Washington

ON network television yesterday a south Texas property developer stood on the still tranquil sea front at Corpus Christi and brushed aside the alarm of city dwellers in the temperate north about the onslaught of Hurricane Gilbert.

"I'd rather be standing here... than sitting on a freeway in Los Angeles that could be destroyed by an earthquake," he said.

Few parts of the US are free from brutal reminders of nature's power. Hailstones the size of a man's fist, tornadoes, floods, droughts, fires, all reflect a weather system often at the mercy of tropical or Arctic extremes.

Unlike impoverished citizens of Jamaica or Yucatan, cleaning up yesterday after Gilbert's devastation, Americans enjoy all the benefits of satellite pictures and a communications network which gives them ample time to flee the path of a storm and the means – cars and cash – to do so.

Nowadays most do and those who stay behind are warned that they are on their own.

The death toll in Jamaica is now put at somewhere between nine and 25 – chiefly by drowning – with widespread damage caused to airports and hotels.

Flimsier structures, inhabited by the poor, inevitably suffered most, with some estimates putting the homeless at 500,000 of the island's 2.5 million people, with 20 per cent of homes destroyed and 80 per cent left roofless. Waves as high as 23 feet were reported. As relief supplies began arriving damage was estimated at $300 million. Sugar and banana farming also suffered badly.

Venezuela and the Dominican Republic were the first to suffer. The British dependency of the Cayman Islands was also hit by the storm – which touched 175 mph on Tuesday. No lives were lost.

Mexico's Yucatan peninsula also sustained less damage than was expected, though at least 25 people are feared dead and many more are missing.

As elsewhere on Gilbert's 1,800-mile westward path across the Caribbean – including southern Cuba – tourists were removed to safety.

Yesterday Gilbert was crossing the Gulf of Mexico towards the Corpus Christi area – 300 miles south of Galveston – and, on present projections, was expected to make a landfall by mid-morning today on either the US or Mexican side of the Rio Grande basin whose major coastal town is Brownsville.

Described as "the mightiest storm to hit the Western hemisphere in this century," Gilbert's eye was described by air force weather analysts as unusually narrow, just eight miles rather than 20–25 miles – and thus more like a tornado, a smaller but more devastating type of storm which arises on land.

The effect of a narrow low pressure eye, sucking warm wind from the ocean to altitudes of 50,000 feet, is to intensify surrounding winds and with it the high waves which cause most death and damage.

The National Hurricane Centre on the frontline in Miami is taking a very grave view.

The only other Category 5 hurricane to hit the US took 408 lives in Florida in 1935. In 1979 Hurricane David killed 3,000 in the Caribbean but swept ashore harmlessly in South Carolina. Allen in 1980 killed 200 people in Haiti but only 28 in the US.

Yesterday people could be found planning to stay and sit out the experience because Allen had not been as bad as expected. "Everyone got ready – and then, nothing," said another citizen of Corpus Christi. But by then most people had already left town.

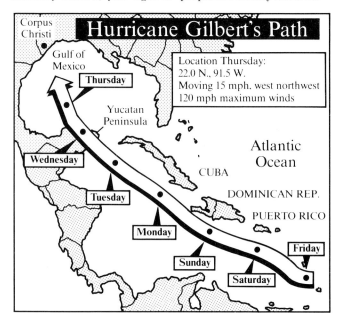

1 According to the person interviewed on TV in South Texas, ...
   a) Los Angeles is a less dangerous place than Texas
   b) Texas is a less dangerous place than Los Angeles
   c) the hurricane will destroy the city
   d) hurricanes are not dangerous
2 In the USA, extreme weather conditions are experienced in ...
   a) all parts of the country   c) few parts of the country
   b) almost all parts of the country d) the northern states
3 American citizens are in a better position than Jamaicans because they have ...
   a) better roads and stronger houses
   b) better weather
   c) faster cars
   d) transport and money to escape from a storm
4 Those Americans who don't escape from the storm are ...
   a) insured against the danger   c) unaware of the danger
   b) made aware of the danger   d) protected from the danger
5 According to the report, Hurricane Gilbert will reach the coast at around ...
   a) 8 a.m. today   c) 12 noon today
   b) 10 a.m. today   d) 2 p.m. today
6 A tornado usually ...
   a) causes less damage than a hurricane   c) travels faster than a hurricane
   b) causes more damage than a hurricane   d) travels more slowly than a hurricane
7 When a hurricane strikes, most damage is caused by ...
   a) high winds   b) falling trees and buildings   c) rain   d) the sea
8 In the past, hurricanes have killed ...
   a) fewer people on Caribbean islands than in the USA
   b) more people on Caribbean islands than in the USA
   c) the same number of people on Caribbean islands as in the USA
   d) very few people on Caribbean islands and in the USA
9 In 1980, Hurricane Allen turned out to be ...
   a) as serious as expected in the USA
   b) less serious than expected in the USA
   c) more serious than expected in the USA
   d) unexpectedly serious in the USA
10 The total number of lives lost in Hurricane Gilbert (up to the date of this report) is about ...
   a) 9   b) 25   c) 50   d) 200

B Find the words or phrases in the article that have the following meanings. The numbers show which paragraph you should look at. The first is done for you as an example:

quiet (1) *tranquil*   number of people killed (6)
refused to take seriously (1)   reach the coast (11)
attack (1)   make more extreme (13)
poor (4)   serious (14)

★ Remember that when you're reading a passage without a dictionary, there are sure to be some words you don't understand. Always try to work out their meaning from the context.

12.8 Exam practice

Make all the changes and additions necessary to produce sentences which make a complete story. The first is done for you as an example:

1 USA / many criminals become as famous / politicians.
   In the USA, many criminals have become as famous as politicians.
2 You hear / story / Edwin Chambers Dodson?
3 He be antique dealer / Hollywood / customers include / many famous film stars.
4 He lead / secret life / bank robber.
5 He rob more banks / any other man / American history.
6 He hold up more banks / Jesse James / Bonnie and Clyde.
7 He take part / 64 robberies / California and make $300,000.
8 He / be known / 'Yankee Bandit' because he wear / blue New York Yankees baseball cap / most / his robberies.
9 He / send / prison / 15 years after he plead guilty / eight robberies.
10 He still be / prison now.

★ In this kind of exercise there may be passives and other difficult verb forms to cope with. Make sure you check your completed sentences through, just as carefully as you check your composition.

12.9 Here is the news . . . *Listening*

You'll hear a news broadcast. Decide whether the following statements are true (**T**) or false (**F**), according to the broadcast.

1 The drug arrests in Bolivia were made in the north of the country.
2 The arrests were part of a joint operation between Bolivia, the USA and the UN.
3 Three planes crashed during the operation.
4 Nearly $2\frac{1}{2}$ tons of cocaine were found by the authorities.
5 In Europe more storms are expected soon.
6 In 24 hours there should be no more delays with air traffic.
7 In 24 hours there should be no more problems on the roads.
8 Next weekend is a holiday and traffic will be held up.
9 Damage in France is estimated to be over 15,000 million francs.
10 No foreign cars can travel through Switzerland during the weekend.
11 The hijackers of the airliner left the plane late last night.
12 The plane will be flown back to Athens by Captain Georgiou.
13 129 people were held hostage during the hijacking.
14 The hijackers have already left Algiers.
15 Prices of shares in Tokyo have gone up.

12.10 Giving your opinions *Composition*

A When you're writing a composition that asks you to give your opinion about a topic, you'll probably need to explain what you mean.
Write two more sentences, adding an explanation or reason to each opinion.

1 I hardly ever read a newspaper ...
because I find that I get a much better picture of what is going on in the world by watching the news on television. Television news is also much more up-to-date than a newspaper and only the most important items of news are reported.
2 It would/would not be a better world if there were no nuclear weapons ...
3 Nuclear power stations are a good/bad thing because ...
4 The government should change/not change the law on drugs ...
5 If a criminal has committed a very serious crime ...
6 The only solution to terrorism ...

B Here are four typical exam questions. Work in pairs and make notes of the points you could make if you wrote these compositions:

1 How does the problem of pollution affect your country and what can be done to improve the situation?
2 Should young people take a break of one or two years between leaving school and continuing with further education?
3 Very few women are members of parliament or government ministers. Why is this so and should it be changed?
4 What do you think of the view, expressed in some countries, that marriage is going out of fashion?

C Write 120–180 words on ONE of these topics beginning as follows:

1 'One of the most serious problems facing the world today is ...'
2 'One of the most serious problems facing my country today is ...'
3 'I read in the paper/heard on the news that ...' (Choose a topic or event that is in the news at the moment and give your opinions about it.)

As in 12.4, time yourself as you write this composition. With this kind of composition, it's absolutely essential to make notes before you start writing. And don't forget to check your completed work through when you've finished.

★ The examiner will be assessing the quality of your English, not your ideas. But if you ignore the question and introduce irrelevant material (or include a passage you seem to have learnt by heart), you will lose marks.

12.11 Exam practice
Interview exercises

★ The purpose of the Interview in the exam is to give the examiner a chance to hear you speaking English. If you don't say very much (because you're feeling shy or nervous) the examiner won't be able to hear how good your English normally sounds. That's why it's essential to do some practice interviews 'under exam conditions'.

Work in pairs for these activities and imagine you're taking part in the exam. One of you could play the role of examiner, perhaps.

A

Answer these questions about the photographs:
- What's happening in the pictures?
- What do you think has just happened?
- What do you think will happen next?
- How do you think each of the people is feeling?
- Which of the people would you support in such a situation?
- What could you say to each of them if you were there?
- How often do such things happen in your country?

B Look at these newspaper headlines. Which of the articles would you be interested in reading and why? What do you think each article is about?

Royal baby shock
Film star's guilty secret
800 metre record broken
Peace talks break down
Jumbo crashes in Mediterranean
Prime minister dies in air disaster
Hurricane hits Mexico
Holiday sunshine traps drivers in nationwide traffic jams

C Look at these cases where the law is being broken.

1 Put them in ORDER of seriousness and explain the REASONS why you consider some to be less serious than others.

2 What PUNISHMENT do you think should be given to someone who breaks the law in each case? (If you think 'it all depends', what does it depend on?)

- A motorist drives faster than the permitted maximum speed
- A passenger travels by train without a ticket
- A motorist parks on a double yellow line
- A motorist isn't wearing a seat belt
- A gang of youths attack an old lady and take her purse
- Someone keeps your wallet which fell from your pocket
- A group of terrorists kill one of their hostages
- An office worker takes some stationery home from the office
- A motorist drives after drinking a couple of glasses of wine
- A burglar breaks into your flat and steals your valuables
- A company doesn't declare all its income for tax
- A shopper takes some goods from a large department store without paying
- A husband kills his wife's lover
- A motorist drives after drinking a whole bottle of wine
- A student sells drugs to fellow students

12.12 *Have* and *give*   *Verbs and idioms*

A Which of the endings below go with these beginnings? Some of them go with more than one of the beginnings, sometimes with a different meaning:

Alex had ...   **Charlie gave us** ...
Barry was having ... **Carol gave** ...

a quarrel with Tim   an order   a sigh   a good time   permission
a good performance   a meal   a drink   his/her opinion   a headache
his/her hair cut   a chance   a look   an interview   a good idea
the information   never been abroad   an accident   a rest   a swim
the details   a newspaper   no imagination   better be careful

B Fill the gaps with suitable forms of the phrasal verbs below:

give
1 When I'd read the books I .... them .... to her.
2 Smoking again? I thought you .... smoking.
3 A man was standing on the corner .... leaflets to everyone.
4 This information is secret, don't .... it .... to anyone.
5 The criminal .... himself .... to the police.
6 Check your work through before .... it .... at the end of the exam.
7 After a bloody battle, the defeated army .... and peace talks began.
have
8 He .... his best suit .... for the interview.
9 When you've finished with the cassette, I'd like to .... it .... again.
10 It's been very nice .... you .... Do come and see us again!

give away   give back   give in   give in   give out   give up   give up
have round   have on   have back

177

13 People

13.1 It takes all sorts... *Vocabulary*

A Work in small groups. Ask your partners these questions:
- What kind of person do you think you are?
- What sign of the zodiac were you born under? Do you think this affects your character?
- What kind of people do you get on with best?
- What kind of people do you find it hard to get on with?

B Choose the word or phrase that best completes each sentence.

1 She's a very .... person – always smiling and in a good mood.
   cheerful   delighted   glad   pleased
2 He's a very .... person – I wish he was a bit more easy-going.
   bad-tempered   furious   mad   wild
3 Don't tell her off – she's very .... and she may start to cry.
   responsive   sensible   sensitive   sympathetic
4 People enjoy his company because he's extremely ....
   adorable   likeable   lovable   sympathetic
5 If you've got a problem, go and talk to her – I'm sure she'll be ....
   patient   sympathetic   tolerant   warm-hearted
6 He has excellent taste in clothes and always dresses ....
   cleanly   healthily   smartly   tastily
7 When his wife started seeing more of the tennis coach, he became very ....
   arrogant   envious   jealous   selfish
8 The twins keep pretending to be each other – they're such .... children!
   evil   miserable   naughty   wicked
9 Thank you for my beautiful present. It was very .... of you to buy it for me.
   charitable   generous   loyal   reliable
10 If you give him a message make sure he writes it down because he's very ....
   absent   forgetful   mindless   preoccupied
11 You have to be quite .... to stand up in front of an audience.
   self-confident   self-conscious   selfish   self-satisfied
12 She's a very .... little girl – her parents give her everything she asks for.
   consented   discriminating   generous   spoilt
13 He's a dreadful person – I can't .... him.
   stand   suffer   support   swallow
14 Everyone agrees that he's a very .... man.
   beautiful   gorgeous   handsome   pretty
15 When she first went to work in another city, she felt very ....
   abandoned   alone   lonely   single

178

16 Most people feel .... before an examination.
   absent-minded   anxious   eager   nervy
17 How long has Sarah been .... with Peter?
   going back   going in   going out   going up
18 They fell in love at first ....
   glimpse   look   sight   viewing
19 How long have they been .... ?
   betrothed   engaged   financed   intended
20 When are they going to .... ?
   get married   marry them   marry each other   marry themselves
21 Peter has asked Michael to be his .... at the wedding.
   best man   bridesmaid   eyewitness   godfather
22 Sarah has invited all her .... to the wedding.
   compatriots   in-laws   parents   relations
23 Her parents have been married for 25 years and today is their ....
   anniversary   birthday   jubilee   marriage
24 The people in the flat upstairs are always having noisy ....
   debates   discussions   noises   rows
25 When her mother remarried, she got on very well with her new ....
   ancestor   forefather   foster-father   step-father
26 A diagram that shows the members of a family and their relationship is called a family ....
   branch   line   river   tree

★ In the exam there may be two answers that both appear to you to make sense in the context provided – if in doubt, choose the one that fits BEST.

C Work in pairs. Draw your own family trees, showing your grandparents, uncles and aunts, brothers and sisters, nieces and nephews. Then join another pair and tell them about your partner's family, while your partner tells them about yours.

D Work in small groups. Describe the following people, but not in this order. DON'T name them because your partners should try to guess the name of each person you describe, or their relationship to you.

- One of your favourite relatives
- A well-known public figure
- One of your closest friends
- Someone your partners don't know
- One of your favourite film stars, singers or musicians

E Work in small groups. What qualities do you admire most in other people?
Put these qualities into order of importance:

Ambition	Creativity	Good looks
Honesty	Independence	Intelligence
Loyalty	Sense of humour	Strength
Tenderness	Understanding	Warmth

- What other important qualities are missing from this list?

13.2 What is Dateline?   *Reading*

A Read this text and answer the multiple-choice questions on the next page.

What is **Dateline**

Dateline is the computer dating service that takes the chance element out of man-woman relations. In a single flash of electronic brilliance it provides a supply of partners who are absolutely right for you — partners whose looks and conversation appeal to you from the first and with whom you feel quickly at ease, friends who are likely to grow closer with every meeting.

How's it done? Simple. By taking careful note of what you are like and following your guidance on the kind of man or woman you get along best with, we select, from the tens of thousands of profiles in our store exactly those who are destined to be your kindred spirits.

There's nothing magic about it. It's a matter of applying science to nature. By the laws of probability there are certainly people in the world who are physically and mentally right for you, just as there are stars in the universe similar to ours. All one has to do is to find them. Dateline has the unique power — thanks to modern computer science — of finding the few-in-thousands who can communicate with you at a deep level of understanding.

■ The Age We Live In

Dateline — the most significant advance in modern relations between the sexes. It is part of the new life-style. It combines all that is new and socially advanced with the traditional ideas of restraint and integrity that belong to any organisation dealing in personal relationships.

Take the Dateline questionnaire. It has been carefully compiled with the aid of experts in psychology and social sciences, using the most up-to-date research of British and American universities, to provide the most accurate and least prying method of assessing personalities.

Take the Dateline computer system. It's a variation on the systems used for launching missiles and rationalising the operations of banks. You can't get more accurate or more impartial than that. It's our own computer too, programmed and operated only by our own experts.

Altogether Dateline is the most exciting social advance for single people since the granting of the vote. Join it and your days will really come alive.

■ The Shifting Society

Social life is changing more rapidly than ever before. The older generation spent their lives more or less in one place.

School, work and family life grew out of the same environment people were born in. You knew everyone in your district and it wasn't too difficult to pick the friends who suited you, and who shared your interests. Even so, when society was more static the opportunities for widening your circle were still restricted, and life wasn't so varied as it is today.

Now we're in the space age. The old 'school-work-early marriage' syndrome is disappearing. A whole new generation of mobile young people is at large in the world. They're people with initiative, independent of their home background, able to change jobs and locations, to take up studies and pastimes, and to pursue their careers all over Britain and overseas if they want to. Many do just that, taking their freedom in both hands and making the most of the world's opportunities. Dateline is for them, and in this case, 'them' means you.

■ What Sort of People join Dateline?

Everyone joins Dateline: showbiz personalities, artists, Lords, musicians, soldiers, cooks, stockbrokers, property-men, models, nurses, athletes, business executives of all kinds, teachers, secretaries, students, librarians, dancers. The only qualification you need is to be unmarried.

Most of our members are busy, successful, intelligent people with enquiring minds and varied interests. They've usually got plenty of their own friends, who, perhaps, they know too well to get romantic about. Others, through pressure of work, or through a shy disposition, or because they find themselves in a strange new career environment, are short of interesting company, and want to make a fresh social start. Through Dateline they can do it. Dateline puts you in touch with new faces, a different crowd, and completely refreshes your social life.

More important for many people is the scientifically-based probability of meeting the man or woman you've always dreamed about, and simply falling in love. Yes, it does happen: so frequently you shouldn't be surprised when it hits you personally. Every week Dateline receives scores of letters from happy couples matched by our computer. Already more than ten thousand known marriages can be attributed to Dateline, and perhaps thousands more that we haven't been told about.

■ How Do You Join Dateline?

Complete our questionnaire. Designed by experts in computer sciences and psychology, it takes about 15 minutes to fill in, longer if you're in an extra-thoughtful mood, but it's fun. The 200 questions are very thorough and for a good reason. The more you tell us about yourself and the kind of people you most like, the more accurate our computer can be and the closer to your ideal will be your dates.

■ What Kind of Questions?

First, basic straightforward questions on your age, physical build, appearance and social background. Then a few on education, social habits and occupation. Next a chance to list all your special interests. And finally, the personality test in three parts. There's also a space for any additional information about yourself that you care to give.

Side by side with the profile of yourself formed by the answers to this set of questions, you fill in a profile of your chosen man or girl, marking the qualities you prefer from the list given. All this careful planning goes a long way to ensure that the people you meet through Dateline will be exactly your kind.

Send for your questionnaire, and from there on, Dateline takes over.

1. Finding your ideal partner is like finding
   A a needle in a haystack.
   B a star like ours in the universe.
   C the answer to your prayers.
   D 50 pence when you've lost 10 pence.
2. Dateline's computer will find you a partner who
   A looks like you.
   B will like you.
   C will laugh at your jokes.
   D looks attractive.
3. Dateline's computer is
   A only used by Dateline's own staff.
   B also used for launching missiles.
   C also used by banks.
   D only used for arranging dates.
4. Life nowadays is different because
   A older people don't move around much.
   B young people have the vote.
   C young people travel abroad a lot.
   D marriages happen later in life.
5. Compared with the past, it is now
   A less difficult to find friends.
   B much easier to find friends.
   C much more difficult to find friends.
   D no more difficult to find friends.
6. The world is full of
   A accidents for young people.
   B chances for young people.
   C jobs for young people.
   D risks for young people.
7. Most of Dateline's members
   A have too many friends.
   B are lonely.
   C dislike their acquaintances.
   D have lots of friends.
8. Dateline couples
   A generally fall in love.
   B regularly fall in love.
   C sometimes fall in love.
   D often fall in love.
9. Dateline is responsible for thousands of marriages
   A a day. B a week. C a month. D a year.
10. In the questionnaire there are 200
    A accurate questions.
    B complete questions.
    C exhaustive questions.
    D nosy questions.

B Work in small groups. Look at this coupon and then ask your partners the questions below.

```
FREE
START HERE ▼1
I am over 17
Single ⏥ Widowed ⏥ Divorced ⏥
Your Sex ⏥ put M or F
Your Height ⏥ ft ⏥ ins.
Your age ⏥ yrs
Age you would like to meet ⏥ min
BLOCK CAPITALS      ⏥ max
First Name _____
Surname _____
Address _____
        _____
        _____
        _____
Occupation _____
Religion _____
```

- 'All you need is love' (a Sphere paperback) — stories of real people matching and meeting through Dateline.
- A full colour guide to how Dateline can work for you.
- Details of just one of the many Dateline members who could be your 'Perfect Partner'.

I enclose 3 first class stamps.

2 Tick ✓ which characteristics best describe you.

3 Tick ✓ those activities you enjoy, put a ✗ against those you dislike, and leave blank those where you have no preference.

ARE YOU:
- Warmhearted
- Serious
- Considerate
- Shy
- Romantic
- Fashion conscious
- Practical
- Conventional
- Reliable
- Adventurous

DO YOU ENJOY:
- Wine bars/Eating out
- Pubs
- Sports/Keep Fit
- Politics/History
- Reading
- Travelling
- Science/Technology
- Cinema
- Pets/Animals
- Pop/Rock music

- Jazz/Folk music
- Classical music
- Theatre/Arts
- Watching TV
- Smoking
- Drinking
- Being with children
- Homemaking
- Gardening
- Countryside

Dateline Dept (SEN) 23 Abingdon Rd. London W8 6AH. Tel: 01 938 1011.

THE WORLD'S LARGEST AND MOST SUCCESSFUL AGENCY

- Would you be honest about filling it in? Or would you make yourself out to be more attractive, interesting or intelligent?
- Can one find a perfect partner for life through an agency like Dateline?
- Is it possible to find a perfect partner for life by an arranged marriage (where your spouse is chosen by your parents)?

13.3 Difficult questions   *Grammar*

A Rewrite the sentences in such a way that they still mean the same:

1 You should be very careful.   You'd better ...
2 I'm not very happy.   I wish ...
3 Please use a dictionary.   I'd like ...
4 You told me to do that.   It was ...
5 It's advisable to arrive a few minutes early. I suggest ...
6 Why haven't you done the work yet?   It's time ...

Did you find those tricky? Well, questions like those do come up in the Use of English paper. If you try to remember the grammar points in this section, you should be able to cope with questions like those. But don't forget that losing a couple of marks on questions like those may not be a great disaster – it's the questions you CAN answer that will help you to succeed in the exam.

B Look at these examples and fill the gaps with your own ideas:

better AND best
You'd (had) better do some revision.   = You should / I strongly advise you to ...
It's better to revise carefully than trust to luck.   = better of two alternatives

It'd (would) be better to do question 2 before 1.   = better of two alternatives
It's best to make notes before you start writing.   = best of several alternatives
You .... several pens to the exam, not just one.
It .... the answer than to leave a blank space if you don't know.
It .... early on the day of the exam.

I'd rather / prefer / like
I'd (would) rather wear a sweater than a jacket.
I'd rather you didn't smoke in here.
We'd prefer you not to smoke, if you don't mind.
They wouldn't like you to use a dictionary.
Would you rather I .... today or tomorrow?
Would you like me .... for you?

wish, if only AND hope
He wishes he were/was more intelligent.
He wishes (that) he had worked harder, but it's too late now.
I wish they wouldn't smoke – it makes me cough.
I wish to make a complaint.   Who do you wish to speak to?
She wishes she .... on holiday.
I wish .... more time before the exam, but there isn't.
If only there wasn't/weren't so little time left!
If only we .... in advance what questions would be asked!
I hope to get the job.   I hope (that) I get the job.
I hope we all ....

It's time
It's time to go home.   It's time we went home.
It's time .... some revision.   It's time .... a break.

suggest
I suggest (that) you (should) use a dictionary.
He suggested using a dictionary.
They suggested .... not worry about the exam.
What do you suggest .... after it's all over?

C   Rewrite these sentences, beginning with the words on the right.
1 Please don't interrupt me when I'm speaking.   I'd rather ...
2 It would be a good idea to phone and ask for information.   We suggest you ...
3 Don't be so frank – be tactful.   It's much better ...
4 Please let me know your decision today, not tomorrow.   I'd prefer ...
5 Staying at home would be better than going out tonight.   I'd rather ...
6 Please fill in this questionnaire.   I'd like ...
7 We ought to find out how much it's going to cost.   It's time we ...
8 They should book early if they want tickets for the concert.   They'd better ...
9 I've got so much to do today.   I wish ...
10 What a shame you didn't tell me earlier!   If only ...

★ If there are a few difficult questions you can't answer in the exam,
DON'T PANIC – just leave a blank, put a pencil mark in the margin to
remind you where they are and come back to them later. Rub out the
pencil mark.

13.4 Synonyms   *Word study*

A Look at these examples. What is the difference between them?

1 She's a very *nice* person. It was *nice* of her to help me and she was *nice* to you too, wasn't she?
2 She's a very *likeable* person. For example, it was *kind* of her to help me and she was *friendly* to you too, wasn't she?

★ Some words that are perfectly all right in conversation are best avoided if you want to make your writing more interesting.

B Work in pairs.

1 Write down at least TWO synonyms that can be used in place of:
   nice   good   bad   thing   like   dislike

2 Write down at least TWO synonyms you can use instead of these adjectives (to avoid having to repeat the same word in a paragraph):
   large   small   important   intelligent   interesting   strange
   unpleasant   beautiful

3 Write five sentences for your partner (or for another pair) to rewrite more interestingly or more clearly.
4 Join another pair and compare your ideas.

C Sometimes you may not be able to think of exactly the right word you need:
   'The carpenter wanted to tighten the screws, so he used a you know, a whatchamacallit.'

But it's sometimes possible to use another word which still shows what you mean:
   'He used a special tool to tighten up the screws.'

In these examples, what is the word that can be used to describe all the items in the list? The first is done for you as an example:

screwdriver   hammer   spanner   **tools**
sister   cousin   uncle
bread   cake   meat
grass   cactus   bush
rabbit   lion   mouse
lamb   beef   chicken
bus   train   lorry
house   flat   room   hotel
parrot   sparrow   pigeon
copper   steel   iron
breakfast   supper   lunch
autumn   spring   winter

suit   socks   sweater
dollar   pound   franc
rugby   tennis   squash
photography   stamp-collecting   reading
medicine   law   accountancy
parrot   goldfish   cat
wheat   rye   oats
rose   carnation   daisy
ant   bee   wasp
book   newspaper   brochure

13.5 'Due to a computer error...' *Problem solving*

The problem:
Six people joined a computer dating service but there was a computer error. Instead of giving them their perfect partners, it matched them with partners who had the same initials! Not realising this, all the people turned up for their first dates with high hopes.

A Work in pairs. Discuss these questions and make notes:
- How badly mismatched were the couples, do you think?
- What did they have in common and how well do you think they got on?

Name ANDREW APPLEBY   Age 29
Occupation: CIVIL SERVANT
How would you describe yourself?
   CREATIVE, OUTDOOR TYPE
What do you enjoy? POLITICS,
   CLASSICAL MUSIC, TRAVELLING,
   GOOD FOOD
What do you dislike?
   POP MUSIC, JAZZ, PUBS, DISCOS

Name ANNE AMIS   Age 25
Occupation: SECONDARY SCHOOL
   TEACHER
How would you describe yourself?
   PRACTICAL, OUTDOOR TYPE, SHY
What do you enjoy?
   SPORT, FOLK MUSIC, READING,
   TRAVEL
What do you dislike?
   POLITICS, JAZZ, FASHION,
   MEANNESS

Name BILL BANKS   Age 34
Occupation: ACCOUNTANT
How would you describe yourself?
   EXTROVERT, PRACTICAL
What do you enjoy?
   GOOD FOOD, TRAVEL, PUBS, SPORT
What do you dislike?
   POETRY, CLASSICAL MUSIC,
   READING, ART

Name BRENDA BOOTH   Age 24
Occupation: MEDICAL STUDENT
How would you describe yourself?
   CREATIVE, ADVENTUROUS,
   EXTROVERT
What do you enjoy?
   POP MUSIC, FASHION,
   CONVERSATION
What do you dislike?
   SPORT, POETRY, JAZZ

Name COLIN COOMBS   Age 24
Occupation: ART COLLEGE LECTURER
How would you describe yourself?
   SHY, CREATIVE, PRACTICAL
What do you enjoy?
   MUSIC (ALL TYPES), READING,
   SPORT
What do you dislike?
   TELEVISION, PUBS, POETRY

Name CAROLE CLARKE   Age 19
Occupation: LAW STUDENT
How would you describe yourself?
   GENEROUS, SHY, OUTDOOR TYPE
What do you enjoy?
   READING, ART, POP MUSIC,
   POLITICS
What do you dislike?
   SPORT, CLASSICAL MUSIC,
   SCIENCE

B Write four paragraphs of about 50 words each, based on your discussion in A, beginning:

'On their first date, Andrew and Anne ...'
'Although Bill and Brenda ...'
'Colin and Carole probably ...'
'Of the people described, the one I'd most like to meet myself is ......
because ...'

13.6 Using your brain *Listening*

🔊 You'll hear part of a talk about the human brain. Answer the questions below.

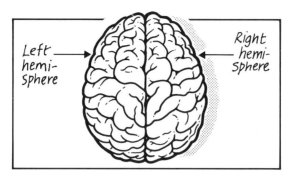

1 The left-hand side of the brain normally controls the .... side of the body.
2 What functions do the two hemispheres of the brain control?

LEFT (rational side)	RIGHT (irrational side)
language	rhythm
....	....
linearity	....
analysis	....
....	space: three dimensions
....	seeing .... of things as a whole
sequencing	

3 In left-handed people, these priorities are often ....
4 The .... is the link between the two hemispheres.
   It is the key to ....
5 The first question the speaker suggests you ask in the experiment is: 'What's ....?'
6 The second question is: 'What piece of furniture is ....?'
7 While someone is trying to answer the first question they will .... to prevent themselves being distracted by ....
8 Unfortunately, the experiment will not be successful if they ....
9 As we get older our memories ....
10 You forget things more easily if your brain doesn't have enough .... or ....
11 Your brain can deteriorate if you don't get enough .... or if your .... is unhealthy.
12 The three Golden Rules of brain power are:
   1 Use your senses and don't only think .... Imagine a problem ....
   2 Use .... of your brain.
   3 Don't say .... because your brain is .... as anyone else's.

★ In the exam, if you haven't got time to write a complete answer down during the first listening, just write the first few words and come back to it later. Otherwise you may not hear the answer to the next question.

13.7 Chapter One *Reading*

A Read this text and answer the multiple-choice questions on the next page.

CHAPTER ONE

My first impression was that the stranger's eyes were of an unusually light blue. They met mine for several blank seconds, vacant, unmistakably scared. Startled and innocently naughty, they half reminded me of an incident I couldn't quite place; something which had happened a long time ago, to do with the upper fourth form classroom. They were the eyes of a schoolboy surprised in the act of breaking one of the rules. Not that I had caught him, apparently, at anything except his own thoughts: perhaps he imagined I could read them. At any rate, he seemed not to have heard or seen me cross the compartment from my corner to his own, for he started violently at the sound of my voice; so violently, indeed, that his nervous recoil hit me like repercussion. Instinctively I took a pace backwards.

It was exactly as though we had collided with each other bodily in the street. We were both confused, both ready to be apologetic. Smiling, anxious to reassure him, I repeated my question:

'I wonder, sir, if you could let me have a match?'

Even now, he didn't answer at once. He appeared to be engaged in some sort of rapid mental calculation, while his fingers, nervously active, sketched a number of flurried gestures round his waistcoat. For all they conveyed, he might equally have been going to undress, to draw a revolver, or merely to make sure that I hadn't stolen his money. Then the moment of agitation passed from his gaze like a little cloud, leaving a clear blue sky. At last he had understood what it was that I wanted:

'Yes, yes. Er – certainly. Of course.'

As he spoke he touched his left temple delicately with his finger-tips, coughed and suddenly smiled. His smile had great charm. It disclosed the ugliest teeth I had ever seen. They were like broken rocks.

'Certainly,' he repeated. 'With pleasure.'

Delicately, with finger and thumb, he fished in the waistcoat-pocket of his expensive-looking soft grey suit, extracted a gold spirit-lighter. His hands were white, small and beautifully manicured.

I offered him my cigarettes.

'Er – thank you. Thank you.'

'After you, sir.'

'No, no. Please.'

The tiny flame of the lighter flickered between us, as perishable as the atmosphere which our exaggerated politeness had created. The merest breath would have extinguished the one, the least incautious gesture or word would have destroyed the other. The cigarettes were both lighted now. We sat back in our respective places. The stranger was still doubtful of me. He was wondering whether he hadn't gone too far, delivered himself to a bore or a crook. His timid soul was eager to retire. I, on my side, had nothing to read. I foresaw a journey of utter silence, lasting seven or eight hours. I was determined to talk.

'Do you know what time we arrive at the frontier?'

Looking back on the conversation, this question does not seem to me to have been particularly unusual. It is true that I had no interest in the answer; I wanted merely to ask something which might start us chatting, and which wasn't, at the same t' either inquisitive or impertinent. Its effect on the remarkable. I had certainly succeeded in arous-

1 The stranger at first looked
   A frightened. B harmless. C shocked. D surprised.
2 When the writer first spoke, the stranger
   A gasped. B got up. C jumped. D screamed.
3 The writer had
   A sat down beside the stranger.   C walked across to the stranger.
   B sat down opposite the stranger. D walked up behind the stranger.
4 The writer asked the stranger for a light
   A once. B twice. C three times. D four times.
5 Before the stranger replied, he
   A adjusted his waistcoat.   C thought for a while.
   B looked for his lighter.   D wondered if the writer was a thief.
6 The stranger gave the writer a
   A delicate smile. B nervous smile. C pleasant smile. D wicked smile.
7 The writer gave the stranger
   A a cigarette. B a light. C a reassuring smile. D his hand.
8 The stranger seemed to be afraid that the writer might be a
   A dull companion. B murderer. C foreigner. D policeman.
9 The writer wanted to start a conversation because he
   A found the stranger fascinating.   C had nothing else to do.
   B found the stranger interesting.   D respected the stranger.
10 The meeting described in the passage took place
   A in a café. B on a bus or coach. C on a plane. D on a train.

B Work in small groups. In your own words, describe the stranger. Then ask your partners these questions:
- Why would you have chosen or not chosen to start a conversation with the stranger?
- Have you ever had a conversation with a total stranger on a long journey or in a public place? How did the conversation start and what did you talk about?
- How usual is it for people to start speaking to strangers on trains or buses in your country?

★ If you don't know the answer in a multiple-choice test, you should guess – remember that you have a one-in-four chance of guessing right!

13.8 Exam practice
Passage with gaps

Fill each gap with ONE WORD only.

The first thing you notice 1 ~~about~~ him is his smile. He's slim, quite tall and very athletic. He talks fast and is very funny. He's 2 ~~an~~ actor, but he usually plays the same kind 3 ~~of~~ roles. 4 ~~In~~ fact, it's difficult to separate the character 5 ~~of~~ the man 6 ~~from~~ the characters he plays 7 ~~in~~ his films. You know that he's going to win every argument and get 8 ~~out~~ of any difficult situation 9 ~~without~~ getting hurt. He's 10 ~~one~~ of today's most popular American film stars.

You can't help 11 ~~being~~ impressed by her good looks and her voice. Her style is modern and 12 ~~her~~ clothes are always very unusual: she sets the fashion 13 ~~rather~~ than following it. She's not only 14 ~~very~~ popular with young people, but she's so talented 15 ~~that~~ even older people appreciate her. The break-up of her 16 ~~marriage~~ came as no surprise to anyone – she 17 ~~gets~~ so much publicity that it's impossible for someone 18 ~~like~~ her to have a private 19 ~~life~~. When ordinary people have similar problems, it's only their friends and 20 ~~relations~~ who get to hear about it.

13.9 Five students
Listening

A You'll hear a conversation between two English teachers. Barbara is telling Chris about some of her students who will be joining his class. As you listen, note down her comments on each student.

	Appearance	Good points	But be careful!
PAUL	Tall,	Helpful,	Makes mistakes,
SUSAN			
MARIA			
HELEN			
PETER			

B Work in small groups. How do you think your teacher would describe each of YOU to a colleague?

C Work in pairs. One of you should look at Activity 38, the other at 49. You'll each have a picture of people to describe to your partner.

13.10 Describing people
Composition

A It's generally easier to write short sentences rather than long ones. Often short sentences are easier to read and understand too. Which of these three paragraphs do you prefer?

1 He is a tall dark-haired man with attractive brown eyes, whose clothes are always smart and who always behaves charmingly even when people are not pleasant to him.
2 He is a tall dark-haired man with attractive brown eyes. His clothes are always smart. He always behaves charmingly even when people are not pleasant to him.
3 He is a tall dark-haired man. He has attractive brown eyes. He always wears smart clothes. He always behaves charmingly. People are not always nice to him.

B Write four short paragraphs, using these ideas:

1 He is ... overweight   mid thirties   selfish   dishonest
   loses his temper   people disagree with him
2 She is ... thin   late fifties   absent-minded
   delightful sense of humour   helps other people with problems
3 He is ... 18   athletic   loves sport   favourite game football
   spare time: going out with friends + going to cinema
4 She is ... 16   studious   enjoys reading   4 brothers + 2 sisters
   hopes to go to university   wants to study engineering

★ In questions like 1 to 3 in C below, the examiner is interested in how well you can express yourself, not in how truthful you are. Imaginary ideas may be more interesting or easier to describe. Try to use words you know, and don't experiment with words you're unsure of.

For example, you could describe a wonderful imaginary aunt in 3 or write about an exciting imaginary meeting in 1 – you needn't even tell the truth about yourself in 2! (NB: In 4 below, you do have to tell the truth.)

C Write 120 to 180 words on TWO of these topics:

1 Describe your first meeting with someone who became a close friend OR who later became an enemy.
2 Write a letter to a new pen friend. Imagine this is your first letter and give your friend a good idea of your appearance, interests and personality.
3 Describe two people you admire or like OR two people you dislike very much. Explain why you feel this way about these people.
4 If you have read one of the prescribed books, explain which of the characters you liked best OR which of the characters you found least attractive.

Write the two compositions together in $1\frac{1}{2}$ hours or separately in 45 minutes each. Don't use a dictionary.
- Make notes before you start.
- Decide how you will begin and end each composition.
- Check your work through afterwards.

13.11 That's a problem!

Interview exercises

A Work in small groups. Look at these pictures. What's going on? What has happened? How can the people solve their problems?

B 🏆 Work in groups of three. Student A should look at Activity 31, student B at 36 and C at 50. You'll each have a problem, which your partners must help you to solve.

Here are some useful expressions:

> Why don't you … ?
> You could …
> If I were you I'd …
> The best thing to do would be …

> That wouldn't work because …
> That's not really possible because …
> I'd like to do that but I can't, because …

13.12 Grammar revision *Exam practice*

A Rewrite each sentence, starting with the words given below.

1. You must be more polite to people.
   It's *important to be polite to people.*
2. She wrote me a letter to tell me she never wanted to see me again.
   The letter *that she wrote to me said she never wanted to see me again.*
3. He's so dull that people fall asleep while he's talking.
   He's such *a dull person that people fall asleep while he's talking.*
4. Although she's the daughter of a rich man, he doesn't want to marry her.
   In spite *of her being the daughter of a rich man, he doesn't want to marry her.*
5. You'll lose touch with him unless you write to him.
   If *you don't write to him, you'll lose touch with him.*
6. 'I'm leaving and I'm never coming back!' she said to me.
   She told *that she's leaving and will never come back.*
7. She's much more amusing than her brother.
   Her brother *isn't as amusing as her.*
8. They first met ten years ago.
   They have *met ten years ago.*
9. During her husband's absence she was very lonely.
   While *her husband was away, she felt very lonely.*
10. He's a liar and a cheat but everyone still seems to like him.
    Everyone *likes him even though he's a liar and a cheat.*

B Complete the unfinished sentences in this dialogue.

Chris: Hi, Robin.
Robin: Hello, Chris, what's up? Are 1 *all right* ?
Chris: Not really, no. I feel a bit depressed.
Robin: Oh dear. Why 2 *are you feeling depressed* ?
Chris: It's my family again. My Uncle George is staying with us again.
Robin: I see, but what 3 *wrong with him* ?
Chris: Oh, *he's* all right. It's just that my father doesn't get on with him. If they're in the same room one of them starts an argument.
Robin: Can't 4 *you do anything to prevent them* ?
Chris: They wouldn't take any notice of me. And to make matters worse, Uncle George is sleeping on the spare bed in my room.
Robin: Why 5 *don't you like* ?
Chris: He snores and I can't get to sleep.
Robin: How 6 *long has he been staying at your place* ?
Chris: He arrived on Sunday.
Robin: And how 7 *long is he going to stay* ?
Chris: Another three weeks at least. Until he gets another ship.
Robin: What 8 *does he do* ?
Chris: He's a merchant seaman. He always stays here when he's on leave.
Robin: Well, you'd better 9 *find somewhere else to stay* ?
Chris: Yes, I'll have to, I suppose! I'm going to be spending a lot of time away from home, until he goes back to sea.
Robin: You could 10 *come and stay at my place* ?
Chris: Really? That'd be wonderful. Thanks a lot.

14 The past

The exercises in this unit are organised in the same order as in the exam:

14.1 to 14.3 will help you to revise for Paper 1 Reading Comprehension.
14.4 will help you to revise for Paper 2 Composition.
14.5 to 14.9 will help you to revise for Paper 3 Use of English.
14.10 to 14.12 will help you to revise for Paper 4 Listening Comprehension.
14.13 will help you to revise for Paper 5 Interview.

14.1 Vocabulary and grammar   *Reading comprehension*

The first part of Paper 1 consists of 25 questions on vocabulary and on grammar. In the exam, allow yourself at least 25 minutes for this exercise – each question is worth one mark out of a total of 55 for the whole of Paper 1.

1 If you can't remember, let me try to .... your memory.
   A arouse   B awaken   C refresh   D stimulate
2 Most of what she learnt at school she's now ....
   A forgotten   B lost   C mislaid   D omitted
3 Aristotle was alive in the fourth century ....
   A AC   B BC   C CD   D DC
4 Her husband claims he is a(n) .... of Queen Victoria.
   A ancestor   B descendant   C follower   D heir
5 Queen Victoria's been dead for about 90 years, ...?
   A has she   B hasn't she   C is she   D isn't she
6 The castle was built in the 12th century and the church beside it is equally ....
   A ancient   B antique   C elderly   D old-fashioned
7 Despite their age, her grandparents are still very ....
   A alive   B childish   C lively   D living
8 My sister's son, Jimmy, is my favourite ....
   A cousin   B nephew   C niece   D uncle
9 The train was delayed so we had to wait for ....
   A ages   B a moment   C a second   D long times
10 I didn't expect you to arrive so soon. How long did the journey ....?
   A continue   B endure   C go   D take
11 We talked about her trip and she said that she .... there before.
   A had never been   B had never come   C never came   D never went
12 It was very kind of you to do the washing-up, but you .... it.
   A didn't have to do   B hadn't to do   C mightn't have done
   D mustn't have done

13 Because of the bad weather we had to .... our picnic.
   A put aside   B put off   C put out   D put up
14 We thought we'd missed the bus but, of course, it arrived ....
   A at the end   B conclusively   C in conclusion   D in the end
15 If you're not sure what the date is today, look at your ....
   A almanac   B calendar   C dairy   D day-book
16 Don't worry, you'll get an answer to your letter ....
   A at last   B one of those days   C sooner or later   D when all's said and done
17 He hasn't come yet, but I'm expecting him to arrive ....
   A at any time   B at no time   C at one time   D at this time
18 It was my first proper holiday for years, so I was really .... it.
   A anticipating   B expecting   C looking forward   D looking forward to
19 It was supposed to rain yesterday, according to the weather ....
   A forecast   B oracle   C prediction   D warning
20 She told me she knew exactly what would happen, but I wasn't ....
   A certainly   B convinced   C secure   D surely
21 I wish I .... more attention in my history lessons at school.
   A had paid   B have been paying   C paid   D was paying
22 We agreed to .... in the main square at 7.30.
   A meet   B meeting   C meet together   D meet us
23 Remember that exams never start late, they always start ....
   A ahead of time   B at the last moment   C in time   D on time
24 I haven't .... an exam for two years.
   A made   B taken   C took   D set
25 Exams are never enjoyable, ...?
   A are there   B are they   C aren't there   D aren't they

★ In the exam, if you can't answer a question, leave a blank, make a pencil mark in the margin and come back to it later. If you still can't answer it, make a guess – you've got a 25% chance of being right!

14.2 1900 *Reading comprehension*

★ Each of the comprehension questions on the passages in Paper 1 is worth two marks – in all there will be fifteen questions making a total of 30 out of 55. In the exam, there may be three or four passages and there will be fewer questions than you have had to answer in this book.

★ It may be best to read the questions through before you read the passage, so that you know what you have to find out. Alternatively, you may prefer to read the text quickly through (to get an idea of what it's about) before you read the questions and then look for the answers in the text.

If you spend too long trying to find a particular answer you may run out of time – it may be best to make a pencil mark beside a tricky question and come back to it at the end.

Read the passage and answer the questions below.

...the nineteenth century brought about the greatest expansion of wealth the world had ever known. Its sources lay in the industrialisation of Europe and the techniques for assuring the continuance of this growth were by no means exhausted or compromised in 1900. There had not only been a vast and accelerating flow of commodities available only in (relatively) tiny quantities a century before, but whole new ranges of goods had come into existence. Oil and electricity had joined coal, wood, wind and water as sources of energy. A chemical industry existed which could not have been envisaged in 1800. Growing power and wealth had been used to tap seemingly inexhaustible natural resources, both agricultural and mineral. Railways, electric trams, steamships, motor cars and bicycles gave millions of men a new control over their environment; they accelerated travel from place to place and eased transport for the first time since animals had been harnessed to carts thousands of years before. In terms of consumption, or of the services to which they had access, or in the enjoyment of better health, even the mass of the population in developed countries were much better off in 1900 than their predecessors a hundred years before.

In spite of this cheerful picture, doubts could break in. Even if what might happen in the future were ignored, contemplation of the cost of the new wealth and doubts about the social justice of its distribution were troubling. Most people were still terribly poor, whether or not they lived in rich countries where the illogicality of this was particularly more striking than in earlier times. Another change in the way men thought about their condition arose over their power to get a livelihood at all. It was not new that men should be without work. What was new was that situations should suddenly arise in which the operation of blind forces of boom and slump produced millions of men without work concentrated in great towns. This was 'unemployment', the new phenomenon for which a new word had been needed. Nor were the cities themselves yet rid of all the evils which had so struck the first observers of industrial society. By 1900 the majority of western Europeans were town-dwellers and they lived in more than 140 cities of over 100,000 inhabitants in 1914. In some of them, millions of people were cramped, ill-housed, under-provided with schools and fresh air, let alone amusement other than that of the street, and this often in sight of the wealth their society helped to produce. 'Slums' was another word invented by the nineteenth century.

(from *The Hutchinson History of the World* by J. M. Roberts)

1. Oil and electricity became available as sources of energy
   A after 1900.
   B before 1900.
   C in about 1800.
   D in about 1900.

2. In the 19th century travel became
   A cheaper and easier.
   B cheaper and faster.
   C cheaper, easier and faster.
   D faster and easier.

3. In 1900 life was better for
   A everyone in the world.
   B most people in Europe.
   C only the rich.
   D non-Europeans.

4. Before 1900 very large numbers of men were
   A always without work.
   B never without work.
   C often without work.
   D rarely without work.

5. The word 'slums' was invented to describe
   A bad housing.
   B poverty.
   C unemployment.
   D wealth.

14.3 The Lost Viking Capital *Reading comprehension*

JORVIK –
LOST VIKING CAPITAL

A thousand years ago York was one of the largest, richest and most famous cities in the whole of Britain. A monk at that time described it as packed with a huge population, rich merchandise, and traders 'from all parts, especially Danes'. People in the 10th century called it Jorvik, and knew it as the capital of the North of England, and one of Europe's greatest trading ports. It owed its prosperity to the hard work and commercial enterprise of Viking settlers from Scandinavia who had captured it in AD 866 and almost totally rebuilt it.

Most of the city's buildings were made of wood, and have long since been demolished, or have burnt down or rotted away. In some parts of modern York, however, near the rivers Ouse and Foss which run through the centre of the city, archaeologists have found that remains of Jorvik do still survive. They are buried deep below the streets and buildings of the 20th century city. Here the damp soils have preserved the timber buildings. Whole streets of houses, shops, workshops and warehouses are to be found, often still standing shoulder high. All the debris and rubbish left by the people of Jorvik in and around their homes is still there, awaiting discovery.

Between 1976 and 1981 archaeologists from the York Archaeological Trust excavated a part of this lost and all-but-forgotten city. The dig took place in Coppergate, before the city's new Coppergate Centre was built. Four rows of buildings were found, running back from Coppergate itself, almost exactly in the same positions as their modern successors. The remains were so well preserved – even down to boots and shoes, pins and needles, plants and insects – that every aspect of life at the time could be reconstructed.

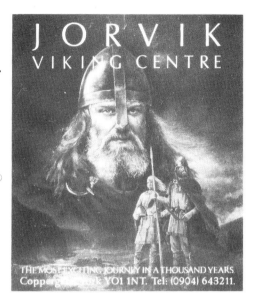

York Archaeological Trust decided to try to tell the story of Jorvik as it was a thousand years ago. To do so it built the Jorvik Viking Centre in the huge hole created by the dig. Two of the rows of buildings were reconstructed as we think they were. A further two were preserved just as the archaeological team discovered them, the ancient timbers set out as they were found in the late 1970s, deep below the new shopping centre, where they have lain for centuries.

In the Jorvik Viking Centre people from the 20th century journey back in time to the 10th century. The journey is done in time cars, which silently glide back through the years, past some of the thirty or so generations of York's people who have walked the pavements of Coppergate, until time stops, on a late October day in 948. For a while modern time travellers explore Coppergate and a little alley, Lundgate, which runs off it. The neighbourhood is full of the sights and sounds and smells of 10th century Jorvik. Townspeople are there, buying and selling, working and playing.

Choose the answer that best completes each sentence about the passage.

1. 1,000 years ago York was
   A more important than present-day York.
   B the most important city in Britain.
   C the most prosperous city in Britain.
   D the principal city of Northern England. ✓
2. Jorvik was first established
   A before the Vikings came to England.
   B 1,000 years ago. ✓
   C in the 8th century by the Vikings.
   D in the 9th century by the Vikings.
3. The buildings that the Vikings built at Jorvik
   A are all still beneath the streets of modern York.
   B have all been destroyed.
   C have not all disappeared. ✓
   D have all vanished.
4. Some of the streets of Viking Jorvik discovered by archaeologists
   A still had walls 1½ metres high. ✓
   B were buried in rubbish.
   C were completely as they were in Viking times.
   D were paved with stone.
5. Coppergate is now
   A a museum   B a park   C a shopping centre ✓   D a street
6. Archaeologists were able to discover exactly
   A how life was lived 1,000 years ago. ✓
   B how the Vikings captured Jorvik.
   C how the Vikings constructed their buildings.
   D what kind of clothes the Vikings wore.
7. Jorvik Viking Centre was constructed .... the place where the dig had taken place.
   A at ✓   B near   C some way from   D a long way from
8. Jorvik Viking Centre contains .... buildings.
   A two   B four   C two rows of   D four rows of ✓
9. Visitors to Jorvik Viking Centre
   A have to queue up for a long time.
   B must be quiet in the museum.
   C should allow plenty of time for their visit.
   D travel back in time. ✓
10. Visitors to Jorvik Viking Centre can
    A buy souvenirs of Viking Jorvik.
    B ask the staff questions about Viking Jorvik.
    C touch the exhibits if they like.
    D walk through the steets of Viking Jorvik. ✓

14.4 Under exam conditions   *Composition – 1½ hours*

★ In the exam it's important to follow the instructions exactly. If the instructions say 'Write a letter to a friend ...', for example, your work must look like a personal letter and NOT like a business letter! This may sound obvious, but it's easy to overlook important instructions when you're in a hurry. So, before you start writing:

1 Make sure you fully understand the instructions for each question. If you don't quite understand a particular question, it's best not to answer it.
2 Decide which of the questions are the easiest for you to answer.
3 Check which grammatical structures may be needed for the subject: conditionals, modal verbs, past/present perfect, etc.
4 Make notes on both questions. If at this stage you find you haven't got enough ideas on one of them, there may be time to choose a different one.

A Choose TWO of the following composition questions. Allow yourself 90 minutes, including time to make notes beforehand and check your work through afterwards. Each composition should be between 120 and 180 words in length. You may not use a dictionary.

1 Write a short story that includes this phrase:
   '... everything seemed to be going well until ...'

2 What was life like in your country 20 years ago? Describe the changes that have taken place and explain how the quality of life has improved and got worse.

3 Imagine that some friends have invited you to go on holiday with them sometime during the next six months. Write a letter explaining why you must turn down the invitation and describing what you will be doing instead.

4 Write a description of a place you once visited and the people you met there.

5 You have been chosen by the other members of your class to present a gift to your teacher and make a speech. Explain why you have chosen this particular gift and thank your teacher for all he or she has done for you. Write down what you would say in your speech.

6 If you have read one of the prescribed books, explain why you enjoyed OR didn't enjoy reading it.
   OR Your teacher will suggest a question on the particular book you have read.

B Your teacher will give you a final mark for the two compositions and also point out what particular points you should be careful about in the exam.

- What are *your* typical 'careless mistakes' of spelling and grammar, which you should notice when checking your work?
- What types of questions do you feel more confident about (e.g. writing a narrative) and which do you dislike (e.g. writing an essay)?

★ In the exam it's a good idea to leave wide margins and to leave two or three lines between each paragraph. Start your second composition on a new page. Then, if you want to add anything or cross a sentence out and rewrite it, you'll have plenty of space.

14.5 Fill the gaps
Use of English

Fill each of the numbered blanks in the following passage. Use only one word in each space.

Many years ago when the summers seemed longer and life was ___less___ (1) complicated, we had rented a cottage by a river in the heart of the country where we were going to ___spend___ (2) three weeks' holiday. There were four of us: me (age 9), Mum and Dad and Mum's ___sister___ (3), Auntie June. Oh, and I mustn't forget to ___mention___ (4) Spot, our little dog. I was allowed to go off by ___myself___ (5) all day, ___provided___ (6) that I promised to be careful and took Spot with me for ___company___ (7).

One day I was out fishing with Spot when we heard a lot of shouting in the ___distance___ (8) followed by a scream and a splash. I was a bit ___frightened___ (9) so I called Spot and we both hid ___behind___ (10) a bush where we could see but not be ___seen___ (11). After a few moments a straw hat came floating down the river, followed by an oar, a picnic basket and ___another___ (12) oar. Then came the rowing boat itself, but it was floating ___upside___ (13) down! A few seconds later my Dad and Auntie June came running ___along___ (14) the river bank, both wet ___through___ (15). Spot started ___barking___ (16) so I came out of hiding and said hello. My Dad got really angry with me for not ___trying___ (17) to catch the boat as it went past. Luckily, however, the boat and both the oars had been caught by an overhanging tree a little further downstream, but not the hat or the picnic basket. So I had to let them ___share___ (18) my sandwiches. Dad and Auntie June both made me ___promise___ (19) not to tell Mum what had happened in ___case___ (20) she was worried.

★ Before you fill any blanks in this kind of exercise, read the whole story through to find out what it's about. Then start filling the gaps. If you're not sure of an answer, pencil it in lightly or leave a blank and come back to it later.

'Mum and dad, can I borrow the wheel tonight?'

14.6 Grammar revision
Use of English

A When you check your compositions through for mistakes, you need to notice spelling errors and grammatical mistakes. Some of these may just be careless mistakes or slips of the pen – others may be harder to recognise.

Work in pairs. Find the mistakes in these sentences and correct them – in some cases there are two or more mistakes.

1 **Careless mistakes and slips of the pen:**
   A The castle contain many treasure and painting.
   B I wonder wich of the misteaks is most serius.
   C My brother and sister has brown eyes but my eyes be blue.
   D Could you tell me what time does it opens?
   E Who did paid for the ticket?

2 **Mistakes that are harder to notice:**
   A After visiting the museum he had not very much time left.
   B His hair is very long, it's time for him to have cut it.
   C I am waiting for you since four hours.
   D They never visited Rome before their first visit in 1987.
   E She never wrote a letter by hand since she has bought a word processor.
   F I am learning English during five years.
   G A suspicious is questioning by the police.
   H Before they had gone out they had been watched the news on TV.

B Finish each of the sentences in this exercise in such a way that it means exactly the same as the sentence printed before it.

1 I'll be busy working while you're on holiday.
   During *your holiday I'll be working*
2 I haven't seen my old school friend for ages.
   It's ages *since I saw my old school friends*
3 It was my first visit to North America.
   I *hadn't been to visited North America before*
4 The ancient Egyptians built the Pyramids.
   The Pyramids *were built by ancient Egyptians.*
5 It'll be necessary for her to give up her job soon.
   Soon she *'ll have to give up her job soon*
6 CLOSED DUE TO ILLNESS said the notice on the office door.
   We found out *that the office was closed due to illness.*
7 In spite of the heat it was an easy climb to the top of the hill.
   We managed *to reach on the top of the hill in spite of the heat.*
8 I'll get ready before your arrival.
   By the time *you arrive, I'll be ready.*
9 It wasn't a good idea for you to put so much salt in the soup.
   You *ought to have put so much salt in the soup.*
10 I'm afraid it's far too salty for me to eat now.
   It's so *salty that I can't eat it now.*

14.7 Word-building revision *Use of English*

★ If there is a word-building exercise in the exam (there may not be), you may have to add both a prefix AND a suffix to the root word. AND you may well have to change the form of a verb to fit the sentence.

A Work in pairs. Here are some examples of tricky questions for you to try. Form another word from the words in capitals to complete each sentence.

1 She got very angry but later she apologised for her .... *im*PATIENT*ence*   PATIENT
2 He is very generous and everyone admires his .... *uh*SELF*lessness*   SELF
3 I didn't want my money back, I wanted a .... *re*PLACE*ment*   PLACE
4 His boss told him off because he had behaved .... *ir*RESPONSIBL*y*   RESPONSIBLE
5 I read an article about .... among school-leavers. *un*EMPLOY*ment*   EMPLOY
6 Her parents .... her to apply for the job. *en*COURAGE*ment*   COURAGE
7 They had an quarrel after .... about who was responsible. *dis*AGREE*ment*   AGREE
8 This knife is very blunt. It needs .... SHARP*ening*

B Now try this revision exercise.
The words in capitals at the end of each sentence can be used to form a word that fits suitably in the blank space. Fill each blank in this way.

1 In some places the weather changes so quickly that it's very .... *un*PREDICT*able*   PREDICT
2 We had a marvellous holiday and our trip to the mountains was .... *un*FORGET*table*   FORGET
3 Two of these tablets should be taken .... DAY *Daily*
4 He remembers every detail of it because he has a .... memory. PHOTOGRAPH*ic*
5 I expect she'll get the job, at least there's a fairly high .... PROBABLE *Probability*
6 I'm not sure at all, I really can't say with .... CERTAIN*ty*
7 There's no .... of the government calling an early election. LIKELY *likelihood*
8 The day she got married was a .... occasion. MEMORY*able*
9 Nobody wears clothes like that any more – they're terribly .... *un*FASHION*able*   FASHION
10 They all passed their exams without the slightest .... DIFFICULT*y*

★ Before you take the exam, make sure you get some practice in doing exercises like these in an Examination Practice book:

It be quite difficult / do / exercise like this / exam.
It is quite difficult to do an exercise like this in the exam.

and

A: Are *you feeling confident* ?
B: Yes, I'm feeling quite confident now.

14.8 Unusual exercises — Use of English

★ One of the exercises in the Use of English paper may be new to you, but the work you have done so far on Vocabulary, Word study, Prepositions and Verbs and idioms will help you to cope with these. Here are three exercises to give you some practice. The golden rules with an unfamiliar type of exercise are:

1 Read the instructions carefully – twice!
2 Look at the examples very carefully.

A Complete these sentences with an expression formed from **make** or **do**. A preposition or particle may or may not be necessary.

EXAMPLE: I'm afraid I have *made* a mistake.

1 I didn't believe their story, I was sure they had *made it up*.
2 There was no wine to drink so we had to *make do with* water.
3 You haven't *done up* your shoelaces – you might trip over.
4 The robbers *made off with* over £1 million.
5 Have you *done* all your work yet?
6 We told the driver we were *making for* the coast and asked for a lift.

B Complete the following sentences with ONE appropriate word connected with the subject of **books**.

EXAMPLE: This book has 210 *pages*.

1 The *title* of this book is *Progress to First Certificate*.
2 He made notes beside the text in the left-hand *margin*.
3 You can use the *index* at the end of a book to find where the information is given.
4 Most dictionaries have two *columns* on a page.
5 The complete novels of Charles Dickens take up twenty *volumes*.
6 Use this card as a *bookmark* so that you can find your place again easily.

C Complete these sentences with one word related in meaning to the number given.

EXAMPLE: It was the *third* time I had seen that film.   3

1 We're going away on holiday for a *fortnight*.   14
2 I've been to that place *dozens* of times.   12
3 The admission prices have *doubled* since I was last there.   2
4 20% is the same as one *fifth*.   5
5 If you cut the apple into pieces, we can each have a *quarter*.   4
6 In the year 2000 a new *century* begins.   100

★ In the exam you are sure to find that there are some questions that you can't answer. Don't get depressed about this. If all the questions were easy, everyone would get 100%!

14.9 Problem solving / Directed writing *Use of English*

A Read this information and consider these questions:
- Which of the cities would suit them best?
- What could they do together – or separately – during a day in the city?

Mr and Mrs Meier and their two children Helen (14) and Richard (16) are staying in London and want to spend Sunday in either York or Cambridge. The Meiers have chosen these cities because they are all interested in history, but they don't all share the same tastes: Helen is artistic and likes looking at paintings, Mrs Meier doesn't like walking, Mr Meier doesn't like museums and Richard likes railways.

In a day, allowing time for travel and meals, there would only be time to see two or three of the sights – not all of them.

York
Historic city with many ancient buildings

- Roman city walls — walk around the city
- York Minster: one of the largest churches in Europe, stained glass windows
- Jorvik Viking Centre: experience the sights, sounds and smells of daily life in Viking times
- The Shambles: old street lined with fascinating shops
- Castle Museum: contains a reconstructed street with shops of various periods
- National Railway Museum: historic engines, carriages and history of railways in Britain

Journey time from London 2 hours — weekend return £45, day return £32

CAMBRIDGE
Historic university city with old colleges

- King's College Chapel: tall windows and superb ceiling
- Colleges – many are open for the public to walk through: peaceful courtyards
- Fitzwilliam Museum: paintings and antiquities
- Kettle's Yard: delightful artist's house full of paintings and beautiful furniture
- River Cam: walk beside river or hire a boat

Journey time from London 1 hour – weekend return £24, day return £16

B Write about 100 words, explaining which city they should go to and what they would do there together (or separately) once they got there.

★ Directed writing is probably one of the hardest parts of the exam. Make sure you read the instructions very carefully (twice). Select the information you think is relevant. There is no perfect answer in this kind of exercise – as long as you can explain and justify your decisions your answer will be satisfactory.

Remember that this exercise only counts for 20–25% of the marks in the Use of English paper – about the same as the Fill the gaps exercise, which is usually question 1 – so don't spend too long on it.

Maybe do it first of all – you can answer the questions in any order you like.

14.10 I remember ...   *Listening comprehension*

You'll hear two people talking about a childhood experience. Answer the questions or choose the alternative that best completes each sentence.

1 Liz's brother is
   A about the same age as her.
   B much older than her.
   C slightly older than her.
   D younger than her.

2 They used to go together to the
   A funfair.
   B park.
   C playground.
   D shops.

3 While she was on one of the swings she realised that
   A it was getting cold.
   B it was starting to rain.
   C she was alone.
   D she was lost.

4 Which of these pictures best shows what happened?

5 The dog tried to
   A bite her.
   B get her teddy.
   C chase her.
   D pull her off the swing.

6 In the end the dog
   A was caught.
   B was hit with a stick.
   C was killed.
   D ran away.

7 After that experience she always
   A avoided the playground if it was empty.
   B told her brother not to leave her.
   C went with her mother to the playground.
   D went to a different, safer playground.

8 Now she realises that her brother had really
   A forgotten about her.
   B gone home to fetch help.
   C left her to be eaten.
   D lost his way home.

9 This experience
   A has almost been forgotten.
   B has had a big influence on her life ever since.
   C has had no effect on her life.
   D still affects her attitude.

10 Which of these pictures best shows what happened?

★ In the exam, you will normally hear each recording twice. Make sure you read the questions through carefully while you're waiting for the recording to be played to you.

★ If you are slightly unsure about any questions, put a light pencil mark beside the answer you think might be best, then listen carefully for the answer to that question on the second listening.

If you have no idea about an answer, don't leave a blank – guess!

'That's the deal then. We give you our gold and you give us something called Spanish omelette.'

14.11 The slave trade
Listening comprehension

🎧 Listen to the radio interview with Professor Nicholson. Put a tick (✓) beside the true statements and a cross (✗) beside the false statements.

1 Professor Nicholson has made a TV film about slavery. ☐
2 According to him, there are still slaves in the world today. ☐
3 The first African slaves were seen in Europe in 1534. ☐
4 Before 1700 the slave trade was dominated by Portugal. ☐
5 Slaves were needed to work on the plantations in the New World. ☐
6 The French and English dominated the slave trade in the 18th century. ☐
7 Six million people were sent from Africa between 1700 and 1800. ☐
8 The plantations in America produced fruit and rubber. ☐
9 Sugar, cotton and tobacco were sent to Europe. ☐
10 Many slaves did not survive the awful journey across the Atlantic. ☐
11 Conditions in the plantations were better than on the ships. ☐
12 The anti-slavery movement started in Europe. ☐
13 English ships stopped carrying slaves in 1809. ☐
14 Slaves in British colonies were set free in 1865. ☐
15 Slaves in the United States were set free in 1833. ☐
16 Some slave owners voluntarily gave their slaves freedom. ☐
17 Liberia was set up as a home for freed slaves who returned to Africa. ☐
18 This interview is about the slaves who were sent from Africa to America. ☐

14.12 Gipsy signs
Listening comprehension

🎧 You'll hear a talk about gipsies and the signs they used to leave for each other outside people's houses. Listen to the recording and DRAW the signs beside their meanings. The first is done for you as an example:

1 Beware of the dog   △

2 Fierce dog

3 Friendly people

4 Friendly, generous people

5 Very friendly, generous people

6 Work to be had here

7 Gipsies not liked

8 Nothing to be had

9 Work available with good pay

10 These people will buy from you

11 This place has been robbed

14.13 A long time ago... *Interview exercises*

A Work in pairs. One of you should look at Activity 14, the other at 21. You will each see different photographs, showing a scene from the past. Find out about your partner's photograph by asking questions.

B Work in pairs. Look at the brochure and answer these questions:
- Would you like to visit this place? Why/Why not?
- What would you enjoy most about it?
- What historical buildings or monuments have you visited? What did you find interesting about them?
- What buildings or monuments should a visitor to your city or area go and see? Why?

"The loveliest castle in the world."
LORD CONWAY

Leeds castle, Kent. Named after Led, Chief Minister of Ethelbert IV, King of Kent, in AD 857.

It is situated about 4 miles to the East of Maidstone on the A20 London-Folkestone Road, in some of England's loveliest countryside.

Built on two islands in the middle of a lake, the Castle was originally a stronghold until it was converted into a Royal Palace by Henry VIII.

Beautifully furnished and lovingly restored, its truly historic atmosphere gently reminds one that it was a Royal Residence for over 300 years.

The surrounding parklands offer many magnificent views and walks as well as a charming woodland garden.

Lunch, tea and light refreshments are available and picnics are welcome in the grounds surrounding the car park area.

Leeds Castle, Maidstone, Kent.

C Work in pairs or small groups. Ask your partner(s) these questions:
- Why do people study history?
- In what ways is studying history relevant to our present-day lives?
- What important historical events have happened in the history of your country? (In Britain everyone learns what happened in 1066 and 1588, for example. What equivalent 'memorable dates' are there in your country's history?)
- What would have happened if those events had turned out differently?
- If someone who had emigrated from your country or city twenty years ago returned now, what changes would they notice?

★ In the exam, the examiner will give you marks for the following aspects of your spoken English:

- **fluency** – Do you speak without too much hesitation?
- **grammatical accuracy** – Do you speak without making too many mistakes?
- **pronunciation** – Can people understand you easily?
- **communication** – Do you communicate your ideas effectively in a conversation?
- **vocabulary** – Do you know enough words to be able to express your ideas?

★ Remember that in the interview you should try to be as relaxed as possible – and as talkative as you normally are in class. The best way to do this is to PRACTISE by taking part in 'mock' interviews.

14.14 Good luck!

In Papers 1 to 4 of the exam,
– keep cool and don't get depressed if there are some questions you can't answer
– use your time sensibly
– read all the instructions and examples very carefully
– check all your written work and correct any careless mistakes you've made
– show the examiners how much you know!

Best of luck and good wishes from

Leo Jones

Communication activities

1 Dictate these names, addresses and phone numbers to your partner. Spell out the difficult names, if you're not sure how to pronounce them. Ask your teacher for help, if necessary.

Ms Fiona Davison, 13 Gloucester Rd, Cheltenham GL9 6GT (0242 819232)
Mr Thomas Twining, 70 St Andrews St, York YO1 8AR (0904 678999)
Mrs G. K. Fuller, 115 W. Harbour Drive, Portsmouth PO3 2PJ (0705 414332)
Miss Helen Konstantinides, 170 El. Venizelou Street, 114 27 Athens, Greece
M. Jean-Pierre Martin, 135 quai de Southampton, 76600 Le Havre, France

2 Here are some ideas you might like to mention to your partners:

> More people will use bicycles in the future:
> no fuel required   no pollution   no traffic jams
> healthy exercise for all   cheap and available for young and old
> heavier traffic will discourage people from using their cars
> everyone can go wherever they want

3 The original version of the story uses the past tense, making it seem true, rather than fiction. Its lack of detail makes it very dull.

What makes the following version of the story better than the one on page 29?

Underline the <u>extra information</u> that helps to improve the story.

<u>'CASABLANCA'</u>
The story is set in Morocco during the war. Rick (Humphrey Bogart) is an American who owns a night club in Casablanca. His ex-girlfriend, Ilsa (Ingrid Bergman), arrives at Rick's with her new husband, Victor Laszlo (Paul Heinreid). Laszlo is in danger there and has to escape to Lisbon, but although they can get plane tickets, they are unable to get visas. Ilsa persuades Rick to help her 'for old time's sake' and he manages to get two visas on the black market but has to sell his club to pay for them. At the end of the film Rick and the chief of police, Renault (Claude Rains) watch the plane take off, carrying Ilsa and Laszlo to freedom.

4 What are the differences between these notes and the notes you made?

<u>GIFT IDEAS FOR CHRIS</u>
Alarm Wallet ✓ – Chris going to USA, doesn't want to lose the money earned at the vacation camp. Would be pleased to receive it. Quite expensive though.
Beach Chair ✗ – Probably not suitable, Chris seems active person, not the sort who would want to lie on the beach reading.
Shopper Calculator ✓? – Chris enjoys supermarkets – maybe a possible gift, fairly cheap, not very exciting though.
Voice Over ✗ – Not suitable, Chris not interested in music.

<u>GIFT IDEAS FOR JO</u>
Alarm Wallet ✗ – Probably not suitable, though if shopping for family might need to make sure money not lost.
Beach Chair ✓ – Suitable for Jo: likes reading + going to the beach. Half the price of Voice Over but more expensive than Shopper Calculator.
Shopper Calculator ✓? – Possibly suitable to make shopping easier, but not what a friend should give Jo. Maybe suggest this to a member of Jo's family??
Voice Over ✓ – Could be suitable – Jo likes music and singing: could enjoy composing own songs perhaps? Quite expensive though.

5 Dictate these words to your partner:

hopeless   abbreviation   butter   lucky   juice   charming   ready   surprise   social   telephone   half

Silent letters: thorough   debt   soften   knot   chalk   scared   vehicle

6 Look at this recipe with your partner and make sure you understand it. Is this something you'd like to make and/or drink?

LASSI – a refreshing Eastern yogurt drink

¼ litre yogurt
¼ litre milk (or water)
juice of 1 lemon
ice cubes
sugar to taste

1 Crush the ice cubes or put them in a food processor.
2 Put all the ingredients, except the sugar, into the food processor or liquidiser and blend well.
3 Add the sugar little by little until the liquid is sweet enough. It should NOT be too sweet!
4 Serve immediately in tall glasses with drinking straws.

Join another pair and explain this recipe to them IN YOUR OWN WORDS. They will be telling you how to make a different refreshing drink.

7

Here are explanations of some of the items on the menu on page 142, so that you can help your partners to understand them. DO NOT just read these descriptions out loud – try to remember them, so that you can answer your partners' questions.
When you're all clear about everything, decide what to order for each course.

Steak and kidney pie   A traditional English pie containing beef and kidneys in a rich sauce – delicious!

Chicken Maryland   Fried chicken, coated with breadcrumbs and garnished with fried bananas – rather strange!

Sherry trifle   Cooked fruit and cake, soaked in sherry and topped with vanilla sauce and cream – very fattening!

8

Here are some ideas you might like to mention to your partners:

> More people will use electric vehicles in the future:
> no petrol needed   no pollution
> small, lightweight batteries will be developed
> quiet and fast enough for city driving
> petrol and diesel vehicles will be banned from city centres

9

The original version of the story contains so little detail that it's impossible to get interested. As it's a personal story, there should be personal details to explain why the night was unforgettable. The exact times and distances are distracting and irrelevant.

What makes this version of the story better than the one on page 29? Underline the main changes that have been made.

I'll never forget the night our car broke down. We were on our way home after a marvellous evening out with some friends. It was well after midnight and we were still miles from home. We tried to get the engine started again, but in vain. There was no traffic on the road at all, so we couldn't get a lift and had to walk all the way home. To make matters worse it started to rain and by the time we arrived we were wet through. But worse was yet to come! It was then that we discovered that we'd left our front door key in the car.

We had no choice but to break a window and climb in. Unfortunately, just as we were doing this, a police car stopped in the road. At first, of course, the policeman didn't believe our story and wanted to take us to the police station, but in the end we convinced him that we were telling the truth. By the time we got to bed it was past three o'clock and we were cold, wet, miserable and absolutely exhausted.

10 Dictate these names, addresses and phone numbers to your partner. Spell out the difficult names, if you're not sure how to pronounce them. Ask your teacher for help, if necessary.

Mr Anthony Fitzgerald, 150 King William Sq., Edinburgh EH2 7JQ
 (031 552 1265)
Mrs Anne Greene, 16 Acacia Ave, Wimbledon, London SW19 4KE
 (01 331 4499)
Mr Mark Butcher, c/o Mrs Finch, 13 North St, Ramsgate CT13 7YZ
 (0843 662701)
Sig. Giorgio Rossi, Via Garibaldi 118, 40125 Bologna, Italy
Mr James Rockford, 4352 Ocean Boulevard, Malibu, CA 40781, USA

11 This is the rest of the passage, with pauses and stressed syllables marked.

Equípment requíred: |
a 30 cm rúler, | stícky tápe, | páper, | scíssors and a pén. |
Procédure: |
Óne. | Cút oút a píece of páper the sáme síze as thís páge. |
Twó. | Yóu will seé alóng the síde of the páge | a scále with divísions márked on it. | Éach divísion shóws a tíme ínterval. | Thése represént fráctions of a sécond. |
Thrée. | Cópy the scále cárefully onto the síde of the píece of páper you have cút oút | and thén tíghtly wráp it roúnd the rúler | só that the scále is vísible. | The bóttom énd of the scále | shóuld be at the bóttom énd of the rúler. | Fíx it secúrely with stícky tápe. |
Fóur. | While you hóld the rúler at the point márked | 'HÓLD HÉRE', | gét the pérson to pláce hís or hér thúmb and fórefinger | on either síde of the zéro líne on the scále. | Téll them to cátch the rúler as soón as it begíns to fáll. | Íf they grip the rúler *befóre* it begíns to fáll, | thís resúlt is nót counted. |
Fíve. | Withoút létting the pérson knów whén you are abóut to dróp it, | reléase the rúler. | The tíme that it toók the pérson to reáct | is shówn in séconds on the scále at the poínt they caúght it. |
Síx. | Repéat the expériment séveral tímes with eách pérson | and récord the resúlts in a chárt. |

12 Unfortunately, delays are quite common on long journeys:
- Alain's ferry might be two hours late, because of rough seas.
- And Bobby's flight could land three hours late, due to fog at the airport.
- And Conny may miss the 06.17 train via Birmingham, if her alarm clock doesn't go off.

Decide what advice you will give to each of them to allow for these situations.

13 Imagine that you've seen this advertisement in the street. Describe it to your partner.

14 Ask your partner these questions about his or her photo, which was taken in 1940.

- What does your photograph show?
- What is happening?
- What has happened?
- What is going to happen?
- What would it be like to be one of the children in the picture?
- What are the differences between life now and life at the time the photograph was taken?
- Would you like to have been alive then? Why not?

1933

15

THE GUARDIAN   Thursday June 23

Yesterday's summary
Wednesday's weather
(Lunch-time reports)

	C	F			C	F			C	F			C	F			C	F
			Budapest	C	19	66	Glasgow	S	18	64	Montreal	R	23	73	Seoul	S	28	82
Algiers	C	26	79	B Aires	S	19	66	Helsinki	S	25	77	Moscow	C	25	77	Singapore	F	31	88
Amsterdam	C	18	64	Cairo	S	31	88	Hong Kong	C	30	86	Munich	S	14	57	Stockholm	F	22	72
Athens	F	17	63	Cape Town	S	27	81	Innsbruck	C	16	61	Naples	S	29	84	Strasbourg	S	19	66
Bahrain	S	35	95	Casablanca	S	23	73	Inverness	S	18	64	New Delhi	F	31	88	Sydney	F	15	59
Bermuda	S	30	86	Chicago	C	32	90	Istanbul	F	23	73	New York	F	36	97	Tangier	F	24	75
Barcelona	Th	22	72	Cologne	F	16	61	Karachi	F	35	95	Nice	S	24	75	Tenerife	F	23	73
Berlin	C	13	55	Copenhagen	F	19	66	Las Palmas	S	24	75	Oslo	Sl	4	40	Tokyo	F	26	79
Biarritz	C	23	73	Corfu	S	28	82	Lisbon	F	21	70	Paris	F	21	70	Tunis	S	32	90
Birmingham	S	21	70	Dublin	S	21	70	London	S	22	72	Peking	C	24	75	Valencia	S	27	81
Bombay	Dr	27	81	Edinburgh	S	19	66	Los Angeles	F	17	63	Perth	C	21	70	Vancouver	C	18	64
Bordeaux	S	25	77	Florence	S	29	84	Luxembourg	S	16	61	Prague	R	10	50	Venice	F	25	77
Boston	R	29	84	Frankfurt	S	18	64	Madrid	F	21	70	Reykjavik	R	8	46	Vienna	F	17	63
Bristol	S	24	75	Geneva	Fg	14	57	Majorca	F	30	86	Rhodes	S	26	79	Warsaw	C	15	59
Brussels	H	15	59	Gibraltar	S	25	77	Malaga	F	29	84	Riyadh	S	41	106	Washington	F	37	99
								Malta	S	28	82	Rome	S	25	77	Wellington	R	12	54
								Manchester	S	18	64	Salzburg	C	12	54	Zurich	F	18	64
								Melbourne	C	15	59								
								Mexico City	C	16	61								
								Miami	F	31	88								

C, cloudy; Dr, drizzle; F, fair; Fg, fog; H, hail; R, rain; Sl, sleet; Sn, snow; S, sunny; Th, thunder.

16 Imagine that you are going to give advice to someone who is going to buy A NEW CAMERA or A PERSONAL STEREO (Walkman). They have never owned one before. What would you tell them? Make some notes.

When you're ready, join another pair.
1 Ask for their advice on buying a new bicycle or a new watch.
2 Then offer them your advice on buying a camera or a personal stereo.

17 Here are three scenes from a film. Your partners have more scenes from the same film. How did the story start, continue and finish? Where do these scenes fit in?

1 Explain your version of the story, beginning: 'This is what happened...'
2 When each of you has given your version, look at each other's scenes and decide on a version of the story that includes all the pictures.

18 Tell your partner this story – as if it really happened to some friends of a friend of yours. DON'T read it aloud word-for-word.

These friends of mine went to the woods to gather mushrooms. They were afraid they might be poisonous, so they fed one to their cat. The cat still seemed OK a few hours later, so they cooked the mushrooms and ate them. When they'd just finished, they looked out of the window and saw the cat lying dead on the pavement. In panic, they rushed to hospital to have their stomachs pumped. On their return they found a note through their door from a neighbour who had accidentally run the cat over in the road.

19 Imagine that you and your partners need a break. Why don't you go away somewhere together? This advertisement in the paper has caught your eye – it seems a wonderful idea.

Tell your partners why they would enjoy a few days at the Springs Hotel.

Escape for a Country Weekend

Think of an elegant and luxurious country house, set in acres of beautiful grounds. Flowers, log fires, cossetting service and a warm welcome from your host. Tennis and croquet of course plus some less traditional amenities like heated swimming pool and sauna.

Dine in a candlelit Restaurant with spectacular views over the floodlit lake.
It's all part of a very special weekend. Two nights' dinner, bed and breakfast, £49.50 per person, including VAT.

North Stoke, Wallingford, Oxon.
Tel: 0491 36687. **The Springs** HOTEL

In the great English Country House tradition

20

Imagine that you've seen this advertisement in the street. Describe it to your partner.

21

Ask your partner these questions about his or her photo, which was taken in 1933.

- What does your photograph show?
- Why has he got the sign on his bike, do you think?
- What has happened?
- What is he going to do?
- What would it be like to be the man in the picture?
- What are the differences between life now and life at the time the photograph was taken?
- Would you like to have been alive then? Why not?
- How serious a problem is unemployment in your country today?

1940

22

Dictate these words to your partner:

approximately   beauty   matter   quickly   edge   cheerful   wreck   lazy   information   cough   halve

Silent letters: height   doubt   whistle   knowledge   calm   heart   exhibition

23 Imagine that you are going to give advice to someone who is going to buy A NEW BICYCLE or A NEW WATCH. They have never owned one before. What would you tell them? Make some notes. When you're ready, join another pair.
1 Offer them your advice on buying a bicycle or watch.
2 Then ask for their advice on buying a new camera or a personal stereo.

24 Here are three scenes from a film. Your partners have more scenes from the same film. How did the story start, continue and finish? Where do these scenes fit in?

1 Explain your version of the story beginning: 'This is what happened: ...'
2 When each of you has given your version, look at each other's scenes and decide on a version of the story that includes all the pictures.

25 These are the correct spellings of the words on the tape:

slipping sleeping   trouble robber   total putting
address doubled   request Christian   angle ignorant
engine average   adventure butcher   careful million
often sudden   immense coming   worry railway   please assistant
pleasure insurance   laughing rough   convince live   theory themselves
twelve while   university yawning

26 Here are just a few ideas on the attractions and drawbacks of some of the jobs listed on page 163. Your partners have different ideas.
AUTHOR: ✓ ✓ ✓   Working at home, no boss
CARPENTER: ✓ ✓ ✓   Your own boss, working with your hands
GOVERNMENT MINISTER: ✗ ✗ ✗   18 hours a day, no holidays
NURSE: ✗ ✗ ✗   Long hours; work can be upsetting
POSTMAN/WOMAN: ✗ ✗ ✗   Not so good in bad weather, dogs may be a problem
SALES REPRESENTATIVE: £££   Excellent, if successful
SECRETARY: £££   Quite good
SHOP ASSISTANT: £££   Not very good
TAXI DRIVER: ✓ ✓ ✓   You're your own boss

When you've looked at these notes, go back to page 163 and continue your discussion – DON'T read the notes aloud.

27

Compare these model paragraphs with your own work.

The ideal gift for Chris would be the Alarm Wallet. As he is likely to earn a lot of money while he is working in the USA, the wallet will keep the money safe. During his journey around the country he needs to be sure that his money isn't stolen and that he doesn't lose it accidentally. I'm sure that Chris would be pleased to receive this as a gift and that it would be very useful. It has plenty of room inside for tickets and loose change – and all the dollars he'll earn in the USA!

As Jo likes music and singing, the ideal gift would be the Voice Over. However, this is very expensive and I could only afford it if several of us shared the cost. So it seems that the Beach Chair would be the best present for her. Jo enjoys reading and going to the beach, so she would certainly find it very useful. There's room in it for keeping drinks and sandwiches cool and, I suppose, for a couple of books. Once she gets to the beach she can unfold it and sit comfortably in the sun.

28

Here are some ideas you might like to mention to your partners:

> More people will use public transport in the future:
> one bus can take 100 people   a train can take 1,000 people
> one car can take only 4 (maximum)
> private cars will be banned from city centres
> heavier traffic will discourage people from using their cars

29

Look at this recipe with your partner and make sure you understand it. Is this something you'd like to make and/or drink?

OLD-FASHIONED LEMONADE – a refreshing drink, rich in vitamin C

4 juicy lemons
500g sugar (brown or white)
1 litre water

1 Peel the lemons thinly, removing only the rind, and squeeze the juice into a large bowl. Add the sugar.
2 Boil the lemon rind in the water for a few minutes.
3 Remove the rind and pour the water over the juice and sugar. Mix well to dissolve the sugar.
4 Pour the liquid into clean bottles and put them in the refrigerator.
5 Shake well before serving. Dilute with cold water to taste.

Join another pair and explain this recipe to them IN YOUR OWN WORDS. They will be telling you how to make a different refreshing drink.

30

Here are just a few ideas on the attractions and drawbacks of some of the jobs listed on page 163. Your partners have different ideas.

- AUTHOR: ✘ ✘ ✘ Income is not regular, no workmates
- CARPENTER: ✘ ✘ ✘ Physically tiring
- GOVERNMENT MINISTER: £££ Excellent, but only when in office
- NURSE: £££ Not good enough
- POSTMAN/WOMAN: £££ Not good
- SALES REPRESENTATIVE: ✓ ✓ ✓ Meeting people; being out of the office
- SECRETARY: ✓ ✓ ✓ Can be interesting, comfortable conditions
- SHOP ASSISTANT: ✓ ✓ ✓ Meeting people, working in a team
- TAXI DRIVER: ✘ ✘ ✘ Unhealthy; some passengers can be difficult

When you've looked at these notes, go back to page 163 and continue your discussion – DON'T read the notes aloud.

31

This is your problem. Tell your partners about it:

– locked yourself out of your car
– keys inside, including house keys – all your money inside – 2 o'clock in the morning

Begin like this: 'Oh no, what am I going to do? ...'

Try to think of drawbacks and objections to each suggestion that is made!

32

Tell your partner how to draw this diagram on page 27.

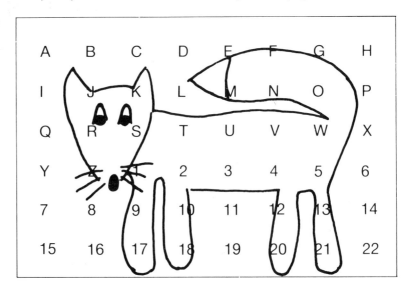

33   Imagine that you and your partners need a break. Why don't you go away somewhere together? This advertisement in the paper has caught your eye – it looks a great idea.

Tell your partners why they would enjoy a few days in an English Country Cottage.

NOT TOO LATE
We can still offer high season vacancies in a choice of 760 cottages throughout England and Wales. For our FREE full colour brochures telephone our Dial-a-Brochure service on FAKENHAM (0328) 4041 or write to:

English Country Cottages
DEPT SO42
FAKENHAM, NORFOLK NR21 8AS

34

35   Here are explanations of some of the items on the menu on page 142, so that you can help your partners to understand them. DO NOT just read these descriptions out loud – try to remember them, so that you can answer your partners' questions.
When you're all clear about everything, decide what to order for each course.

Cottage pie   Minced beef in gravy topped with mashed potato – could be nasty!
Nut and mushroom roast   Nuts, mushrooms and rice made into a kind of loaf and cooked in the oven – tasty and suitable for vegetarians!
Blackberry fool   Cooked blackberries and sugar whipped up with fresh cream and served cold.

36 This is your problem. Tell your partners about it:

– middle of holiday in foreign country – run out of cash – no traveller's cheques – no credit cards – no friends in this country

Begin like this: 'Oh dear, what can I do? ...'

Try to think of drawbacks and objections to each suggestion that is made!

37 CORRECTED VERSION of 1.10 C. As there are no firm rules for punctuation in English, there are a number of possible variations to this version.

Every Tuesday, Friday and Saturday in our part of the city, there's an open-air market in the main square which everyone goes to. Farmers come in from the countryside to sell their fresh vegetables and fruit. Other stalls sell all kinds of things: cheese, jeans, fish and even second-hand furniture. It's almost impossible to carry on a conversation above the noise and shouting as customers push their way to the front, trying to attract the stall-holder's [or stall-holders'] attention and demanding the ripest, freshest fruit or the lowest prices.

38 Take it in turns with your partner to describe each person in your photos – their appearance AND the kind of people they seem to be. Make notes on what your partner tells you.

Start with the person on the left of the group in your photo.

39 With your partner, study the details below and prepare to explain to another pair how SOAP works. What questions do you think you may be asked? Don't join another pair until you have familiarised yourselves with the process.

When you're ready to start, close your book and explain the process FROM MEMORY. Draw a diagram as you explain, if necessary.

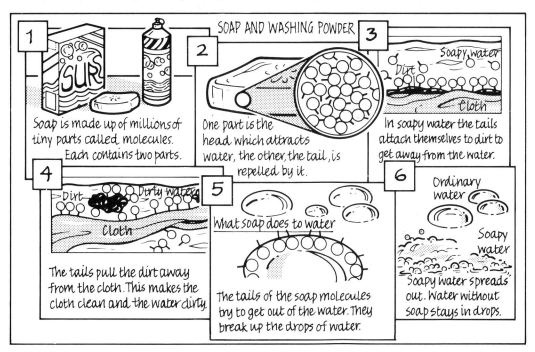

40 Tell your partner how to draw this diagram on page 27.

41

Villa Don Carlos
Marbella, Spain

August 30

Dear John,

It's really lovely here in Spain. The sun's blazing hot and the weather has been perfect. The food's really good too – yesterday we had a marvellous 'paella'. The people too are ever so friendly – we made friends with an old man the other day who helped us to do our shopping (in Spanish) and afterwards we talked to him for ages and he was really interesting.

There are plenty of interesting places to visit nearby. On Sunday we went to a town in the mountains called Ronda, which is full of ancient buildings and was fascinating to explore. We went there by bus which took hours! It was an exciting journey but it's a pity we haven't got a car here, then we could explore the countryside properly. It's such a long drive from England that the best thing would be to hire a car here for a few days.

It really is a shame you couldn't come with us – perhaps next year you'll be able to. As I said, it's a wonderful place and we're having a great time.

Love,
Jenny and Bill x

---

17 Cherry Tree Avenue
Greenwich
London SE11 4IZ

April 1 199#

The Manager
Hotel Romantica
Sea Road
Felixstowe

Dear Sir,

Your hotel has been recommended to me by Mr Charles Brown, who is a regular guest of yours and who has told me quite a lot about the hotel.

I wish to reserve two twin-bedded rooms and one single room for myself and my family (3 adults and 2 children) for 7 nights from July 7th. We should like to have quiet rooms with a bath or shower and which have sea views, preferably with balconies. Would you please inform me of the cost of the rooms with half board and enclose a brochure describing your hotel?

One member of my party is my father-in-law, Mr Black, who will be occupying the single room. He has a small dog which he would like to sleep in his room. Please confirm that this will be convenient. He is also a vegetarian, so please also confirm that you can provide suitable meals for him.

I look forward to hearing from you.

Yours sincerely,
Alan Green

42

Tell your partner this story – as if it really happened to some friends of a friend of yours. DON'T read it aloud word-for-word.

These friends of mine wanted a new carpet, so they went to the shop and chose one and the carpet-fitter came round to fit it while they were out at work. When he had finished he found there was a bump right in the middle. He realised this must be a pack of cigarettes that he'd put down absent-mindedly, so he jumped up and down on the bump till it was flat. The family got home and admired the carpet. Then they asked the man if he had seen their pet canary which was missing. It was then that he noticed his cigarettes on the hall table!

43 Imagine that you and your partners need a break. Why don't you go away somewhere together? This advertisement in the paper has caught your eye – it looks a really nice idea.

Tell your partners why they would enjoy a few days in a villa in Italy.

> **IT'S MAGIC!
> VILLAS IN
> ROMANTIC ITALY**
>
> We've discovered villas in the lovelier parts of Italy, from love nests for two to family villas for up to seven. Our new discovery is the charming village of Atrani, below Ravello —a beautiful old house divided into five high quality apartments with spectacular views from £189. In Cefalu, Sicily, extra studios and apartments on the promenade from £199. FREE colour brochure from:
>
> **Magic of Italy**
>
> Dept. ST, Russell Chambers, London WC2E 8AW. Tel. 01-240 5984 or after hours 01-240 5986.
> ABTA   ATOL 488B

44

45 Here are just a few ideas on the attractions and drawbacks of some of the jobs listed on page 163. Your partners have different ideas.

- AUTHOR: £££ Good, but only if you're successful
- CARPENTER: £££ Not very good
- GOVERNMENT MINISTER: ✓✓✓ Power, serving his/her country
- NURSE: ✓✓✓ Looking after people, belonging to a team
- POSTMAN/WOMAN: ✓✓✓ Popular with the public, fresh air
- SALES REPRESENTATIVE: ✗✗✗ Insecure job, a lot of travelling
- SECRETARY: ✗✗✗ A bad boss can be difficult to work with
- SHOP ASSISTANT: ✗✗✗ Long hours, some customers can be difficult
- TAXI DRIVER: £££ Good, but only when business is good

When you've looked at these notes, go back to page 163 and continue your discussion – DON'T read the notes aloud.

46

Here are three scenes from a film. Your partners have more scenes from the same film. How did the story start, continue and finish? Where do these scenes fit in?

1. Explain your version of the story, beginning: 'This is what happened: ...'
2. When each of you has given your version, look at each other's scenes and decide on a version of the story that includes all the pictures.

47

With your partner, study the details below and prepare to explain to another pair how A CASSETTE works. What questions do you think you may be asked?

Don't join another pair until you have familiarised yourselves with the process. When you're ready to start, close your book and explain the process FROM MEMORY. Draw a diagram as you explain, if necessary.

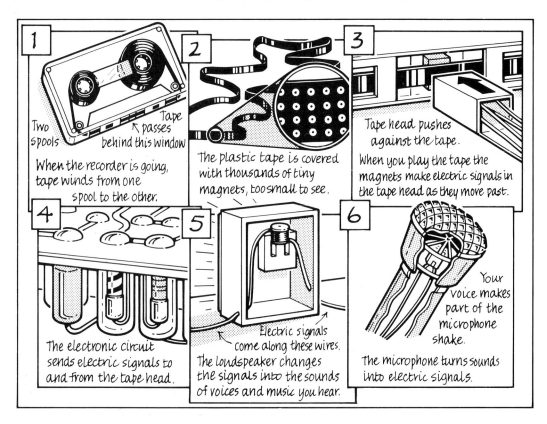

1. Two spools. Tape passes behind this window. When the recorder is going, tape winds from one spool to the other.
2. The plastic tape is covered with thousands of tiny magnets, too small to see.
3. Tape head pushes against the tape. When you play the tape the magnets make electric signals in the tape head as they move past.
4. The electronic circuit sends electric signals to and from the tape head.
5. Electric signals come along these wires. The loudspeaker changes the signals into the sounds of voices and music you hear.
6. Your voice makes part of the microphone shake. The microphone turns sounds into electric signals.

48

Here are explanations of some of the items on the menu on page 142, so that you can help your partners to understand them. DO NOT just read these descriptions out loud – try to remember them, so that you can answer your partners' questions.
When you're all clear about everything, decide what to order for each course.

Lancashire Hotpot   Lamb and vegetables cooked in the oven with a layer of potatoes on top – very tasty!
Chicken Madras   Chicken pieces in an Indian curry sauce – very hot!
Bread and butter pudding   Layers of bread and butter with raisins and cream, baked in the oven till crisp and chewy – delicious!

49

Take it in turns with your partner to describe each person in your photos – their appearance AND the kind of people they seem to be. Make notes on what your partner tells you.
Start with the person on the left of the group in your photo.

50

This is your problem. Tell your partners about it:

– on an excursion – coach has left without you – in the middle of nowhere – no public transport – money and raincoat on the coach – just started to pour with rain

Begin like this: 'Oh my goodness, what shall I do? ...'

Try to think of drawbacks and objections to each suggestion that is made!

To the self-study student

Using the self-study notes

This part of the book contains:
- Self-study instructions on how to use the main part of the book on your own;
- Answers and model compositions or paragraphs;
- Tapescripts for the listening exercises;
- Extra ideas and advice.

Follow this procedure when working on your own:
1. Read the self-study instructions for part **A** of the section.
2. Do the exercise or activity in **A** in the main part of the book.
3. Check your answers with the model answers (if these are given).
4. Look at any extra ideas or advice (shown with this symbol: ▶).
5. Follow the self-study instructions for part **B** of the section.
6. Do part **B** in the main part of the book.
7. Check your answers.
    ... and so on.

Answers and models

The answers, model compositions and model paragraphs in this part of the book will help you to check your answers and learn more. In some cases, where the questions are open-ended, suggested answers are given and variations may be possible. When a model is given, you should compare your work with this – but you should ask a teacher or an English-speaking person to correct your work from time to time, so that you can find out what kind of mistakes you are making.

When you make mistakes or can't answer questions, make sure that you learn from your mistakes. In fact, it's impossible to learn if you don't make mistakes – if you got everything right it would mean you knew everything already!

Working without a teacher

Working alone using the self-study notes will help you to improve your reading, writing and listening skills, but you should try to get someone to read your written work and correct it. If you are using *Progress to First Certificate* completely on your own without a teacher or other students in a class, the self-study notes tell you how you can do the speaking activities using a cassette recorder with a microphone – but if possible you should do some of these with another person.

Working regularly with a partner will give you a chance to discuss what you have been doing and read each other's work. You will find that you will learn a lot from each other and it will help you to feel that you are making progress. If possible, arrange a regular session each week when you can work together.

▶ Whenever you are doing an exercise in cooperation with another student, follow the instructions in the main part of the book.

The self-study notes at the back of the book tell you how to use each exercise in the main part of the book when you are working alone.

Working partly on your own

Parts of *Progress to First Certificate* can be used in class and other parts can be done by you working alone. Your teacher will advise you which parts you should do on your own, depending on how much time is available for work in class – in this case you may be expected to check some of the answers yourself. You should try to work through any exercises for which there is no time in class on your own.

Students who are unable to follow a complete classroom course, through illness or other commitments, will find this book especially valuable. You will be able to catch up on work you miss and perhaps rejoin the class later – or go on working on your own if you are unable to continue attending classes.

What you need

- A piece of card, the same size as this book, to cover up the model answers in this part of the book while you read the self-study notes. This will stop you seeing the answers by mistake.
- An exercise book in which to write your answers to the exercises and your compositions, and a smaller pocket-sized notebook for your vocabulary notes.
- A yellow highlighter pen, for marking the useful vocabulary and expressions in the passages and tapescripts.
- The set of two cassettes for the listening exercises and the pronunciation exercises.
- A cassette recorder (with a microphone) for listening to the cassettes and recording your own voice.
- A good English-to-English dictionary: the *Longman Dictionary of Contemporary English*, the *Oxford Advanced Learner's Dictionary*, the *Collins COBUILD Essential English Dictionary* or the *Penguin Wordmaster Dictionary* are all excellent.
- A good bilingual dictionary – but a tiny pocket-sized one is NOT good enough. Ask for advice on which one to choose if you don't already possess one.
- A good reference grammar book to answer your questions on English grammar: *English Grammar in Use* WITH ANSWERS by Raymond Murphy (Cambridge University Press) or *Basic English Usage* by Michael Swan (Oxford University Press) are recommended.
- Shortly before the exam, you should work through the test papers in *Cambridge First Certificate Examination Practice 3* (Cambridge University Press) and you'll need the accompanying Teacher's Book, which contains the correct answers.

Exam enrolment

If you are entering for the First Certificate exam (which is held in June and December), remember that you will need to enrol for it at least three months in advance. In some centres the last date for enrolment is even earlier. If you are studying in your own country, a British Council office can give you the address of your nearest centre.

Notes and answer key for each unit

1 Shopping

The notes for this unit are longer than later units – they explain how the different types of exercises work and suggest how you should use them. You should do all the exercises in this unit, but in later units you may decide to leave some exercises out.

1.1 Shopping habits   *Vocabulary*

A   Imagine that someone is asking you these questions: say your answers aloud softly to yourself. Use a dictionary to look up any words you need. You may prefer to write down your answers to some of the questions.

B   Do the whole exercise in the main part of the book IN PENCIL or in your exercise book, using a dictionary to look up any words you are unsure of. There will probably be several gaps that you can't fill. When you have finished, check your answers below and correct any mistakes you made.

Then use a piece of paper or card to cover up the right-hand side of the page and test yourself. Can you remember the words which are now hidden by the paper or card?

If you have written the answers in pencil, you can rub them out and do the exercise again during another session – this will help you to remember the new words you are learning. If you have written them in your exercise book, use a fresh page when you do the exercise again.

Answers

(Notice that in 15 and 25 several answers are possible.)
2 signature;   3 shopkeeper;   4 shop assistant/sales assistant;   5 counter;   6 help looking;   7 sale bargain;   8 total;
9 receipt;   10 guarantee;   11 shoplifting;
12 chemist's/pharmacy;   13 trying;
14 size;   15 fit long/short/tight/loose/baggy/uncomfortable;   16 stock;   17 match suit;
18 label;   19 market;   20 discount;
21 greengrocer's;   22 hire purchase;
23 department store   mail order;
24 deliver;   25 boring/fun/tedious/enjoyable/exhausting/a waste of time/unpleasant/tiring, etc.

Try to work out why any answers you got wrong were wrong – and why the answers given above are correct.

C   Write down the names of the shops, using a dictionary where necessary.

(In different countries the goods may be sold in different kinds of shops.)
 2 stationer's/newsagent's/kiosk   bookshop/bookseller's
 3 dairy/grocer's/corner shop   hardware store/ironmonger's
 4 greengrocer's   hardware store/ironmonger's
 5 butcher's   hardware store/ironmonger's
 6 off-licence/wine store   hardware store/ironmonger's/wine store
 7 electrical dealer's/radio shop   music shop/record shop
 8 baker's   grocer's/dairy/corner shop
 9 stationer's   stationer's
10 chemist's/pharmacy   chemist's/pharmacy
11 kiosk/newsagent's/sweet shop   post office/newsagent's

D   Write down the words you would use to describe your own clothes and also the clothes of another person you know well. Again, use a dictionary.

▶ Each time you go shopping, take a look at the shops 'through English eyes' and see if you can put names to everything you see. Perhaps

229

take a pocket dictionary with you. Do this for a different type of shop or department each time.

▶ To help you to remember new vocabulary you should note down any useful English words that you meet in a notebook.

1.2 Enter a different world   *Reading*

Reading exercises

The reading sections in *Progress to First Certificate* usually contain:
A A 'first reading' task which helps you to understand the main points of the passage, often by reading the passage through fairly quickly. In some cases, there are questions about your previous knowledge of the subject.
B A 'second reading' task: reading comprehension questions which help you to develop your reading skills and understand the details of the text, by reading the passage again more slowly and carefully.
C A 'post-reading' task in which you discuss the information given in the passage – this can be recorded on a blank cassette or done with a partner.

Some reading sections also contain vocabulary exercises, which will help you to understand difficult passages without using a dictionary to look up the unfamiliar words. Whenever you read a passage for the first time, it's best not to use a dictionary – you'll find that you can often guess the meaning of unfamiliar words from their context.

▶ The passages in *Progress to First Certificate* come from a wide variety of sources: magazines, newspapers, books, advertisements, etc. However, you should also read more English in books, newspapers or magazines for your own pleasure and to improve your vocabulary and reading skills.

A This is a 'prediction' exercise. This kind of exercise will help you to use your previous knowledge when you read the passage, and will make it easier to understand.
When you have made a note of your answers, read the passage through to see whether you guessed right.

2 T   It's a landmark of London (see paragraph 4)
3 T   See paragraph 3
4 F   'anything from a pin to an elephant'
5 T   Look at the royal crest at the top of the page
6 F   It's the second largest

B These questions check whether you have understood some of the details of the text. To answer the questions, you will have to read the text very carefully.

1 F   'a suitable elephant owner'
2 T   '*no* other store can'
3 F   '500 types of shirts'
4 F   '57 malts'
5 T   'circulating library'
6 T   'funeral service'
7 T   'Los Angeles' – which is in the USA
8 T   '£40 million worth ... annually' – $40 \div 12 = 3\frac{1}{3}$
9 F   '4,000 regular staff rising to 6,000' – they take on 2,000 temporary staff at Christmas
10 T 'will deal with a wider range'
11 F 'from any assistant in the store'
12 F 'the time of delivery will be guaranteed to within one hour'
13 F 'the building ... was started in 1901'
14 F 'reasonable prices'
15 T 'as many cream cakes ... as your greed will allow'

▶ Questions like the ones in **B** will help you to read passages more carefully. Try not to use a dictionary too often. Usually you can guess the meaning of an unfamiliar word from its context – or you may find that you can understand the text perfectly well without knowing the exact meaning of every word.

C Decide how you would answer the questions and say your answers aloud softly to yourself. Perhaps record yourself on a blank cassette.

Some things you might say in answer to the questions

1 Price: things are not necessarily any cheaper in a department store
  Choice: department stores often stock a wide range of products

Service: you get personal service in a department store, which you don't get in a supermarket
Quality: department stores often stock top quality merchandise
Convenience: you can usually look around without being approached by assistants

2 Bread, for example, is usually fresher and may be cheaper if you get it from a local baker.
3 Can you buy a car or a flat or a book, for example? OR would you have to go to a car showroom/garage, an estate agent or a bookshop for these?

1.3 Present tenses   *Grammar*

All the grammar sections in *Progress to First Certificate* are REVISION. The examples and exercises cover the main difficulties that students have with English grammar. More basic and more advanced points are not covered. For a more detailed explanation and further examples, you should refer to your grammar book – *English Grammar in Use* WITH ANSWERS by Raymond Murphy (Cambridge University Press) or *Basic English Usage* by Michael Swan (Oxford University Press) are recommended.

A Fill the gaps with your own examples, as this will help you to memorise the rules that are shown.

Suggested answers

Permanent or regular actions and situations:
I never **drink coffee before I go to bed.**
Every evening I **watch the news on TV and then I have dinner.**

Temporary, developing or changing actions and situations:
At the moment I **am sitting in class doing this exercise.**
I **am taking** a First Certificate course this year.

Actions or situations begun in the past and still true now or continuing now:
We **have spent two** hours on this unit so far.

B As your examples will contain your own ideas, only a few are suggested below.

A few suggested sentences

Thomas doesn't deserve to go out tonight.
These boots don't fit, they're too small.
I don't know what Maria means.   etc.

C This is the most difficult grammar exercise so far in this unit. The numbers in the answers refer to the sentences in the main part of the book.

at the moment – 1
from time to time – 3
occasionally – 2
sometimes – 2
every week – 3
generally – 2
often – 2
.this morning – 1
for a long time – 4
hardly ever – 2

once in a while – 3
today – 1
for a week – 4
never – 2
rarely – 2
usually – 2
frequently – 2
now – 1 (or 2)
since Tuesday – 4

▶ We return to the problems of adverb order in 12.3.

D The error-correction exercises in the grammar sections will help you to recognise mistakes when you're checking your own written work.

2 I am reading
3 I sometimes buy
4 ✓ *no errors*
5 prefers
6 I have been waiting
7 costs
8 ✓ *no errors*

E The answers given here are suggestions only – many variations are possible.

Assistant: Good morning, have you been waiting long?
Customer: No, only for a few moments. Could you help me, please?
Assistant: Certainly. **What can I do for you / are you looking for?**
Customer: I'm looking for a pair of jeans in my size.
Assistant: What **size do you take?**
Customer: I take a size 30, normally.
Assistant: Thirty. Well, we have these Levis on special offer. Do **you like the look of these / these look all right?**
Customer: Oh, very nice, yes, I like that style very much.

Assistant: You can try them on in the changing room over there.
Customer: Oh, right, thanks. I'll just see if they fit.

(*The customer tries them on.*)

Assistant: Do **they fit / they seem all right**?
Customer: Yes, they fit perfectly. How much **do they cost / are they**?
Assistant: £16.99. Is there anything else you'd like to see?
Customer: Yes, have **you got any jackets / a jacket to match**?
Assistant: I'm afraid we're out of stock of the matching jackets at the moment, but we'll be getting some more in soon.
Customer: When **will they arrive / will you be getting them / will they be delivered**?
Assistant: We're expecting a delivery at the end of the week. If you like, I'll put one aside for you when they come in.
Customer: Oh, thanks very much. And I think I'll keep these jeans on now. Do **you take Visa/Access/American Express**?
Assistant: Yes, we take all major credit cards.
Customer: Good, here you are.
Assistant: Thanks. Let me just cut off the label … there we are! And if you could just sign here …

1.4 I had to go to the shops … *Listening*

Listening exercises

Before you listen to the recording, read these notes through carefully and look at the questions in the main part of the book. Then, if necessary, listen to each conversation two or three times.

The recordings on the cassette are all un-simplified, natural conversations or interviews or radio programmes. The speakers talk at their normal speed. Each recording lasts only a few minutes, so it's quick and easy to listen to them several times if you need to. In the exam itself, you'll hear each listening passage twice through.

The questions you have to answer in the exercises or the gaps you have to fill in are the only things you need to worry about. DON'T WORRY if you can't understand every word that's spoken or if parts of a conversation seem very fast to you. No one, not even a native speaker of English, can catch every single word that's spoken in a conversation. So, all you have to do is to concentrate on understanding the information given by the speakers. If you can answer the questions, then you have understood all the important information.

In other words, DON'T PANIC if the voices seem very fast or if the speakers use some words you don't know. Just listen to the recording again a couple of times, looking at the questions in the main part of the book, and you'll soon find that you do understand all that you need to in each conversation. If necessary, pause the recording while you note down the answers.

There is a tapescript for each listening exercise. Don't look at this until you have heard the recording at least twice through.

A Follow this procedure, and do the same with the other listening exercises.

1 Read the questions through.

2 ▭ Listen to the first 20 to 30 seconds of the recording so that you can get used to the unfamiliar voices. Don't try to answer the questions and don't look at the tapescript. (You may find it easier to concentrate if you close your eyes while you're doing this.)

3 ▭ Listen to the recording all the way through and answer the questions. If necessary, PAUSE the tape during the conversation – this will give you time to think about your answers to the questions.

4 ▭ If you have only been able to answer a few of the questions, listen to the whole conversation again and concentrate on finding the answers you missed or were unsure about. Again, PAUSE the tape where necessary.

5 Check your answers. If you have made any mistakes, it means you have misunderstood the speakers or the question.

6 ▭ Listen to the recording again, but this time follow it in the tapescript, checking any wrong answers as you go. Again, PAUSE the tape where necessary. Use a yellow highlighter pen to mark any useful new words or expressions.

7 ▭ Listen to the whole conversation all the way through. Sit back, close your eyes and listen – this will help you to appreciate

and learn the sounds of English conversation, pronunciation and vocabulary.

▶ Looking at the tapescript earlier would make the task much easier – but this will not help you to improve your listening skills.

▶ A low-pitched tone is recorded between each section on the cassette. When the tape is played forwards or backwards fast on CUE or REVIEW you will hear this as a high-pitched *beep* which makes it easy to find where each new section begins on the cassette.

Answers

TRUE: 2, 3, 6, 8, 10, 11; FALSE: 4, 5, 7, 9, 12.

Tapescript

(Don't look at this until you have answered all the questions.)

Narrator: Look at your Student's Book before you listen to the recording. You'll probably need to hear the recording at least twice before you can answer all the questions in the Student's Book.
Ann: Hello, Tim, you look really worn out! What's happened? How come you're so late?
Tim: I'm sorry. I had to go to the shops...used up my whole lunch hour.
Ann: W...why didn't you wait till you got home?
Tim: Oh, no, I'm going out this evening. Honestly, I had to queue at that checkout for fifteen minutes, I swear. I only wanted a couple of things.
Ann: Well, how come you didn't go to the fast one if you only had a couple of things?
Tim: Oh no, the queue was even worse there, it always is.
Ann: You know, you sound as if you hate shopping.
Tim: Oh, I don't know...I don't generally hate shopping as such, I just hate certain kinds of shopping, you know. I don't mind buying clothes and things...er...can't stand buying food.
Ann: I like shopping for food. I don't know, I think...I think, you know, finding a present for somebody else is the hardest thing. You just don't...you just don't know where to start, you know?
Tim: Oh, I don't mind that. Oh no, I like that, I like buying presents and things, as long as I've got some time, you know. I don't like the sales, mind you, they're the pits.
Ann: Oh yeah! Or the shops, you know, just before Christmas – the crowds!

Tim: Awful! Oh yeah, I hate 'em. What I like... what I like and what you don't see much of these days is those little shops, you know, little corner shops and things, where you get...where, you know, where the bloke knows you and you get a...sort of...personal service...
Ann: And they're little and they're crowded and you always have to wait a long time – no, no come on, a big supermarket's the best thing, you've got...you've got the whole range of everything you might possibly want, the prices are lower, you've got to admit that, come on.
Tim: Yeah, yeah.
Ann: You've got the car park – you can just drive in, load your shopping into the car, drive away again. It's easy, there's no hassle.
Tim: Yes, it's too easy. It's too easy to spend all your money. I mean they...they...sort of...lull you with a...sort of...horrible music and stuff and you end up...I mean there's so much there. You...you buy the stuff you don't really want, you spend all your money!
Ann: Haha. Well, you know, I...I think shopping can be hard work though anyway, I agree with you there. I order a lot of things, you know, from catalogues. You can look through, you know, in your own spare time and phone in and then...and then it arrives at your doorstep. It's all so easy. Now, that's what I like, it's easy!
Tim: That's what I mean! It's too easy. I tell you it...it's sending you to sleep, it's brainwashing you. One day we'll have...we'll have computers and we'll be able to order everything we want from our...from our living room and it'll be delivered by robots to our doors. And you'll never leave home, you'll never meet anybody! Not for me, I...I prefer the personal touch.
Ann: Well, I think perhaps we'd better get on with some work.
Tim: Perhaps you're right.

(Time: 2 minutes 25 seconds)

B You may need to use a dictionary to do this vocabulary exercise.

a bottle of mineral water; a box of matches; a can of Coke; a carton (or bottle) of milk; a jar of honey; a bar of chocolate (not really a 'container', but it is how chocolate is sold – note that a 'box of chocolates' is a box containing layers of small chocolates); a packet of biscuits; a tin (or can) of peas; a tube of toothpaste.

1.5 Abbreviations and numbers
Word study

A Use a dictionary to check any abbreviations you don't know.

c/o	care of
cont'd	continued
GMT	Greenwich Mean Time
incl.	including/inclusive
info.	information
intro.	introduction
max.	maximum
min.	minimum
misc.	miscellaneous
PTO	please turn over
RSVP	please reply to this invitation (French: *répondez s'il vous plaît*)
VAT	value-added tax
VIP	very important person (a celebrity)
vocab.	vocabulary
Xmas	Christmas

▶ The use of full stops in abbreviations in English is often optional – GMT is also sometimes written G.M.T., for example. If the abbreviation consists only of capital letters, the full stops are often omitted in modern English. If the abbreviation is a short form of a longer word, the full stop is usually necessary.

▶ The best way to learn abbreviations is by noticing them when you come across them. Most abbreviations can be written in their full form if you prefer.

▶ Use a dictionary to find out what these English abbreviations mean – some dictionaries contain lists of abbreviations at the end.
   a.m.   p.m.   i.e.   e.g.   St   Rd   Ave   Sq

B Notice that spelling and the use of hyphens are important here.

144	a hundred and forty-four
113	a hundred and thirteen
227	two hundred and twenty-seven
850,000	eight hundred and fifty thousand
5.75	five point seven five
1,992	one thousand nine hundred and ninety-two
$\frac{7}{8}$	seven-eighths

$1\frac{1}{4} + 2\frac{2}{3} = 3.9167$ one and a quarter plus two and two-thirds equals three point nine one six seven

$4\frac{3}{4} - 2\frac{1}{2} = 2.25$ four and three-quarters minus two and a half equals two point two five

C This exercise practises understanding numbers when they are spoken. Examples 1 to 6 are telephone numbers, examples 7 to 12 are normal numbers, 13 to 16 are times and 17 to 20 are prices.

Play the tape and PAUSE it after each sentence while you write down the numbers you hear. Then listen to the whole recording again to check what you wrote.

2	617930	12	3.142
3	01 225 8915	13	3.45
4	044 202 892671	14	10.50
5	0473 993313	15	7.35
6	879615	16	7.15 (or 7.17?)
7	5,180,477	17	£45.99
8	617,930	18	$12.15
9	40,515	19	£140 + VAT
10	14,550	20	90p
11	17,170,660		

D Use your cassette recorder with a microphone and a BLANK cassette (not one of the *Progress to First Certificate* tapes):
1 Record all the information that is given in Activity 1 (page 209) on the cassette.
2 A little later, play it back to yourself and write down the information, pausing the tape frequently.
3 Look again at Activity 1 and check whether you got all the information correct – were any mistakes your fault as a reader or your fault as a listener?
4 Do the same with the information in Activity 10.

1.6 Advertisements
Speaking and listening

A Write down your reactions to the advertisement or, if you prefer, just say what you think to yourself. What would you say to another person about it?

B Look at Activity 13 and record your description of the advertisement on a blank cassette. Then listen to your recording and use a dictionary to find any words you needed to describe the advertisement. Then do the same with Activity 20.

C 🎧 Listen to each commercial separately – it is not necessary to understand every word. These commercials are all authentic and may contain unfamiliar vocabulary.

PAUSE between each commercial to check your answers. Look at the next set of words and gaps before you listen to the next commercial.

When you've checked all your answers, listen to all five commercials while looking at the tapescript.

Finally, listen to them again with your eyes closed – and enjoy them!

1 10 a.m. to 5 p.m.
2 olive oil   olive oils   natural
3 cool   hot   portable   conditioners   sweat
4 spring   orange   seriously
5 fries   hamburgers   pineapple   anything   ketchup   more   more   waste   thick   smooth   dinner

Tapescript

1
Harrods would like to suggest five places to spend this Bank Holiday Monday, August 29th: our ground floor, our first floor, our second floor, our third floor and our fourth floor. Harrods: open 10 a.m. to 5 p.m. for people who would like to spend this Bank Holiday spending.

2
Have you discovered that wonderful Italian, Filippo Berio? I mean Filippo Berio Olive Oil, of course. Pure olive oil is perfect for frying and extra virgin olive oil is divine in salad dressings. Filippo Berio is just so incredibly versatile that naturally you wouldn't choose to cook without it. Filippo Berio Olive Oils: the natural choice.

3
Man: The heatwave was all over the front pages, I was my usual cool self.
Woman: Darling, the heat in the office is unbearable. I need someone to cool me down quickly.
Man: The lady was hot. It was another job for the Heatbusters. In less time than it takes an ice cube to melt, a portable air conditioning unit was installed and working. The lady simmered down.
Woman: You Heatbusters are so wonderful! Why don't we s...?
Man: It was time to leave. Portable air conditioning on hire. For written details call Freefone Heatbusters – no sweat.

4
noises
1st man: No, no they're not right. Sorry.
2nd man: How about – *noise*?
1st man: Oh, no, no, no, no.
2nd man: What exactly are you trying to achieve?
1st man: Well, the sound of an orange dropping, preferably a big juicy Citrus Spring orange.
2nd man: How about – *noise*?
1st man: Mm, what was that?
2nd man: Well, it's actually a grapefruit but...um...I reckon if I work on it...
1st man: Hmm, people'll spot it. How about the second half of the melon with the first one we had? *noise* Not really.
2nd man: I could do you a raspberry.
1st man: No, thanks, Mike.
2nd man: Look, why don't you just say it tastes great? You know the sort of thing: 'A sparkling blend of spring water and natural orange juice'. Um, I mean, this is a seriously fruity drink.
1st man: If it was that easy, we'd have done it, Mike.
2nd man: More?
1st man: Yeah, keep going. *noises* No. No. Interesting. No...
3rd man: Citrus Spring – *noises* – the seriously fruity drink.
1st man: That's it! Perfect!
2nd man: Love it.

5
Men: Doowahbeketchup, bedoowah, bedoobedoobe...
Girls: Gee, Lucy, was that Dirk Studebaker outside your house last night?
Lucy: Uhuh.
Girls: What on earth did you do to get him out of his car?
Lucy: Can't you guess?
Girls: Oh, Lucy, you didn't!
Lucy: Yes, I did!
I cooked him dinner: frankfurters and fries, with two hamburgers and for a surprise, we had some gammon with a pineapple ring, that's what I cooked him.
Girls: Did you miss anything?
Lucy: Don't think so.
Girls: Was the ketchup on the side of his plate?

Lucy: It was Heinz, it was Heinz on his plate.
Girls: Well, ah well, oh well, oh
   give me more, give me more
   of that Heinz Ketchup taste.
   Eat it all, eat it all,
   'cause it's too good to waste.
Men: I do like a dollop of ketchup, of Heinz...
Girl: Are you seeing Dirk again tonight, Lucy?
Lucy: You betcha!!
All: Heinz is the ketchup, so thick and so
   smooth,
   Heinz is the ketchup for dinner for two...

(Time: 3 minutes 50 seconds)

D Look at some magazines and find some attractive and amusing advertisements. What would you say about them in English? Perhaps record yourself.

E Record your descriptions on a blank cassette.

1.7 Which gift? *Problem solving*

Parts **A**, **B** and **C** of this section lead up to the paragraph-writing task in **D**.

A Think about the questions before you do **B**.

B There are no 'correct answers'. Use a dictionary to look up any words you don't understand.

C MAKING NOTES is an essential part of any writing task – it gives you a chance to arrange your ideas in a sensible order and to decide on the order in which you will present them.

When you have made your notes look at the model notes in Activity 4. These are not 'perfect notes'. Different people have different ways of making notes.

D Write the two paragraphs and compare your work with the model paragraphs in Activity 27. Again, the models are not 'perfect answers' and many variations are possible – indeed you may find aspects of them that you want to criticise.

1.8 Using prepositions – Revision *Use of English*

This exercise covers some common uses of prepositions and adverbs that you should already know.

(Note that more than one answer is possible in some cases.)

2 of; 3 of; 4 for; 5 for; 6 about/on;
7 on; 8 off; 9 by; 10 of; 11 at/over;
12 for; 13 by; 14 out of; 15 off;
16 on; 17 off; 18 by/on; 19 off;
20 for; 21 with; 22 at; 23 about;
24 by to; 25 in; 26 of; 27 off;
28 of; 29 at; 30 over; 31 on;
32 under/over; 33 with.

1.9 Buying a camera *Listening*

A If you use a pencil (and have a rubber handy) you can correct any mistaken ideas when you're doing **B** later.

B Follow the same procedure suggested for 1.4 on page 232.

Tapescript

Salesman: ...camera? Yes certainly, madam, this one actually is on special offer this week. It's a good deal at 19.95, so...er...you know, you've struck it lucky. Er...I suppose you'd like to know a bit about...er...
Customer: Oh please, yes. How...how do you load it?
Salesman: How it loads? OK, well look, you ...first of all, it's dead simple, anyone can sort of operate these, you know, they're really...even I can, you know...ha ha...I hope! Anyway, you open it up at the back here, OK? That's where you put in the film cassette. No problem, you just press that and it closes up. And then you set the film speed, you see, if you've got a fast film or a slow film you want to use it either to 100 or 400 and you use this switch here, you see, where it says 100, where it says 400.
Customer: When do you want to use 100 and when do you want to use 400?
Salesman: Well, it depends. I mean, if it's very dark, for example, you'd use 400 or if it's, you know, it's ordin...most often you'd use 100, you know. But if you've got any problems, just

> **ACME INSTAMATIC CAMERA £29.95**   ~~£29.95~~
> INSTRUCTIONS   **SPECIAL OFFER £19.95**
> 1 Load film cassette.
> 2 Set film speed to _100_ or _400_
> 3 Press WIND lever till _1_ appears in the small _window_
> 4 Set focus to symbol of _people_ for close-ups or _mountains_ for landscapes.
> 5 Press shutter very _slightly_
>   If _green_ light appears, shoot picture.
>   If _red_ light appears, switch to _flash_
> 6 Wind film on for next shot.

ask whoever you're going to buy the film off, OK?
Customer: Uhhuh.
Salesman: So then the next thing you want to press the Wind lever until the number 1 appears. You see, in the little window there.
Customer: That's for the first picture?
Salesman: That's right, you've got it, you've got it. You see, it's dead simple. And then you set the focus to the picture, you know, depending on who you're going to take photos of, right?
Customer: Uh...no.
Salesman: Well, I mean, say...say you want to take a picture of me...
Customer: Yes.
Salesman: That's just a portrait picture, you see. You turn it to People...
Customer: Oh right.
Salesman: There, right? If you want to take a big landscape, then...then you put it on Mountains ...dead easy.
Customer: I see, I see. Close-ups or landscapes?
Salesman: That's right, yeah. Then you...then you press the shutter very slightly...yeah...as you look at the subject. Now if the green light appears – do you want to hold it? Here...
Customer: Yes. Right, thanks...I've got it.
Salesman: Right...OK, now if you look through there, if a green light appears in the frame...
Customer: Oh yes, it's appeared!
Salesman: That's right. Well, you go ahead and shoot, you see. But you won't have any luck at the moment because there's no film in there, you see.
Customer: Ha ha.
Salesman: Anyway, if the red appears in the frame, then you have to switch to Flash before shooting.
Customer: Flash?
Salesman: Yeah, well, you just press that little button there and a little, you know, flash thing comes out but you have to buy...
Customer: Oh I see...
Salesman: ...have to buy...you know...it's quite straightforward.
Customer: Have to buy a bulb?
Salesman: Yeah, you have to buy a bulb, yeah. And then finally when you've finished, you just wind the film on before the next shot.
Customer: Oh, that's marvellous. Very simple. Oh, I think I'll have it. Thanks very much.
Salesman: Jolly good, OK, madam. How are you going to pay? By cheque or cash?
Customer: Oh...um...could I pay by Access, please?
Salesman: Certainly.

(Time: 2 minutes)

C Note down the advice you'd give on just one of the items suggested in Activities 16 or 23. Then imagine that you're talking to a friend on the phone and record yourself giving advice. Listen to your recording and decide how you could improve what you said.
   Then try again, but this time with advice on a different purchase.

▶ Keep this recording. You can listen to it again in a few months' time to find out how much your spoken English has improved!

1.10 Starting out...   *Composition*

A The sixteen spelling mistakes are underlined and corrected below:

Please let me know your <u>adress</u>.   **address**
My brother is <u>ninteen</u> years old   **nineteen**

One day he's <u>hopping</u> to go to <u>Amerika</u>.
   hoping   America
It was a <u>realy wonderfull</u> meal!   **realy**
   wonderful
I <u>recieved</u> your letter this morning.   **received**
He <u>want</u> to improve his <u>knoledge</u> of <u>english</u>.
   wants   knowledge   English
Concorde <u>flys accross</u> the Atlantic in 4 <u>ours</u>.
   flies   across   hours
Some people find <u>speling especialy dificult</u>.
   spelling   especially   difficult

★ These notes in the Student's Book are 'useful tips' and 'points to remember' or, later in the book 'advice on exam techniques'.
  The importance of checking written work through carefully is a point that will be emphasised over and over again.

B   Notice that capital letters are used incorrectly as well as apostrophes, commas, etc. The punctuation mistakes are corrected in this version of the text:

Harrods is London's most famous department store. You can buy almost anything there and it's one of the landmarks of London. People come to eat at its restaurants and look round its 214 departments, but not everyone comes to buy. Many of the people who go there are just having a look at the enormous range of goods on display and at the other customers.

▶ Make sure that you know the names of the most common punctuation marks in English: colon, exclamation mark, inverted commas, hyphen, etc.
  Use a dictionary to find out any you are unsure of:

! ? . , ; : ' "
— — ( )

C   The corrected version of the unpunctuated paragraph is in Activity 37. Some variations are possible.

D   Think about the questions before beginning E.

E   Write the two paragraphs, following the instructions in the main part of the book.

▶ If possible, with this and in later composition exercises, ask a teacher or an English-speaking person to read your work and advise you how it could be improved.

1.11   *Look* and *see*   Verbs and idioms

A   This section deals with some common synonyms of LOOK and SEE. As we are dealing with synonyms, several variations are possible.

2 watched;   3 gazed/looked;   4 see/recognise/notice;   5 recognise;   6 noticed/seen/recognised;   7 watch;   8 seen;   9 see;   10 looks.

B   Use an English-to-English dictionary to look up any words that you don't understand.
  Many phrasal verbs can be replaced with equivalent 'normal verbs' – as this exercise shows. Quite often the phrasal verb is more informal than its 'normal' equivalent.

3 looking for;   4 Look out;   5 look up to;   6 see to;   7 looking into;   8 saw through;   9 look up;   10 look in;   11 look through it/look it through;   12 looking forward to.

▶ Here are some more examples of the four types of phrasal verb:
1 The same as a verb + preposition:
  look for   look into   and also   *answer for   watch for*
2 Intransitive phrasal verbs (with no object) – none in this exercise, but: *go away   come back   the plane took off*
3 'Separable' phrasal verbs:
  see off   see through   look through   and also   *pick up   take off a coat*
4 'Inseparable' phrasal verbs (these include the ones with a preposition and a particle):
  look forward to   see to   and also   *do with   do without*
Notice that, structurally, type 1 and type 4 are the same.

▶ A good English-to-English dictionary contains definitions and examples of every phrasal verb. There are thousands of these, but you only need to know the ones covered in *Progress to First Certificate* for the First Certificate exam.

Before you begin Unit 2 ...

▶ Before you go on to the next unit, look back through the exercises in this unit and decide which ones seemed most difficult. If possible, go through these exercises again now.

Remember that doing exercises in pencil or in your own notebook means that you can do them again easily (by rubbing out your answers or using a fresh page).

2 Leisure activities

2.1 Entertainment and sport — *Vocabulary*

A Make notes on your own answers to the questions – and on your friends' and relations' interests.

B Questions 4 to 17 concern entertainment and 18 to 24 concern sports. Notice that there are several possible answers in questions 16, 17 and 24. Check that your spelling is correct when you go through your answers.

2 recreation/relaxation; 3 collecting taking; 4 comedy; 5 thriller; 6 plot; 7 director; 8 screen stage; 9 reviews; 10 audience; 11 musical; 12 interval performance; 13 video; 14 villain; 15 channel; 16 hi-fi/stereo/record player/compact disc player/personal stereo/Walkman, etc.; 17 pop/rock 'n' roll/opera/folk music/jazz/classical music/orchestral music, etc.; 18 match; 19 referee whistle applause crowd/fans/supporters (NOT audience); 20 team supports; 21 cup prize; 22 draw score; 23 court course; 24 baseball/basketball/hang gliding/windsurfing/volleyball/badminton/athletics/soccer, etc.

C Find out about all the sports you are interested in, using a dictionary.

▶ Next time you watch television or go out for the evening, try looking at the world 'through English eyes' and see if you can put English names to the things and people you see or hear. Note down any useful new words connected with the topic of leisure, entertainment and sport in your notebook.

2.2 Fitness or fun? — *Reading*

A 1 walking; 2 beer; 3 health and fitness clubs; 4 sports and leisure centres.

B

Annual expenditure per head of population:

Motor vehicles	£180
Beer	£150
Spirits & wine	£140
Smoking	£110
Electricity	£90
Gas	£75
Bread	£75
Sports	£60
DIY goods	£50
Newspapers & magazines	£40
Pets	£25
Gambling	£20
Bingo	£5
Cinema	£2.50

Number of people who regularly take part in leisure activities:
(total population of UK 55 million)

Walking	9.5 million
Snooker & pool	4.7 million
Indoor swimming	4 million
Outdoor swimming	4 million
Darts	3.8 million
Fishing	1.7 million
Going to football matches	1.3 million
Keep fit, aerobics & yoga	1.2 million
Football	1.2 million
Squash	1.2 million
Golf	1.2 million

C Note down your answers to the questions. Read the passage again to remind yourself about the popularity of different sports in Britain.

2.3 Articles   *Grammar*

This section REVISES the main problems that students often have with using articles in English. For more information and further examples refer to *Basic English Usage* by Michael Swan (Oxford University Press) or *English Grammar in Use* by Raymond Murphy (Cambridge University Press).

A Refer to section 92 of *Basic English Usage* or 69–70 in *English Grammar in Use*.

These are countable nouns: suitcase   lesson
These are uncountable nouns:
    bread   butter   food*   blood   milk*   salt
    money   luggage   accommodation (count-
    able in US English)   mathematics
    education   health
These could be either:
    glass (windows are made of glass / a glass of milk)
    fire (fire is a great danger / what a nice fire!)
    room (there's no room / this is a nice room)

* Note that in some special cases these words can be countable:
    Hamburgers and frankfurters are fast foods. (i.e. kinds of fast food)
    Three coffees and two chocolate milks please. (i.e. ordering in a café)

B *Suggested answers*

THE
Liverpool/Everton is **the** best football team in the world. (Many variations possible!)
What time does **the sun/moon** rise?

How many students are there in **the class/school/college**?
We are taking **the** (**First Certificate**) exam in **June/December**.

The director of the film *Psycho* was Alfred Hitchcock.

- **the** Pacific, **the** Rhine, **the** Nile, **the** Mediterranean, etc.
- **the** Alps, **the** Rockies, **the** Cyclades, **the** Philippines, **the** West Indies, etc.
- **the** National Theatre, **the** Royal Opera House, **the** Hilton, **the** British Museum, **the** Odeon, etc.

A
- A leisure pool usually has **a wave machine/a water slide**.
- She's **a relation/cousin/colleague** of Peter's.
- She's such **a delightful/charming/rude/fussy** person.
- My father's **an accountant/a baker/a seaman**.
  My mother's **a teacher/managing director/housewife**.
- **A manager/teacher/politician/An army officer** has to be a good leader.

0 – zero article
- **Dictionaries/Computers/Reference books** are useful.
  Discos/Lorries/Aircraft/Children are noisy.
- Mars, Venus, Asia, West Germany, China, Texas, Bavaria, etc.
- Greek, Chinese, Welsh, Arabic, Guaraní, etc.
- Everest, Mont Blanc, Lake Constance, Lake Superior, etc.
- Richmond Park Avenue, Shaftesbury Road, Regent Street, etc.
- Queen's Park, Liverpool Street Station, Heathrow, etc.

C This error-correction exercise is similar to what you should do when checking through your own written work.

2 I'm looking for some accommodation with an English family.
3 More women are involved in politics in Britain than in other countries. (not true, by the way)
4 Most people agree that women can do the same work as men.
5 To get to the library, go along Elizabeth Road and take the first right.
6 Violence is a very great problem in the world today.

D *Complete story*

Last week I went to **an** exhibition of **Ø** paintings at **the** Tate Gallery in London. I'm not really **a** great art lover but I'd read **some/a** lot of/lots of good reviews of the exhibition and I was keen to see it. When I arrived, there were already some/lots of/a lot of people waiting outside for the doors to open. I joined the queue and in the end the doors opened and we went inside to see the show.

Now, I must be honest and admit that many of the paintings disappointed me. Although I spent a lot of/lots of/some time looking carefully at Ø each one, I had some difficulty in understanding what the artist was getting at. Finally, as I was looking rather stupidly at one of the paintings and trying to decide if it was the right way up or not, an old gentleman came up behind me and started to explain the whole thing to me. He kindly answered all of Ø my questions and we talked for over an hour. Then he said he had an appointment and had to go, so we shook hands and said goodbye. I went round the gallery once more and now I found that all the paintings seemed really beautiful.

It was only as I was leaving the gallery that I found out who the old man was – his self-portrait was on the posters advertising the exhibition!

E Some variations are possible in the answers below.

2 Please don't send the results of the exam to my/an address in the UK.
3 Bring an example of a good and a bad advertisement to (the) class tomorrow.
4 The President of France and the Queen will open / have opened / opened the Channel Tunnel.
5 A group of taxi-drivers have won a million pounds in a/the lottery.
6 A man has found a valuable painting in a garden shed.

▶ Look again at the mistakes you made in this section and, if necessary, refer to your grammar book.

2.4 What sort of films do you enjoy? *Listening*

A 📼 Follow the suggested procedure for 1.4. Remember that you don't have to catch all the words to be able to answer the questions.

Don't look at the tapescript until you have filled in all the ticks and crosses.

▶ As Bob's voice is much harder to understand than Susan's, perhaps note down only Susan's likes and dislikes during your first listening, then note down Bob's during the second listening.

	BOB	SUSAN
Thrillers	✓	✗
Action films	✓	✗
Horror films	✗	✗
Love stories	✓	✗
Films with subtitles	✓	✗
Comedies	✓	✓
Cartoons	✓	✗
Black and white films	✗	✓

	BOB	SUSAN
Harrison Ford	✓	✓
Clint Eastwood	✓	✗
Sylvester Stallone	✓	✗
Robert Redford	✗?	✓
Eddie Murphy	✓	✓

(Bob doesn't actually say what he thinks of Robert Redford – but perhaps his tone of voice suggests that he doesn't like him.)

Tapescript

Bob: ...all right...er...so what do you feel like doing this evening? We could...er...have a meal – are you hungry?
Susan: Nnn...
Bob: I know, do you feel like...um...how about going to the cinema?
Susan: Ah, that's a good idea, yes. I...I'd love to see a film, I haven't been to the cinema for ages.
Bob: No, no, I haven't either. OK, what...what sort of films do you like? Erm...how about thrillers? I enjoy a really good thriller. What was that one with...um...that one with Harrison Ford, you know about...you know, that strange sect? *Witness.* Harrison Ford – he's always good, isn't he?
Susan: Yes, *Witness,* yes. Now I like Harrison

Ford and..er..I don't know about *Witness*, no. Mmm..I'm..it was a good film, but I'm not really very keen on that..that..sort of..kind of film.

Bob: Mm, so th..then..then you won't..what if I suggested action films, you wouldn't like that either?

Susan: Action? Wh..what do you mean by action films?

Bob: You know..um..w..er..Clint Eastwood, that sort of thing.

Susan: Oh, no, no, I can't stand films like that.

Bob: Oh, I like those, you see..um..violent – *Rambo 1, 2, 3*.

Susan: Oh no, definitely, no, no, definitely not, no. I can't stand old..um..whatsisname..um ..Sylvester Stallone. I can't stand it when you see people getting killed and all the violence and everything, no. I think it's pointless and horrible.

Bob: Well, n..I..I quite..I quite like him. I don't mind you see, I don't mind some violence on the screen, though it's not real life after all. But if it's, well, if it's too bloody I have to shut my eyes. Bit squeamish.

Susan: Oh, absolutely, but you know the worst films of all th..are horror films. Ugh! I went to see a horror film – now what was it called? – um..*Nightmare on Elm Street*. Ohh! Did..I went to see it last year..er..I had to keep my eyes shut almost the whole way through the film.

Bob: Yeah, I know, that sort of film gives me nightmares, I just..So what..what..what *do* you like, what shall we go and see? I mean, love stories? I quite like a good love story.

Susan: No, no! Can't stand romantic films. *Unless*, unless Robert Redford's in them.

Bob: Oh, come on! Susan, you don't like him, do you? I'm really surprised!

Susan: Robert Redford, he's my absolute favourite! I absolutely adore him.

Bob: Haha.

Susan: Actually, I don't really like American films at all really, no. I quite like foreign films, but not when they've got subtitles.

Bob: Oh, I disagree with you there, I mean, I don't mind subtitles at all. In fact I prefer it, I like to hear foreign languages being spoken. I quite like French or Spanish films, for example. Now, what does that leave us? Comedies? You must like comedies, surely.

Susan: Well, yes. I love comedies. Now, one of my favourites is Eddie Murphy.

Bob: Ah, now then, now then, he's brilliant. Did you see *Coming to America*?

Susan: Oh, yes! Wasn't it brilliant! And what about *Crocodile Dundee*, did you..did you see *Crocodile Dundee*?

Bob: Oh, I did. I didn't..I didn't really enjoy that quite as much.

Susan: You didn't enjoy *Crocodile Dundee*?

Bob: Oh, it was..well..stupid, wasn't it? Unbelievable, I thought.

Susan: Oh, come on, that was the whole point!! It *was* a comedy you know!

Bob: Oh, yeah, I take your point but I didn't enjoy it, OK? Well..er..that doesn't leave us much, does it?

Susan: Not really.

Bob: Cartoons – you know, Walt Disney? Kind of thing. I love cartoons. But you don't see many new ones these days, only the old Walt Disney ones.

Susan: Oh, did you see that Roger Rabbit film?

Bob: *Who Framed Roger Rabbit*? Oh, that was fantastic, wasn't it? The way the real people and the..the cartoon characters acted together, it was fabulous.

Susan: Oh, actually you know, I didn't really enjoy it. Do you know, I don't really understand what the attraction is of cartoons, I..I really don't. You know..what I really like, no, what I really like are the old black and white films. You know, the classics, the Humphrey Bogart, the Hollywood classics.

Bob: Mm, well, I've got to confess I prefer modern films really – I don't like black and white..well..it's old-fashioned.

Susan: Well, I don't really know what we're going to do, do you?

Bob: No.

Susan: Do you know what?..I don't think we should go to the cinema at all. I think we should go out for a meal instead.

Bob: I'd quite like to go to the cinema. Have you got a local paper, so we can see what's on?

Susan: Oh! Well, I don't know, I haven't got a..a paper. I know, why don't we just ring up the cinema and find out what's on?

Bob: You've always got the best ideas. Then we can decide properly and sort out exactly...

(Time: 4 minutes 10 seconds)

B You may need to pause the tape while you're writing your answers.

Tapescript

Narrator: You'll hear a recorded message.

Recorded voice: ...now be repeated. Thank you for calling. This is the Maybox Film Centre with recorded information on films showing from today until Thursday next.

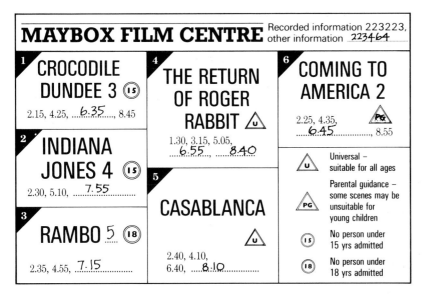

Screen One is showing *Crocodile Dundee 3*, starring Paul Hogan, Certificate 15: showing at 2.15, 4.25, 6.35 and 8.45.

Screen Two is showing *Indiana Jones 4*, starring Harrison Ford, Certificate 15: performances begin at 2.30, 5.10 and 7.55.

Screen Three is showing *Rambo 5*, starring Sylvester Stallone, Certificate 18: performances at 2.35, 4.55 and 7.15.

Screen Four is showing *The Return of Roger Rabbit*, Certificate U: performances at 1.30, 3.15, 5.05, 6.55 and 8.40.

Screen Five is showing *Casablanca*, starring Humphrey Bogart and Ingrid Bergman, Certificate U: performances at 2.40, 4.10, 6.40 and 8.10.

Screen Six is showing *Coming to America 2*, starring Eddie Murphy, Certificate PG: performances at 2.25, 4.35, 6.45 and 8.55.

If you require further information, please call this number: 223464. This programme information will now be repeated. Thank you for calling. This is the Maybox Film Centre with recorded information on films showing from today...

(Time: 1 minute 45 seconds)

2.5 Using prefixes *Word study*

In case you are not sure of the meanings of the prefixes:
co = with
mid = in the middle
over = too much
under = not enough
re = again
self is connected with *oneself* or *itself* – look at the examples and see what they have in common
sub = below
un = doing the opposite action – not quite the same as *un* in *unkind* (= not kind) or *unfamiliar* (= not familiar)

A In some cases the words can be written as one word or with a hyphen. There are no fixed rules on this.

co	co-driver
mid	mid-afternoon, mid-morning, mid-winter, midway
over	overcharge, overexcited
under	underdone
re	rearrange, remarry
self	self-control, self-service
sub	sub-standard
un	unbutton, unfold, unscrew, unwrap

B 2 co-author; 3 overconfident; 4 mid-sentence; 5 rebuilt; 6 underpaid; 7 overworking; 8 unlock; 9 sub-zero mid-winter; 10 overeat overweight.

2.6 Safety at sea *Listening*

A Looking at the questions before you listen will make it easier to do the task in **B**.

B

1 Match the signals to the pictures:
   a) 'I am OK.' – picture C
   b) 'I need assistance.' – picture A
   c) 'I have a diver down. Keep clear and proceed at slow speed.' – picture B
   d) 'Faster!' – picture F
   e) 'Slower!' – picture E
   f) 'Speed OK.' – picture G
   g) 'Back to jetty.' – picture D
2 nod your head
3 shake your head
4 Advice to the water skier:
   a) watch the skier   drive the boat
   b) above water
   c) start
   d) let go of the rope and sit down
   e) curl yourself into a ball
   f) they can help to keep you afloat

Tapescript

Jenny: After a series of accidents involving water skiers, it's clear that there need to be stricter rules and controls. Chuck Brown is a lifeguard. Chuck, what advice would you give to people who are taking part in water sports?

Chuck: Well, Jenny, er...first of all you have to know the signals that...er...you should use if...if you get into trouble. Now, it...it's difficult to hear shouts alone above the noise of waves, er...boat engines, breathing apparatus if you're wearing that, and so on.

Jenny: I see, could you give us some examples?

Chuck: Well, if you're diving...er...you need to use these signals. Now, 'I'm OK,' is the hand up with thumb and forefinger making an O, like that. Um...the 'I need assistance'...er...signal is...er...you put the fist up and you move it from left to right above the water. Now, er...if...if you're on a boat you should be flying the right international signal which is a flag. Um...Flag A: that's white on the side nearest the mast and it's blue on the other side.

Jenny: And what does that mean?

Chuck: That indicates 'I have a diver down...er...keep clear and proceed at a slow speed' for other boats around.

Jenny: Yes, and what about skiers?

Chuck: Well...um...anybody who's going to be water skiing should be taught several signals. First of all, the signal to go faster: you hold your palm up and motion upwards *or* just nod your head.

Jenny: Yes.

Chuck: The signal for slower is the palm down, you motion downwards *or* you shake your head. Now, if you want to indicate that the speed's OK, you give the OK signal with your thumb and forefinger making the O, as...er...I just told you about. If you want to go back to the jetty, just point with your arm downwards. Like that, down towards your side like that.

Jenny: I see, uhuh. Well, so much for signals. But water skiing can be quite dangerous, can't it?

Chuck: Well, not if you follow the basic safety procedures and you know what you're doing. Um...well, there are three points really. There should always be two people in the boat. Now, that's one person to watch the skier and the other to drive the boat...er...they call them the helmsman. Um...before you start, your ski-tips must be above the water, so you don't get dragged down immediately. If you're the skier you have to give a clear signal to the helmsman (that's the driver, the person who's driving the boat) when you're ready to start.

Jenny: And I suppose even the best water skiers fall into the water quite often, what should you do if you fall?

Chuck: When you fall! Well, if you start to fall forwards you should let go of the rope and sit down. Um...if you're falling sideways, you should just curl yourself up into a ball. And very important: recover the skis immediately. Get a hold of those skis because they can help to keep you afloat.

Jenny: I see, right. Well, thank you very much, Chuck.

Chuck: Not at all.

(Time: 3 minutes 15 seconds)

2.7 The Month in View   *Reading/Problem solving*

This passage is a magazine article. It contains a number of difficult words and unfamiliar names of actors and performers – but you will be able to answer the questions WITHOUT this knowledge. This section will help you to cope with a difficult text IN SPITE OF the difficulties.

A Look through the passage quickly, without worrying about unfamiliar words.

(The words or information that provide the clues are included.)
1 Nov 16 – burglary   Agatha Christie
2 Nov 10 – French

3   Nov 4 – invented   ballpoint pen   safety pin   etc.
4   Nov 23 – Bomb   nuclear war
5   Nov 4 – Painters   paintings
6   Nov 26 – Sixties   since the war
7   Nov 18 – women   women

B   2   F – he copies other painters' styles; 3   F – the character wants to escape from home;   4   T;   5   T;   6   F – the writer finds humour in the situation;   7   T;   8   F – it's on twice a week;   9   T;   10   T.

C   Note down your answers to the questions.

D   Before you write the two paragraphs, make some notes on the points you will make. When you have finished your paragraphs, compare them with the model paragraphs below.

Model paragraphs

(These are not 'perfect', just suggested versions of what you might write.)

```
The programme I'd most like to see is
'Year of the French'. This interests
me because I like to find out about
the way people in other countries
live and their attitudes. I've never
heard of Marie-Paule Belle, but I'd
like to find out more about French
pop music. Friday's programme about
a skiing policeman sounds fascinating,
too.

The programme I'd least like to see
is 'Stuntman Challenge'. Although
stunts in films are always exciting,
it's their place in the story that
makes them worth watching. The
idea of people challenging each
other to do dangerous things seems
pointless and stupid to me, not
thrilling.
```

2.8   Position and direction   *Prepositions*

A   Make sure you understand the meaning of each preposition in the lists, using a dictionary if necessary. Write a sentence using each one you had to look up the meaning of.

B

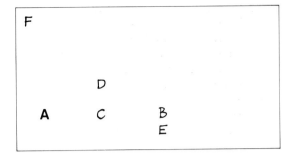

C   Add more letters to the diagram and then write a sentence to describe where each one was placed.

D   Look at Activity 32 and, using a blank cassette, record yourself explaining the route that a pencil should take to draw the picture. Pause the tape when you need to stop and think. (This may be much harder than you expect – but quite enjoyable.) Then listen to what you said and try following your own instructions to draw the same picture on page 27.
Do the same with the picture in Activity 40.

2.9   The jogger's wallet   *Listening*

This listening exercise introduces the theme of telling a story, which you will have to do in the communication activity in 2.10 and, in writing, in the composition exercise in 2.11.

▭   Listen to the story and decide on the correct sequence of pictures. Then listen to the tape again a couple of times, enjoying the story and concentrating on the way the speaker tells the story. Notice how the speaker involves his listener in the story.

The correct sequence of pictures is:
E   F   C   D   A   B

Tapescript

Man: OK, OK. Now listen to this then. Now, this...this is a story about a friend of mine, a New Yorker who...he lives near Central Park, so every morning he goes out jogging. Right? He goes out jogging. Now he was jogging this morning, this one morning very early at his usual...the way he usually ran, you know,

245

jogging along there, and he was surrounded by, you know, lots of others, there are always lots of people jogging in Central Park. And suddenly, out of nowhere, this jogger...kind of bumped into him and...and shot past him. Well, he didn't think much except that...er...suddenly...he thought he felt something...he felt something missing, so he discovered...he tapped his pocket and he discovered that his wallet was missing. Huh? So he said to himself, 'Now, this has never happened to me, this...I've got to...I...I can't let this happen.' So he saw the guy that had hit him and said, 'That...he must have been the one,' and he ran up to him and he...and he grabbed him and he...and he shook him and he said 'Give me that wallet!' like that. Well, the guy was terrified, it was really threatening, and the other guy obviously wasn't stronger than him and...and thank God he didn't pull a knife or anything like that. And s...immediately, immediately the guy reached in his pocket and he produced this wallet which my friend took and felt very happy about it, pocketed the wallet and ran home.

Well, he...he went home, and he took his shower as he usually did to get ready to go to work and then he got his...putting his clothes on and he patted his jacket pocket a...and...it w...in his pocket was his own wallet. The wallet he had taken in the guy...from the guy, the wallet was in his back pocket belonged to somebody else – he'd taken the other guy's wallet! He felt dreadful!

(Time: 1 minute 45 seconds)

2.10 Telling a story *Communication activity*

A and **B**   Note down your answers to the questions.

C   Look at the pictures in Activity 17. Make notes on the story you think is shown there. Then, using a blank cassette, record your version of the story, beginning: 'This is what happened...'

Now look at Activities 24 and 46 – how do these scenes match your recorded version of the story? Record a new version, including all the scenes.

2.11 Writing a narrative *Composition*

A   There are no grammatical errors or spelling mistakes in the story.

Activity 9 contains an improved version of the story. The version on page 29 lacks detail and is very boring to read – and the precise times and distances are irrelevant and distracting.

Underline (or highlight) the main changes that have been made in the version in Activity 9. There are no 'correct answers' but doing this will help you to notice the expressions and structures that are used.

B   Again there is an improved version to look at later, in Activity 3.

The first version uses the past tense (which makes it seem a true story, rather than the plot of a film) and is not very interesting to read. The improved version contains extra information, which you should underline or highlight – this is to draw attention to the details and there are no 'correct answers'.

Normally, the plot of a film or book is told in the simple present tense.

C   Write your own composition.

D   If possible, ask another person (perhaps an English-speaking person or a friend whose English is reasonably good) to read and mark your work.

If this is not possible, check your own composition through a week or so later. By this time, you will probably be able to find mistakes of spelling and grammar in your work that you can correct yourself.

2.12 *Make* and *do* *Verbs and idioms*

A   Use a dictionary if necessary.

Bill made ...
   Shirley laugh   a cake   a noise   a mistake
   an arrangement   a comment   a decision
   a good impression   me an offer   a promise
   a statement

Shirley did ...
   Bill a favour   the washing-up   her duty

the shopping   an exercise   her homework
a good job   badly in the test   her best
very well   nothing at all

B The definitions given in the answers below are simply rough definitions – consult a dictionary for more detail and further examples.

1 do with   = need or want
2 doing up   = redecorate (we can also do up a shoelace or coat)
3 done   out of = cause to lose by cheating or trickery
4 do without   = manage without having something
5 make out   = see with difficulty
6 make up for = repay or compensate for
7 making for   = going in the direction of / heading for
8 making up   = invent a story
9 made off with = steal

▶ Before you start work on Unit 3, look back through the exercises in this unit and decide which of them were particularly difficult. If possible, go through these again now – or make a note in your exercise book of the ones you think you should do again later.

3 Nature and the environment

3.1 Plants and animals *Vocabulary*

A *Some suggested answers*

2 Fruit: apple, plum, pineapple, apricot, melon, raspberry, strawberry, blackcurrants, cherry, etc.
3 Vegetables: cabbage, potato, cauliflower, aubergine, onion, etc.
4 Trees: fir, beech, palm, cypress, eucalyptus, etc.
5 Flowers: buttercup, daffodil, crocus, dandelion, orchid, etc.
6 Wild animals (mammals): lion, wolf, fox, elephant, deer, monkey, dolphin, etc.
7 Domestic animals: cow, sheep, chicken, horse, donkey, etc.
8 Pets: cat, dog, canary, hamster, gerbil, etc.
9 Birds: blackbird, robin, stork, crow, swallow, kingfisher, etc.
10 Young animals: cub, kitten, lamb, foal, etc. (there are not many of these)
11 Reptiles: snake (adder, python, cobra, etc.), crocodile, tortoise, turtle, etc.
12 Insects: bee, mosquito, cockroach, beetle, locust, moth, flea, etc.
13 Fish: trout, sole, sardine, cod, anchovy, red mullet, etc.
14 Other sea creatures: lobster, mussel, squid, prawn, shrimp, jellyfish, etc.

B Do the ones you know first and come back to the others later.

2 harvest   crops   picked;   3 mountains;
4 hunting;   5 pollution   poisons;
6 forecast   intervals;   7 fog;   8 misty;
9 temperatures   frost;   10 gale/storm/hurricane/night/evening;   11 breeze   shade;
12 thunder   lightning;   13 shower;
14 scenery   valleys   climate;   15 coast   cliffs.

▶ Next time you go to a park or into the country, look at the world 'through English eyes'.

3.2 The balance of nature *Reading*

A Make a note of all the animals and plants you can think of that might be found in a wood or forest.

C natural community (i); woodland (a); dominated (b); species (h); tissues (e); flesh (d); link (f); organisms (c); decomposers (g).

D oak (a kind of tree); bramble (a kind of large plant); moss (a kind of simple plant); lichen (a kind of simple plant); algae (a kind of

247

simple plant); trunk (part of a tree); snail (a kind of small animal); aphid (a kind of insect); caterpillar (a kind of insect); lacewing (a kind of insect); shrew (a kind of small animal); vole (a kind of small animal); fungi (a kind of simple plant).

E TRUE: 1, 3, 4, 5, 8; FALSE: 2, 6, 7.

F Decide what you would say if you were asked these questions and make a few notes. Then, using a blank cassette, record your views.

3.3 The past *Grammar*

A *Suggested answers*

SIMPLE PAST:
I **saw** a film about animals on TV last Wednesday evening.
In 1988 I **spent** my summer holidays in **Italy**.

PAST PROGRESSIVE:
We **were playing** cards when the lights went out.
As the sun **was shining** we decided to go for a drive.
While you **were waiting for** the bus, we walked all the way here.

USED TO:
Before the war, more people **used to work** on the land.
When I was a child, we **used to have** a dog.

PAST PERFECT:
It rained all day but I **had forgotten** to pack an umbrella.
After I **had read** the book, I made some notes on it.
They were still friends even though they **had been** apart for ten years.

PRESENT PERFECT:
We **have** already **studied the first** two units in this book.
She **has made** five phone calls since lunchtime.
Have you (**ever**) **visited** Britain?

B

2 I **went** to the zoo last weekend.
3 When **did you leave** school?
4 Where **did you go** on holiday last year?
5 She **was** born in 1975.
6 Our family **used** to live in a smaller flat when I **was** younger.
7 Our broken window **hasn't been** mended yet.
8 The rain started **while they were playing** tennis.

C *Suggested answers*

(Some variations are possible.)
2 When the farmer had started his tractor, he began to plough the field.
3 While I was walking in the country it began to rain / the rain began to fall.
4 After we had had lunch, we went for a walk by the river.
5 They used to have a dog (but they haven't got one now).
6 Before I went to the zoo (last year), I had never seen a real tiger. / Before I saw a tiger in the zoo last year, I had never seen one.

D Read the story in Activity 18 through carefully. Then retell the story in your own words, recording it on a blank cassette.

Then read the story in Activity 42. Close your book and retell it in your own words – but this time IN WRITING. Compare your version with the original and then check if you made any spelling mistakes.

3.4 The Earth at risk *Listening*

B You will need to hear the interview more than once to fill all the gaps as this is quite a long recording and may be quite difficult to understand.

1 firewood   domestic;   2 rain;   3 soil;
4 wheat   maize;   5 tropical forests;
6 food   Europe   America;   7 poor exhausted;   8 the USA   furniture;   9 rare plants   medicines;   10 world;   11 Nepal India   rainfall;   12 1 ten   twenty international;   2 controlled;   3 softwoods hardwoods.

Tapescript

Interviewer: Brian Cowles is the producer of a new series of documentaries called 'The Earth at Risk' which can be seen on Channel 4 later this month. Each programme deals with a different continent, doesn't it, Brian?

Brian Cowles: That's right, yes, we went to...er...we went to America, both North and South and then we went over to Africa and South-East Asia.

Interviewer: And what did you find in each of these continents?

Brian Cowles: Well...er...starting with...er...Africa, our film shows the impact of the population on the environment. Generally speaking, this has caused the Sahara Desert to expand. It's a bit of a vicious circle...er...we find, people cut down trees for firewood and their domestic animals eat all the available plants – and so consequently they have to move south as the Sahara Desert expands further south. I mean, soon the whole of Mali will become a desert. And...er...in East Africa: here the grasslands are supporting too many animals and the result is, of course, there's no grass – nothing for the animals to eat.

Interviewer: Mm, yes, I see. Um...and the...the next film deals with North America?

Brian Cowles: That's right. In the...er...USA, as you know, intensive agriculture requires a plentiful supply of rain for these crops to grow, I mean if there isn't enough rain the crops don't grow. And growing crops stabilise soil, without them the top soil just...it just blows away. I mean, this is also true for any region that is intensely farmed – most of Europe, for example. But the USA is the world's breadbasket – American farmers grow huge quantities of extra wheat, maize and soya beans to feed the world – consequently, if there isn't enough rain there, other countries can't buy enough food for their people to eat.

(*Questions 5 to 10* ↓)

Interviewer: And what did you find in South America?

Brian Cowles: In South America (a...as in Central Africa and Southern Asia) tropical forests are being cut down at an alarming rate. Th...this is done so that people can support themselves by growing food or to create ranches where cattle can be raised to exp...to be exported to Europe or America as tinned meat. The problem is that the s...the soil is so poor that...um...that only a couple of harvests are possible before this very thin soil becomes exhausted. And it can't be fed with fertilizers like agricultural land in Europe.

Um...for example, in Brazil in 1982 an area of jungle the size of Britain and France combined was destroyed to make way for an iron ore mine. I mean, huge numbers of trees are being cut down for export as hardwood to Japan, Europe, USA...I mean...to make things like luxury furniture. These forests can't...er...they can't be replaced – the forest soil is thin and unproductive and in just a few years, a...a jungle has become a waste land. Tropical forests contain rare plants (which...er...we can use for medicines, for example) and animals – one animal or plant species becomes extinct every half hour. These...er...forest trees...I mean ...also have worldwide effects. You know, they convert carbon dioxide into oxygen. The consequence of destroying forests is not only that the climate of that region changes (because there is less rainfall) but this change affects the whole world. I mean, over half the world's rain forest has been cut down this century.

(*Questions 11 and 12* ↓)

Interviewer: So, Brian, would you agree that what we generally think of as...er...as er...natural disasters are in fact man-made?

Brian Cowles: Yes, by and large,...er...I mean, obviously not hurricanes or earthquakes, but take flooding, for example. I mean, practically every year, the whole of Bangladesh is flooded and this is getting worse. You know, the cause is that forests have been cut down up in Nepal and India...I mean...higher up-river in the Himalayas. Trees...er...would hold rainfall in their roots, but if they've been cut down all the rain that falls in the monsoon season flows straight into the River Ganges and floods the whole country. The reason for flooding in Sudan is the same – the forests higher up the Blue Nile in Ethiopia have been destroyed too.

Interviewer: Well, this all sounds terribly depressing. Um...what is to be done? I mean, *can* anything be done, in fact?

Brian Cowles: Yes, of course it can...er...first, the national governments have to be forward-looking and consider the results of their policies in ten or twenty years, not just think as far ahead as the next election. Somehow, all the countries in the world have to work together on an international basis. Secondly, the population has to be controlled in some way: there are too many people trying to live off too little land. Thirdly, we don't need tropical hardwood to make our furniture – it's a luxury people in the West must do without. Softwoods are just as good, less expensive and can be produced on environment-friendly 'tree farms', where trees are replaced at the same rate that they are cut down.

Interviewer: And, presumably, education is

important as well. People must be educated to realise the consequences...um...of their actions?
Brian Cowles: Yes, yes of course. But educating people who are struggling to survive is difficult. I mean, you can't say 'Don't cut down these trees because you'll only get one harvest' – one harvest will keep them alive for another year.
Interviewer: Yes, I see, well, thank you, Brian.

(Time: 5 minutes 35 seconds)

3.5 Using negative prefixes

Word study

A

un-	uncomfortable, unexpected, unfamiliar, unknown, unlucky, unpopular
in-	inaccurate, inconvenient, intolerant, invisible
im-	impatient, impersonal, improbable
dis-	disapprove, dislike, disobey
mis-	mispronounce, misspell

▶ Write five sentences using the new and useful words you have come across in this section.

B 2 impatient; 3 inconvenient; 4 unreasonable; 5 inefficient; 6 misunderstood; 7 misspelt; 8 disliked.

▶ We return to this aspect of word formation in 12.7.

3.6 What's the weather going to be like?

Problem solving

A

Alan
Monday	London: 01 444 3456
Tuesday	Paris: *no number*
Wednesday	New York: 0101 212 909 3900

Betty
Monday	Oslo: 010 47 2 776 2121
Tuesday	Rome: 010 39 6 685 3890
Wednesday	Brussels: 010 32 2 861 1970

Colin
Monday	Los Angeles: 0101 213 345 8729
Tuesday	Geneva: *no number*
Wednesday	Vienna: *no number*

Tapescript

Narrator: You'll hear three recorded messages from your friends.

Alan: Hello, this is Alan. Listen, I'll be in London on Monday, Paris on Tuesday and New York on Wednesday and Thursday. You can get in touch with me in New York on Wednesday at this number: 0101 212 909 39 double O. I'll go over that again: 0101 212 909 39 double O. In London, that's Monday, the number is 01 treble 4 3456, well you know that one. In Paris I won't be...er...contactable on the phone.

Betty: Hi, this is Betty. I'm just leaving now...er...and I'm going to be in Oslo on Monday, er...in Rome on Tuesday and in Brussels on...er...Wednesday and Thursday. Now...um...if you need to get in touch, my phone number in Oslo is 010 47 2 776 2121. Er...now...in Rome it's 010 39 6 685 3890. Oh...er...and in Brussels it's 010 32 2 861 1970.

Colin: Er...hello, this is Colin. Um...look, I'm going to be in Los Angeles on Monday, er...then in Geneva on Tuesday and in Vienna from Wednesday for the rest of the week. If you need to get in touch, my number in Los Angeles is: zero 1 zero 1 31...no, oh, let's start that again: that's zero 1 zero 1 213 345 8729. Um...but you won't be able to get me on the phone in Geneva or Vienna, I'm afraid.

(Time: 2 minutes 20 seconds)

C This chart summarises all the information about the weather in each place.

	FORECAST	Monday	Tuesday onwards	Actual weather on Wednesday
Alan	London	cloudy 18	thundery showers	sunny 22
	Paris	sunny 24	mostly sunny	fair 21
	New York	rain 28	rain at times	fair 36
Betty	Oslo	cloudy 22	rain at times	sleet 4
	Rome	sunny 26	warm and sunny	sunny 25
	Brussels	cloudy 18	warmer, sunny	hail 15
Colin	Los Angeles	cloudy 21	dry and sunny	fair 17
	Geneva	cloudy 22	mostly sunny	fog 14
	Vienna	sunny 20	showers then fair	fair 17

D *Model postcards*

Brussels, Wednesday evening, 22 June
Dear Eddie,
Arrived here this morning from Rome. Here at lunchtime there was a hailstorm and it was quite a contrast from the lovely sunny weather in Rome yesterday and of course, as I expected, it's much cooler.
But Rome was an even greater contrast from Oslo. As you know, I was there on Monday and the forecast had said it might rain but that it would be reasonably warm — but in fact it was freezing and there was sleet!! As I only had a light raincoat I was glad I was only staying there for one day.
I'll see you in a couple of days.
Best wishes,
Betty

Vienna, Wednesday 22 June

Dear Eddie,
Well, here I am in Vienna after stopping over in Geneva on my way from Los Angeles. They say the sun always shines in Southern California, but while I was there it wasn't very nice at all — everyone said it was more like winter there. Yesterday in Geneva it wasn't too bad — mostly sunny in fact and quite warm but it was foggy when I left this morning. Here in Vienna it's not very warm but at least it's dry.
I'll call you on Saturday when I get back.
Best,
Colin

3.7 Compound prepositions — *Use of English*

2 apart from/except for;   3 by means of;
4 except for/apart from;   5 due to;
6 According to;   7 ahead of;   8 on behalf of;   9 instead of;   10 in addition to/as well as;   11 As for;   12 As regards.

▶ Do you know these compound prepositions?
   away from   because of   in front of
   out of   owing to   in spite of   despite

3.8 The Greenhouse Effect — *Reading*

A 1 fossil fuels   trees   atmosphere
2 heat   space   trapped;   3 vapour   absorbs;   4 surface   reflect   snow;
5 store   warming   expand.

B TRUE: 1, 2, 5, 6, 7, 8; FALSE: 3, 4, 9, 10.

3.9 Making notes *Composition*

A No particular style of notes is recommended here – you should experiment with various styles to find out which suits you best.

B *Model notes*

"CLOSE ALL ZOOS"

I AGREE BECAUSE...
- unpleasant, depressing – especially old-fashioned zoos
- cruel to keep animals in small cages – lions: Africa, open spaces
- climate – winter: tropical animals
- entertainment (like circus) – people laugh at animals performing (bananas, swinging, etc.) & people make animals nervous – don't respect them

I DISAGREE BECAUSE...
- modern zoo parks – large enclosures
- scientific research
- preserving + breeding rare species – stop some becoming extinct
- education about animals – better than films or books

C If possible, ask someone to read your work and mark it.

Model composition

Some zoos are rather unpleasant, depressing places. This seems to be particularly true of the more old-fashioned ones where large animals are kept in tiny cages for the amusement of the public. This kind of zoo is cruel – a lion is an animal that lives in the open spaces of Africa and cannot enjoy being a prisoner. In the winter, zoos in colder countries do not provide a warm enough environment for animals from hot countries. Worst of all, it seems to me, is the way some zoos are regarded as places of entertainment, like circuses, where people are encouraged to laugh at animals as they 'perform' their funny tricks (eating bananas, swinging from rubber tyres, and so on), make them frightened or angry by teasing them and don't respect them as our fellow creatures.

On the other hand, it seems to me that people who say that all zoos should be closed are overstating the case. Many modern zoo parks do keep animals in large enclosures and try to make them feel at home. Some zoos are valuable centres of scientific research, where rare species can be preserved and encouraged to breed. In many cases, this policy has led to the reintroduction of animals into areas where they had almost become extinct. Zoos are also a unique form of education, where children (and adults) can learn about the behaviour of animals in a more effective and enjoyable way than seeing films or reading about them.

3.10 For or against? *Listening*

A

1 'Keeping pets in cities'
   Points FOR: Dogs can protect you from thieves and intruders
   Dogs can be good company
   Take their owners for walks
   Points AGAINST: Cruel to keep bird in cage
   Cruel to keep dog shut indoors all day
   Dogs pollute pavements + parks – unhealthy for children and sports

2 'Everyone should stop eating meat'
   Points FOR: Cruel to kill animals, e.g. young lambs
   Unnecessary to have meat – protein from nuts, beans, etc.
   Land used to raise animals could be used for growing corn or wheat – just as good for you
   Points AGAINST: Meat very important biologically + is tasty
   You can't tell people not to eat meat if they want to
   Most vegetarians eat fish – also cruel?

3 'There should be stricter worldwide control of pollution'

Points FOR:
- Pollution is a world problem – rivers, air, oceans
- Pollution crosses frontiers
- Ozone layer being destroyed by gases in aerosols – forbidden in some countries, permitted in others

Points AGAINST:
- Not such a big problem – only a tiny amount of pollution on a worldwide scale
- Oceans and space immense – can absorb all this stuff
- Pollution concentrated in certain areas
- Local people should protest and clean it up

Tapescript

Narrator: You'll hear three conversations. Here's the first.

Interviewer: Excuse me, could I just stop you for one moment and ask you both please your opinion on...um...pets? What is your opinion of keeping pets in the city?

Man: What? Dogs and cats? Well, I've got a dog and...er...I'm all for it. A dog can protect you from thieves and intruders and...um...he's very good company, he's a very lively little dog and...er...of course, he takes me for walks! Haha. Gives me all the exercise I need...

Woman: Yes, yes, but...I mean...it is...it is cruel to keep a bird in a cage, I mean, or even a dog...a dog that's shut inside all day. I mean, particularly in London, dogs pollute pavements and...and in the parks...I mean...they're really unhealthy for children, people running, for sports...I mean...

Man: But don't you think this is something to do with the owner, how he actually...

Narrator: Two.

Interviewer: Excuse me, do you agree that everyone should stop eating meat?

Man: Yeah, I do. I think it's really cruel to kill animals because, I mean, we see these nice woolly lambs, right? And they're less than a year old when they're actually taken off to a slaughterhouse and killed. I mean it's unnecessary to have meat for protein. I mean, we can get protein from nuts, beans, that sort of thing. Look at it from the agricultural point of view: to raise one cow you need all that land and all that land could be used for growing corn or wheat – just as good for you.

Interviewer: Thank you.

Woman: Well, I...no I'm sorry, I don't agree at all. I mean, I...I think...well, yes all right it may be cruel to...to slaughter very young animals but I think meat's very important biologically, I think we need it. And it's tasty...I mean...there's no way you can replace that with anything else, is there? I mean, that soya protein stuff it is just horrible. The other thing is, I don't think that you can actually tell people what to do you see, you can't tell everybody not to eat meat if they want to, there's nothing you can do...

Man: Well, I'm not telling them.

Woman: Well, yeah, well, that's what this lady's suggesting, isn't it? And...and what about fish? Now, have you noticed, most vegetarians will eat fish, now why isn't that considered cruel? I mean, think about it...

Narrator: Three.

Interviewer: Er...excuse me, I wonder if you could spare a moment, please? Do you think there should be stricter worldwide control of pollution?

Woman: Oh yes, I certainly do. Um...many countries have strict control but others haven't as yet and I think it's high time they had because it is a world problem. Um...pollution goes into our rivers, the air, the oceans, it crosses frontiers. The ozone layer is being destroyed by gases in aerosols that are actually forbidden in some countries and...and permitted in others. It's permitted in our country and I think it's disgraceful, something should be done about it before it's too late.

Interviewer: Right, thank you. What about you, sir?

Man: Ha, well I don't think it's such a big problem as these prophets of doom would say – sorry about that, honey! Look there's only a tiny amount of pollution happening on a worldwide scale. Th..the oceans are immense, space is immense, it can absorb all this stuff. Pollution is concentrated, I'll give you that, in certain areas, now it's up to the local people in those tiny areas to protest against it and to clean it up!

Interviewer: Thank you very much...

(Time: 3 minutes 30 seconds)

B Imagine that a radio reporter stops you in the street and asks you for your views. Using the notes you made on one of the interviews (and your own opinions), record what you would say on the topic. Look at the useful expressions below.

Listen to your recording and decide how it can be improved. Then do the same with another of the topics.

It seems to me that …
I'd say that …
I agree that …
Don't you think that … ?
I don't agree that …
It's not true to say that …
It's ridiculous to say that …

sentences – and not just a few words. Listen to the recording and decide how you could improve your answers.

C Look at the picture in Activity 34. Record your answers to the questions.

▶ You can hear some useful ways of 'filling silence' in many of the listening exercises. For example:

you know   you see   er   well   actually   in fact   sort of

3.11 How sweet!? *Picture conversation*

▶ In the exam, part of the interview will involve talking about a photograph. This section will help you to get used to doing this and to finding things to say – one word answers are not recommended in the exam!

The interviewer will not just ask you questions about the content of the picture but will encourage you to give your opinions.

A *Suggested questions*

1 Why do you think it's wrong to keep animals in captivity / hunt or shoot animals / train animals to do tricks?
2 What can be done to prevent trees being killed by acid rain?
3 What would it be like to be a visitor / an animal in this zoo?
4 Why do you enjoy / not enjoy going to the zoo/circus?

B Record yourself answering the questions. Try to answer each one with two or three

3.12 *Get* *Verbs and idioms*

A 1 get rid of; 2 get better; 3 got a headache; 4 got the sack; 5 getting dark; 6 get the joke; 7 get ready; 8 got home late; 9 get to sleep; 10 get someone else to do it.

B 1 get on with = continue; 2 get on with = live happily together; 3 get round to = find time; 4 get out of = avoid; 5 get across = communicate   getting at = suggest; 6 getting down = make someone feel depressed; 7 get around/round = find a way of solving; 8 get by = survive; 9 get off = alight; 10 getting on = manage/make progress; 11 get through = make connection on phone; 12 get together = meet/assemble.

▶ Write your own sentences, including any phrasal verbs that are new to you.

4 Transport and travel

4.1 On the move — *Vocabulary*

▶ Before you begin **A**, make a list of as many different forms of transport as you can. Then grade them in order of preference. What would you say if someone asked you, for example: 'Why do you prefer cycling to going by bus?'

A Notice the US English terms among the answers below – these may be of interest, but are not necessary for the exam.

1 fares;
2 trams (US streetcars);
3 tunnel;
4 return (US round trip);
5 pavement (US sidewalk);
6 footpath;
7 petrol (US gas)   motorists;
8 seatbelt/safety belt;
9 boot (US trunk);
10 mirror   off;
11 engine   bonnet (US hood);
12 way   roundabout;
13 lights   lane;
14 caravan   (US trailer/mobile home);
15 straight;
16 space;
17 car sick;
18 sign;
19 pedestrian crossing;
20 trip   journey   journey.

B This part is similar in style to the FCE exam, except that in Paper 1 there are only four alternatives to deal with.

▶ Make sure you look at the WRONG alternatives in this part – and in such exercises in later units. There are many useful words among them. Can you explain WHY the wrong answers are wrong in each context?
For example, in **B** 1:
- Why is *by-pass* wrong in this context?
  Because a by-pass goes round a city or town – like a ring road, in fact.
- And why is *highway* wrong in this context?
  It's not completely wrong, it's just not a British English term – but it could be used in American English.
- And why is *main road* wrong in this context?
  Because a main road is a general word for an important road – not as wide as a motorway.
- And why is *main street* wrong in this context?
  Because a main street is an important road in a town or city, not one that goes a long distance.

1 motorway (US highway/freeway/interstate);
2 tube (US subway), also *underground*;
3 coach (US bus);
4 turning;
5 brake.

C

cruise = visiting different places by ship
trip = a short journey or a journey made on business
tour = visiting different places, often with a guide
flight = by air
crossing = by ship between two ports
voyage = a long distance by ship
excursion = a short pleasure trip, usually with a group
outing = a short pleasure trip

D Think about the questions for a few moments. Then record your answers to them on a blank cassette.

▶ Next time you travel anywhere, try to put an English name to everything you see.

4.2 The Orient Express — *Reading*

This passage contains quite a lot of difficult vocabulary, but the questions in **A** and **B** will help you to understand the main points in spite of this.

255

A

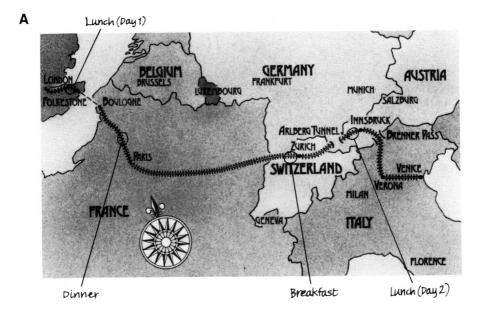

B TRUE: 2, 5, 6, 9, 10; FALSE: 1, 3, 4, 7, 8.

C This exercise will help you to appreciate the style of the passage. Use a pencil or highlighter for this. Perhaps look up any words you don't understand – these may be the very ones that create this impression of luxury and elegance.

Some selected phrases

- magnificent English 'Pullman' cars waiting grandly
- lunch in all its splendour with the Alpine panoramas in all theirs
- Exquisite food flawlessly served in surroundings of magnificent opulence
- Courteous and professional to a fault
- Course after tantalising course cooked to perfection by superb French chefs
- with your cabin miraculously transformed
- reading lamp left thoughtfully aglow
- your steward will tiptoe past your cabin
- dizzying Arlberg Pass and its 6½ miles of amazing tunnel
- towering forests, and peaks you have to crane to see, alternate with pretty waterfalls and rushing streams to take your breath away

D Using a blank cassette, record a description of a journey you regularly make – starting from the moment you leave your home right up to the moment you walk through the door at your destination.

Listen to your recording and try to decide what you could have said differently or better. Then have another go, but this time describe the journey in the OPPOSITE direction right up to your arrival home.

4.3 Revision of modal verbs *Grammar*

A There are a number of points here that may cause difficulty. Some of these are explained among the suggested answers below. For example, there is a difference in meaning between lack of obligation (*You needn't do it if you don't want to*) and an obligation not to do something (*You mustn't do it, even if you want to*).

Suggested answers

Ability/inability:

I can't find my pen anywhere – **Can/Could** you help me to **look for** it?
I **was** unable **to** finish all my work yesterday, but I hope **to finish / to be able to do** it tomorrow.

■ Notice that *was able* is used rather than *could* in some positive sentences. For example:
He thought he could climb the mountain

easily. = He thought it would be possible (but perhaps he didn't succeed).
He was able to climb the mountain easily. = Past ability + success

Possibility/Certainty/Impossibility:
Your bus **can't have** been two hours late, surely?
Might it be difficult to get a seat at such short notice?
Jane is always so careful, she **can't have/ couldn't have** forgotten to check the timetable – the train **must have** been delayed.

■ Notice that the ideas of 'certainty' and 'impossibility' can also be referred to as 'deduction' (e.g. You must be joking. / You can't be serious.). Strictly speaking, if you are completely certain about something you wouldn't use a modal verb at all:
It will rain today. = I am certain it will rain.
She was joking. = I know she was joking.
His plane didn't land on time.

■ Notice the difference between the idea of possibility that something is **not** true:
That may not/mightn't be correct. = It's possible that it's not correct.
He may not/mightn't have done it. = It's possible that he didn't do it.
and **impossibility**:
He can't have done it. = It's impossible that he did it.
That can't be correct. = I'm sure it's not correct.

Permission/Refusing permission:
You **mustn't smoke** when you're in a non-smoking seat.
You **weren't allowed to / couldn't use** a calculator in the maths test because it was against the rules.

Obligation or responsibility:
You **don't have to / needn't stand up** on the bus unless all the seats are occupied.
In the exam **do we have to / have we got to / must we write** in pen or are we allowed to use pencils?
You **ought not to / shouldn't spend** so much time listening to music when you **ought to be / should be** working.

■ Notice that there are different degrees of obligation and in many cases either *must*, *have to*, *have got to*, *should* or *ought to* can be used.

Basically, the differences are as follows:
MUST expresses strong obligation:
  You must go home now. = I am ordering you to go.
  I really must leave. = I am ordering myself to go.
HAVE TO expresses obligation from 'outside':
  I have to finish this today. = According to the rules or someone's orders.
  Don't you have to leave before 6? = (perhaps) You've got a train to catch or an appointment somewhere else.
HAVE GOT TO means the same as HAVE TO.
SHOULD expresses a duty or what is the right thing to do:
  You should be careful on the way home. = I advise you to be careful.
  I should work harder. = It would be the right thing for me to do.
OUGHT TO means the same as SHOULD.

▶ A full explanation of the 'rules' of usage of modal verbs would take up several pages. Please consult *Basic English Usage* by Michael Swan (Oxford University Press) or *English Grammar in Use* by Raymond Murphy (Cambridge University Press) for more examples and explanations.

B *Sentences with errors corrected*

(Some variations are possible.)
1 You don't need to / needn't worry about meeting me at the station, I'll get a taxi.
2 Ought I to / Should I phone the airport to find out if there might be / are any delays?
3 Were you able to find the papers you lost?
4 I don't/won't have to show my passport to get a rail ticket.
5 I was able to / managed to buy my ticket after queueing for five minutes.
6 You needn't / don't have to write anything down unless you want to. (If the original sentence ended ... *unless you really want to* it wouldn't really be wrong.)
7 I checked the timetable so I can't be wrong about the departure time!
8 You don't spend as much time as you should on your homework.
9 Could/Can you tell me where I can catch a bus to the railway station?

C This is the kind of exercise you may have to do in the exam.

1. You shouldn't eat food as you walk down the street in Japan.
2. I shouldn't have spent so much money on records.
3. Do I have to pay for my ticket now?
4. Can you tell me how much luggage I am allowed to / I can take on the plane?
5. Her car can't have broken down again.
6. You needn't stand / won't have to stand on the train if you have reserved seat.
7. You must have made a mistake when you added up the total.
8. Will you be able to get to the airport at 6.30 a.m.?
9. You needn't have / shouldn't have travelled first class.
10. We couldn't go / weren't allowed to go onto the platform.

D You may be able to think of other words that fit in some of the gaps (e.g. *happened* in gap 3).

1 Have; 2 did; 3 was; 4 had;
5 would; 6 was; 7 had; 8 might;
9 had; 10 was; 11 must; 12 was;
13 had; 14 would; 15 can; 16 has;
17 does; 18 do; 19 ought; 20 must;
21 could; 22 would; 23 is; 24 can.

4.4 Getting the message *Listening*

A Don't worry about the unfamiliar place names – in real life such announcements are full of place names.

1. a) Lyndhurst Road: Remain on platform 4;
   b) Portsmouth: Go to platform 2;
   c) Romsey: Go to platform 3.
2. a) Poole: Yes; b) Dorchester South: Yes;
   c) Christchurch: Yes – and you must change at Brockenhurst.
3. a) Parkstone: Change at Bournemouth;
   b) New Milton: Change at Brockenhurst;
   c) Millbrook: Remain on platform 4 for the next stopping train.

Tapescript

Narrator: Imagine that you're waiting on platform 4 at Southampton station and listen to this announcement.

Announcer: This is Southampton. Southampton. The train at this platform, platform 4 is the 17.38 Network Express to Weymouth, calling at Brockenhurst, Bournemouth, Poole, Hamworthy, Holton Heath, Wool, Moreton, Dorchester South, Upwey, and Weymouth. Change at Brockenhurst for Sway, New Milton, Hinton Admiral, Christchurch, and Pokesdown. Change at Bournemouth for Branksome and Parkstone. Remain on this platform for the next stopping train calling at Millbrook, Redbridge, Totton, Lyndhurst Road, and Beaulieu Road. Cross the footbridge to platform 2 for Netley, Fareham and the Portsmouth line. Cross the footbridge to platform 3 for Romsey and Salisbury.

(Time: 1 minute 20 seconds)

B

Tapescript

Recorded voice: ...now be repeated. This is the road report for the Bristol Area for Saturday 24th November, compiled by the Automobile Association. There are emergency road works on the southbound carriageway of the M5 motorway between junctions 17 and 18. These are likely to last throughout the weekend. Southbound traffic will be diverted to the northbound carriageway and there are likely to be long delays in both directions, particularly on Saturday.

Delays can also be expected on the main A38 Bristol to Taunton road near Bristol Airport due to resurfacing work on Saturday afternoon and Sunday.

The Carnival at Wells on Saturday afternoon is likely to cause delays to traffic on the A371 to the west of the city, but traffic on the A39 and A37 is unlikely to be affected.

Motorists are also advised to avoid the centre of Bristol all day Saturday, where traffic connected with the International Power Boat Races is likely to cause severe hold-ups.

There was a serious accident on Friday evening on the M4 between junctions 18 and 19 causing long delays to traffic. Both carriageways have now been reopened and no delays are expected on this motorway.

That is the end of this recorded road report, which will now be repeated. This is the road report for the Bristol area...

(Time: 1 minute 25 seconds)

258

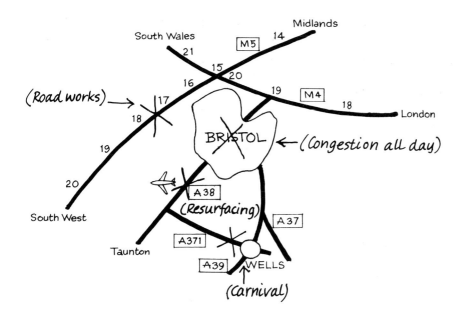

4.5 Using suffixes – Adjectives
Word study

A Use a dictionary to look up any unfamiliar words.

▶ Notice that the word stress changes in the -ical words, but not in any of the others:
biólogy → biológical
grámmar → grammátical
álphabet → alphabétical
geógraphy → geográphical   etc.

-al	musical professional traditional
-ical	alphabetical grammatical mathematical
-able	breakable comfortable enjoyable obtainable washable
-ful	colourful hopeful painful restful successful thoughtful
-less	careless fearless restless useless
-ish	foolish greyish oldish smallish tallish youngish
-y	bumpy draughty noisy rainy sleepy smelly sunny

B 2 thoughtful; 3 musical; 4 childish; 5 sunny; 6 readable; 7 geographical; 8 reddish; 9 unreliable; 10 unforgettable.

4.6 *Come* and *go*   *Verbs and idioms*

A 1 come; 2 go; 3 take; 4 Come bring; 5 carry; 6 delivered; 7 fetch.

B 1 came across; 2 came up against; 3 came about; 4 go with; 5 comes in goes out; 6 has been going out with; 7 gone off; 8 has gone off; 9 went off; 10 went in for; 11 Come on; 12 go on go over.

4.7 Avoid the queues   *Reading and discussion*

A The word-play in this advertisement is very common in British advertising.

1 Eleven Qs are missing.
2 British Airways flights to Paris, Amsterdam and intercontinental destinations (i.e. flights beyond Europe).
3 It's very large and so it's less busy and there are fewer queues.
4 You can wheel your trolley directly to the car park (no lifts, stairs or escalators), which holds 3,200 cars and is easily accessible.
5 Terminal 1.
6 There is a frequent bus service.

259

B These are just the type of questions you might be asked in the exam Interview about your experiences and opinions. Record your answers to the questions.

4.8 InterCity services *Problem solving*

A Notice that there may be several possible routes and times which are equally suitable. Conny's arrangements are quite simple, so perhaps begin with hers if you aren't very good at timetables.

Model notes on each person's route

ALAIN

Trains

The 07.55 is the ideal train, but he'd probably miss it - if he did catch it he could catch the 10.30 from Euston, arriving in Glasgow at 15.44. 08.55 probably OK unless ferry late - arrives London 10.19. Allowing 40 minutes to cross London, he might just make the 11.00 from King's Cross, if not he'd get the 11.35. That means he'd arrive in Glasgow at 17.18 or 18.21, changing trains in Edinburgh. A more relaxing way might be to go to Euston and catch the 13.00 direct train, arriving in Glasgow at 18.30, but if he's really in a hurry that's not the best one.

Planes

Catching the 08.55 from Portsmouth and taking the Underground to Heathrow Airport would get him there in time to catch the 12.15 plane, arriving at Glasgow Airport at 13.25 and then by coach to central Glasgow arriving about 2 p.m. If he caught the 07.55 from Portsmouth he could even be there by 1 p.m.

BOBBY

The best route is the direct one (especially if he's got a lot of luggage) and he may just catch the 10.17 and be in Manchester at 14.05. But by the time he gets through customs it may be 10.30 or later, so he can get the Gatwick Express at 10.35 or 10.50, arriving Victoria at 11.05 or 11.20. The train to Manchester from Euston at 12.50 will get him there at 15.25. He might just make the 11.50, which arrives in Manchester at 14.36.

CONNY

The best direct train is the 06.17 from Bristol, arriving in York at 10.46. No point in going via London.

B *Model notes on each person's route*

ALAIN

If the ferry is two hours late, he might just make the 09.55, but even if he missed it and caught the 10.55 that should get him in London in time to catch the 13.00 from Euston. Alternatively, the 13.15 plane from Heathrow would get him to the centre of Glasgow by 3 p.m.

BOBBY

If he's three hours late, he can get the 13.47 direct train, arriving in Manchester at 18.05. If he misses that he could get the 14.20 Gatwick Express and then get the 16.00 from Euston, arriving in Manchester at 18.33.

CONNY

If she misses the 06.17, she'll have to go via London. The 07.40 arrives at Paddington at 09.06 and then she can catch the 10.00 from King's Cross, arriving in York at 12.11. However, to be on the safe side, the earlier 07.00 from Bristol would be better, enabling her to catch the 09.35 from King's Cross, arriving in York at 11.54.

C *Model letters/postcards*

Dear Alain,
    When you get to Portsmouth, you should get the bus from the Ferry Port to the railway station. You might just make the 7.55 to London, but if not there's another train at 8.55. When you arrive at Waterloo, get the Underground to Heathrow Airport and you'll be in time to catch the 12.15 plane, arriving at Glasgow Airport at 13.25. There's a coach from there to the centre of Glasgow and you'll get there at about 2 p.m. If you caught the 7.55 from Portsmouth you could even be there by 1 p.m.
    If you don't want to go by air, and you do catch the 7.55, you could catch the 10.30 from Euston direct to Glasgow, arriving at 15.44.
    If your ferry is late, there are trains at 5 minutes to every hour from Portsmouth to London Waterloo, arriving about 1½ hours later. From there you can take the Underground to Heathrow (planes leave there every hour) or go to Euston and catch the

```
13.00 which arrives in Glasgow at
18.30.
        Have a good journey!
        All the best,


Dear Bobby,
        If your plane lands at Gatwick on
time, you should hurry through customs
and try to catch the 10.17 direct
train, which will get you to
Manchester at 14.05. If you're a bit
late, you should take the Gatwick
Express (every 20 minutes) to London
Victoria. Then take the Underground to
Euston, where you can take the 11.50
or the 12.50. If all goes well, you'll
arrive in Manchester at 14.36 or
15.25.
        If your plane is delayed, there's
another direct train from Gatwick
Airport station at 13.47 which would
get you to Manchester at 18.05.
        Have a good journey!


Dear Conny,
        If you have to get to York in
good time for your interview at 12.30,
you should take the direct train via
Birmingham, leaving Bristol at 6.17
a.m. and arriving in York at 10.46.
There's no point in going via London.
        If you missed that, you'd have to
go via London. The best train to take
is the 7.00 to London and then take
the Underground to King's Cross to
catch the 9.35 from King's Cross,
arriving in York at 11.54.
        Good luck with your interview!
        Best wishes,
```

4.9 How do I get there? *Listening*

A Study the map for a little while before you listen to the recording.

Tapescript

Woman: Hallo, Acme Agency. Can I help you?
Driver: Yeah, I hope so...um...look, I'm bringing round some deliveries this morning. I think you're expecting them and...er...I've got a bit of a problem. Um...I'm in Trumpington Street in a van at the moment but I can see up the road...er...to King's Parade that it's a one-way street and I...I...I don't have a clue as to how to get to you. Is there anyone in your office who can...um...you know...?
Woman: Yes, yes, I can probably help you. Whereabouts exactly are you in Trumpington Street?
Driver: Er...by er...Pembroke Street. Um...yeah, that's right. Because I've got this map here but it's a very stupid map because it has...it doesn't tell you where the one-way streets are, you know.
Woman: Yes and...and some of the...streets have become pedestrian precincts. It's changed a lot recently.
Driver: Yeah.
Woman: Look...um...go up Pembroke Street... Yes...Do you see that?
Driver: Yeah...yeah, sure.
Woman: And that becomes Downing Street... Yes...Now follow along Downing Street until you hit a T junction...
Driver: Yes.
Woman: St Andrew's Street?
Driver: St Andrew's Street.
Woman: That's right. Now turn left into St Andrew's Street and then immediately right down...
Driver: Immediately right? That's Emmanuel Street.
Woman: That's it. Past Emmanuel College. Then keep going and if you go straight to the end of Emmanuel Street, you'll see on your left the Bus Station.
Driver: Right. Got yer.
Woman: Now don't...don't turn into the Bus Station. Turn right away from the Bus Station and then left...er...first left.
Driver: Well, that's a bit dodgy 'cause I haven't got that on my map, but carry on, carry on.
Woman: Ah, well maybe you should draw it in.
Driver: Yeah, all right.
Woman: Right...go back to the bottom of Emmanuel Street.
Driver: Right.
Woman: Now turn right round the corner of Emmanuel College and draw in a road directly opposite going first left. That road will curve round with Christ's Pieces, which I think is marked on your map, on your left. Christ's Pieces on your left.
Driver: Quite right.
Woman: Right, in fact Christ's Pieces is set into a park and there's a car park on your right. Now keep going straight ahead until you hit a roundabout.
Driver: Yeah.
Woman: And then take the second exit.
Driver: The second exit. OK.
Woman: That will bring you into Jesus Lane. Can you see that?
Driver: Ah, I can see Jesus Lane, that's at the top of my map, yeah, right.
Woman: Fine. Follow Jesus Lane right round, Sidney Sussex College will be on your left...
Driver: Yeah, with you.

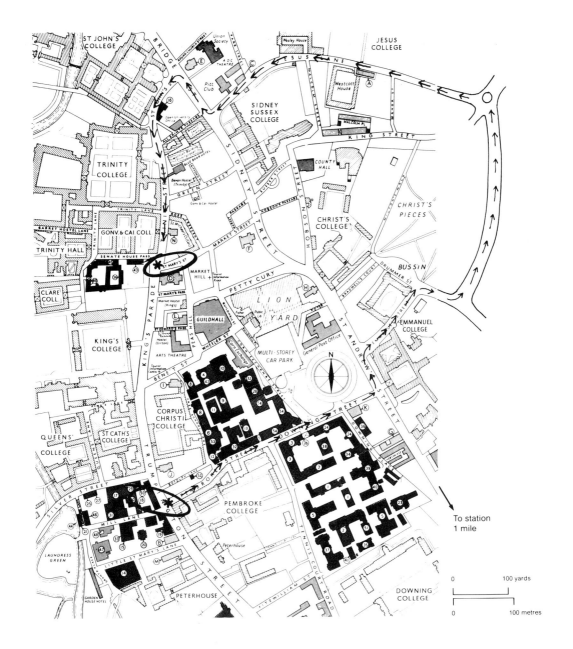

Woman: And you hit a T junction. Right, Sidney Street's on your left.
Driver: Yeah, that's Bridge Street and Sidney Street?
Woman: Bridge Street and Sidney Street, right. Turn right into Bridge Street and then take the first left down St John's Street.
Driver: Yes!
Woman: Go down St John's Street, along Trinity Street, where St John's Street becomes Trinity Street, right? Right to the end there and we're on the corner of Trinity Street and St Mary's Street. Can you see it?
Driver: Yes, yes, no problems now. Well, thanks very much. I'll be there in a few minutes I hope.
Woman: OK.
Driver: If I don't get lost again, eh?
Woman: Yes, good luck!
Driver: Bye.
Woman: Bye.

(Time: 2 minutes 40 seconds)

B Imagine that you are on the phone, like the woman in the recording, and the caller wants to know the route he must take on foot to get from St Mary's Street to the Bus Station, and so on. Record what you would say, using a blank cassette.

▶ As well as using the street plan of Cambridge, use a map of your own town or city. Explain the best routes to the various points of interest.

4.10 Layout of letters, directions — *Composition*

A *Suggested answers*

This is clearly a matter of opinion, but some of the more helpful bits of the *first letter* are perhaps:
 'Ask the driver to tell you'
 'I enclose a map' + the map itself is very useful

And some of the less helpful bits are:
 'expensive' – how expensive?
 'cheap, but slow' – how slow?
 'you'd have to change twice' – where?
 Jan doesn't recommend a best option

Some of the more helpful bits of the *second letter* are:
 'there's no easy way'
 'I'd suggest taking the underground'
 'When you come out of the station ...' etc. – the clear directions
 'there's a stop opposite Greenwood Station'

'If you get lost ... phone me at work' + the number

Some of the less helpful bits are:
 'You'll have to change twice' – where?
 No map

B There is no model composition, as the two letters in the main part of the book are models in this case, and show how personal letters are laid out.

4.11 Using prepositions – 1 — *Use of English*

1 for; 2 with about; 3 for; 4 of;
5 with about; 6 in; 7 from; 8 for;
9 about; 10 from; 11 of; 12 on;
13 of; 14 of; 15 for.

4.12 Transport in the future — *Communication activity*

Look at the notes in Activity 2. Imagine that you've been asked to give your views on the topic. Record what you would say, using a blank cassette.
 Then do the same with the ideas in Activities 8 and 28.

5 Somewhere to live

5.1 Make yourself at home! — *Vocabulary*

A Look round your room and name the main pieces of furniture (wardrobe, cupboards, etc.) and equipment (lamps, typewriter, etc.) in English.

B 1 swimming pool/games room/study/large garden, etc.; 2 neighbours; 3 detached/semi-detached/terrace/two-storey/family;
4 storeys floor; 5 accommodation;
6 outskirts suburbs; 7 move cottage/farmhouse, etc.; 8 mortgage (US home loan); 9 rent landlord/landlady; 10 cupboards (US closets)/storage space; 11 bookcase shelves; 12 central heating living room/lounge; 13 wardrobe/chest of drawers;
14 cosy/spacious/homely (GB)/welcoming/tidy, etc.

C 1 cellar; 2 blinds; 3 drive; 4 shed;
5 lawn.

5.2 Different places *Listening and speaking*

A

1 In a small flat in the city centre.
2 In a small semi-detached house in the suburbs, 10 km from town.
3 The garden, the lack of noise and the shops nearby.
4 Walking to work, the entertainments and the facilities.
5 The noise and the traffic.
6 Travelling to work and being dependent on public transport or a car.
7 In a larger flat in the city centre.
8 In a little cottage in the country.

Tapescript

Charles: I'm going to have to do something about my flat, you know.
Ruth: Why?
Charles: It's just much too small...I live in the middle of the city centre, you see.
Ruth: Oh I see, well I live in a small...semi-detached house in the suburbs. It's about ten kilometres out of town.
Charles: Oh, do you like it?
Ruth: Oh, I love it. I like having a garden, being able to sit in it and relax. You know, away from the noise of the city. And good shops, there are good shops nearby, I like that.
Charles: Course I like being able to...to walk to work...I've got all the entertainments and the facilities of the...you know, living in a city, they're all nearby like the cinemas and banks, shops, those sorts of things, you know.
Ruth: Oh yes...But...er...isn't it noisy?
Charles: Oh yes, it's terrible. Oh well, that's what I dislike about it: the noise and the traffic.
Ruth: Mm, but still if you live out like I do, I...there's still disadvantages. I dislike having to travel into the city to work and, you know, I'm always dependent on public transport or I have to go by car.
Charles: Yeah, I think the...thing that I really...er ...feel most about my flat is that it's just not big enough and I...You see, you talk about sitting in the garden, well I've...I haven't even got a balcony...Well, really I just wish I...you know, what I'd like to do most of all is get a bigger flat but still be in the middle of the t...of the city.
Ruth: I...I'd like not to have to go into the city at all. I wish I could afford to give up work and go and live somewhere in the country. You know, that's my dream: a little cottage in the heart of the country.

(Time: 1 minute 20 seconds)

B Make some notes on your answers to the questions. Then record what you would say if you were being asked them – try to do this without pausing the tape.

5.3 The future *Grammar*

A *Suggested answers*

PREDICTIONS + GENERAL FUTURE:
I'm sure the weather **will improve** towards the end of the week.
She is very clever, so I expect that she **will do well in** her exams next summer.
If you don't hurry up, the bus **will have left/gone** before we get to the bus stop!

Following a time conjunction:
If you **write them down**, you'll find it easier to remember the new words.
When my friend **arrives / gets here**, I'll tell her all about my plans.
By the time our guests **arrive / turn up**, all the food will have been eaten.

▶ Notice that, in CONVERSATION, the short form *'ll* is often used after names and question words:
Thomas'll be there.   Alison'll know the answer.   Who'll tell us?
but usually only WRITTEN after pronouns:
Thomas will be there.   Alison will know the answer.   Who will tell us?
He'll be there.   She'll know the answer.

FUTURE EVENTS that we can 'see coming':
Look out! That dog **is going to** bite you!
Look at those black clouds – it **is going to rain** soon.

INTENTIONS and PLANS:
I am going to do the work later, when I've got more time.
Your room is in a terrible mess – when **are you going to tidy it?**

ARRANGEMENTS:
I can't meet you this evening because **I'm going to a concert / going out**.

264

Mr and Mrs Jones **are coming** to dinner tomorrow.

FIXED EVENTS on a timetable or calendar:
The plane from London **lands/gets here** at 9.30.
Tomorrow, according to my diary, the sun **rises/sets** at 5.09.

PROMISES, SUGGESTIONS and OFFERS:
Give me your suitcase and **I'll put it** in the boot of the car for you.
I'll pay you back/repay the money you lent me next Friday.

B *Corrected sentences*

1 If the telephone rings, I'll answer it.
2 After the floor has been cleaned, I'll polish the furniture.
3 This evening I'm going to / I'll tidy up my room.
4 By the time you get home we will have finished dinner.
5 We'll be waiting for you when your plane lands at the airport.
6 Elizabeth is going to have a baby next month.
7 The new by-pass will be finished in the spring.
8 You won't be able to unlock the door if you don't remember your key.

C You may have to do an exercise like this in the Use of English paper. Look at the examples carefully before you begin.

Suggested answers

(Some variations are possible. In the places marked with a * *going to* can be used.)

2 Our latest news is that next week we are moving* house!
3 Our new flat is on the outskirts of the city.
4 The flat (itself) is not any larger but we'll be able to grow vegetables in the garden.
5 We hope there won't* be any problems with noisy and nosy neighbours, as there are now.
6 We'll* be glad to escape from the noise and traffic in the city centre.
7 My journey to work will* take longer, but I'll* enjoy the fresh air and privacy.
8 We'll* (be able to) take the dog for a walk across the fields every evening.

9 On Sunday 14th we're having* a flat-warming party.
10 Will you be able to come?
11 We're looking forward to seeing you any time after 7 p.m.
12 P.S. You won't (be able to) find our new flat without some directions.
13 If you phone me I'll tell you how to get there.

5.4 A nice place to live *Reading*

A Don't use a dictionary while you do this exercise.
TRUE: 2, 3, 4, 5, 7, 8; FALSE: 1, 6, 9, 10.

B 2 courteous; 3 squeezing; 4 agents; 5 award; 6 manners; 7 needless to say; 8 citizens; 9 consolation.

▶ Use a dictionary now to check the meanings of any unfamiliar words in the passage.

C Different countries have different ideas of what is polite. Imagine that you are talking to a British person who is coming to work in your country. What kinds of behaviour are considered polite in your country? Make some notes, then record what you would say on a blank cassette.

5.5 High-rise buildings *Listening*

A PAUSE the tape while you're writing your answers.

Tapescript

Interviewer: …over the past few years there seems to have been a swing against the popularity of high-rise buildings. Professor Hill, why do you think this is?
Professor: Well, first of all, I think we must make a clear distinction between residential and commercial buildings, OK?
Interviewer: Yes.
Professor: The first skyscraper was itself an office block built in Chicago in 1883 and there were really three reasons for this being built. Firstly, the enormously high price of land; secondly, there was a fair amount of cheap

NOTES

Where and when was the first skyscraper built?
Chicago in 1883
Why was it built? 1 High price of land
                   2 Cheap steel
                   3 Invention of the lift (elevator)
Where is the world's tallest apartment block?
Lake Point Towers, Chicago
Where is the tallest in the UK?
Shakespeare Tower, Barbican, London
How do people who live in tower blocks feel?
Isolated and lonely
What kind of flats are vandalised?
Council flats
How can vandalism be prevented?
  1 Encourage tenants to be proud of their homes
  2 Not housing families in high-rise blocks
  3 Building more low-rise flats
  4 Blowing up vandalised flats

---

steel about. And the third reason was that they'd invented the passenger elevator, the lift, in 1857.

Interviewer: So they could get to the top?

Professor: Exactly, yes. And where land is in fact still very expensive – especially in the centre of cities – high office buildings are still being built. And some companies get prestige from operating from a large modern beautiful building.

Interviewer: Yes, well, what about...um... dwellings?

Professor: Well, some luxury flats are still being built and the highest in the world is at Lake Point Towers in Chicago...um...the highest in the United Kingdom is the Shakespeare Tower, Barbican, in the City of London. But in the public sector housing – that's council flats – they're no longer being built at the rate they were in the 60s and early 70s. And the reasons for this are quite numerous: people feel very isolated in them and lonely and they have this terrible feeling of being cut off from the real world.

Interviewer: Understandable.

Professor: Yes, and so many of these flats were getting vandalised and smashed up – the windows were being broken, lifts damaged and so on. And oddly enough perhaps this doesn't seem to happen in privately-owned blocks, they...they tend to be much more secure. But perhaps that's because they've got porters or even guards to protect them.

Interviewer: Yes, what do you think can be done to prevent vandalism?

Professor: Well, vandalism can only be prevented by encouraging the tenants to take a pride in where they live, to feel that they own their environment. Not housing families in these large high-rise blocks – perhaps only single people or at least only childless couples. And...um...building more low-rise accommodation and, I have to say, that...er...in the last resort if all else fails, by blowing up the blocks which attract the vandals.

Interviewer: That seems a wee bit drastic.

Professor: Well, in many cases, it's the only thing that can be done.

Interviewer: Well, Professor Hill, thank you very much.

Professor: Thank you.

(Time: 2 minutes 35 seconds)

5.6 Using prepositions – 2   *Use of English*

1 deal with;   2 depends on;   3 engaged to married to;   4 forgive Bill for;   5 exchanged it for;   6 insisted on;   7 interfere with;   8 introduce you to;   9 involved in/with;   10 hope for;   11 interested in;   12 confidence in;   13 lack of;   14 longing for.

▶ Look up any new words in a dictionary – and look carefully at the examples given there as well as the definitions.

5.7 Spelling and pronunciation: Vowels
Word study

A Say the words aloud to yourself.
guest break hole steal through

B Say the words aloud to yourself. You need to recognise the phonetic symbols (/æ/ /ʌ/ /ə/, etc.) to find how words are pronounced when using a dictionary.

🔊 The completed lists are recorded on the cassette as a key to the exercise. Don't listen to this till you have completed the exercise.

Answers + Recording script

æ	/bæd/	**bad** damage + scandal marry
e	/bed/	**bed** pleasure leisure lent/leant + bury/berry weather/whether guessed/guest merry check/cheque
aɪ	/baɪt/	**bite** height guide eye/I + climb it/climate right/write by/buy/'bye
ɑː	/kɑːm/	**calm** heart + laugh castle half guard
ɔː	/bɔːd/	**bored**/board warm caught/court + wore/war shore/sure source/sauce walk warn/worn raw/roar
ɜː	/bɜːd/	**bird** worm + turn work
aʊ	/naʊ/	**now** crowd + plough allowed/aloud
ɔɪ	/bɔɪ/	**boy** point + destroy employer
eə	/ðeə/	**there**/their scarce where/wear + stares/stairs fare/fair pair/pear
ɪə	/hɪə/	**here**/hear steer + cleared atmosphere sincere
eɪ	/meɪk/	**make** sale/sail break/brake + paint wait/weight male/mail waste/waist
əʊ	/nəʊt/	**note** joke whole/hole + folk soap nose/knows
iː	/ʃiːp/	**sheep** piece/peace + ceiling sealing sieze/seas weak/week receive meat/meet seen/scene
ɪ	/ʃɪp/	**ship** sink mystery + guilty business witch/which mist/missed
ɒ	/pɒt/	**pot** what yacht + not/knot knowledge quality wander
uː	/buːt/	**boot** truly threw/through + soup blue/blew root/route new/knew
ʊ	/pʊt/	**put** should wood/would + cushion butcher pull push
ʌ	/kʌt/	**cut** worry money + blood tongue country one/won thorough wonder

(Time: 3 minutes 30 seconds)

C *Corrected words*

1 sure week to; 2 truly wait for; 3 dreadful pours sauce; 4 their armchair through; 5 Which two right; 6 leant against climbed; 7 ceiling painting urgently.

D 🔊 Listen to the tape and add the missing words. (In the recording the missing word is spoken again after each sentence.)

2 wonder; 3 wandered; 4 height; 5 guards; 6 knowledge; 7 walking; 8 caught; 9 damage; 10 receive.

5.8 Finding a flat
Listening and problem solving

A Make notes on your answers to the questions. By the way, Windsor, Sandringham and Balmoral (together with Buckingham Palace) are residences of the British Royal Family.

B 🔊 Listen to the recording a couple of times and make notes. Pay attention to the responses that the speakers give to each other (e.g. 'Mm, yeah') to find out whether they agree with each other or not.

Compare your notes with the model notes below.

Tapescript

John: Well, OK, darling, we've seen 'em all, what do you think?

Jill: Well, I think we really ought to talk about the money first. I mean, well, the one in…the one in Balmoral Way, now that…that did seem…I mean that was an awful lot of money compared with the others. I mean they were …they were both quite reasonable, I thought. But do you think we could afford to pay that much?

John: Well, it's…sure, it's more than…than I expected to pay but it…well, you could do without a few things, you know. Just…er…so that we could…Then I think we'd be able to afford it. But which of the kitchens did you like of all of them?

Jill: Kitchens, well the biggest one was that one in Windsor Avenue, but...I mean it did need a lot doing to it, didn't it? I mean, shelves, units and everything. Er...the other one I liked was the...was Sandringham Gardens, now that was...that was big, wasn't it, that one and it was facing south. Um...but the trouble with the other one *[i.e. Balmoral Way]* was that although it was...you know...it had...I mean...it was terribly well equipped, but it was very small and dark.

John: Oh, yes, yes, that's very true. You know what I liked about Windsor Avenue was the garden it had. You know, having a garden for m...garden flat for me would...would be *great* because it would mean we could sit out in the summer and...and, you know, it's wonderful...

Jill: Yes, yes, I know, but...I mean...but that one at Sandringham Gardens had a *lovely* big balcony an...and that would be gorgeous too when it's lovely weather.

John: Mm...balcony's OK, they're too small. It's a pity about Balmoral Way...you know...it had the park across the road. I guess that'd be all right for walks and things, having the park, but...

Jill: Yes, yes, and I must say the view over the park from there was lovely, wasn't it, you see? I mean, y...you could see the hills as well, couldn't you...well, I mean...you know...

John: Mm...mm...that's right.

Jill: ...quite far away but you could see them. And it...much nicer than that car park, which was...you know...Sandringham Gardens, remember that's all you could see out of the window there?

John: Yes, unbearable. That's true. That's true. You know something else we ought to discuss is th...the way each one of these places is positioned...each...where...how...how they are. Balmoral Way...er...it was close to the station. It...it'd be quite a short walk to catch the train you know, to get into town in the morning. Windsor Avenue...er...must be two miles away from the station, that's too much of a walk, specially if you have to do it twice a day.

Jill: Ah, yes, but just remember that you did say you wanted to take up cycling.

John: Haha!

Jill: Yes! You see, and you could easily do that in...in about a quarter of an hour on your bike. A...and the...exactly the same goes for Sandringham Gardens. Now that would only be about ten minutes to the station on your bike.

John: Yeah, but you know bicycling is fine in weather but I'm not sure I want to bicycle in the snow or the rain and in this country that's what you've got to count on. Now, what about the shops in addition to all that? If you're close to the town centre you can get anything you want and there at Balmoral Way you're just around the corner.

Jill: Yes, but I mean there were some really sweet little shops...er...near Windsor Avenue, weren't there?

John: Mm.

Jill: And...and there was the supermarket, the Co-op.

John: Oh, yes.

Jill: I mean, cer...I mean Sandringham Gardens ...it...I mean it just...I mean...the shops weren't there, were they?

John: No.

Jill: And that newsa...opp...that newsagent that was opposite, now that was the only shop that I saw.

John: That's true. One thing that worried me about both the Sandringham Gardens and the Windsor Avenue places was that they both needed a lot of work, you know, being done. Wallpaper and paintwork – revolting in both of them!

Jill: Yes, yes, I know but it was only a flat. I mean, it wouldn't take very long to redecorate that.

John: I don't know, it looked like a pretty big job to me. Anyway, the Balmoral Way flat...it...it'd just been freshly painted, it still looked...you know...I thought it looked pretty good.

Jill: Yes. And actually the rooms were a very good size, weren't they?

John: Mmm, yes.

Jill: I mean, they all felt quite spacious and that was...that was the one with the extra bedroom, wasn't it? For guests. Yes.

John: That's right, that's right. And what about all the traffic going past in that road? Seemed very noisy, I think we ought to think about that. Did you notice it?

Jill: Mm, yeah, I certainly did an...and it did seem very very peaceful, didn't it, at Windsor Avenue comparatively?

John: Yes, yes.

Jill: Still...still, I think I've made up my mind which of them I like best.

John: I think I have too. Let's hope we decide on the same one!

Jill: Haha!

(Time: 3 minutes 50 seconds)

It's a matter of opinion, but the flat they probably preferred was Windsor Avenue –

its garden was a particularly attractive feature.

Model notes

BALMORAL WAY
- expensive - they could just about afford it
- kitchen quite well equipped but small and dark
- public park opposite
- nice view of park + hills
- very near station
- near town centre + shops
- freshly decorated
- spacious rooms
- extra bedroom
- noisy traffic

SANDRINGHAM GARDENS
- kitchen quite big + facing south
- balcony
- view over car park
- 10 mins from station by bike
- only newsagent's shop nearby
- needs redecorating (maybe not a problem)

WINDSOR AVENUE
- biggest kitchen but needs a lot doing to it: shelves, units, etc.
- garden - they could sit out in summer
- 2 miles from station (but John could cycle in 15 mins)
- small shops + Co-op nearby
- needs redecorating (maybe not a problem)
- peaceful

C In the model paragraphs BOTH sides of the argument are included in sentences beginning 'Although …'. This may not be necessary as this information is not really relevant.

Model paragraphs

Jill and John might have chosen 7B Windsor Avenue because of its large kitchen and the nearby shops. But the main attraction of that flat was its garden - a place to sit on warm days and enjoy the peace and quiet of the neighbourhood. Although it was some way from the station, John could get there in a few minutes by bike. The one drawback seemed to be that it needed redecorating.

They might have decided against 44C Sandringham Gardens because it was so far from the station, though John could have cycled there in ten minutes. Although its kitchen was bright and it had a balcony, the main drawbacks were that there were no shops nearby, apart from a newsagent's, and the view of the car park was unbearable.

They might have rejected 13A Balmoral Way because it was expensive, but apart from this it had no garden and the kitchen seemed small and dark. Although it had an extra room, felt spacious, was near the shops and the station and had a good view over the park opposite, it was on a busy road and would be very noisy.

D Record a description of your dream house on a blank cassette.

5.9 Welcome to G__! *Reading*

A

1 not far;   2 deep;   3 under an hour's walk;   4 sleepy;   5 a short walk;   6 don't depend on tourism;   7 not changed its atmosphere;   8 wants to keep it a secret.

5.10 Starting and ending well *Composition*

A The suggested answers below are a matter of opinion and some are more suitable than others. Some of the unsuitable ones would be suitable in a different type of composition.

Suitable opening sentences: 1, 3, 4? 5, 6?, 9, 10?

B Suitable closing sentences: 1, 3?, 7, 8, 9.

D There is no model composition in this case. Look again at the passage in 5.9 on G__ as your model. The description of G__ is much longer (432 words) than you will need to write in the exam (120–180 words).

5.11 Grammar revision

(Some variations are possible.)
2 When I was a child we lived in the country.
3 We have been living in this district for eight years.
4 The furniture has to be moved from this room.
5 After we have had our summer holiday, we'll redecorate our flat.
6 Someone must have forgotten to lock the door.
7 After we had finished spring-cleaning we went out for a meal.
8 While we were having our meal, we discussed what to do at the weekend.
9 You hadn't painted this room last time I was here.
10 You shouldn't have painted the walls pink. *or* You should have painted them a different colour.

▶ Check any mistakes you made by referring to your grammar book.

6 Science and technology

6.1 Talking about science *Vocabulary*

B 1 atoms; 2 element; 3 compound;
4 radioactive; 5 chemistry physics biology; 6 formula; 7 experiments;
8 laboratory; 9 workshop demonstration;
10 theory practice; 11 proved;
12 practical; 13 technique; 14 electronic;
15 hardware software; 16 disc/tape/floppy disc/hard disc/magnetic tape/cassette;
17 instructions; 18 button/switch;
19 adjust/reduce/increase; 20 serviced break down repaired/mended/fixed/put right;
21 robots; 22 components/parts;
23 carpenter screwdriver/plane/drill;
24 screws/nails glue; whatsit/wotsit/thingumabob/thing/gadget/mechanism/device.

▶ Notice the pronunciation of these words (which are normally NOT used in writing):
whatchamacallit /wɒtʃəməkɔːlɪt/
thingumajig /θɪŋəmədʒɪg/ whatnot /wɒtnɒt/
wotsit /wɒtsɪt/ thingumabob /θɪŋəmɪbɒb/

C Make notes on how some equipment or gadgets are used. Then record an explanation of how they work. Use a dictionary.

6.2 For a pint, just add water *Reading*

A Read this information before you read the newspaper article:

The traditional ingredients of beer are: malted barley, hops, yeast and water (though sugar may sometimes be added and even various chemicals). The hops give the drink its bitter flavour. The ingredients are mixed together and the yeast ferments, forming alcohol from the sugar contained naturally in the malted barley. Eventually, when the fermentation is complete, the liquid is filtered to remove the excess yeast and sediment and put into barrels or bottles.

B 1 c 2 b 3 b 4 b 5 c 6 b 7 c 8 c

6.3 Using the passive *Grammar*

B

ACTIVE	→ PASSIVE
They did it yesterday.	→ It was done yesterday.
They were doing it last week.	→ It was being done last week.
They have already done it.	→ It has already been done.

They will soon do it.	→ It will soon be done.
They will soon have done it.	→ It will soon have been done.
They had done it earlier.	→ It had been done earlier.
They have to do it at once.	→ It has to be done at once.
They may not have done it yet.	→ It may not have been done yet.

C

1 The process has been patented by Fischer.
2 The concentrate will only be sold to bottling companies.
3 Bottlers will be required to use water specified by Fischer.
4 The trade name can be chosen by the bottlers.
5 These particles can only be seen through a microscope.
6 The first laser was produced by Charles Townes in 1960.
7 Computers are being used in all kinds of work.
8 Dangerous chemicals have to be kept in a safe place.
9 The laboratory shouldn't have been left unlocked.
10 Intelligent life is unlikely to be discovered on other planets.

D Write sentences about each invention or discovery. There are no model answers, as each sentence will contain your own ideas.

Dates for your information:
bicycle 1840   computer 1943
jet engine 1937   laser 1960
margarine 1869   printing press 1455
Scotch tape 1930   telephone 1876
television 1926   thermometer 1593

6.4 Serendipity   *Listening*

A 1 a 2 c 3 c 4 b 5 a 6 c
7 a 8 b 9 c 10 c 11 b 12 b

Tapescript

Presenter: ...good luck plays a part in scientific research too. In this case it's often referred to as **serendipity**, which according to my dictionary is 'the natural talent that some people have for finding interesting or valuable things by chance'. Debbie Charles has been looking into this for us. Debbie.

Debbie: That's right, Jenny. In fact, you know, most important discoveries in the world of science and technology came about by some sort of lucky accident. Starting with the wheel, presumably.

Now let's just look at a few of these, starting with...er...**penicillin**. Now, Alexander Fleming found some mould growing on a laboratory dish which he'd...er...absent-mindedly left on a windowsill. Now, he found that this mould stopped the spread of bacteria, which as you know is the cause of illnesses like pneumonia. And modern antibiotic drugs based on penicillin save millions of lives every year.

And then there's **radar**. Now, all sea and air transport depends on radar for navigation and safety – and armies depend on it for defence as well, of course. Radar was discovered during the war while British military scientists were trying to find a death ray, which was...er...some sort of radio wave that could be used to kill people. They didn't find a death ray, but they did find a technique.

And then there's...er...**Teflon**, which is a substance which is used in non-stick frying pans. Now, this was discovered by accident in a laboratory by DuPont scientists, who were doing research into gases to use in refrigerators. Now, they discovered that a plastic coating had formed on their equipment and this was unaffected by heat and it was also very slippery. Now, no use was found for this until some time later a French researcher used it in a frying pan – and...er...Teflon's also used in space vehicles.

And then there's **artificial sweeteners**: now, from saccharine to the more modern sweeteners, all of these (for example...er...Cyclamate and Nutrasweet, etc.) were discovered by accident. The usual pattern was that scientists were...were doing another experiment and they happened to taste one of the by-products, which they found to be sweet. Some of these sweeteners are thousands of times sweeter than sugar, you know.

And then there's **chewing gum**, which was discovered while scientists were looking for a substitute for rubber. And again there seemed at the time to be no apparent use for this product of the...er...Mexican Sapodilla tree! But serendipity made this product – there's no country in the world where chewing gum isn't available.

Presenter: Haha, no, but...er...I'm not sure that

that is quite as beneficial to mankind as the others that you've talked about!

Debbie: Oh, maybe not. But here's one more very useful product. You know those...er...little yellow stick-on notes we use in the office and...er...for leaving phone messages and so on? Er...**Post-It Notes**, they're called I think. Well, a researcher at 3M (which is the firm that makes Scotch tape) was doing research into adhesives and glue, and...er...he discovered a substance that seemed to be completely useless. I mean, it was...was quite sticky but it wouldn't stick permanently to anything. You know, that's what adhesives obviously are supposed to do. And in fact, however long he left the adhesive sticking to various surfaces, it didn't make a mark on the surface and the bond became no more and no less effective. All other adhesives either get more sticky or less sticky with age, you know. Now, he was a member of a church choir and he always had to use slips of paper to mark the place where each of the hymns was in his hymn book – and the slips of paper kept falling on the floor. So he used these bits of sticky paper with this...er...'useless' adhesive on to mark his place in the hymn book. And then he realised that other people could find a similar use...

Presenter: Brilliant!

Debbie: No, just serendipity!

Presenter: Haha. Yah. Thank you, Debbie.

(Time: 3 minutes 50 seconds)

6.5 Helping people to understand   *Pronunciation*

Although you will NOT have to read aloud in the exam, your pronunciation will be marked during the Interview. These reading aloud exercises will help you to improve your pronunciation, so that people can understand you more easily.

This section emphasises the importance of PAUSES and STRESS.

B 🔲 Listen to the first part of the recording.

Tapescript

The text is read aloud with pauses in the wrong places, silly intonation and many words wrongly stressed:

Quick reactions ARE imporTANT IF you're an airline
pilot. A motorist? or even a cyclist? – and OF course IN sports fast
reactions ARE especially
valuable this simple
BUT effective reaction timer makes
use of THE principle ...

(Time: 35 seconds)

E Record your reading on a blank cassette. Compare your reading with the recording that you listened to in **C** and **D**.

6.6 Reaction times   *Directed writing*

A If you have carried out the experiment on some friends or members of your family, use your own table.

B *Model paragraphs*

1   An experiment was carried out in which we tested each other's reactions. To begin with, we cut out a piece of paper and copied a scale onto the edge of the paper. The paper was wrapped round a ruler and secured with sticky tape. Then each member of the group had to catch the ruler between their thumb and forefinger as it fell. The speed of their reaction was shown in seconds on the scale at the point they gripped it.

2   We found that there was a big difference in reaction times between members of the group and between each person's left and right hand. The person with the quickest reactions was Chris (average 0.11 seconds), though she failed to catch the ruler at all on one of her attempts. The person with the slowest reactions was Anne (average 0.17 seconds). Bill's average was 0.15 seconds and mine was 0.14 seconds, and it was surprising that my left-hand reactions were faster as I am right-handed.

3   We thought that the experiment was interesting and surprisingly enjoyable. Before we started we were quite doubtful, as the idea seemed rather silly and childish, but once we got started and were concentrating hard and trying to do

our best, we discovered we were talking English to each other in a very natural way. The actual results of the experiment were quite interesting, and we wondered whether one could develop the speed of one's reactions by exercises or more practice.

6.7 Using prepositions – 3
Use of English

1 with about for; 2 of to;
3 on with; 4 to for; 5 in for;
6 with; 7 from for; 8 from with;
9 for; 10 of for to; 11 to;
12 for from.

6.8 Chips with everything?
Reading

A 1 c 2 b 3 b 4 b 5 a 6 b 7 c 8 b

B change – convert; bring advantages for – benefit; in danger – at risk; lack of differences – uniformity; simple – unsophisticated; do better than – surpass; painful – wounding; not taking part in – opting out of; intelligent – smart; feeling of not belonging – alienation.

6.9 I'd better explain how it works
Listening

 1 a 2 b 3 b 4 a 5 b 6 a

Tapescript

Ted: Now, Annie, while you're here looking after the house, you may want to use the dishwasher.
Annie: Oh, that'd be lovely, yes. It'll save me a lot of bother.
Ted: Now, it's not as easy as it looks. So I'd better explain, you know, then you won't break anything.
Annie: Oh, right. Go on then.
Ted: Now listen, put all the cups and glasses in the top rack, not the bottom one, otherwise they'll all rock about and get broken. We made that mistake when we first bought it. Er...plates and cutlery all go in this bottom rack and you sort of slot them in.
Annie: Er...now does it matter whether...do the bigger ones go at the back?
Ted: You've got it!
Annie: Right?
Ted: No, actually, what...what you do is you put the large plates on the right. Not on the left.
Annie: Oh, the right.
Ted: You know why you don't put them on the left?
Annie: No.
Ted: Be..because if you do, the door won't close.
Annie: Ha ha. I'd have probably found that out, wouldn't I?
Ted: Now...er...cutlery in the two little baskets there. Oh...handles downwards. Otherwise they don't get washed properly.
Annie: Oh, really...mm...
Ted: Um...now...er...Oh, don't try to...
Annie: Oh, wait a minute. You know, I think I'm going to write this down, actually, because...
Ted: Well, it's not that difficult.
Annie: Isn't it?
Ted: No, no.
Annie: All right. OK. Well, go on then.
Ted: I mean, I'll leave the manual here, just in case...
Annie: Oh OK, yeah. Ta.
Ted: All right? And then you've got it. But anyway...Oh, don't try to put a large plate on the...on the far right nearest the side.
Annie: Why?
Ted: Well, if you did that, you can't slide the rack in. Well, you'd probably...
Annie: Oh, I see, of course.
Ted: Now...er...
Annie: What about the powder?
Ted: Oh yes...ahha...good point. Otherwise you won't...won't be able to wash anything. Now...er...measure out a...a...a full scoop of powder. You know, fill it right up...um...because otherwise it won't be enough powder...
Annie: OK. One full scoop, yeah.
Ted: Full scoop.
Annie: Right.
Ted: Now, the powder container is here in the door of the dishwasher. Put the powder in there.
Annie: Uhhu...Right.
Ted: Close the flap. And the flap'll auto...automatically open when the...when the programme flicks round to Wash.
Annie: Oh I see. Now...er...how do I actually start the whole thing going?
Ted: Dead simple.
Annie: Yeah.

Ted: Turn the control knob to three.
Annie: Three?
Ted: Number three, that's important, number three. Pull it out to start the machine going, right?
Annie: Yeah.
Ted: And the whole cycle lasts about an hour. So you just leave the things in there...um...and in fact it's best to leave the things longer than an hour to...to dry completely, if you can do that.
Annie: Oh, I see. Well...
Ted: OK?
Annie: Yeah, that's fine! Yeah, I think I've got that. Thanks!

(Time: 2 minutes 10 seconds)

6.10 How does it work? *Communication activity*

Study the information in Activity 39. Then record an explanation in your own words. Listen to your recording before doing the same with the information in Activity 47.

6.11 Explaining a process *Composition*

A The first paragraph lacks detail and the second has rather too much irrelevant detail. Try to avoid these faults when writing the composition in **B**.

B The model composition below is about microwave ovens. If you want to write on the same topic, you may have to do some research.
   Alternatively, if you choose to write about a different topic, it may help you to read the model composition before you start.

Corrections

SPELLING: What was the affect of this? ✗ effect
PREPOSITIONS: I'm interested for science. ✗ in
VERB FORMS AND ENDINGS:
  I was gave it. ✗   If I would be rich... ✗
  I was given it.   If I were rich...
  She live in London. ✗
  She lives in London.
ARTICLES: I'm interested in the science. ✗
  I'm interested in science.

Model composition

MICROWAVE OVENS
Microwaves are a type of short-wave radiation, rather like radio waves. They are produced by a device called a magnetron which is housed inside the oven. The microwaves are reflected by metal surfaces but absorbed by food. They cause the molecules of the food to vibrate billions of times a second, making the food heat up and cook. Larger amounts of food take longer to cook, so microwaves are especially effective when cooking small portions.
   The advantages of microwave cooking are that it is both quicker and cleaner than conventional cooking. Food that has already been cooked can be reheated at any time without loss of flavour or juices, and frozen food can be defrosted and cooked very easily.
   Microwave ovens use less energy than conventional methods of cooking and are very safe. As soon as the door is opened, they automatically switch off and microwaves cannot normally leak out of the door while they are operating - despite some frightening stories about this!

6.12 *Keep* and *take* *Verbs and idioms*

A took ...
   some photographs, a holiday together, a long time, control of the situation, action, no notice of each other, the engine to pieces, care of the children
kept ...
   calm, house for their father, quiet, their tempers, their hands in their pockets, listening, an eye on each other

B The synonyms given below are approximate only. Refer to a dictionary for more exact definitions and further examples.

1 keep up = continue;   2 keep on with = continue;   3 keep away from = not go close to;   4 kept on = continue;   5 keep up with = go as fast as;   6 took in = trick/deceive;   7 take up = start an activity;   8 took to = start to like;   9 take over = be in charge;   10 take off = leave the ground;   11 takes up = fill;   12 take in = absorb/understand;   13 take away from = subtract;   14 take after = inherit a characteristic.

7 Good health!

7.1 In sickness and in health — *Vocabulary*

A 1 thermometer; 2 infectious/contagious/catching cure/remedy/medicine; 3 swollen/painful/bruised/tender/sore; 4 surgery/waiting room/office (US); 5 medicine/tablets/pills; 6 sneezing/sniffing/having to blow your nose; 7 plaster/bandage/dressing/Band-Aid (US)/Elastoplast (GB); 8 ambulance; 9 operation; 10 fillings; 11 exercise; 12 temperature/headache/stomachache; 13 diet; 14 stomach/tummy; 15 be sick/throw up.

B 1 prescription; 2 injection; 3 spots; 4 game; 5 headache.

C 1 off your food   out of sorts   under the weather; 2 bruise   bump   cut; 3 physically fit   living a healthy life   in good shape; 4 affect   damage   ruin; 5 dizzy   faint   funny.

7.2 What to do about flu — *Reading*

A TRUE: 1, 4, 7, 8, 9, 14 (dirty plates and cutlery can spread infection), 15; FALSE: 2 (they can't kill viruses), 3 (24 hours to several days), 5 (don't force yourself to), 6 (it can become serious for elderly or sick people), 10 (the text would say if this was advisable – but if it helps, why not?) 11 (they can be), 12 (only one year), 13 (winter).

B Do this as a writing exercise. Write down your questions and the advice you'd give. Then compare your ideas with the suggested questions and advice below.

Some questions

Have you got a headache?
Do you feel weak or shivery?
Are you sweating a lot?
Do you feel sick?
Have you lost your appetite?
Have you got a high temperature?
etc.

Some advice

It's best to stay indoors.
You'd better keep away from other people.
If I were you I'd take a few days off work.
The best thing to do is to go to bed.
You ought to take it easy.
etc.

C Record the advice you would give, as if you were talking to your friend on the phone.

7.3 Comparing and contrasting — *Grammar*

B Try to use a VARIETY of the structures shown in the examples in **A**, and not just 'more … than'. Here are two examples:
   In 1950 there were far fewer retired people in Britain than there are now.
   In 2025 there will be over twice as many retired people in Japan as there are now.
When you have written your ten sentences, compare them with the examples given in **A**. As this exercise is open-ended, there are no model answers given here.

C *Errors underlined and corrected*

1 *no errors*
2 July in Cairo is far <u>more dryer as</u> Athens.   **drier than**
3 The daytime temperature in Tokyo in July is the same <u>than</u> New York.   **as**
4 There are <u>much</u> differences between the weather in Cairo and Tokyo.   **many**
5 The weather in Athens in July is <u>more warmer</u> than London.   **warmer**
6 New York is <u>more cold</u> in winter <u>as</u> London.   **colder   than**

D

1 London isn't as hot as Cairo in July.
2 There aren't as many rainy days in Buenos Aires as (there are) in New York.

3 More rain falls in Athens than in Tokyo in January.
4 Buenos Aires is cooler than New York in July, but drier. / Buenos Aires isn't as warm as New York in July, but it's drier.
5 About the same amount of rain falls in London and New York.
6 In London summer nights are much cooler than Cairo.
7 A sprained wrist is not as serious as a broken leg.
8 AIDS is the most frightening illness you/anyone can imagine.
9 A cold is less serious than flu.
10 Not as many people die from flu as 50 years ago.

E Write two paragraphs: one on the similarities and the other on the differences. Or, if you prefer, write ten sentences.

7.4 Sleep and dreams *Listening*

A TRUE: 1, 3, 5, 6, 9, 12; FALSE: 2, 4, 7, 8, 10, 11.

Tapescript

Interviewer: ...now, sleep, like the way our brains work, is something of a mystery, but some recent research into sleep has given us a few more answers. Dr Terry Harrison has just published a book called *Sleep*. Dr Harrison, how many kinds of sleep are there?

Dr Harrison: There are three types of sleep: light sleep, deep sleep and REM sleep. Now, light sleep is 'optional' – we can do without it and yet quite a lot of our sleeping time is spent sleeping lightly. Our brains in fact require deep sleep, not REM sleep, to restore them.

Interviewer: And dreams occur when you're just about to wake up, don't they?

Dr Harrison: A lot of people think this but it...it is in fact wrong. Dreams take place during REM – and that's rapid eye movement sleep. That's every 90 minutes or so throughout the night. And they usually go on for several minutes.

Interviewer: Why do we dream?

Dr Harrison: Again, opinion is divided. One purpose of dreams seems to be to help sleepers to solve problems in their waking lives. Er...we all know the most common dreams that we experience...er...falling, flying, being chased, for instance. And in these dreams like falling or being chased, the dreamer's not usually hurt or caught, is he?

Interviewer: Now, not everyone does dream, do they?

Dr Harrison: Research has in fact shown that everyone does dream at some point, according to my research anyway. But many people can't *remember* their dreams. In fact, most people forget their dreams very quickly after waking up. Now, if I asked you to tell me about your dreams last night now, you probably couldn't remember, could you?

Interviewer: ...No, no, actually I can't.

Dr Harrison: Yet, alternatively if I asked you as soon as you'd woken up you would have been able to tell me.

Interviewer: I see. And how much sleep do we really need? Er..eight hours is supposed to be what everyone requires.

Dr Harrison: Yes, in fact most people require less than eight hours' sleep a night...er...six or seven is enough for many people. And there are many successful people who need only a few hours sleep a night. Erm..I can think of Napoleon, and there's Winston Churchill...er...Margaret Thatcher all managed...er...to manage on four hours a night – leaving them more time than their enemies to keep one step ahead!

Interviewer: Haha. Now, what about problems like er...snoring and talking in your sleep? Are there any cures?

Dr Harrison: Ah, no, no there is no cure for snoring apart from waking up. And...er...talking in your sleep is something most people do at some time in their lives, it's not a problem exactly and it occurs in all kinds of sleep, not just when you're dreaming.

Interviewer: Now what about people who have two sleeps, one sleep during the day (a siesta) and another sleep at night? Now, presumably they get more sleep than the people who only sleep at night?

Dr Harrison: It's very simple, if you...if you split your sleep into two parts, you need less sleep. If you take a siesta and sleep for say two hours, you only need to sleep for four or five hours at night. And that's presumably why people in Mediterranean countries seem to be able to keep going until 2 a.m. or even later. But a sleep during the day has to be long enough to allow time for deep sleep. So the benefit of a ten-minute nap is only psychological, not physical. It may make you feel better, but it doesn't really do you any good at all.

Interviewer: Dr Harrison, thank you.

Dr Harrison: Thank you.

(Time: 3 minutes 5 seconds)

7.5 Using suffixes: Actions and people
Word study

A
- **-ise** individualise summarise symbolise
  (Note that these can also be written **-ize**)
- **-en** flatten lessen loosen sharpen soften tighten
- **-ify** purify simplify

B
- **-er** bróadcaster cléaner mánager sínger skíer teácher
- **-or** diréctor inspéctor instrúctor vísitor
- **-ant** assístant inhábitant
- **-ist** ártist cýclist scíentist týpist

C 1 loosen tighten; 2 scientist assistant; 3 widened motorist; 4 employer employees; 5 sharpening; 6 sterilised heating; 7 rider cyclist; 8 inhabitants.

7.6 Welcome to the health farm!
Listening

A TRUE: 1, 2, 6, 7, 9; FALSE: 3, 4, 5, 8, 10.

Tapescript

Dr Lawrence: Good afternoon, everybody, I'm Jane Lawrence, I'm Doctor Jane Lawrence, the administrator and medical officer. I hope you're all going to be very happy here. I must explain first that you've got to participate in all the activities we offer and no absences from the premises will be permitted. Every morning everybody has to weigh in and your progress will be monitored. Your diets are adjusted according to the progress you make – that is, how much weight you lose. Now first of all, I'd like to introduce Mr O'Hara, the sports organiser. Mr O'Hara.

Mr O'Hara: Good afternoon. Now my motto is: healthy bodies are fit bodies. And from the look of you lot, you are certainly going to need our programme of compulsory sport and exercise routines. By the way, I also organise the social activities programme, which includes dances and cross-country treasure hunts.

Dr Lawrence: Thank you, Mr O'Hara. Now I'd like to explain the rules of the house. I'm afraid no visitors are allowed; lights out at 11 p.m.; breakfast at 7.15 a.m. Could I introduce you to Miss Burns, who is our catering manager.

Miss Burns: Good afternoon. Well, I think you'll find the food here is wholesome and well-cooked. The amount that you will receive is given in strictly controlled portions according to the amount of weight that you lose each day. However, guests on the intensive one-week course will only be served with lunch and a salad dinner, I'm afraid. There will be no cakes, sweets or bread served at all.

Dr Lawrence: Thank you, Miss Burns. Now I'd just like to point out one final thing: all post received will be opened by the reception staff to prevent smuggling of extra food. I'm afraid that's been necessary because of our bad experiences in the past. Let me wish you a pleasant stay here with us and if you have any questions about the course you are on, please come and see me in my office.

(Time: 2 minutes 10 seconds)

7.7 Suppleness, strength and stamina
Problem solving

B With these profiles (as in the exam) some of the information given is not directly relevant to the task: the idea is to SELECT the relevant information.

C *Model paragraphs*

```
My advice to Anna is to take up
swimming. This will help her to
develop her stamina as well as
improving her muscle power and
suppleness. The best way to go about
it would be to get together with a
friend and go to the local swimming
pool together two or three times a
week. Dancing would be unsuitable as
she doesn't like pop music.

If Richard wants to keep fit he should
take up yoga to improve his
suppleness. This is something he can
practise at home on his own, or he
could join a class. If he can afford
the time he could walk to work every
day, but this wouldn't really help him
with his stiffness problem. Swimming
might also be a good idea for him.
```

⟫→

The best thing for Eric to do would be to learn to swim, then he could go for an early morning swim every day to keep fit. If this is not possible, he could become a football referee. Referees have to do a lot of running around, but they don't need to be as young as footballers. Another idea for Eric would be to take up tennis, especially if his hotel has a tennis court.

What I do to keep fit is spend ten minutes every morning doing simple keep-fit exercises: arm swinging, sit-ups, knee-bends and so on. I also run on the spot for two to three minutes, which is more energetic than running for the same amount of time. I usually swim once a week, but I don't really enjoy swimming up and down a pool. In fact, that's the trouble with most ways of keeping fit on your own: although they are necessary, they tend to be rather boring!

7.8 A pain in the neck   *Reading*

B 1 c   2 b   3 c   4 d   5 c

7.9 At...   *Prepositional phrases*

1 at first = to begin with;   2 at least = not less than;   3 at last = finally;   4 at first sight = when first seen;   5 at a profit   at a loss;   6 at war   at peace;   7 at a time = not all together;   8 at any rate = in any case/anyway;   9 at once = immediately;   10 at the same time = simultaneously.

7.10 Staying healthy   *Picture conversation*

There is a model conversation recorded on the cassette – listen to this AFTER you have done **A** and **B**.

A and B

Write down six questions about the first picture and six about the second. Then record your answers to the questions.

Now listen to the model conversation, which shows the kind of conversation that might take place in the exam Interview. (As both speakers are British, this is not a REAL exam Interview.)

Tapescript

Man: ...Mm, look at these two photos here.
Woman: Mm? Oh yeah.
Man: What's your reaction to the first picture?
Woman: Which one? The woman keeping fit...er...jogging?
Man: Yeah. Why is she alone do you think?
Woman: Haha, well, perhaps she couldn't get anyone to go with her – or perhaps she's ahead of her companion and he's not such a fast runner.
Man: So...um why do you think she's wearing headphones, then?
Woman: Oh, is she? Oh, yes. Well, I mean, jogging's not very interesting, is it? And music helps to keep you going – I mean, the rhythm ...the rhythm can help you keep you going at a steady...steady pace.
Man: Yeah, you mean you don't fancy...er...swapping places with her, then?
Woman: Haha, it could be me. I do try to go jogging every evening after work, but I don't go on my own. No, I always go with my boyfriend, I think it's safer. Actually, it's quite good for me 'cause he's faster than me and I have to run to keep up with him. Haha.
Man: Haha, so wh...why do you do it, then?
Woman: Well, I don't...don't really enjoy it but if I didn't do that, I'd have to do something else to keep fit.
Man: Well, why don't you do something different then?
Woman: Well, I think the main advantage is that you only need a good pair of running shoes.
Man: That's true.
Woman: You just go outside and start running, and it's free and you can more or less do it any time you like – even if it's raining or snowing or blowing.
Man: That's true, fair enough. OK, so...um... what's your reaction to the other one then, the other picture?
Woman: Let's see...well, when I first saw it, I thought it was just a normal cigarette packet, you know with the warning on the side, but then I realised it must be from an anti-smoking campaign.
Man: Ah, now why do you say that?
Woman: Well, look, I mean there's so many warnings – your love life, your appearance, your children's future, your taste, your wage packet, your unborn baby.
Man: Yeah, but I...I mean I don't quite understand all that. I mean, how can...how can

smoking, for instance, damage your love life?
Woman: Ah, well, makes your breath smell, doesn't it? Haha. Your mouth tastes horrid – have you ever kissed a smoker? I have. Never again!
Man: Well, all right, then, how about...erm...this damaging your appearance: how does smoking do that, then?
Woman: Oh, come on! I mean, look at people who smoke, look at their hands! And teeth: they're all sort of horrible yellow colour.
Man: All right, all right. H..how can it affect your children's future?
Woman: I'm not really sure. Well, I mean, what do they call it? Passive smoking. I mean, if you smoke and your children are in the same room then they're inhaling the smoke that you're blowing out, aren't they?
Man: I see...mm. Yeah, I remember, I..I mean..I worked in an office once where I was the only non-smoker – it was, it was awful.
Woman: Yes, I mean, smokers...I mean..they don't always realise that what they're doing doesn't just damage them but it damages the health of other people around them. I feel quite strongly about that.
Man: What about the other points, then? Um...how can smoking damage your taste?
Woman: Ah, well you see...

(Time: 3 minutes 20 seconds)

7.11 Doctor's orders *Listening*

B

```
Fresh fish    ✓         Bread ✓ (less)
Canned fish   ✗         Margarine ✗
Fish and chips ✗        Butter (unsalted) ✓
Fresh meat    ✓         Tomato ketchup ✗
Salt          ✗         Coffee ✓

Apples    ✓             Grapes ✓
Bananas   ✓             Carrots ✓
Potatoes  ✓             Crisps ✗
Sausages  ✗             Hamburgers ✗
Tea       ✓             Beer ✓
```

Tapescript

Doctor: ...Fine, thank you. So, Mr Brown, you're going to have to change your diet quite considerably. Um...let's just look at this list that you've made of the things that you normally eat. Mm, dear, well you're going to...er..going to have to avoid these fast foods you've been having, like...um...hamburgers and...er...fish and chips and so on. Um...and you should try to eat rather less bread, too. And if you do eat bread, can you make sure that you don't have any margarine or salted butter – unsalted butter's all right. Um...oh and none of this ketchup, all right?

Now, you can eat fish, but not...not if it's in cans, it must be fresh fish. And...um..meat is all right but...um...again, only fresh meat and grilled is best, but as I said, don't eat hamburgers and sausages, they're even worse. Now...er..fresh fruit and...er..vegetables of all kinds are...are excellent, but...um...make sure that you don't cook the vegetables in...in salted water. Now, there's no harm at all in eating potatoes, even chips but definitely not crisps, OK?

Now...er...let's see, what else? er...ye...oh yes, you can...you can drink whatever you like, no...no problems there and...um...chocolate should be OK too. Um...but the most important thing is not to put any salt on your food. In fact, if you've got any salt in the house, just...just throw it away. And if you do what I say then...um...you should start feeling better in about three to four weeks, so...um...come and see me in a month from now.
Patient: Yes, well thank you, doctor. Goodbye.

(Time: 1 minute 55 seconds)

D This is an exam-style Open Dialogue exercise. Read it all the way through before you start writing. Many variations are possible for the last two questions that the doctor asks.

Suggested answers

Doctor: When **do you usually get them?**
Doctor: What **do you take for them? / do you do about them?**
Doctor: How long **have you been suffering from them?**
Doctor: Why **haven't you been to see me before this?**
Doctor: Have **you been working any harder than usual?**
Doctor: Have **you said anything to your boss about this?**
Doctor: What **would you like me to do?**
Doctor: Would **two weeks' rest be better?**
Doctor: **Well, if you like I could recommend that you take a month off work, how about that?**
Doctor: **And make sure you get plenty of rest and fresh air.**

7.12 What would you say? — *Composition*

B Notice the style of the speech and how it is different from a written passage, welcoming people. Compare Dr Lawrence's speech with the 'Welcome!' section on page 1.

D *Model composition*

```
Good evening, everyone, and welcome!
I'd just like to say a few words about
what we're going to do on this course,
in particular about our aims and
methods.
    First of all, I think the one
thing you all have in common is that
you think you aren't fit enough - am I
right? Good! Well, our purpose is to
make you fit by introducing you to
easy exercises that you can do with us
here every week and at home every day.
Now, none of these exercises are going
to need special equipment or skills
and you'll be able to adapt them to
your own requirements. For example, if
you particularly want to develop your
strength then some of our muscle-
building exercises will be more
suitable than some of the stretching
exercises, which help to develop
suppleness.
    Well, that's enough from me, so
let's get started. You can ask me
questions in the break later. Now,
spread out so that you don't touch
anyone else and put your legs apart.
That's right. Now lift both arms up in
the air and swing them down and up
again...
```

7.13 *Put* — Verbs and idioms

1 put on = switch on; 2 put up = provide accommodation; 3 put off = distract; 4 put out/off = switch off; 5 put off = postpone; 6 put up = raise; 7 put on = gain; 8 put down = write down; 9 putting back = replace; 10 put away = remove to proper place; 11 put forward put back = change to later/earlier time; 12 put through = connect to phone extension; 13 put up with = tolerate; 14 put off = discourage.

7.14 Fill the gaps — *Exam practice*

1 of; 2 in; 3 on; 4 on; 5 at; 6 with; 7 in; 8 from; 9 through; 10 in; 11 by; 12 in; 13 to; 14 onto; 15 after; 16 in; 17 of; 18 without; 19 by; 20 from.

8 Holidays

8.1 Getting away from it all — *Vocabulary*

B 1 brochures; 2 view; 3 balcony; 4 sunbathing; 5 flight; 6 takes off; 7 land; 8 package; 9 fluently; 10 phrase book; 11 sign; 12 excursions; 13 cruise; 14 souvenir; 15 agency; 16 understood; 17 resort; 18 protect; 19 beach; 20 self-catering.

C 1 day-trippers holiday-makers sightseers; 2 bed and breakfast full board half board; 3 active busy energetic; 4 lazy relaxing restful; 5 choice range variety.

D Make notes and then record your answers, giving reasons.

8.2 Brazilian Contrasts — *Reading*

A the atmosphere of old Brazil – Salvador; historic buildings – Salvador; a rapidly growing city – São Paulo; a statue of Christ – Rio; one of the world's most famous views – Rio; a cable car ride – Rio; unusual architecture – Brasilia; a samba show – Rio; a magnificent waterfall – Iguaçu; wonderful costumes – Rio.

B 1 No: 'by scheduled service'; 2 Early morning; 3 Day 2: afternoon city tour AND Day 11–13: Carioca night tour; 4 Brasilia; 5 Narrow, cobbled and winding up and down the hills; 6 By one million new inhabitants every year; 7 The noise: 'the distant roar of the Falls increases to a deafening crescendo'; 8 Evening; 9 4–7 February; 10 No: 'For carnival supplements see price box below'.

C 1 Luxor Continental; 2 Yes: '290 rooms … high rise'; 3 No: '50 yards from … Copacabana Beach'; 4 Not necessarily: 'Rooms vary in size and location'; 5 No: 'with shower only'; 6 No: 'modern accommodation'.

8.3 *If* sentences *Grammar*

A

TYPE 1:
If you **decide / have** to go to the USA, you **will need / 'll need** a visa.

TYPE 2:
If you **had** £1,000 to spend, where **would you go** on holiday?

Type 2 or Type 1
If **I go** abroad next summer, I **'ll need / 'll have to get** a new passport.
If **I went** abroad next summer, **I would need / would have to get** a new passport.

TYPE 3:
If you **had asked** me to confirm the booking, **I would have sent** you a letter.

Types 2 and 3 in the same sentence:
If I'd been (had been) born in 1975, I'd be **XX years old** today.

'd as the short form of *had* and *would*:
1 would   had;   2 would;   3 would would;   4 would   had.

B *Errors underlined and corrected*

1 If I <u>would have</u> known, I could have helped you.   **had**

2 If <u>it's</u> my birthday tomorrow, <u>I'll</u> invite my friends out for a meal.   **it was / it were   I would**   or **As** it's my birthday + no changes
3 *no errors*
4 If the weather had been better, we <u>had</u> gone to the beach yesterday.   **would have**
5 If you <u>will need</u> any help, please let me know.   **need**
6 *no errors*
7 If I hadn't just been on holiday, <u>I would have had</u> more money now.   **I would have**
8 Where <u>you would</u> go if you <u>can</u> go anywhere in the world?   **would you   could**

C

2 If you go to Britain, you'll be able to speak English all day long.
3 If you sunbathe all day long, you'll get sunburnt.
4 If I hadn't got a holiday job this summer, I could / would be able to go on holiday.
5 Unless you book in advance, you won't find any accommodation.
6 If I had enjoyed my holiday there, I would/ might go back.
7 If you had told me where you were staying, I could have got in touch.
8 Pack a jumper to wear after dark in case the evenings are cool.
9 If you come on holiday with us, you'll enjoy it.

D Make some notes and then record your answers. Alternatively, perhaps write a paragraph about what you would do.

E Look at Activity 19 and note down what you would say to persuade a friend to go to the place shown. Then record this as if you were on the phone to your friend. Then do the same with the information in Activities 33 and 43.

Listen to all three parts of your recording – which sounded most convincing?

8.4 Getting away from it all? *Picture conversation*

Record all three parts of this section on a blank cassette. Then listen to your recording. What did you do well and less well? What improvements could be made?

8.5 Island-hopping *Listening*

A

	Attractions	Drawbacks
Athens	Museums, classical sights	Noisy, hot in summer
Corfu	Night life, direct flights	Touristy
Rhodes	Quiet outside town, good hotels in town, cheap villas and rooms in Lindos, direct flights	Busy in main town
Paros	Pretty, good beaches, unspoilt outside town, clear water	Six hours on ferry from Athens
Santorini	Beautiful scenery, direct flights, black sand beaches	Climb to capital, 10 hours on ferry, a bit frightening
Zante	Green, unspoilt, wild flowers, friendly people, direct flights, small beaches (?)	

Tapescript

Travel agent: Good afternoon. Can I help you, sir?
Client: Oh yes, good afternoon. Well, I hope you can, yes. Um...I'm thinking of going off to Greece this summer...
Travel agent: Yes.
Client: ...and really I need some advice. I mean, if you've got any maps or whatever.
Travel agent: I see, yes, certainly, yes, of course I can help because in fact I've been to Greece several times myself on holiday there. I think it's a marvellous place...
Client: Oh, good.
Travel agent: ...and I did see quite a lot of the islands as well as the mainland. Now...er...let's get a couple of facts sorted out first: how long do you actually want to go for?
Client: Well, I've got two weeks free. Um...and ideally, of course, I want...er...to have time to see the sights and so forth but...er...I want to relax as well, you know...
Travel agent: I see.
Client: ...so if we could manage a bit of both.
Travel agent: Yes, yes, certainly. Um...well, we'll talk about the...er...sightseeing first, shall we? Um...of course the most obvious place is Athens.
Client: I was going to say, yeah.
Travel agent: Right, er...now if you want to have a look at this map here...
Client: Ah, yes.
Travel agent: So...now you can see exactly where Athens is.
Client: Yes.
Travel agent: It's very noisy, I have to tell you that, very hot in the summer, but there are marvellous museums and the classical sites are quite fantastic. It's very best...er...c...to combine ...this with a quite...a quiet island, so you spend one week in Athens and one week on an island.
Client: Oh, I see. Oh, how about Corfu? I mean, that's...er...is that all right?
Travel agent: Y...yes it is. Um...I hesitate to recommend it because it's terribly touristy. I mean, it actually depends what you want and what you like. There's certainly plenty of night-life and things to do.
Client: Mmm.
Travel agent: But in fact more tourists visit this island than the whole of the rest of Greece put together...
Client: Oh, good gracious!
Travel agent: The one advantage about Corfu is that there are direct flights...Um...in fact, I think the place I'd recommend most is Rhodes.
Client: Oh, yes, yes. Somebody told me about Rhodes.
Travel agent: It's very busy near the town itself but elsewhere it's very quiet, even in the summer. The best way to see the rest of the island is to hire a car and if I were you I'd

probably stay in Rhodes Town itself or in Lindos.
Client: Oh, I see.
Travel agent: There are good luxury hotels in Rhodes Town and there are very reasonable villas and rooms in Lindos. And again there are direct flights there.
Client: Oh, that's useful to know. But...er...what about the places that aren't quite so well-known? I mean, some of these little islands.
Travel agent: Mmm. Well, as you can see, there are a lot to choose from. Um...I'll tell you a little about my favourite islands.
Client: Mmm.
Travel agent: Er...Paros...
Client: Oh now...
Travel agent: Now can we find that there?
Client: There's Poros here.
Travel agent: No, we mustn't confuse the two. This is Paros there, which is just south of Mykonos.
Client: Yes, I see.
Travel agent: Now, to get there you fly to Athens and take the ferry, which takes six hours to get across. But it's a very pretty island, there are good beaches and it's quite unspoiled outside the main town. The best way of exploring the island is either by hiring a moped or a motorbike. And the swimming's marvellous because the water's very clear.
Client: Oh smashing...Great, where else?
Travel agent: Er...Santorini, now that's...
Client: Oh, that's down the bottom there.
Travel agent: ...one of the southern ones there. That's unbelievably beautiful. Very impressive scenery. The island's actually an extinct volcano and in fact you can still see it smoking in the bay.
Client: Oh, gracious!
Travel agent: The town itself is built on top of the edge of the crater and the cliffs plunge into the sea below, so you can imagine how the scenery really is very impressive.
Client: Fantastic...yeah.
Travel agent: Er...there's one slight problem about this place is that to...to get from the ferry up to the capital, which is called Thira, you have to climb up the track or ride on a donkey. So, you know, that's something to take into account. The ferry from Athens takes longer, it takes about ten hours, but in fact you can now fly there direct as well. Oh and...and the other marvellous thing about this place is that the beaches are black sand...
Client: Good gracious me!
Travel agent: ...which is breath-taking, but I also found it a little bit frightening at first. Um...
Client: Where else?

Travel agent: Yes, the other island I'd recommend to you is Zante. Er...it's a very very sweet island, very green, completely unspoiled. There's amazing wild flowers, the beaches are small and the people are very very friendly.
Client: Oh, that sounds really my sort of thing.
Travel agent: Oh, does it? Yes, it's lovely. You can fly there direct or you can fly to Athens and take the ferry or a plane from there. Um...if you, you know, wanted to ignore the city centres altogether, you could do what we did last year, which was 'island-hopping' – going from one island to another by ferry, spending a day or two on each.
Client: Oh super!
Travel agent: That way, you see, that way you don't get a chance to get fed up with them and we had a marvellous time.
Client: Mmm!

(Time: 4 minutes)

B Record a short talk about the attractions of your own country or region.

8.6   Three more islands! *Problem solving*

B Note down the advice you would give to all three people.

C Each paragraph should be about 50 words, though the model paragraphs below are nearer 100 each.

As usual with these problem-solving activities, the models are not 'correct answers' – the reasons why Kim would like Madeira are given, for example, but there may also be good reasons why another island would be suitable.

▶ Instead of writing 'If I could go to one of the islands ...' you may prefer this one: 'If I could go anywhere in the world on holiday, the place I'd go to is ...'

Model paragraphs

(The fourth is on the alternative topic suggested above.)

```
I'd advise Gerry to go to Kos. Even if
he goes in the middle of the summer,
he'll discover that it's peaceful and
quiet. It's quite a large island, so
there will be plenty to do and the
```

beaches won't be over-crowded. He can explore the island by hiring a bicycle. The main problem would be the heat. In the middle of summer the sun shines all the time and the temperature is 30° or more. If he doesn't like hot weather, perhaps he could go there during the Easter holidays.

If I were Kim I'd go to Madeira. In the autumn the weather is pleasantly warm but not too hot. Kim would enjoy walking in the mountains and seeing the wild flowers, for which the island is famous and which flower all year round. Kim would enjoy the fantastic scenery and visiting the little villages, and the lack of beaches wouldn't worry her. I think Madeira would suit Kim very well - much better than the other islands, in fact.

My advice to Sandy would be to go to Majorca. There's plenty to do there and it has wonderful scenery and great beaches as well as places to go for a good night out. There's a wide range of different things to do, which would make it ideal for an active person like Sandy. The one problem about going in April or May is that it won't be very hot at that time of year, so from that point of view perhaps Kos might be better.

If I could go anywhere in the world on holiday, the place I'd go to is the west coast of Scotland - not for sunbathing and discos, but for the scenery, which is magnificent. Even in summer it can be cool and may rain a lot and be windy, but between the showers when the sun shines it is gorgeous. In summer the days are incredibly long too, and it doesn't get dark till quite late in the evening. The best way to see the country is by hiring a car and driving up the coast road.

8.7 By ...   *Prepositional phrases*

1 by far = far more popular than anywhere else;   2 by sight = recognise   by name = know their names;   3 by plane   by ship;   4 by heart = memorise;   5 by accident;   6 by train   by car;   7 by day   by night = during the day/night;   8 by surprise;   9 by chance;   10 by all means = certainly;   11 by mistake;   12 by post   by hand = deliver personally;   13 by yourself = alone/on your own.

8.8 An excursion programme   *Listening*

A

Tapescript

Tour leader: Good morning, everyone. Er...ha...sorry to...er...interrupt breakfast. I've got here a few changes to the excursion...er...programme, which I think you've all got. Um...I might as well go through them all and then you'll know

	Depart		Return
Sunday	14.00	Edinburgh city sightseeing *(no need to book)*	16.30
Monday	9.00	(Braemar Castle) and (Aberdeen)	17.30
Tuesday	~~8.30~~ 7.45	Glencoe and Fort William	17.30
Wednesday	8.00	Inverness and Loch Ness	~~17.30~~ 18.30
Thursday	14.00	Edinburgh city sightseeing tour	16.30
Friday	~~9.15~~ 7.00	~~Galashiels and the Borders~~ *cancelled* Glasgow and River Clyde steamer trip	~~16.00~~ 17.45

where you are. In fact, they make absolutely no difference to the tours: in fact they...they improve them, which is basically why we've made the changes. Now, your Monday 9 o'clock...um...where you've got the Braemar Castle...er...Aberdeen: what we're going to do is we're going to swop round there and we're going to go to Aberdeen first and then on to Braemar, returning here at 17.30. Now we move to Tuesday. Ah...the only difference there...I'm going to make an earlier start for Glencoe and Fort William: ah...7.45 instead of 8.30. Ah...Wednesday: yes, the...the Inverness and Loch Ness – one of my personal favourites, I think...um...everyone – um...instead of returning at...er...17.30, we'll come back a...a a little bit later there on that one...er...18.30...give us a bit more time actually at Loch Ness. Hope we spot the monster, eh? Ha! Well...er...Thursday...um...now this is...this is our...our big day in Edinburgh, where we're doing the city sightseeing. Um...also...er...we're going to do an Edinburgh this afternoon – that's today, Sunday, we're going to do an Edinburgh...um...because...er...we...we had nothing planned for today, but we're going to do an Edinburgh as well. Er...same time, no need to book. Er...now unfortunately on Friday we've had to cancel your Galashiels and your Borders. Er...but instead we're substituting Glasgow, leaving at 7 for Glasgow and then I think a fitting end to your holiday, one I think you're going to go for: the River Clyde Steamer Trip. Yes, on an actual River Clyde steamer. Re...returning at...at 17...17.45. Er...I hope those are all satisfactory. Sorry we've had to make these changes, but I think you'll find that they'll improve the holiday and make it even better than it already is. Oh, now I...can I remind you that the...the excursions are of course optional, you know, but I'm sure you'll all want to go on them. Er...and would you decide which ones you want to go on by lunchtime today. Thanks very much, everyone, enjoy the rest of your breakfasts.

(Time: 2 minutes 25 seconds)

8.9 Spelling and pronunciation: Consonants *Word study*

B Pause the tape between each group of twelve words so you can catch your breath. The correct spellings are in Activity 25, but don't look there until you have done all three parts of the exercise. (There is no Tapescript

for this exercise, as the correct spellings are all in Activity 25.)

C Here are some more examples of 'silent letters' that don't come up in **D**:
through   straight
crumb   thumb
postman   fasten
know   knock   knit   knickers
stalk   talk   would
far   father   farther   confirm (only in some British accents and not in American English)
honour   dishonest   exhausted

D Look at Activity 5, which contains some words that may cause spelling difficulties. Read out the words and record yourself on a blank cassette. Then play back the cassette and write down the words, pausing the tape frequently. Check your spelling by looking at Activity 5 again.
    Do the same with the words in Activity 22.

8.10 Writing letters *Composition*

A There are no spelling mistakes or grammatical errors in the two 'students' compositions'.

▶ There is no model composition in this case, but compare your work with the letters in Activity 41.

8.11 Duty-free goods *Listening*

1 <u>Airports</u>

Amsterdam	£8.50
Athens	£7.50
Gatwick	£10
Heathrow	£10
Madrid	£9
Manchester	£10.50
New York	£9.50
Paris	£9
Rome	£10
Tokyo	£12
Zurich	£10

<u>Airlines</u>

British Airways	£10.50
Air France	£10

Alitalia	£10
Iberia	£9.50
JAL	£10.50
KLM	£9.50
Olympic	£8.50
Swissair	£10.50
Varig	£8

2 they don't carry such a large stock;
3 a local supermarket;   4 souvenir;
5 Do I really need this?   Is it really cheaper?;
6 higher   normal.

Tapescript

Presenter: If you're going abroad this year and you're going by air, you'll probably do what every air traveller does – stop at the duty-free shop or buy duty-free goods on the plane. But not all duty-free shops offer the same value, as Jonathan Harris now explains.

Jonathan: That's right, Stella. I've been...er...I've been looking at prices in...er..duty-free shops and on airlines in various countries. Now, I've taken the average shopping basket that most travellers would buy...er...the most common purchase is one bottle of whisky and...er...200 cigarettes and I've found out the prices vary enormously depending on where you shop. Now, let's say you buy £10 worth of goods at the airport in London – it's the same at both Gatwick or at Heathrow. Now, if you bought exactly the same things at Amsterdam Airport, those goods would cost you £8.50 and if you bought them at the airport in Athens they'd only cost you £7.50. In Madrid they'd cost £9, and in Paris they'd be £9 too. In New York they'd be £9½ *[Note: the speaker is an American]* and in Zurich and in Rome exactly the same price as you'd pay for them in London. Now, the only airports more expensive than London are Manchester, where that £10 basket of goods would cost you £10.50, and in Tokyo where you'd pay £12.

Presenter: Mmm, that's quite a variation, isn't it? Well, is it any cheaper actually on the plane?

Jonathan: Well there is just as much variation from airline to airline there, too. Er...most expensive I found were British Airways, Swissair and JAL (that's the Japanese Airline). Here the £10 worth of goods at Heathrow would cost you £10.50. Now, Air France and Alitalia charged just the same as Heathrow prices. Um...Iberia and KLM were £9.50 and...er ...cheapest of all were the Greek Airline Olympic at £8.50 and Varig (that's a...a Brazilian airline) at £8.

(Questions 2 to 6 ↓)
But there is a problem with airlines and that's they just can't carry the stock that a shop on the ground can – so if you...er...smoke a particular brand of cigarettes or you prefer a particular brand of Scotch, you can't depend on them to have it. And...er...then again, if you're at the far end of the cabin from where they start down with the trolley, by the time they get down to you they may have nothing left.

Presenter: Right, so is there any advice that you'd like to offer?

Jonathan: Ah...yes, there are a couple of things. In some countries you may find that it's cheaper to look around the local supermarket before you leave, because very often prices locally are cheaper than here anyway and that's got to do a lot with their tax structures. Um...in addition to that, surely a bottle of the...er...local drink...er...whatever it is, is a nicer souvenir to take back home than the same old bottle of Scotch whisky that you'd get back in the United Kingdom anyway.

Presenter: Er...what about other duty-free purchases?

Jonathan: Well, there I'd say: Think before you buy – think twice in fact and ask yourself two questions:

The first one is this: Do I really need this? Things like perfume, after-shave, silk ties and so on are things you can do without and in fact if you weren't at the airport or on the plane you probably wouldn't buy them anyway.

Second question is this: Is it really cheaper? Many of the...er...electronic goods...er...tape recorders, calculators, Walkmans – and I've got caught on this one – on display at 'duty-free prices' are probably cheaper i...in a normal shop where the prices are discounted. You'll be saving VAT by buying at the airport but you're probably also paying a higher price anyway.

Presenter: Thanks very much, Jonathan.

(Time: 4 minutes)

8.12   Break, bring, call, cut
Verbs and idioms

A

Kit broke ... a window   Jan's heart   the ice   the news to us

Lee called ... a doctor   the dog Rover   to see Sandy

Chris brought ... Lee to the party   the book to Sandy (+ possibly: a doctor, a piece of paper, the ice, the news to us)
Sandy cut ... a piece of paper   the grass   himself/herself

B 1 broken down; 2 broke off; 3 broke up; 4 brought about; 5 brought up; 6 bring them down; 7 bring them back; 8 called off; 9 call in; 10 call it off; 11 call for; 12 call me back; 13 cut down; 14 cut out; 15 cut off.

night; 3 *verb:* cross; 4 *adverb:* eventually, finally; 5 *articles:* a the.

B (Some variations are possible.)
1 usual; 2 himself; 3 moment; 4 airport; 5 road; 6 time; 7 lounge; 8 flight; 9 made; 10 desk; 11 end; 12 free; 13 technical; 14 fly; 15 ages; 16 information; 17 night; 18 expense; 19 night; 20 happened; 21 asleep; 22 stranded; 23 passengers; 24 reason.

8.13 Fill the gaps   *Use of English*

A *Possible answers*

1 *adjective:* splitting, bad, terrible; 2 *noun:*

9 Books and reading

▶ If you are NOT studying one of the prescribed books for the exam, the exercises in this unit are still relevant.

▶ For a complete list of this year's books, refer to the current Cambridge Examination Regulations obtainable from your Local Examinations Secretary.

9.1 A good read   *Vocabulary*

B 1 library   bookshop/bookstore; 2 author; 3 paperback; 4 title   cover; 5 biography (*or* an autobiography).

C Note that it is the BEST alternative that has to be chosen – as in the exam. In some questions other answers may not be quite as good as the 'best' one.
   Make sure that you find out the meanings and uses of the 'wrong' alternatives.

1 literature; 2 characters; 3 verse; 4 rhymes; 5 table of contents; 6 index;

7 chapters; 8 publisher; 9 message; 10 well-written; 11 favourite; 12 put it down; 13 get into; 14 minor; 15 borrow.

D 1 central   main   principal; 2 entertaining   readable   true-to-life; 3 amusing   believable   likeable; 4 convincing   realistic   true-to-life; 5 about real life   non-fiction   textbooks; 6 appreciate   bear   stand.

9.2 Call for the Dead   *Reading*

A Although the simplified version omits a great deal of detail and some difficult words, there are also some additions:
   An anonymous letter   **Communist** Party   clear him **of the accusation**

B
2 He had been woken up in the middle of the night by a phone call – version B.

287

3 He had learned the skill years before/long ago – both A and B.
4 An anonymous letter had been received accusing Fennan of being a (Communist) Party member – both A and B.
5 Friendly – both A and B.
6 Because he was anxious/in a bit of a state – both A and B.
7 No – both A and B.
8 Suicide – both A and B.

9.3 Joining sentences *Grammar*

A IDENTIFYING RELATIVE CLAUSES:
Notice that you can use either *that* or *which* when referring to things, and either *that* or *who* when referring to people.

B NON-IDENTIFYING RELATIVE CLAUSES:
Hamlet , **which** is a famous play by Shakespeare , is a tragedy.
Hamlet's father , **who** dies before the play begins , appears to Hamlet as a ghost.
Hamlet's mother , **whose** husband has died , marries her husband's brother.

C (Some variations are possible.)
2 New York, which I'd love to visit one day, is a wonderful city.
or New York is a wonderful city, which I'd love to visit one day.
3 Ms Fortune, whose body was found in the cellar, was a writer.
4 I met an old friend, who told me all about a book he'd just read.
5 The car that/which was found at the airport was / had been stolen.
6 Science fiction books, which some people love and others hate, are about the future and space travel.
7 The book (that) you recommended to me was very good.
8 A simplified edition, which is shorter than the original, is (also) easier to read.

D CONJUNCTIONS and PREPOSITIONS:
Notice that *as* can be used as either a time conjunction or a reason conjunction.

E
1 In spite of the (enormous) difficulties she managed to escape.
2 It is such a wonderful story that I'd recommend it to anyone.
3 As I wanted my friends to know when I'd be arriving, I phoned them.
4 While I was sitting in bed reading, my friends were dancing.
5 Although the book is over 500 pages long, I'm going to try to read it before next week.
6 Before I go and see the film, I'm going to read the book.
7 After the heroine had escaped from the villain, she rescued the hero.
or After escaping from the villain, the heroine rescued the hero.
8 During my summer holiday / my holiday in the summer I read a lot of books.

F (Some variations are possible.)
1 which; 2 about; 3 whose;
4 who/whom; 5 who; 6 whose; 7 of;
8 After; 9 up; 10 who; 11 time;
12 to; 13 but; 14 During; 15 between;
16 but; 17 until; 18 When; 19 after;
20 to.

9.4 Reading habits *Listening*

A 1 85% electronic noise;
2 inexpensive/cheap portable;
3 bookmark; 4 one airport plane beach; 5 established authors/best-selling authors; 6 Plot A is *Savages*, Plot B is *Zoya*, Plot C is *Alaska*, Plot D is *Glamorous Powers*, Plot E is *To Be The Best*.

Tapescript

Presenter: According to a recent survey, 85% of American adolescents, quote 'can no longer take in a printed page if their act of reading does not have an accompanying background of electronic noise' end of quote. And many students nowadays seem to need a background noise of headphone music to cut out outside distractions. But are we reading less these days? Will the days of books soon be over? Mike Osborne reports.
Mike: Well, there are two questions really. Er first, will other entertainments – er computer games, videos, TV and so on – stop people reading? And second, will the new technology – that's electronic publishing, information on computers and books recorded

on cassettes and so on – will these things provide substitutes for the printed page?

Well, the main advantage that books have over all these media is that they're relatively inexpensive and they're very portable. I mean, you can take a book with you wherever you go, it doesn't...it doesn't break down if you get sand inside it, and you don't need batteries ...you can put it down and pick it up whenever you like – the only equipment you need is a bookmark.

Now, according to the survey, many people only buy one book a year – as holiday reading. Er...they probably buy it at the airport on their way to the sun and they...they read it in the airport (while their flight is delayed) on the plane and on the beach, of course.

Nevertheless, books by best-selling authors are selling more and more copies every year, not fewer. All the signs are that people are spending more and more money on books. Now, the most popular books are books by established authors – that's writers who've developed a product that their readers know they'll enjoy and whose books they'll 'collect'.

(Question 6 ↓)
So I thought I'd give you a few examples of some recent best-selling paperbacks by authors who sell hundreds of thousands of copies of every book they write:

First, there's *To Be The Best* by Barbara Taylor Bradford. Now, this book centres around a wealthy family and the action switches between Hong Kong, Australia, America and Yorkshire. It's basically about a woman who has to become more ruthless than her grandmother.

The second book is *Zoya* by Danielle Steele. This is about a Russian countess who escapes from the Russian Revolution in St Petersburg and becomes a ballerina in Paris. The book follows her career to America where she faces her toughest struggle yet in the business world of present-day New York.

Then there's *Alaska* by James A. Michener. This is a story of Eskimos and of Russian and American explorers and colonists struggling to survive in a hostile environment. The action spans thousands of years and is a blend of historical fact and fictional narrative.

Savages by Shirley Conran is about five women on a tropical island who see their husbands killed in front of their eyes. They escape into the jungle and eventually find that they're involved in a mysterious international plot.

And lastly, *Glamorous Powers* by Susan Howatch is about a man who becomes a priest after playing many different roles in life. He falls in love with a woman and they have to struggle to find their happiness.

Of course, the one thing that all these books have in common is that they're all over 500 pages long, which is fine if you're used to reading. But the problem is that many people aren't. Reading tends to be something you enjoy more as you get older – but if you don't develop a taste for it when you're young, you may never discover the pleasures of getting involved in a good book. Now, technology and its influence on reading is, as I said, another question. Will people who study need to buy textbooks in the future? Or will they just sit in front of computer screens and get all the information they need...

(Time: 4 minutes)

9.5 Using suffixes: Abstract nouns *Word study*

A Nouns from verbs:

-ation	association demonstration starvation translation
-ion	connection objection reflection
-ment	astonishment embarrassment encouragement improvement
-al	approval proposal removal survival
-ance	acceptance assistance disappearance

▶ Notice that nouns can also be formed from verbs by adding **-ing** as in these examples: painting   sailing   skating   learning English.

B Nouns from adjectives and nouns:

-ness	blindness carelessness cheerfulness sadness selfishness shyness weakness
-ence	confidence intelligence patience silence
-ity	availability probability reality suitability
-y	accuracy efficiency fluency photography
-ship	leadership membership ownership sportsmanship
-hood	motherhood parenthood

▶ Another way of forming nouns is by adding **-ism** as in these examples: Buddhism

Catholicism   Communism   Marxism
Socialism   vegetarianism   sexism.

C   2 translation;   3 violence;
4 weakness;   5 description   childhood;
6 kindness   honesty.

9.6   Holiday reading   *Problem solving*

C   Each paragraph should be about 50 words long. As usual, the model paragraphs below are not 'correct answers'.

Model paragraphs

Anna may be rather too young to have appreciated Jupiter's Travels, in particular the 'journey to the centre of the author's soul'. However, the author's adventures were probably quite exciting for her to read about. A better choice for her might have been Hills of Kalamata: its Greek setting and romantic plot might have been just right for her to read on the beach.

The Human Factor sounds as if it is the kind of book that needs a fair amount of concentration to appreciate. If Bob is the sort of person who reads a lot, I think he might have enjoyed it during his walking holiday. On the other hand, even though the plot is exciting, a more conventional thriller like Send No More Roses might have been a better choice.

Colin's choice of holiday reading was unfortunate because Send No More Roses is a thriller and, for a student of literature, a book like Empire of the Sun might have been a better choice as it is both exciting and well-written. According to the blurb on the cover it is one of the major novels of the twentieth century.

I'm sorry I took Hills of Kalamata with me because I really hate romantic novels. Generally they're badly written and the plot is unbelievable. Although I was interested in its descriptions of 'the most primitive part of Greece', I found the characters lifeless and the plot predictable. It was a complete waste of time. I wish I'd taken Empire of the Sun instead.

9.7   *In*...   *Prepositional phrases*

1 in common = share qualities;   2 in danger;
3 in a hurry;   4 in all = total;   5 In general
= in most cases;   6 in particular = especially;
7 in secret;   8 in debt = owe money;
9 in difficulties;   10 in public   in private;
11 in a way = partly   in other words;
12 in tears = crying/weeping   in prison.

9.8   The Captain and the Enemy   *Reading*

A   1 b   2 c   3 c   4 c   5 c   6 b   7 d
8 c

B   2 gym shoes;   3 recklessly;
4 slithered;   5 abrupt;   6 in a bit of a quandary;   7 reluctant;   8 conceal;
9 obscure;   10 from hearsay;   11 ajar;
12 trim.

9.9   Talking about books   *Listening and speaking*

A

Title	Author
A Taste for Death	P. D. James
Boy	Roald Dahl
Catch 22	Joseph Heller
Cider with Rosie	Laurie Lee
I Know Why the Caged Bird Sings	Maya Angelou
Surfacing	Margaret Atwood

B   TRUE: 1, 5, 6, 7, 8, 10, 11, 12, 15, 16;   FALSE: 2, 3, 4, 9, 13, 14.

Tapescript

Narrator: David, what kind of books do you like?
David: I must admit, I...there's nothing I enjoy more than a good thriller. I mean, there are some marvellous writers around like Agatha Christie and of course her marvellous creations of Miss Marple and Hercule Poirot, but in fact my favourite writer is P.D. James. She is, I believe, one of the finest thriller writers that we've got in England at the moment. And

certainly my favourite book of hers is *A Taste for Death*. Er...it comes...the title of the book comes from a saying 'There's this to say for blood and breath, it gives a man a taste for death'. And I love the way she uses language and doesn't talk down, I believe, to the reader. And you get this marvellous story in *A Taste for Death*: an MP found dead in a church together with a tramp, and apparently the two are unconnected but as the story moves on, you realise that their lives become closer and closer...interweaved. And it's just a gripping read from start to finish. I think that's what I enjoy most in a book: the fact that you can pick it up and just be gripped by it from beginning to end.

Narrator: Jocelyn, what sort of books do you enjoy?

Jocelyn: Well, I suppose I like novels and biographies best. And if I was pressed, my favourite author would be Margaret Atwood, who's a Canadian author. She's...er...an award-winning author, she...she's won awards from all over the world and my favourite book would be *Surfacing*, which is her second book, and it's about a woman who returns to an island in the Canadian wilderness and she undergoes a...a sort of a personal transformation. I suppose I like Margaret Atwood because she's...er...she's very witty and she makes very sharp observations from a woman's standpoint – she makes me laugh. But there's always...um...a meaningful edge to her writing: the laugh catches in your throat, if you like.

Narrator: Ken?

Ken: I suppose the kind of reading I enjoy most are travel books and autobiographies and I think my favourite author for this particular genre is Laurie Lee. Er...but I think the book I enjoyed most with...was *Cider with Rosie*. It's about his childhood in a Gloucestershire village, and I enjoyed this because it's very evocative of an era which now seems totally lost to us. Um...he writes about the seasons which seemed to be more clearly defined than they are now, you know, very hot summers and cold winters and there are some wonderful descriptions of the countryside and it's often very funny and...er...there are some extraordinary characters in the village, often very eccentric...um...like neighbours, and er...his brothers and sisters. And I think...er...the reason I like it so much is because it has a very nostalgic appeal to me.

Narrator: Jill, what do you enjoy?

Jill: I enjoy reading autobiography and...er...my favourite writer at the moment is...Maya Angelou. Um...the first book in the series of her life is called *I Know Why the Caged Bird Sings*. Um...she's a black American writer and...er...the book is about her life as a child in the Deep South. Um...I enjoyed it because...er...she has a very simple way of writing about a very complicated and exciting life.

Narrator: How about you Blain?

Blain: Well, I like reading comedy books. Basically I like to laugh when I'm reading and I've enjoyed a lot of good American authors – Salinger, Thurber – but I think probably the greatest author of the twentieth century, and I think his greatness is based on one book is Joseph Heller. I think *Catch 22* is probably the finest, the funniest book I've ever read. And one of the things I like about it is because it says so much as well, it's a great satire and it...er...has a lot to say about modern life and particularly about the reasons why people go to war. Um...it's probably the book I've enjoyed most and the most often. I've read it several times and I read parts of it a lot.

Narrator: And finally, Judy, it's your turn.

Judy: Um...I like reading lots of different sorts of books, I like...um...thrillers and spy stories and so on, I like biographies very much. I read...um...Roald Dahl's biography, the two...it comes in two parts – the first one's called *Boy* and the second one I think is called...um...*Flying Solo*. But *Boy* in particular I...I liked enormously. He's written it for children as well as for grown-ups and...um...the style appears to be very simple – I don't mean by that that he writes down to children, 'cause he certainly doesn't, but this simplicity makes it very very direct and...and some of the...the memories that he...that he brings back are...um...are amazingly vivid. There's...there's one I remember and was amazed that the publishers allowed it to go through. It's a description of a headmaster who was a particularly savage sort of man who in fact became an Archbishop of Canterbury eventually, but it is one of the most frightening childhood...er...remembrances I think I've...um...I've ever come across and...um...that's why I like Roald Dahl's writing so much. It's...it's very honest.

(Time: 5 minutes 35 seconds)

C Suggested answers

YOU: Who **are** your favourite authors?
YOU: Do **you** only read spy stories, then?
YOU: And what **are you** reading at the moment?
YOU: What's the title of the book?
YOU: What's it about?

YOU: Where **does the action of the book take place?**
YOU: What **happens to the boy in the story?**
YOU: Is **it a depressing book?** It sounds as if it is.
YOU: Then **what are you enjoying / have you enjoyed about it?**
YOU: **Would you recommend it to me?**
YOU: Will **you lend it to me when you've finished it?**

D Record your own answers to the questions that the Friend asked in C.

9.10 Writing about a book *Composition*

A *Suggested answers*

1 In the extract from *The Captain and the Enemy*, most of the paragraphs show that a different speaker is talking. 'I slid …' marks a return to the main stream of the narrative. The only possible breaking point in the first paragraph might be after '… for the first time.'

2 In the two versions of *Call for the Dead* each line of dialogue (or Smiley's thoughts in brackets) is a new paragraph. The second paragraph in each version ('The taxi turned …' 'The cab turned …') marks a return to the main stream of the narrative after the digression in the previous paragraph.

▶ There are no fixed rules for paragraph structure. You should try to develop your 'feelings' for what seems right – the tasks in **A** will help you to do this.

▶ Normally a new paragraph begins when a new idea is introduced. One advantage of paragraphs is that they 'break up' the text and make it easier to read.

B If you aren't studying a prescribed book, answer question 8, which is the one that is the model composition in this case.

Model composition

```
                          13 Richmond Avenue
                          Cambridge CB2 2RU

                          15 May 19##
```

```
Dear Peter,
         I felt I simply had to write
to you about the enclosed book which
I'm sure you'll enjoy reading.
         As you'll see from the cover
it's by David Lodge and it's called
"Nice Work". It's all about two people
who live close to each other in the
same city. One is a female university
teacher who lectures about English
literature, the other is the male
managing director of a factory. They
have nothing in common but they are
thrown together when the teacher
becomes the industrialist's 'shadow'
and spends one day each week with him
as part of a scheme to increase
cooperation between the university and
local companies. I won't spoil it by
telling you what happens in the end!!
         You'll enjoy the humour of
the relationship and the contrast
between the world of the university
and real life in the factory.
         When you've read it, let me
know what you think.
         Best wishes,
```

9.11 You know that book I borrowed … *Listening*

A 2 a month; 3 garden;
4 radiator; 5 bath; 6 out of print;
7 replace the book (Peter ignores what Jean has told him!); 8 damaging them;
9 returned it with a flat tyre; 10 she won't lend anything to him.

Tapescript

Peter: Hi, Jean!
Jean: Oh, hallo, Peter.
Peter: I've brought that book back you lent me. You remember the…er…the Eric Ambler.
Jean: About time, isn't it? I lent you that book two months ago.
Peter: Oh, it was only a month, wasn't it? Last month…
Jean: No, it wasn't, it was longer than that.
Peter: Look, before you get…er…
Jean: Wh…what's this?
Peter: I knew you were going to say that. What happened was…what happened was, I was reading it in the garden, right? And I…I just left it out. And it rained. But I've dried it out over the radiator. I think it's…
Jean: Peter! It looks as if you've dropped it in

the bath and then dried it out on the radiator!
Peter: Look, you can turn all the pages. It's fine. Anyway...
Jean: When I gave it to you, it was as good as new!
Peter: Yeah, I know, I know. Look, I...I'm really really sorry...
Jean: Peter, do you realise that this book's out of print? I can't get hold of another copy, you know.
Peter: I'm really sorry, I mean, I do feel a bit guilty about it...
Jean: I should think so! I mean, I know I've read it but I like to keep all the books I've read and I never throw them away.
Peter: Yeah, well it's...it's only a paperback. I mean, if you...if you feel like that, I mean, I...Look, I'll tell you what: I'll buy you a new one. OK?
Jean: Oh, that's not the point. You're always losing things and damaging them. Do you remember when you borrowed my bike? You brought it back with a flat tyre.
Peter: Oh, come on! I think you're being a bit...
Jean: Well, it's true!
Peter: ...unreasonable. It's only a paperback book.
Jean: I'm not being unreasonable. It's you who's being unreasonable. You've got the most casual attitude of anyone I know...
Peter: I've offered to buy you a new one!
Jean: You never take anything seriously...Listen, it's the last time I'm going to lend you anything and that's final!

(Time: 1 minute 15 seconds)

9.12 **Fall** and **hold**   *Verbs and idioms*

1 falls for = be attracted to;   2 fell out with = quarrel;   3 fell over = fall on the ground;   4 fall in with = agree to;   5 fallen through = fail before completion;   6 held up = rob;   7 holding on to = grasp;   8 hold on = wait;   9 held up = delay;   10 hold out = continue in spite of difficulties.

10 Food and drink

10.1 **Talking about food**   *Vocabulary*

B 1 cooks;   2 raw;   3 food processor/electric mixer/maid/husband, etc.;   4 chopped/sliced;   5 stirred;   6 bread and cakes: baked; vegetables: steamed/boiled/microwaved/eaten raw; meat: fried/roasted/stewed/grilled/boiled;   7 vegetarian;   8 kettle/saucepan/pan/electric kettle;   9 peel/cut/slice;   10 bowl;   11 oven;   12 sour;   13 washing-up/clearing-up;   14 beef/veal/chicken/lamb/pork/ham/bacon/turkey;   15 sour, salty, bitter (*All flavours are a combination of the four tastes.*).

C (In some cases these are 'best' answers and others may be just possible.)
1 hot;   2 dishes;   3 recipe;   4 rare;   5 additives;   6 wine list;   7 greedy;   8 helping;   9 avoid;   10 gone off.

D *Some suggested answers*

FRUIT
strawberry, raspberry, pineapple, apple, pear, apricot, peach, melon, blackcurrant, blackberry, banana, grape, grapefruit, plum, greengage, orange, lemon, lime

VEGETABLES
potato, pea, cauliflower, cucumber, cabbage, carrot, onion, celery, broccoli, asparagus, artichoke, mushroom, tomato, lettuce, spinach

DRINKS
tea, coffee, beer, lager, bitter, wine, whisky, brandy, lemonade, orangeade, orange juice, tonic water, mineral water, vermouth, cider, milk

10.2 **Eating out**   *Reading*

A Your experience of eating out in your own

country may be different from the UK, where the *Good Food Guide* is published.

B (Answers according to the *Good Food Guide*.)
1 The restaurant may be turning customers away and it's a legal requirement.
2 Your table may be given to someone else and it's good manners.
3 So that the restaurant can prepare for the child's requirements.
4 To see whether the prices include cover charge, service and VAT.
5 In case you regret a hasty choice later.
6 To benefit from their expert knowledge.*
7 Because it's polite and they may object to your smoking, for example.
8 Because the restaurant can try to improve.*
9 Because the bad food was probably not his fault.
10 So that good restaurants can gain customers and bad ones lose them.

* This is implied but not stated explicitly in the article.

C Record your answers to the questions. For example, is it polite in your country to eat in the street, cut up meat and eat it with a fork, mop up sauce with bread, etc.?

10.3 -*ing* and *to*___ *Grammar*

A

-*ing* as the subject of a sentence:
Travelling/Going abroad is interesting.
Washing up/Clearing up after a meal is boring.

-*ing* after prepositions:
I'm looking forward to **going** to Spain on holiday.
I can't get used to **having/drinking** tea without milk.
I've got an upset stomach after **eating too much**.

Verbs + -*ing*:
I avoid **eating/dining/staying** in expensive hotels.
I couldn't help **laughing** when he fell over.
I dislike **washing up/doing the dishes** after a meal.
I always enjoy **trying/tasting** new dishes.

Verbs + *to*___:
I can't afford **to stay/to eat** at the Ritz.
We managed **to get/to find/to reserve** a table by the window.
We decided **to have/to stop for** a drink in the pub.
He tried **to open/to unscrew** the lid.

Verbs + -*ing* or + *to*___ with no difference in meaning:
I don't like **eating/dining** alone in restaurants.
After the meal we continued **talking/chatting**.
Which dessert do you intend **to have/to choose**?
I **hate/like/prefer to drink/drinking** black coffee.

Verbs + -*ing* or + *to*___ with a difference in meaning:
stop -ing and *stop to*___
Their mother told them to stop **talking/shouting/being rude**.
I was half-way through my meal but I had to stop **to answer** the phone.
*remember to*___ and *remember -ing*
You should have remembered **to send/to give** Jill an invitation to the party.
I remember **posting** the letter yesterday evening after work.

***to*___ after adjectives:**
I was glad **to meet/to see** my old school friends again after so many years.
We were surprised **to get/to receive** a bill for £45.
It's easier **to get** from here to the centre by bus than **to go** by car.

***too ... to*___ AND *... enough to*___**
The tray was too heavy for me **to carry/to manage/to lift**.
Boiled eggs are easy enough **to cook**.

B
1 I'm looking forward to seeing my friends on Friday.
2 It's essential to phone the restaurant if you want a table for ten.
3 I'm not used to eating at restaurants.
4 Would you prefer to sit by the window or outside on the terrace?
5 They didn't stop smoking all through the meal.

6 I didn't remember to bring my wallet with me, have you got / did you remember to bring yours?
7 It's easy to boil an egg.
8 I'd like you to get me some water, please.
9 I can't afford to eat in expensive restaurants.
10 I don't mind you sharing my pizza.

C In this kind of exercise in the exam, this symbol: / means that at least one word is missing – but other words may have to be changed too, especially verbs.

(Some variations are possible.)
2 I always look forward to going to see them and enjoy spending the day with them.
3 My grandmother likes to grow (*or* growing) all her own vegetables.
4 She never prepares a meal without using fresh vegetables and refuses to use any ingredients which have artificial additives.
5 When we arrived we decided to go for a short walk before sitting down to lunch.
6 I love walking in the country, even though I dislike walking when I'm in the city.
7 When we got back, the table was laid in the garden for lunch and we all began to eat and talk and we went on eating and drinking all afternoon!
8 I'm not used to eating a lot, but everything was so delicious that I just couldn't stop eating!
9 I managed to eat a great deal more than I (had) intended to eat.
10 When we had all finished eating, we sat round the table and went on talking till it got dark.

10.4 A memorable meal *Listening*

A TRUE: 1, 3, 7, 8, 9, 12, 13; FALSE: 2, 4, 5, 6, 10, 11, 14, 15.

B Record your own description of a meal, like the ones you heard in the recording.

Tapescript

Narrator: Judy, tell us about a meal you remember.
Judy: Um...last...last Boxing Day, I'd invited...er...my parents, my sister, my aunt and my brother and his family for lunch and I was really looking forward to this because it was having all the family together and I love the idea of lots of people round a table, but...er...I think I'd gone a bit far. There were twelve of us as it turned out with...um...my children and husband as well and so it was a bit of a squash round the table. But the main problem was my brother's children, who were aged about two and four, and they were awful. They screamed the whole time, they didn't like the food that I'd produced, they knocked the glasses over, they ate with their fingers – they were awful. And what I had planned as a lovely, happy family meal turned out to be...um...I think one of the most disastrous meals I've ever produced.
Narrator: Anne.
Anne: Er...my most memorable meal...er...was ...um...takes place in the West Indies in a tiny island called Nevis. I went out there to stay with some friends who were running a hotel and I'd had a very long, arduous journey to get there from Heathrow and the last lap had been quite frightening in a very tiny rickety plane and I didn't get there till very late at night and...er...they'd saved some food for me and we sat out on the terrace with the tree-frogs croaking in the palm trees and these wonderful, exotic smells coming from the countryside around us. Er...I don't remember what we ate but it was like suddenly arriving in paradise, it was really wonderful, and I won't...will never forget it.
Narrator: Blain.
Blain: This summer I spent two weeks holidaying on Crete for the first time. I hated the food in Crete: the meat was tough all the time, the salads were identical no matter wherever you had them and everything, whether it was meat, potatoes or salads, were covered in huge lashings of oil and grease. My most memorable meal happened on the first day, the first two hours back in the UK, when I sped straight from the airport to the nearest McDonald's. I got in, and crunched into a juicy Big Mac with the mayonnaise squirting out, the tomato sauce squirting out, I had handfuls of great chips, I loved it.
Narrator: Jill.
Jill: Well, my most memorable meal was in Greece. We used to go to a little taverna for lunch every day and then on our very last night we went to the same taverna in the evening for an evening meal. And it was very beautiful, it was on a deserted beach...um...there were hens and cats and cockerels wandering about, we sat under olive trees...um...with little lights in

them and the whole atmosphere was wonderful. The owner's name was Harry. Um...we had a delicious meal and then we asked him to...um ...order a taxi for us, but instead of a taxi he...um...brought wine, more wine, and...er... about an hour later more wine came. And we kept asking for a taxi but no taxi came, just more wine and more food. And at the end of the meal, we were all pretty drunk and he said it was all on the house because he 'enjoyed us all so much'.

Narrator: Ishia.

Ishia: I think I've had my most memorable meals in Italy but possibly my most memorable meal in Italy was in the South. And I was working there and I went to an extraordinarily marvellous...um...restaurant and had ten courses, something I've never done before nor since. Er...four or five of them were pasta courses and included...er...pasta and raspberries, pasta and champagne with mushrooms, and pasta and smoked salmon and caviar. It was absolutely wonderful and the most remarkably good part about the meal was that I didn't have to pay for it.

Narrator: Coralyn.

Coralyn: Er...a very memorable meal that I had recently was memorable, not so much for the food...um...but for the situation which again was...um...rather comic...er...not funny at the time. Um...I'd cooked this meal...mm...my boyfriend and I had cooked a meal and invited two other couples, it was a Sunday lunch and we'd cooked a *cassoulet*, which had got various bits of spicy meat and sausage in it, and we knew one of the couples very well and the other couple less well and we sat down and had our starter, can't even remember what that was, we got ready to bring the *cassoulet* to the table and I remember making a joke about ...um...'That's good...lucky...it's a very meaty dish, I hope nobody's a vegetarian!' Two mouths opposite dropped open and of course this couple we didn't knew...know very well were vegetarians. But they hadn't told us that they were vegetarians, so I don't know quite how they expected us to know. Um...it got very embarrassing at this point because I made a...another joke about fishing the meat out of the *cassoulet*, which instead of meeting with laughs in response, got stony looks. The husband said, 'No, actually that won't do at all, anything cooked with...er...' I said, 'Oh no, absolutely, no, I'll think of something.' Went in the kitchen and there was nothing really to come up with. It all got more and more embarrassing because this couple were not laughing or sort of getting into the spirit of things. I felt like throwing the *cassoulet* over their heads...um...but all was saved at the end of the day by my very good-natured boyfriend who went in the kitchen and improvised with a *risotto* containing I don't quite know what, but...um...good for him, he came up with something and it all ended happily ever after.

(Time: 6 minutes)

10.5 *On* ... and *out of* ...   *Prepositional phrases*

1 on time   on business;   2 out of order = not working;   3 on holiday/on vacation   out of doors;   4 on your own;   5 on the house = free, no charge;   6 on purpose = deliberately;   7 out of date;   8 on the telephone;   9 on the other hand *or* on the whole;   10 out of work = unemployed; 11 out of reach;   12 out of stock = not available;   13 on duty;   14 on the whole.

10.6 The humble spud   *Reading*

B   1 b   2 d   3 c   4 c   5 a

C

1 After boiling or steaming them.
2 While they're still warm.
3 When they're crisp and brown.
4 After you've preheated the oven, washed the potatoes and rubbed oil on them.
5 When they're tender (after about 1 or 1½ hours).
6 When they're on the table (the guests can do it themselves).

D   Record your answers to these questions and the ones in **A**.

10.7 In a restaurant   *Listening and Interview exercises*

A 🎧 (In the exam, you won't have to understand or be able to spell French or Italian words!)
1 a gin and tonic   sparkling water;

2 tomatoes olives; 3 veal breadcrumbs; 4 chopped potatoes onions; 5 layers pasta meat oven cheese; 6 wine cream starter main course; 7 grated bacon fried eggs; 8 moules marinière Spanish omelette green; 9 Greek salad lasagne; 10 fresh orange juice a half bottle of the house red wine.

Tapescript

Waitress: Good evening. Would you like to see the menu?
Anne: Oh, yes, please.
Waitress: Er...do you want a drink before you start?
Philip: Oh, I think so, yes. Um...I'll have a gin and tonic, how about you?
Anne: I think I'll just have a sparkling water.
Waitress: Right, thank you.
Anne: Mmm, let's have a look. Oh, I see they've got pizzas.
Philip: Mm, yeah, I think I fancy some fish tonight actually.
Anne: Do you? Hey, Philip, what does a Greek salad consist of?
Philip: Greek salad? Um...it's got cucumber, tomato, olives and...um...you know, that *feta* ...er...goat's cheese.
Anne: Oh, I don't like goat's cheese. Er...oh, what about 'Vienna Schnitzel', what is that?
Philip: Oh...er...I don't know. We could ask the waitress. Oh, hold on, do you know what...er...Spanish omelette is?
Anne: Oh yes, it's an omelette made with eggs, of course, and then it's got chopped potatoes and onions in it.
Philip: Mm, sounds good.
Anne: It is.
Philip: What about...er...'Lasagne al Forno'?
Anne: Oh, well, I know it's some sort of pasta, but I'm not quite sure what...well, we'll have to ask the waitress...

Waitress: ...Are you ready to order?
Anne: Oh...er...yes. Could you just tell me something. What is 'Wiener Schnitzel'?
Waitress: Er...yes, it's a thin piece of veal coated in egg and breadcrumbs and then it's fried in oil.
Philip: And...er...what's...um...'moules marinière'?
Waitress: That's...um...mussels cooked in wine with onions and a little cream. You can have it as a starter or as a main course.
Philip: Mussels, mm. Er...and what's...er...'Rost...Rösti'?
Waitress: 'Rösti', yes that's grated potatoes, bacon and onions fried together. You can have it with two fried eggs on top as a main course, you can have it with your main course instead of French fries, if you like.
Philip: Oh, right.
Anne: And...er...just one thing. What's 'Lasagne al forno'?
Waitress: Yes, that's thin layers of pasta and meat sauce with a béchamel sauce, baked in the oven with cheese on top.
Anne: Oh. Oh, well...gosh...Yes, all right. I'll have ...um...moules marinière as a starter, please, and then I'd like the Spanish omelette with a mixed salad...um...no, no. Could you make that a green salad?
Waitress: Yes.
Philip: And...er...I won't have a starter. If I could have the lasagne as a main course and a...um...mixed salad to go with it.
Waitress: Right. So that's one moules marinière as a starter, a Spanish omelette, a lasagne and two mixed salads.
Anne: Er...no mine was a...a green salad, actually.
Waitress: Oh, right...OK.
Philip: Yes, and...and could I...sorry...could I have a Greek salad instead of a mixed salad. But as a starter, is that all right?
Waitress: Right, yes, that's fine. Anything to drink?
Philip: Er...what do you fancy, red wine?
Anne: Oh, no, I won't have any wine, I'm driving. Have you got apple juice?
Waitress: Oh, I'm afraid not, but we have fresh orange juice.
Anne: Oh, that'll be fine, thank you.
Philip: Mm, and could we j...er...a half bottle of the...er...house red?
Waitress: Right, fine.
Philip: Thanks.

(Time: 2 minutes 55 seconds)

B A model version of this conversation is recorded on the cassette. Listen to this first of all.

After listening carefully, write down a description of the dishes YOU would choose from the menu on page 142, giving your reasons.

Tapescript

Narrator: This model conversation gives you an idea of how the conversation about the menu might develop.
First woman: Shall we have a look at the menu? I'm so hungry.

Man: Yeah, OK. Boy, there are a few things here that I don't understand.
Second woman: There's a lot of this stuff I don't understand. What's all this then?
First woman: Well, what about the starters? Hey, do you know what 'prawns'...
Man: The appetisers.
First woman: Appetisers, oh. 'Prawns' are what?
Man: They're like large shrimps.
Second woman: Oh, they're delicious with avocado.
First woman: Really? Mind you, I like the sound of 'melon and orange salad'.
Man: Hey, hey, look at the main courses. What is 'Lancashire hotpot'?
Second woman: I've heard of that. That's...um a...sort of lamb and vegetables cooked in the oven, sort of broiled and the potatoes are sliced on top and put in a layer. It's delicious.
First woman: It sounds good. And what's this one: 'steak and kidney pie', do you know what that is?
Man: Yeah, that now is a typical English dish – it's made of beef which is cut up into pieces along with pieces of kidney in a rich brown sauce. It is lovely. And that is traditionally English.
First woman: Sounds delicious!
Second woman: The one I don't understand is 'cottage pie'.
First woman: Er...I've come across that before. That's minced beef in gravy and it's got mashed potato on top. I don't know if that's going to be that good, although this does look like a good restaurant, don't you think?
Second woman: Yeah...OK. Now, do either of you know what's this: what's 'nut and mushroom roast'?
Man: Well, it's a vegetarian dish...er...hasn't got any meat in it – made of nuts, mushrooms and baked in the oven like a cake. Might be quite nice. Er...but the other one I don't know here is 'chicken Madras'. Anyone know that?
First woman: No.
Second woman: Yes, that's an Indian dish. I can tell you that's...um...it's, I think it's pieces of chicken...

(Time: 1 minute 50 seconds)

10.8 Compound words   *Word study*

A   *Further examples*

long-haired   curly-haired
super-   power   store
multi-   purpose   storey   national   coloured
mini-   bus   lecture
wine waiter   football pitch   racing circuit
athletics track   tennis racket

B
first	first floor first name first course
high	high-class high-level
home	home-grown home-produced
middle	middle-aged middle-sized
second	second-best second-hand second cousin
self	self-discipline self-respect self-service
well	well-known well-off

▶ There are no fixed rules about using hyphens in English. Notice that the examples with *self-* normally have a hyphen even though they are nouns.

C   coffee beans   exercise book
food processor   instant coffee
intelligence test   railway station   recipe book
restaurant owner   salad dressing
savings account   sports ground   story telling
tea bag   television set   tennis court
tomato soup   wholemeal bread
yogurt carton

D   breadcrumbs   chairman   dishwasher
headache   housekeeping   playground
postman   seafood   taxpayer   teapot
toothache   toothbrush   toothpaste

E   1 high-speed/high-powered;   2 coffee cups;   3 toothpaste;   4 stomachache;   5 first cousin;   6 well-done;   7 girlfriend;   8 home-grown;   9 old-fashioned;   10 salad dressing

10.9   A nice cake   *Listening*

B

Tapescript

Harry: Jill, that wonderful cake...um...we had last time we met. You promised to give me the recipe for it. Have you got it?
Jill: Mm, I haven't forgotten. I've written it all out for you – well, at least I've written out the

RICH DUNDEE CAKE

- 220g flour
- 1½ teaspoons of mixed spice (ground cinammon, nutmeg, cloves)
- 150g butter
- 150g sugar
- 3 eggs
- 300g mixed dried fruit (raisins, currants, sultanas)
- 50g glace cherries
- 1 tablespoon of sherry
- 1 tablespoon of rum
- 50g ground almonds
- 50g split almonds

12	A	Remove cake from tin.
10	B	Test after 2 hours with knitting needle.
3	C	Beat eggs and add to creamed butter and sugar.
8	D	Arrange split almonds on top.
5	E	Add remaining ingredients.
4	F	Fold in flour and mixed spice.
1	G	Measure out all ingredients.
13	H	Allow to cool completely before cutting.
9	I	Cook in preheated oven (160°C) for 2½ hours.
11	J	If ready, remove from oven and allow to cool for 15 mins.
6	K	Grease a medium-size cake tin.
7	L	Pour mixture into cake tin.
2	M	Cream butter and sugar in large mixing bowl until light and fluffy.

ingredients for you...Have you ever made a cake before?

Harry: Yes, yes...

Jill: Oh good.

Harry: ...on occasions, yes.

Jill: On occasions? So this is going to be quite an adventure, then?

Harry: Oh yeah, yeah. I can't wait to do it, actually.

Jill: Well, have you got a largish mixing bowl? It needs to be quite big...

Harry: Yeah.

Jill: ...because it's quite a big cake. Er...so you just need a mixing bowl, wooden spoon and a medium size cake tin.

Harry: Right, no problem, yes.

Jill: Right...so, well, you measure out the ingredients and the...I've put all the measurements on here.

Harry: Right.

Jill: So, first of all, you put the butter and the sugar into the bowl. And that's the hard work because you have to sort of cream it all together with a spoon and keep beating and beating and beating until it's really light and fluffy.

Harry: Yes.

Jill: Then you beat the eggs...and pour them in.

Harry: How many eggs is it? Oh yes...

Jill: Three.

Harry: Three.

Jill: Three eggs, yes. Pour them in and beat them into the creamed sugar and butter.

Harry: Yep.

Jill: Now, when it comes to actually putting in the flour and the mixed spice, dispense with the wooden spoon and get an ordinary...er... table spoon...

Harry: Why do you do that?

Jill: Well, the...the secret is to fold in the flour, you see...You don't beat it in, you fold it in...Er...so you fold in the flour very carefully...

Harry: Right.

Jill: ...rather than beating and then add your sherry, rum, fruit, and the ground almonds. I usually grind mine up in a...in a coffee grinder. They're nicer if you buy them whole and grind them yourself.

Harry: OK, right.

Jill: And then again you sort of fold in all that and you...you grease very very well the bake...the bake...the...er...the cake tin.

Harry: Sure.

Jill: Er...you can actually line it with greaseproof paper if you want but I usually...

Harry: That's to stop it sticking?

Jill: To stop it sticking, yes. And if you're really lucky and you've got one of those with a bottom lifts up, it helps it when you want to take it out at the end of all the cooking time. Anyway, you pour it in – but do make sure it's very very very greasy. Pour the mixture in and arrange your split almonds on the top...Cook it in a slow oven – preheat the oven by the way...

Harry: Ah, right.

Jill: ...to about 160 degrees Centigrade. And cook the cake for about two...two and a half hours. But after two hours, take it out of the oven and test it with a knitting needle or a skewer or something by just putting the needle into the top of the cake, pulling it out and if there's any cake on it, it's not cooked. So put it back again and test it every 15 minutes thereafter until it's cooked.

Harry: Right, OK.

Jill: Let it stand for about 15 minutes and remove it from the tin.
Harry: Yes.
Jill: And then wait until it's completely cooled before...trying it. Well, that's if you can...you can manage to wait!
Harry: Well, that's great, thanks very much. I can hardly...er...hardly wait to get home and try it myself. Thanks very much!

(Time: 2 minutes 50 seconds)

C Look at Activity 6. Study the recipe carefully. Then close your book and record your explanation of how to make 'Lassi', pausing the tape if you need to look back at Activity 6.

Do the same with the recipe in Activity 29 (old-fashioned lemonade).

10.10 Revision exercise *Grammar*

1 A meal is being prepared for us now.
2 As the table has been laid, you can sit down now.
3 White bread is not supposed to be as good for you as brown.
4 I've never had a worse meal than the one I had at my brother's flat. / I've never had such a bad meal as the one I had at my brother's flat.
5 If you hadn't arrived so early, the meal might / would have been ready.
6 If we get there early, we'll be able to get a table.
7 If there had been any coffee left, we wouldn't have had to have tea / we could have had coffee instead of tea.
8 Although I'm on a diet, I love chocolates so much that I'll just have one.
9 During dinner there was a power cut.
10 When they arrive, I'll make some tea.

▶ There are more exercises like this in *Cambridge First Certificate Examination Practice 3*.

10.11 How to make a national dish *Composition*

A Here we're looking at STYLE – and the way that the style of a composition should be right for the imagined reader. There are no fixed rules about this, and you should try to develop a 'feeling' for what seems appropriate in different situations.

Suggested answers

1 Spoken by an adult to a child (suitable style for 'Write what you would say to a child')
2 Spoken to a group of adults
3 Spoken to a friend
4 Spoken to a stranger – rather formal style
5 Written in a magazine or newspaper
6 Written in a recipe book
(5 blended with 6 would be suitable style for 'Write instructions for a friend'.)

B As a very complicated dish may take too long to explain, choose something fairly plain.

C In this case you may find you have to write more than the 150-word limit – as in the model composition below. By the way, the model composition might be clearer if each step was numbered.

Model composition

```
                    44 Arcadia Ave
                    Greenwood

                    2 April 19##

Dear Les,
        You asked me to send you the
recipe for a typical national dish.
The one I've chosen is something I'm
sure you'll enjoy cooking and eating,
but it's one you've probably never
tried before. It's called:

Blackberry Fool

To make it you need:
   ½ kilo fresh blackberries (frozen
   ones will do)
   200 g sugar
   3 eggs
   ½ litre milk
   ¼ litre cream

Cook the fruit on a low heat with half
of the sugar until soft (about 15
mins).
        Meanwhile, beat the eggs with the
rest of the sugar in a bowl. Heat the
milk to just below boiling point and
pour it slowly onto the eggs and
sugar, stirring all the time. Then put
the bowl into a pan of almost boiling
water and keep stirring until the
```

mixture thickens (about 5 mins). Then remove the bowl and put the custard you have made in the fridge.
Rub the cooked fruit through a sieve and put the purée you have made in the fridge.
When everything is cold, whip the cream. Then fold the cold custard into the puree and then fold in the cream too.
Serve in a large glass bowl or individual glass dishes.

It's quite tricky to make but you'll find it's absolutely delicious!

Best wishes,

10.12 Leave, let, pull and run *Verbs and idioms*

A 1 let; 2 pulling; 3 pull; 4 leave; 5 leave; 6 let; 7 leave; 8 runs/ran; 9 left; 10 run; 11 let; 12 runs.

B 1 let in = allow to enter; 2 let down = disappoint; 3 leave out = omit; 4 let off = allow to explode; 5 pulls up = stop; 6 pulled out = extract; 7 pulled down = demolish; 8 running over = kill or injure   ran into = collide with; 9 run out of = have no more; 10 run after = chase; 11 ran into = meet unexpectedly; 12 run away with = leave secretly or illegally.

11 Work and business

11.1 Earning a living *Vocabulary*

B (These are the 'best alternatives'.)
1 qualifications; 2 firm; 3 profession; 4 career; 5 apply (there is no such word as *applicate*); 6 fill in; 7 referees; 8 staff; 9 employee; 10 overtime (there is no such word as *overhours*); 11 permanent; 12 promoted; 13 training; 14 earn; 15 pension; 16 department; 17 routine; 18 a salary; 19 profit; 20 goods.

C 1 makes manufactures produces; 2 dismissed fired sacked; 3 became unemployed lost their jobs were made redundant; 4 experience personality qualifications; 5 computer typewriter word processor.

11.2 How to create a good impression ... *Reading*

A DOs – all items except 6 and 11, which are DON'Ts. (7 and 10 are things you should not forget.)

B 2 c 3 c 4 b 5 a 6 b 7 c 8 c 9 a 10 b 11 c 12 a 13 c

C Record your answers, as if you were being asked the questions in the exam Interview. Some of the differences between a job interview and the FCE Interview are:
• Candidates and examiner don't shake hands.
• There's no need to take your certificates with you.
• You won't be asked technical questions.

11.3 Reported speech *Grammar*

A Reporting Statements
3 She said that **she hadn't found a job that suited her yet.**
4 She told me **that she would telephone them and ask them to send her an application form.**
5 I found out **that she hadn't got the job she had applied for.**
6 She admitted **that she had done very badly at the interview.**
Note: *that* can be omitted in all the above sentences.

B Reporting Orders, Promises, Offers, Requests and Advice

3 He wanted me **to type the letter out for him**.
4 I offered **to do it on my word processor**.
5 I reminded him **to send it by first-class post**.
6 He persuaded **me to make a photocopy of it for him**.

C Reporting Questions

3 I asked her if it **was her first interview**.
4 She asked me what the **most important thing to remember at an interview was**.
5 I wanted to know **what she was going to wear for the interview**.
6 I wondered **how she would feel before the interview**.
7 I asked her if **she had got the job when I saw her after the interview**.
8 I tried to find out **why she didn't look pleased**.
9 She said she was disappointed because **it wasn't really the kind of work she wanted to do**.

▶ Notice that there are no question marks in a reported question and the word order usually changes.

D (Some variations are possible.)

1 He said that he wasn't enjoying his work.
2 He told me (that) he hadn't remembered to post the letter the night before.
3 She said (that) she wanted me to get there early the next day.
4 She asked me if I had already phoned our clients or if I would / was going to do it later.
5 She reminded me to order the supplies she needed.
6 He wanted to know when the delivery van would arrive.
7 She persuaded me/us to phone them.
8 He admitted (that) it was / had been his fault.
9 She threatened to scream if we didn't stop laughing.
10 He promised to make the phone call first thing tomorrow/the next day.

11.4 Four candidates   *Listening*

B

Tapescript

Dennis: Well, then Margaret. Four quite interesting people. What's your verdict?
Margaret: Well, I think before we make any decision, we should compare notes, you know, see what...we think.
Dennis: Yes, fine, fair enough, let's...er...take them in alphabetical order, shall we?
Margaret: All right. What do you think?
Dennis: Well, that is...er...Mr Anderson, isn't it? Well, he seems pretty well-qualified, don't you think?
Margaret: Yes, yes, qualified, well-qualified...and pleasant, I thought.
Dennis: Yes, oh, exceedingly so, yes. Plenty of experience in...in our field too, that's very very important.
Margaret: And he seemed a reliable sort of chap.
Dennis: Yes. Do you think perhaps he's been a little too long in his present job?
Margaret: Could be...I mean, he...he didn't come over as very imaginative...Perhaps he's lacking in drive.
Dennis: Yes, I think...er...I think possibly so.
Margaret: What about Miss Ballantyne?
Dennis: Ah, Miss Ballantyne, now the...she's very interesting, I think. She was...er...after all recom-

	GOOD POINTS	BAD POINTS
Mr Anderson	Well-qualified, experienced, reliable	Unimaginative, lacking in drive, too long in present job
Miss Ballantyne	Recommended, hard-working	Aggressive?? (or nervous)
Mr Collins	Good sense of humour, did well at school, asked good questions, would learn quickly	No experience, too well-qualified?
Miss Davis	Serious, imaginative, intelligent	Unreliable? 5 jobs in 2 years

mended to us by Mr Fowler of Acme Engineering.
Margaret: Mm. I liked her. She seemed a hardworking sort of person, you know the type. Oh yeah, I liked her.
Dennis: Mm. What did you think about her...er...her personality at...at the interview? I...I didn't think that was too good, did you?
Margaret: Oh, what worried you?
Dennis: Well, she seemed a...a little...little aggressive.
Margaret: Oh, you thought she seemed aggressive?
Dennis: Yes. That didn't come over to you?
Margaret: No, no, not at all.
Dennis: That...that's very interesting.
Margaret: Maybe that's a male point of view. I thought she seemed rather nervous, not at all aggressive.
Dennis: Ah, yes. I...it just...I don't know, I...I was just thinking that, well, you know, she's not giving a very good interview. Therefore probably not giving...doing herself justice. And then I...Sorry, go on.
Margaret: Mm, I was going to say, what about Mr Collins?
Dennis: Mr Collins, ah yes, now that's a very nice sense of humour. I...I liked him very much...Mm...The on...the only thing against him of course is that he...he has no experience in our line of work. I don't know, do you think there's any value in that?
Margaret: I don't know. He seemed intelligent and...and would learn very quickly.
Dennis: Yes...yes. Of course, he did very well at school and...and...and then college, of course.
Margaret: Yes, and he asked us some very good questions.
Dennis: Yes, that's true.
Margaret: You know, one thing bothered me.
Dennis: Yes?
Margaret: I think he's too well-qualified.
Dennis: Too well-qualified? Do you think so?
Margaret: Yes, could be.
Dennis: Yes, even...despite the fact that he has no experience? I would have thought that the one might have balanced the other, no?
Margaret: I don't know, we could try. What about Mr Dav...Miss...Miss Davis?
Dennis: Miss Davis...yes. Yes, very very pleasant...Um...she worries me a little bit. Er...that...point, I mean she was very honest about it but she's after all had five jobs in the past two years...Makes me feel a little cautious, you know.
Margaret: Yes, she could be a bit unreliable, but then...She...she seemed to have a serious sort of nature. She seemed...seemed serious about us too. Seemed interested in our kind of work.
Dennis: Yes...yes and...and she was very intelligent...very intelligent ideas. And a very good imagination. I thought some of her points were very imaginative.
Margaret: Right, well...So of the four, yes, what do you think?
Dennis: Well, it seems to me that of the four ...given what we've taken and thinking about it, that the best for the job is probably...

(Time: 3 minutes)

11.5 Fill the gaps *Use of English*

1 the; 2 ever; 3 was; 4 hear; 5 bit;
6 although; 7 in; 8 not; 9 whole;
10 those; 11 ground; 12 effort;
13 anything; 14 again; 15 said;
16 that; 17 own; 18 since; 19 spite;
20 telling; 21 all; 22 listened; 23 hard;
24 time; 25 back; 26 ways.

11.6 Situations vacant *Problem solving*

A Here are a few notes of explanation on the advertisements:
1 INN ON THE PARK: *beverage* = drinks
2 ATTENTION: *the Services* = army, navy, air force *commission* = money paid as a percentage of sales *incentives* = extra money for higher sales *advancement* = promotion
3 TWO YEARS AGO: *broke* = had no money, bankrupt *five-figure income* = £10,000 per year or more
4 THE SELFRIDGE HOTEL: *rota* = staff take it in turns to work different days/hours
6 STEWARDESSES: *sailboat* = yacht *will train* = training will be given *resumé* = CV (curriculum vitae, career history)

B Notice that the opening words may require the use of certain structures.

Model paragraphs

```
The best job for Anne would be to find
out more about the part-time job in
number 7. She has all the right
qualifications and, assuming she has
no objection to using her car and
working on Sundays, the job might be
```

very interesting. The pay is reasonable but she should find out how much she would have to spend on petrol and other expenses. The work itself is not described and she should find out exactly what is involved.

Bob would perhaps enjoy the job of Room Service Order Taker at the Inn on the Park. He seems to have no previous experience, but he is well-educated and no doubt he could cope easily with the work. The danger is that he might quickly get bored with the work and lose patience with guests who are too fussy.

Cherry might like to apply for the job of secretary at the language school. She is perhaps over-qualified for the job but it sounds like an interesting job with a chance to meet people from all over the world. However, she may not speak German well enough to get the job. But a person with Cherry's experience should have no difficulty in finding a suitable job.

Doris should write a letter and send her photo to T.W. Charters in Miami. As a stewardess she could have a real break from the monotony of working in an office and enjoy the excitement of cruising in a sailing yacht. She might meet all sorts of fascinating people on board and ashore. On the other hand, there may be unexpected risks involved in living on board a boat.

11.7 Word stress + Joining up words   *Pronunciation*

▶ 🔲 **A** and **B** are recorded on the cassette. These exercises will help you to improve your stress and help you to speak more fluently by joining up words instead of pausing between each word. These features of pronunciation are assessed in the Interview.

A 🔲

Verbs and -ing forms
These bananas are impórted.
He insúlted me.
I objéct to being insúlted.
They perfécted a new method.

Nouns and adjectives
Ímports have risen this month.
That was a terrible ínsult.
Unidentified Flying Óbject
Your work is not quite pérfect.

Smoking is not permítted.
His work is progréssing well.
They protésted about the situation.
Listen to the recórding.
He is suspécted of the crime.

You need a pérmit to fish in the river.
Prógress to First Certificate
They held a prótest meeting.
Have you heard their new récord?
He is the main súspect.

B 🔲

ádvertising   advértisement   attráction
certíficate   cómfortable   communicátion
députy   désert   dessért   desírable
détails   devélopment   expérience   gírlfriend
himsélf   informátion   intélligence   machíne
pérmanent   phótograph   photógraphy
qualificátion   recéptionist   reservátion
secretárial   sécretary   télephone   teléphonist
témporary   themsélves   tóothache
végetable   yoursélf

C 🔲 *Suggested answers*

1 Stréss is just as impórtant in a convérsation as when you're réading sómething alóud.
2 Knówledge of at léast óne fóreign lánguage is required in this jób.
3 The unemplóyment fígures are hígher agáin this mónth, it sáys in the páper.
4 I héard on the néws that éxports are úp agáin this yéar.
5 Mále sécretaries were replaced by wómen in the Fírst Wórld Wár.
6 Fínd oút as múch as póssible about the jób befórehand.
7 Shów some enthúsiasm whén the jób is expláined to you.
8 Nó one is góing to emplóy you if you lóok as if you've wándered oút of a dísco.
9 The wáy you ánswer will show what kínd of pérson you áre and if your educátion, skills and expérience mátch whát they're lóoking for.
10 It tákes most péople a lóng time to perféct their pronunciátion in Énglish.

D After you have followed the instructions in the main part of the book, read each of the sentences aloud and record yourself on a blank cassette.

Suggested answers

1 Stress is just as important in a conversation as when you're reading something aloud.
2 Knowledge of at least one foreign language is required in this job.
3 The unemployment figures are higher again this month, it says in the paper.
4 I heard on the news that exports are up again this year.
5 Male secretaries were replaced by women in the First World War.
6 Find out as much as possible about the job beforehand.
7 Show some enthusiasm when the job is explained to you.
8 No one is going to employ you if you look as if you've wandered out of a disco.
9 The way you answer will show what kind of person you are and if your education, skills and experience match what they're looking for.
10 It takes most people a long time to perfect their pronunciation in English.

▶ You will not have to read aloud in the exam, but reading aloud is an excellent way of improving your pronunciation. Read the whole of the passage in 11.2 aloud, which is written in a conversational style.

11.8 First jobs   *Listening*

A   1 c   2 a   3 a   4 b   5 b   6 c   7 c   8 a   9 a   10 c

Tapescript

David: Do you remember the...er...the very first job you ever had?
Jill: Yes, I certainly do. I wasn't very good at it, actually. Um...it was as a secretary, I was supposed to be a secretary but I hadn't done very much secretarial training, and I went along – it was a design studio – and in fact I wanted to be a designer, so I used to sit around doing drawings all the time where I should have been typing letters, shorthand and typing. And...er...my boss went away for three weeks' holiday and there was...um...a horrible woman put in charge and...er...she was very very nasty and got me into terrible trouble with my boss, who came back and gave me a big lecture and I ran home in tears and then I didn't go back and then several...several weeks later I had a letter from him, saying: 'Please come back because the...' – now what did he call her? Something horrible, anyway – 'She's gone' he said.
David: So you went back?
Jill: 'And would you like to come back?' – No, I didn't. Tell me about yours.
David: Oh mine, oh, straight out of school I worked in a library for six months, which was so boring it was untrue and the...the only excitement we got out of the day was seeing people come in the door which was at the far end and we would all decide between ourselves what sort of book they were going to take out, right? So they'd come up to the desk and you'd...you'd sort of say: 'Oh, she's going to get an Agatha Christie.' 'No, no, no she's into cars', you know. And then of course it would turn out to be something totally different. We...we used to have a point system, you know, you'd score points according to...Apart from that I would never ever go back to work for a library, but what I do know now is how to get...how to find my way round in a library. So if you find yourself in a library you don't know, you can find your way around. That's the only part I enjoyed about it.

Richard: Well, the first job I had and certainly one of the best was straight after school and before I went to university, I had some months off, and I was fixed up with a job in Berlin as a postman in...in a...a quarter of Berlin called Spandau...Spandau. Er...and it was a lovely job. I find postmen the world over tend to be very friendly sort of people and the...there were a group of us Englishmen in there and the German postmen were wonderful, they sorted all our mail for us and everything, and took us round, and got drunk with us after the round and...And...er...it was strange for me 'cause I'm not used to getting up quite that early but I lived about an hour and a half away, the other side of the city, I had to get up at five in order to be there for half past six, do the round and I was back in bed by about one o'clock in the afternoon.
Jocelyn: Was it well paid?
Richard: Well, it...for someone who'd just left school it was quite well paid, yes. Er...it was...um ...and a German postman has to do far more than an English postman. They have to take the old-age pensions round and hand them out and collect various moneys and things, so it's a much more responsible job and I was amazed that they were giving me all this responsibility

305

– an English schoolkid, basically, carrying thousands of pounds around with me, accountable for it in theory. But it was great fun.

Jocelyn: Well, my first job was about the same time really, I suppose, I was leaving school, but I...I made a lot of money but it was an awful job...it was selling encyclopedias door-to-door in the United States and the pressure to sell was incredible. I mean, you had to go back every night and...and...and produce the goods and I found that I just used to burst into tears. I mean, they would drive you into an area that...where you didn't know the streets, you didn't know where you were, and they said: 'Well, we'll pick up up in four or five hours', and there was no sort of steady wage, you had to sell in order to make any kind of money at all. And at first I was so timid I'd, you know, I'd ring the doorbell and I'd expect them to slam the door in my face and of course they did. And after a while I thought: 'The only thing that's going to save me is a sense of humour here'. So I would make jokes, I would run through the sprinklers on the lawn and this seemed to...um...interest them. So I found myself getting asked in and I would spend the evening talking about everything else other than encyclopedias and then sort of towards the end I'd sort of say: 'Oh by the way...' And they'd buy them. It would be...yeah...

Richard: So you made a living out of it?

Jocelyn: Yeah, I did, I did. Well, I put myself through college on it.

Richard: Fantastic!

(Time: 4 minutes)

B Record a description of your own first job.

11.9 The secretary *Reading*

A 1 d 2 a 3 a 4 c 5 b 6 d 7 b 8 a 9 c 10 a

11.10 A typical working day *Listening*

A Albert Wilson is an underground train driver. Gordon Spencer is a writer.

B Pause the tape before the interview with Gordon Spencer begins.
TRUE: 2, 4, 6, 7, 10; FALSE: 1, 3, 5, 8, 9.

C TRUE: 2, 4, 6, 9; FALSE: 1, 3, 5, 7, 8, 10.

▶ In the exam the questions are likely to be harder, BUT you don't have to get 100% right.

Tapescript

Interviewer: Albert, tell us about a typical working day in your job.
Albert: Well, if you're on the morning shift, er...you might have to get up as early as four to be at work by five, you know, which is when the first train leaves. But, you know, not all the trains start that early...er...they leave every ten minutes or so up to about seven. So if you're driving a later train, you wouldn't report for work until...oh...you know, six forty-five ...er...in the case of driving at seven o'clock. But oh...er...it all depends, you know. Er...you know, I find the work itself is quite tiring. Even though you're sitting down all the time, you have to remain alert the whole time and it's a big responsibility because there are only two or three minutes between each station. This means you're always starting and stopping or accelerating and slowing down. I...er...I wouldn't say it's a very healthy job, really, you know, because...er...you know, the lack of air and lack of ventilation. You know, although the line I'm on at the moment, it runs as much above ground as it does below ground. You know, it's quite nice out in the country there sometimes. But...er...more because of...er...th...you know...because of the strain on the nerves is the health thing really. It's the strain on the nerves. You get...er...headaches quite often. On the whole, though, I don't mind the work. Though I don't suppose I...I don't really enjoy it. Er...I don't mind being on my own most of the time, you know. You get a chance to chat to your mates in the refreshments breaks you get between journey. But...er...I suppose the advantage of the work is that you...you don't have to answer to anyone. You know, you're your own boss, there's no one telling you what to do the whole time.
Interviewer: What...what's the pay like?
Albert: Oh, the pay very good. I think it's very fair for what...for what we do. Um...and the other advantage is if you're on a morning shift you're free the whole afternoon, you know...you know, with my hobbies and...er...all that kind of thing, and helping the wife out with the shopping, it's great. But if you're on the evening work it can be a real problem.
Interviewer: Why...why is that?
Albert: Well...you know, because you're too

tired, er...you know, working and this means you can't spend...er...time with your mates except on your days off, as well, that's another thing. I...I suppose I get about two days off a week, sometimes three. And four weeks holiday. You...you try to take the...er...the family to the seaside on one of those weeks, really. Because, you know, I get...er...I get free travel anywhere in London for myself and my family, that's another thing. So on rest days we try to go out for the day with the family if the weather's nice and we take a picnic to the park or something like that.

Interviewer: Well, thank you very much, Albert. Next we have Gordon Spencer. Gordon, would you tell us how you spend a typical working day?

Gordon: Yes, indeed, the...er...I suppose the only time I ever stick to a really strict routine is when I'm actually writing a book. I suppose I get up at six, yes, it's always fairly early, have breakfast, swim and then off I go to my writing hut which is about five miles from home.

Interviewer: A writing hut?

Gordon: Yes, it's marvellous, you see, it's a little place where I can actually shut myself away, be absolutely private and quiet. There's no telephone there or anything like that and I can really concentrate on writing.

Interviewer: Oh, I see.

Gordon: Er...work, yes, well, I suppose it starts round about...about seven. Um...I make rough drafts in longhand and...er...type up these drafts every day immediately afterwards. You see, I don't leave anything over until the next day. I always sort of complete what I'm doing on the day. Now the books, as you'll know if you've read them, are always based very carefully on the research that I do.

Interviewer: I think that's quite evident from the sort of stories that you write.

Gordon: Well, I have notebooks absolutely chock full of information about people and places kept locked away in the writing hut. I keep them all in a big safe there. Now, I work through the day for about eight hours and I stop only to make tea or have some biscuits or something like that. And then I stop at three o'clock. Dead stop at three o'clock and home I go, home I go, cycle home and I have a swim and a . . . and a sauna.

Interviewer: I expect you need it after that, don't you?

Gordon: Well, it's...er...it's not a doddle, writing a book. At...er...five o'clock, you see, I then eat. My wife's got the meal ready. And...er...well, after that we settle down and relax a bit.

Interviewer: And what sort of time do you go to bed? What time does your day actually finish?

Gordon: Oh, I suppose, not too late, about ten o'clock if I've got to be up at...er...six the next morning.

Interviewer: Mm. How long on average would you say it takes you to write a book?

Gordon: Well now, the actual writing of a book takes, what, about five or six weeks, I suppose if you...if I work seven days a week. Er...my output is one book a year and that's always in July and August. And the rest of the year I spend...well, well, what do I spend...er...yes, I spend it relaxing at home or travelling abroad doing research for the next one.

Interviewer: I see, well thank you very much, Gordon Spencer.

Gordon: A pleasure.

(Time: 5 minutes)

11.11 Writing a formal letter — Composition

B The first writer has made the following 'mistakes':
- The name and address of the reader don't appear on the left-hand side.
- The letter begins 'Dear Sir' although we know the name of the reader is Ms Brown. (If you know the name of the person, you should use it.)
- 'Yours sincerely' isn't suitable as an ending if the opening is 'Dear Sir' or 'Dear Madam'.
- The writer isn't 'selling' him/herself hard enough.
- A little more personal detail about previous experience would be a good idea.
- The letter is shorter than an exam composition should be (though in real life this is not a fault, of course!).

The second writer seems more suitable for the job, though the details of the time he/she is available are probably unnecessary.

C There is no model composition in this case: refer back to the second letter in **B** if necessary.

Make sure you time yourself, make notes and check your work through afterwards.

11.12 Set, stand and turn — Verbs and idioms

A 1 stands; 2 turned; 3 stands;
4 stands; 5 set; 6 turned; 7 stand;
8 set; 9 stand; 10 set; 11 turned;
12 set; 13 turn; 14 turned.

B 1 set out = start a journey; 2 set up = found/start; 3 sets out = explain;
4 standing in for = be a substitute; 5 stand for = tolerate; 6 stand up to = resist;
7 stood for = be a candidate for; 8 stand by = support; 9 stood up = rise to one's feet;
10 turn up = arrive; 11 turn over = go to the next page; 12 turned down = reject.

11.13 Different kinds of jobs — Interview exercises

▶ You aren't expected to know everything about an unfamiliar topic for the exam. There are ways of dealing with unknown items, like saying to the examiner: 'I haven't **come across** this word/tool/profession before.' And this may be safer than pretending you know something you don't.

B Look at Activity 26. In your own words, record a short talk using the ideas there. Then look at Activity 30. Listen to your recording and imagine that you are reacting to the views expressed in the recording. Record your 'reply' as a short speech. Do the same with the ideas in Activity 45.

Finally, listen to the whole recording, which may sound as if three people are having a discussion!

▶ If you are doing the Interview some time before the written papers of the exam, make sure you look at the FINAL EXAM ADVICE for the Interview at the end of Unit 14 on page 208.

12 In the news

12.1 The press, politics and crime — Vocabulary

▶ Buy an English-language newspaper and read it before you do this exercise. Also, if possible, listen to the news on the BBC World Service. This will help the whole topic to come alive.

B 1 article; 2 headlines; 3 editorial;
4 newsreader; 5 hostages; 6 revolution;
7 earthquake; 8 weapons; 9 support;
10 democracy; 11 election;
12 government; 13 Prime Minister;
14 arrested; 15 stolen; 16 lawyer;
17 jail; 18 guilty; 19 jury;
20 socialist.

12.2 The robber gendarme — Reading

A (*Gendarme* is a French word for policeman; *bingo* is a kind of gambling game; a *home loan* is the same as a *mortgage* – money borrowed from a bank to buy a home.)

B *Correct sequence*

1 Played bingo; 2 Found himself in debt;
3 Decided to rob bank; 4 Was afraid to rob bank; 5 Robbed bank; 6 Alarm raised by manager; 7 Paid part of his debts;
8 Reported for duty; 9 Arrested.

C 1 d 2 c 3 c 4 b 5 d 6 a

12.3 Word order *Grammar*

▶ The points covered in parts **A** to **D** are a very tricky area: there are no firm rules. Hopefully, by now, you have developed a 'feeling' for the position where adverbial phrases can be placed in sentences. Some places feel 'just right' or 'comfortable', others feel 'not quite right' and others feel 'wrong'.

Doing the exercises in **A** to **D** will help you to realise that, in fact, you already have this 'feeling'.

A ADVERBS and adverbial phrases
The gaps (—) in the chart are the positions where the adverbs are not normally placed in the example sentence, as explained in **B**.

B
If you read these sentences that were 'missing' from the chart in **A**, you'll probably agree that they sound 'wrong':
He was arrested never. ×
He yesterday was arrested. ×
He by the police was arrested. ×

C
The first group of adverbs (*almost* to *seldom*) are all mid-position adverbs. The rest can be placed in various positions. In some cases the adverbs simply don't make sense in the context – so there is no 'comfortable position' in these cases.

Decide on just one or two positions where each adjective can be placed in each sentence. There's no need to worry about every possible position – just a couple that feel 'comfortable' or 'right'.

▶ IMPORTANT: DO NOT worry about any possible positions that you have missed – only the ones you have got wrong.

Suggested answers
(Some of these may seem less 'comfortable' than others.)

1 **They** *2* **didn't** *3* **arrive** **on time** *4* **.**
5 **She** *6* **was** *7* **able to finish her meal**
8 **.** *9* **We** *10* **knew** *11* **that the work**
12 **would** *13* **be very difficult** *14* **.**

almost: 2, 7
always: 3, 4, 6, 7, 10, 11, 13
hardly ever: 7, 10, 13
just: 2, 7, 10, 13
nearly: 2, 7
never: 6, 7, 10, 12, 13
rarely: 2, 6, 7, 10, 12, 13
seldom: 2, 6, 7, 10, 12, 13

as usual: 1, 4, 5, 7, 8, 9, 11, 12, 13, 14
certainly: 1, 2, 5, 6, 7, 9, 10, 12, 13
definitely: 1, 2, 6, 7, 10, 11, 12, 13
frequently: not 3
maybe: 1, 5, 9, 11
normally: all
obviously: all
often: all
one day: 1, 4, 5, 8, 9, 11, 13, 14
on Friday: 1, 4, 5, 8, 9, 11, 14
perhaps: all
possibly: not 3
probably: not 3
really: all
still: 1, 2, 5, 6, 7, 9, 10, 11, 12, 13
usually: all
yesterday: 1, 4, 5, 8, 9, 11, 14

D
(Variations are given, though others may be possible.)
1 She worked hard to finish the essay.
2 You hardly ever read about my country in the newspapers.
3 Unexpectedly, it was a hard task that took a long time to finish.
   It was a hard task that took an unexpectedly long time to finish.
   It was an unexpectedly hard task that took a long time to finish.
   It was a hard task that unexpectedly took a long time to finish.
   It was a hard task that took a long time to finish, unexpectedly.
4 He walked slowly into the room and clapped his hands.
   Slowly he walked into the room and clapped his hands.
5 They did the work very well on their own.
   They did the work on their own very well.
6 There is normally not much news in the paper on Saturday.
   Normally, there is not much news in the paper on Saturday.
   On Saturday there is normally not much news in the paper.
7 We will definitely hear the election results on TV on Sunday.

On Sunday we will definitely hear the election results on TV.
8 We always listen to the evening news on the radio during dinner.
   During dinner we always listen to the evening news on the radio.
   We always listen during dinner to the evening news on the radio.

E IT and THERE

There was (loud) **applause at the end**.
It wasn't me who **broke the window**.
It was **the tall man who started the fight**.
It's also **interesting to read good news**.
It is said **that crime is increasing**.

F (Some variations are possible.)
1 It isn't as easy as it looks to rewrite sentences.
2 It was the right-wing party who/that won the election.
3 It was kind of you to help me.
4 There's no need to read the paper unless you want to.
5 There isn't much difference between the policies of the two parties.
6 It was the left-wing candidate who was unexpectedly elected.
7 There were unfortunately no survivors of/from the air disaster.
8 It was George Bush who was elected President in 1988.
9 It is believed that 100 people have been killed.
10 There will probably be no change in the weather.

12.4 What happened? *Composition*

B *Model composition*

```
I was just crossing the road the other
morning on my way to take part in a
demonstration when a man on a bike
nearly ran into me - I was astonished
to see that he was wearing a bowler
hat and had a big rucksack on his
back. He didn't apologise but just
waved his umbrella at me and rode on.
'That looks pretty dangerous, I hope
he doesn't fall off,' I thought. Well,
two blocks further on I discovered
that he hadn't fallen off, but that
the sight of him must have distracted
two motorists who had lost control of
their cars and collided. Although both
cars were damaged, I was glad to see
that no one was hurt. I overheard the
drivers explaining to a policeman
about the cyclist but I could tell
from his expression that he didn't
believe a word of it. However, I
couldn't stop because I didn't want to
be late for the demo. Luckily I got
there just as the march was starting
and took my place among the other
students as we all started marching.
```

▶ In the exam, an 'impression mark' is given for each composition. For the complete marking scales used by the examiners, see the Teacher's Book of *Cambridge First Certificate Practice 3*, which also contains some authentic candidates' compositions with the marks that were awarded.

12.5 Better safe than sorry! *Listening*

A 1 95%; 2 60%; 3 two thirds;
4 a) locks; b) front door key; c) chain;
d) insured; 5 1½ million; 6 25%;
7 a) doors boot; b) valuables boot;
c) windows; d) well-lit; 8 a) forget the number; b) two to three.

Tapescript

Man: Erm...er...good evening, everyone. My name's Matthew Jackson, I'm the area crime prevention officer. I...I'd just like to talk to you for a few minutes. Er...we hear a lot on the television and in the papers about the increase in violent crime. Now, it's true that it is increasing, but the facts are that about 95% of crimes are against property, not against people. Now, you can reduce the risk of losing your property by taking simple precautions in your home and when away from your home. For example, according to a recent survey, 60% of homes do not have window locks. Now, this means that a thief can just break a window, open the catch, climb in. Two thirds of all burglars get in through a window. So to increase the security of your home, make sure you have locks on all your windows. Have a lock on the front door that can only be opened and closed with a key. Have a chain on the front door and make sure your property is insured.

Now, i...in Britain over 1.5 million cars are broken into or stolen each year. That...that's six cars every two minutes. Now, if you regularly park your car in a city street, there is a one in four chance it will be stolen or broken into. So, when you leave your car you should always lock all the doors and the boot and take your valuables with you or lock them in the boot. And if the car's empty, close the windows completely – don't even leave them open a fraction. And if you can, make sure you park in a well-lit street at night.

Now, i...if you have a bicycle it must be locked up securely with a good lock whenever you leave it unattended. N...not a combination lock, you know, where you have to remember a number, because...well...you may forget the number and they're absolutely useless because it...it only takes a thief two or three minutes to open one.

Now, as for making sure of your own personal safety: first of all, remember that criminals are looking for easy opportunities and again there are simple precautions you can take, for instance, always go out...

(Time: 2 minutes 30 seconds)

12.6 Opposites   *Word study*

A disagree   disapprove   uncomfortable
harmful   dishonest   unkind   illegal
unlucky   impolite   irregular   irrelevant
unsafe   unwilling

B The opposites here are all different words. In some cases there are a number of possible answers.
modest   ugly   expensive   kind   victory/beat   succeed   lead   melt/thaw   love/adore/like   well/healthy   win   quiet/silent   polite   fresh   loose   fast asleep

C This exercise contains a mixture of words, some of which have opposites formed with a suffix and others with opposites that are different words.
raw/uncooked   safe   similar/identical   truth/non-fiction   solid   immature   unnecessary   support   impersonal   unpleasant/nasty   impolite/rude   smooth   untrue/false   invisible   loser   correct/right

12.7 Hurricane Gilbert   *Reading*

A Don't use a dictionary while reading the article.
1 b   2 b   3 d   4 b   5 b   6 b   7 d
8 b   9 b   10 c

B refused to take seriously – brushed aside; attack – onslaught; poor – impoverished; number of people killed – death toll; reach the coast – make a landfall; make more extreme – intensify; serious – grave.

12.8 Exam practice

2 Have you heard the story of Edwin Chambers Dodson?
3 He was an antique dealer in Hollywood whose customers included many famous film stars.
4 He led a secret life as a bank robber.
5 He robbed more banks than any other man in American history.
6 He held up more banks than Jesse James and Bonnie and Clyde.
7 He took part in 64 robberies in California and made $300,000.
8 He was known as the 'Yankee Bandit' because he wore a blue New York Yankees baseball cap during most of his robberies.
9 He was sent to prison for fifteen years after he had pleaded guilty to eight robberies.
10 He is still in prison now.
(*This is a true story, by the way.*)

12.9 Here is the news ...   *Listening*

In the exam, the following procedure is used:
1 You have 15–20 seconds to read the questions.
2 You hear the recording for the first time.
3 There is 15–20 seconds silence before you hear it again.
4 You hear the recording for the second time.
5 There is 15–20 seconds more silence.

Try to do this listening exercise 'under exam conditions'.
TRUE: 2, 6, 8, 10, 13, 15; FALSE: 1, 3, 4, 5, 7, 9, 11, 12, 14.

Tapescript

Woman: Nine hours Greenwich Mean Time. The news read by Wendy Gordon. A hundred and twenty-five people involved in drug manufacture and smuggling have been arrested in Bolivia. The Greek airliner hijacked to Algeria is on its way back to Athens.

In an attempt to stop the flow of cocaine and other drugs from Bolivia to the USA, a series of arrests have been made in Santa Cruz in the east of the country. Among the 125 people arrested are Miguel Castro, believed to be the leading figure in the manufacture and export of cocaine to the USA. According to the US Drug Enforcement Agency, who have been working in close cooperation with the United Nations and the Bolivian army, three planes loaded with drugs have been destroyed in a raid on an airfield and more than 2.5 tons of pure cocaine has been seized in other raids.

The worst of the heavy rains and thunderstorms that have been sweeping parts of Europe during the past week appears to be over. Exceptionally heavy rainfall brought flooding to many parts of Germany, Switzerland, Northern Italy and France and chaos to rail and road transport. Air traffic too has been affected with flight delays at airports. Although most flights are expected to be back to normal by this time tomorrow, there are expected to be serious delays on the German and Italian motorways over the forthcoming holiday weekend and train services are unlikely to be normalised for several days. A government spokeswoman in France announced that the damage to homes and property is expected to be at least four thousand million francs. It is reported that at least five people have lost their lives. Experts agree that casualty figures are low because emergency warnings were issued on the day before the storms began. The federal government in Switzerland has urged motorists and rail travellers not to travel during the next few days and no international traffic will be allowed on the main north–south motorway routes across the country until next Tuesday.

The Greek airliner that was hijacked and flown to Algeria on Tuesday is now on its way back to Athens. After nearly 48 hours on the tarmac at Algiers airport, the five hijackers were persuaded to leave the plane in the early hours of this morning and the relief crew who have been standing by took over from Captain Georgiou and his crew. The Olympic Airways Airbus A310 airliner is due to land in Athens in an hour from now. Our correspondent who has been following the hijacking reports that the six members of the crew and the 123 passengers on the airline, which was on an internal flight from Athens to Crete, are all well. There is no information about the hijackers, but it is believed that they will be allowed to leave the country though their proposed destination is unknown.

Share prices in Tokyo rose sharply after the government's announcement that import restrictions are to be lifted. In brisk trading the Nikkei share index was up 25 points at the end of today's trading. The value of the dollar against the yen rose by 2.3 cents to 133.6 yen to the dollar. Sterling rates remained unchanged at 1.78 dollars to the pound.

And now to end the news, here again are the main points: 125 drug manufacturers and smugglers have been arrested in Bolivia. Storms and flooding in Europe appear to be over. Despite widespread damage to property and transport facilities, relatively few lives have been lost. The Greek airliner hijacked to Algeria is on its way back to Athens. All the passengers and crew are safe. Share prices have risen sharply in Tokyo.

And that's the end of the news from London.

(Time: 4 minutes)

▶ Listen to the news on the BBC World Service.

12.10 Giving your opinions *Composition*

A In the exam, you don't need to write a brilliant essay – all that's required is that you communicate your ideas and justify them to some extent.

Suggested answers

(These do not necessarily reflect the author's views!)

2 It would be a better world if there were no nuclear weapons because the entire world could be destroyed if someone pressed the wrong button or if a world leader went crazy.
3 Nuclear power stations are a good thing because, unlike coal-fired power stations, they do not add carbon dioxide into the environment. On the other hand, …
4 The government should change the law on drugs so that people are afraid to use them

as well as sell them, because, at the moment, it's only the dealers who are likely to be punished, not the users.

5 If a criminal has committed a very serious crime such as murder he should be sent to prison for the rest of his life with no chance of being released on parole.

6 The only solution to terrorism is to call for world action against terrorists so that there is nowhere they can be safe. If this is done, and every government enforces this law, terrorists will become outlaws in every country.

C Write your composition 'under exam conditions' – with no interruptions and no dictionary.

As the choice is so wide, there is no model composition here and you should ask someone to mark your work for you.

12.11 Exam practice   *Interview exercises*

All three parts of this section are recorded on the cassette as a 'model mock interview'. The speakers are playing the roles of 'Candidates' and 'Examiner', but as they are all native speakers this is not really what would happen in the exam – however, it may give you an idea of the kind of conversation you could have with the examiner.

Note that the Examiner does not encourage Candidates B and C to justify their ideas and seems satisfied with receiving very brief answers – consequently, the interviews don't develop into conversations. Can you suggest how Candidates B and C could have expanded on their replies?

A Record your answers. Then listen to this part of the interview on the cassette.

▶ One problem in the exam is that you don't know what you're going to be asked. However, examiners don't try to catch you out or make you feel uncomfortable – what they do is encourage you to speak and put you at your ease.

B This kind of exercise gives you a chance to speak about the kinds of things you like to read about in the paper and explain why. Each headline suggests a different field of interest. You are not expected to provide the 'right answers'.

In **B** and **C**, record your answers – keep talking for two or three minutes, if possible. Then listen to the model conversation on the cassette.

▶ In the exam, the examiner will be assessing the following aspects of your spoken English: Fluency, grammatical accuracy, pronunciation of sentences, pronunciation of individual sounds, communication skills and vocabulary.

For the complete marking scales used in the exam, see *Cambridge First Certificate Examination Practice 3* Teacher's Book.

Tapescript

Narrator: These model conversations give you an idea of the form that the examination interview takes. A: Picture Conversation.

A

Examiner: What do you think's happening in these pictures?

Candidate A: Um...yes...in the first picture...er...I see a guy in a car. He looks like he's arguing maybe with a policewoman, who perhaps is giving him...um...a ticket or...

Examiner: Why...I mean...what do you think's happened?

Candidate A: Erm...perhaps he's just been caught driving too fast – speeding...

Examiner: Mmm, good.

Candidate A: Or parking somewhere where he shouldn't. Um...

Examiner: And the other one?

Candidate A: Ah, the other picture. Um...this boy looks as though he's sad or guilty about something...um...

Examiner: Can you think of why perhaps?

Candidate A: Yeah...er...well, the conductor of the train...um...is either giving him or asking him for his ticket. Um...perhaps he didn't buy one – perhaps he's breaking the law.

Examiner: So what do you think will happen next in that case?

Candidate A: In the case of the second picture...um...I should think the conductor would take the man's name and address and...er...perhaps ask him to buy a ticket.

Examiner: Right. And in the first one?

Candidate A: Er...the first one...um...looks as though the argument's going to go on...for some time.

313

Examiner: How do you think each of the...each of the people in the photograph is feeling at this time?

Candidate A: Er...well, I think in the first picture ...the guy is very angry. I think he feels the situation is unjust. Um...second picture, it's hard to say – you see the man might be a traveller...um...a foreigner who just isn't used to being in the country so he might feel unsure...guilty...

Examiner: Right...OK, so...and which of these...of these people in these pictures do you feel that you could support in...in such a situation?

Candidate A: Um...I think I'd...I'd be able to support...er...the guy in the first picture...um...because I've been given a parking ticket many times when I've felt that it wasn't necessary to do so. Because sometimes you just cannot park anywhere...

Examiner: So you know how he feels?

Candidate A: ...and you have to park there, yeah...

Examiner: You've been there?

Candidate A: Yes, I have.

Examiner: And what could you say to...to each of them if you were actually there with them in that situation?

Candidate A: Um...I'd say, 'Try to put your case over as calmly and as sensibly as possible. Um...don't argue too much with...um...people in authority because it can get them angry and then it could go against you. Um...but try to work out the best way to solve the situation.'

Examiner: Good. And...er...do these...er...sort of things happen very often in your country?

Candidate A: Oh yes, yes, a lot of the time. Um...I've been asked...um...sometimes for instance, I'm travelling on the subway in Toronto and...er...there's so many people travelling you can't buy a ticket, so you have to just get on the train otherwise you'll miss it and then the conductor comes along and says, you know, 'Hey, where's your ticket?' And you have to try and explain and they just have to believe you, I suppose, that you're an honest person.

Examiner: Sounds as though it's the same the whole world over! Thank you very much.

Candidate A: I think so! Thank you.

(Time: 4 minutes)

B

Examiner: Can you tell me which of the articles here you'd be interested in reading?

Candidate B: Yes, I'd...read first of all the...um...the one about the prime minister dying in an air disaster.

Examiner: Right.

Candidate B: And the one about the peace talks breaking down. And possibly the one about the hurricane hitting Mexico.

Examiner: Yeah...OK, that first one about the prime minister dying in an air disaster: why would you be interested particularly in reading that?

Candidate B: Well...I think, first of all I'd want to know who the prime minister was and then, whoever it was, I think it...it would obviously be...be very important news...um...for a prime minister to be killed – very serious news.

Examiner: Right, second choice: 'Peace talks break down'.

Candidate B: Um...well, I...I'm a member of the Peace Movement and interested in that area of things so...er...obviously that would be...um ...something of interest to me immediately, of...of great concern.

Examiner: Mm. And now which was your third choice?

Candidate B: The hurricane hitting Mexico.

Examiner: Oh yes, and why are you so interested about that?

Candidate B: Well, that's really only because I...I went on holiday to Mexico once for a couple of weeks so...um...I know it a little bit and...er...I'd like to know whether that part of Mexico was affected so...Maybe a...a silly reason but that...that would have been the...

Examiner: No, understandable. If we look at the...the list of headlines here, perhaps you could just briefly tell me what you think each article is about? Now, the 'Royal baby shock'.

Candidate B: Um...I would think that was...um- ...someone who found out that the...one of the royal babies had developed some disease, something like that, some illness.

Examiner: Yes. Second one: 'Film star's guilty secret'.

Candidate B: I should imagine that's...um the discovery that a film star...or a confession that a film star has had an affair or a relationship.

Examiner: Good. '800 metre record broken'.

Candidate B: Um...that must be a...a sprinter or a runner who's broken...a sprinting record.

Examiner: Now we'll leave the next one because you've already told me about that one. Er...'Jumbo crashes in Mediterranean'.

Candidate B: Mm...that must be...er...an aeroplane disaster.

Examiner: I think so. And lastly: 'The holidays...holiday sunshine traps drivers in nationwide traffic jams'.

Candidate B: Yes, well, that must be all the people driving out to enjoy the...the good weather and...er...spending most of their time in the car.

Examiner: Mm, thanks very much.
Candidate B: Thank you.

(Time: 2 minutes 20 seconds)

C

Examiner: Could you just look at this list of cases and tell me which one...which cases you think are more serious than others?
Candidate C: Yes, right. Um...well, I think a motorist driving after dr...after drinking a whole bottle of wine is...is more serious than a motorist driving after drinking a couple of glasses of wine.
Examiner: Right.
Candidate C: And I think that a motorist parking – sorry, a motorist driving faster than the permitted maximum speed is more serious than a motorist parking on a double yellow line.
Examiner: OK. One...one other comparison.
Candidate C: Um...a gang of youths attacking an old lady and taking her purse is more serious than someone keeping your wallet which... which fell from your pocket.
Examiner: Good, now...um...why do you think...er...a motorist driving faster than the permitted maximum speed is more serious than a motorist who parks on a double yellow line?
Candidate C: Well, a motorist who drives faster than the permitted maximum speed could cause an accident in which somebody could be killed, whereas if he parks on a double yellow line it's going to cause an obstruction, and not a death.
Examiner: Mm...OK. Can you tell me, if you look at that list, um...which are the most serious cases of all there?
Candidate C: Well, I would say a group of terrorists killing one of their hostages was serious and I would say a husband killing his wife's lover was serious.
Examiner: Good. And which are the most trivial ones there, do you think?
Candidate C: Perhaps the motorist not wearing a seat belt...um...or...Let me see...Again, one I mentioned before, someone keeping a wallet which fell from your pocket.
Examiner: Right. Now, finally, I'm going to...er...ask you four of these cases, and I'm going to ask you what punishment you think should be given to...er...to someone who breaks the law in each of these cases. Now, first of all, a motorist who parks on a double yellow line, what punishment should he receive?
Candidate C: I would say...a small fine.
Examiner: Right...um...what about someone who keeps your wallet which fell from your pocket?
Candidate C: Um...I would say a small fine again.
Examiner: Mm...and a company that doesn't declare all its income from...for income tax?
Candidate C: I would say a large fine.
Examiner: And finally, what about a husband who kills his wife's lover?
Candidate C: I'd say imprisonment, depending on the case, possibly for life.
Examiner: Mm...er...what would this depend on?
Candidate C: Well, we don't know the reason he killed the wife's lover: it might have been self-defence, there might have been reasons that would mean that you would give him a lower sentence.
Examiner: OK, thank you very much.

(Time: 3 minutes 15 seconds)

12.12 *Have* and *give* — Verbs and idioms

A
Alex had ...
a quarrel with Tim   a good time   permission
a meal   a drink   a headache   his/her hair cut
a chance   a look   an interview   a good idea
the information   never been abroad
an accident   a rest   a swim   the details
a newspaper   no imagination   better be careful

Barry was having ...
a quarrel with Tim   a good time   a meal
a drink   his/her hair cut   a look
an interview   a rest   a swim

Charlie gave us ...
a good time   permission   a meal   a drink
a headache   a chance   a look   a good idea
the information   the details   a newspaper

Carol gave ...
a sigh   a good performance   his/her opinion
— AND, if an indirect object (e.g. *to her friend*) is added:
an order   permission   the information
the details

B 1 gave back = return;   2 had given up = quit, sop;   3 giving out = distribute;
4 give away = reveal;   5 gave up = surrender;   6 giving in = hand in;   7 gave in = surrender;   8 had on = wear;   9 have back = have returned;   10 having round = have as a guest/visitor.

315

13 People

13.1 It takes all sorts ... *Vocabulary*

A, C, D and **E** Record your answers.

B In this exercise there may be more than one answer that appears to be right – you should choose the 'best' one, as in the exam. Make sure that the answers you choose fit the context grammatically.
1 cheerful; 2 bad-tempered; 3 sensitive;
4 likeable; 5 sympathetic; 6 smartly;
7 jealous; 8 naughty; 9 generous;
10 forgetful; 11 self-confident; 12 spoilt;
13 stand; 14 handsome; 15 lonely;
16 anxious; 17 going out; 18 sight;
19 engaged; 20 get married; 21 best man;
22 relations; 23 anniversary; 24 rows;
25 step-father; 26 tree.

13.2 What is Dateline? *Reading*

A Some of these questions are tricky, to give you a little foretaste of what you may have to cope with in the exam.
1 B ('just as there are stars in the universe')
2 B
3 A ('only by our own experts')
4 D ('The old "school-work-early marriage" syndrome is disappearing')
5 D ('the opportunities for widening your circle were still restricted')
6 B ('making the most of the world's opportunities')
7 D ('plenty of their own friends')
8 D ('Yes, it does happen: so frequently you shouldn't be surprised')
9 D ('every week ... scores of letters')
10 C ('very thorough')

13.3 Difficult questions *Grammar*

A
1 You'd better be careful.
2 I wish I was happier / wasn't so unhappy.
3 I'd like you to use a dictionary.
4 It was you who told me to do that.
5 I suggest (that) you arrive a few minutes early.
6 It's time you did the work.

B *Suggested answers*

better AND best
You'd better take several pens to the exam, not just one.
It's better to guess the answer than to leave a blank space if you don't know.
It's best to arrive/get there early on the day of the exam.

I'd rather / prefer / like
Would you rather I did it today or tomorrow?
Would you like me to carry it for you?

wish, if only AND hope
She wishes she were/was on holiday.
I wish there were/was more time before the exam, but there isn't.
If only we knew in advance what questions would be asked!
I hope we all pass / get through / do well.

It's time
It's time to do / we did some revision.
It's time to have / we had a break.

suggest
They suggested that we did/should not worry about the exam.
What do you suggest doing / we do / we should do after it's all over?

C
1 I'd rather you didn't interrupt me when I'm speaking.
2 We suggest you phone and ask for information.
3 It's much better to be tactful than frank.
4 I'd prefer you to let me know your decision today, not tomorrow.
5 I'd rather stay at home than go out tonight.
6 I'd like you to fill in this questionnaire.
7 It's time we found out how much it's going to cost.
8 They'd better book early if they want tickets for the concert.

9 I wish I didn't have/hadn't got so much to do today.
10 If only you had told me earlier!

13.4 Synonyms *Word study*

A The meaning of the second sentence is much clearer.

B *Some suggested answers*

nice: pleasant, attractive, satisfying, friendly, likeable, agreeable
good: splendid, excellent, terrific, perfect, fine, great, marvellous, wonderful
bad: terrible, dreadful, awful
thing: object, topic, article, item, subject
like: love, appreciate, enjoy, value
dislike: hate, loathe, detest, dread, despise

large: big, enormous, huge, immense, great
small: little, tiny, unimportant
important: serious, vital, essential
intelligent: clever, bright, brainy, brilliant
interesting: exciting, entertaining, fascinating
strange: unusual, unfamiliar, odd
unpleasant: disgusting, annoying, terrible, frightening, nasty
beautiful: attractive, good-looking, pretty

C sister etc. – relations/relatives; bread, etc. – food; grass, etc. – plants; rabbit, etc. – animals/mammals; lamb, etc. – meat; bus, etc. – vehicles; house, etc. – buildings/dwellings; parrot, etc. – birds; copper, etc. – metals; breakfast, etc. – meals; autumn, etc. – seasons; suit, etc. – clothes/garments; dollar, etc. – currencies; rugby, etc. – sports/games; photography, etc. – hobbies; medicine, etc. – professions, etc. – parrot, etc. – pets; wheat, etc. – cereals; rose, etc. – flowers; ant, etc. – insects; book, etc. – publications.

13.5 'Due to a computer error ...' *Problem solving*

▶ Do this section on your own under exam conditions, leaving out the discussion in **A**. Allow 30 to 40 minutes for this.

B ▶ Many students find that it's a good idea to read the information for the Directed Writing question first of all in the exam (even though it's usually the last question) and make notes on it. Then they do all the earlier questions, before writing the paragraphs. Others prefer to leave the Directed Writing question to the end, when they know how much time they have left.
Which do you prefer?

▶ The Directed Writing task is worth 20–25% of the total marks in the Use of English paper, so if too much time is spent on it at the expense of the other questions, marks may be lost on the other questions.

Model paragraphs

```
On their first date, Andrew and Anne
may have got on reasonably well. There
isn't too great an age gap between
them and they both describe themselves
as outdoor types. The problem may have
been what to talk about. The only
interest they have in common is travel
and Anne wouldn't have enjoyed it if
Andrew talked about politics. I hope
they didn't go to a pub or a disco,
for Andrew's sake.

Although Bill and Brenda are both
extroverts, there's a ten year
difference in their ages and they
don't have much in  common. They may
have enjoyed talking about travel but
Brenda doesn't share Bill's interest
in sport. Their mutual dislike of
poetry is unlikely to have improved
their conversation much.

Colin and Carole probably got on quite
well. Of course, they don't share
exactly the same interests but they
both like reading and pop music.
Carole dislikes classical music,
though, which is a pity. They are both
shy people. Perhaps Colin is a bit old
for Carole, though. They probably
found something to say to each other
about Carole's course and Colin's job
on their first date.

Of the people described, the one I'd
most like to meet myself is Colin,
though not as a marriage partner of
course! He's quite a lot younger/older
than me but he seems a pleasant sort
of person. I'm interested in all kinds
of music and reading, as he is, but
not sport and although I dislike
poetry, I quite like watching
television and going to pubs
sometimes.
```

13.6 Using your brain   *Listening*

▶ 🖭 Do this under exam conditions, with a 20-second break between the two playings. In the exam itself you would not normally have to write down so much as here, though.

1 right-hand

2 LEFT (rational side)   RIGHT (irrational side)
   language   rhythm
   numbers   colour
   linearity   **imagination**
   analysis   **daydreaming**
   logic   space: three
   lists   dimensions
   sequencing   seeing **collections** of
                             things as a whole

3 reversed;   4 corpus callosum   successful thinking;   5 12 multiplied by 137;   6 directly above this chair in the room upstairs;   7 look to the right   visual information;   8 close their eyes;   9 do not get worse;   10 stimulation   exercise;   11 fresh air/oxygen   lifestyle;   12 Three Golden Rules: 1 in an abstract, rational way   visually;   2 both halves;   3 you can't solve a problem   just as good as.

Tapescript

Man: ...you see the human brain weighs about 1½ kilos. It contains ten to fifteen thousand million nerve cells. Now, each nerve cell can connect with any number or combination of other neurons – that's what you call a nerve cell, a neuron – the total number of possible connections, of course, is enormous. Now, if you want to type that number so you'd have...get an idea of how many combinations there are, you'd have to start by typing a one, then follow that with ten million kilometres of zeros.

   Every human brain has an unlimited potential – only a small fraction of neurons are used for...er...everyday routine tasks like eating, moving, routine work, etc. The rest are constantly available for *thought*.

   Now, our brains consist of various parts, some of which control routine functions. But the important parts that make us into those marvellous thinking machines, we like to think we are, are the two hemispheres or the two sides of the brain: the left and the right. Now, the left hemisphere controls the right half of the body, that's right, the left controls the right, and the right controls the left half. Normally, the left half of the brain is dominant.

   Now, the left side, which is known as the rational side, controls the...these functions: language, numbers, linearity, analysis, logic, lists and sequencing.

   The right side, which is known as the irrational side, sometimes people call it the artistic side of your brain, controls those things ...er...which are...well, less specific perhaps: rhythm...er...er...colour, imagination, daydreaming, space: spatial dimension, three-dimensional thought...erm...seeing collections of things as one, as a whole. One interesting thing is that left-handed people often have a dominant right hemisphere, and in this case the priorities of the things I've just mentioned are all reversed.

   The corpus callosum is very important. That's: corpus C O R P U S callosum C A L L O S U M – you should make a note of that, it's very important – that's the link between the two hemispheres in the brain and it's the key to successful thinking, linking the two parts of the brain, so you don't use them independently.

   By the way, you...you could try this experiment – you'll see the two halves being used. Ask someone two questions, one to do with numbers...er...you could say 'What's 12 multiplied by 137?', and the other one to do with space. For example, you could say, 'What piece of furniture is directly above this chair in the room upstairs?' OK? Now, while they're trying to answer the first question, that was the...the numbers one, they'll probably look to the right to prevent being distracted by visual information, and while they're trying to answer the second, that's the spatial one about what's upstairs above the chair, they'll probably look to the left. But of course, some people just close their eyes and that ruins the whole test!

   According to experts, as we get older our memories do not get worse. Er...that's just an old wives' tale. In fact, we forget things at *all* ages. Now, if you *expect* your memory to be bad or to get worse, it probably will. Lack of stimulation, brain exercise and lack of interest can mean that you forget things more easily. Lack of concentration simply. Ah, lack of fresh air can also lead to your brain being less efficient because it gets starved of oxygen, and an unhealthy lifestyle – take note – can also damage your brain: er...alcohol, smoke, um...pollutants in the air like lead, er...chemicals in food, they can all add to a generally deteriorating condition of the brain.

You've probably heard a lot of people say, 'I'm not brainy' or 'That's too difficult for my brain' – but this is not true because everyone's brain has an equal potential.

There are a few rules – Golden Rules of brain power. One: use your senses. Don't only think in an abstract, logical way. Try to imagine a problem visually. Second rule: use both halves of your brain. For example, if you're faced with...er...an abstract, logical problem, try thinking about it imaginativ...er ...try thinking about it imaginatively. Or if you're faced with a creative problem, try to analyse it. Think logically about it. And don't ever say you *can't* solve a problem because your brain is just as good as anyone else's.

(Time: 5 minutes 45 seconds)

13.7 Chapter One *Reading*

A 1 A 2 C 3 C 4 B 5 C 6 C
7 A 8 A 9 C 10 D

B A description of the stranger:
The stranger seems very nervous as though he is scared of the writer. He is wrapped up in his own thoughts and rather unwilling to talk to the writer. He is smartly dressed, has small pale well-manicured hands and a charming smile. His teeth are like broken rocks.

13.8 Exam practice *Passage with gaps*

In the exam, this kind of exercise is more likely to be a story than a description.
1 about; 2 an; 3 of; 4 In; 5 of;
6 from; 7 in; 8 out; 9 without;
10 one; 11 being; 12 her; 13 rather;
14 very/extremely/terribly, etc.; 15 that;
16 marriage; 17 gets/receives/has; 18 like;
19 life; 20 relations/relatives/acquaintances/colleagues.

▶ Where more than one answer makes sense and fits grammatically, you do get a mark for whichever one you choose, even if one of them is 'better' in the context. However, you should never write more than one word in each gap.

13.9 Five students *Listening*

A In this exercise there is a great deal of writing to do and it is NOT a 'typical exam exercise'.

Tapescript

Chris: Barbara, before you go, could you tell me about these students who are coming into my class?
Barbara: Oh, yes. Now, let me think, well there's ...er...Paul. He's...er...he's the tall slim...slim lad with fair hair. Very...very friendly face, lovely smile...He's...er...particularly good with group activities, he's a very helpful person to have in

	Appearance	Good points	But be careful!
PAUL	Tall, slim, fair hair, friendly face, lovely smile	Helpful, speaks fluently, interesting ideas	Makes mistakes, speaks first and thinks later
SUSAN	Dark hair, dark eyes	Lively, quick, bright	Doesn't always talk in English, sometimes talks too much
MARIA	(Susan's sister) Looks similar but longer hair and plumper*	Sensible	Sulks when she makes mistakes, feels inferior to Susan
HELEN	Pretty, nice smile	Good written work, laughs at jokes	Shy – needs encouragement – own little world
PETER	Older, moustache, glasses, wavy dark brown hair, jacket or suit	Takes notes, serious, determined to learn	Asks difficult questions

* plump = rather fat

the class and very helpful with the other students. He...er...speaks fluently, but does make a lot of mistakes! Doesn't seem to mind making mistakes, mind you. He asks a lot of questions...er...tends to speak first and think later, he's a bit impetuous. But he's got lots of interesting ideas.
Chris: Good.
Barbara: Er...Susan...Susan. Now, she's very lively, quick, very bright. Now she talks all the time but not always in English.
Chris: What, is she difficult or anything?
Barbara: N...no...She's quite young but she does behave in quite a grown-up way really for her age. She...ah...it can be a bit difficult to actually shut her up sometimes and make her listen to you but she's...er...
Chris: Ah, right.
Barbara: She's...er...very nice. And she's...um... what does she look like? Just as...yes, she's dark hair, dark eyes.
Chris: Right, well...er...is there...any other girls in the...
Barbara: Yes, there's Maria, that's Susan's sister.
Chris: Yes.
Barbara: Actually, it's quite difficult to tell them apart although...er...Maria is slightly older. She's a bit...a bit plumper and has longer hair...than Susan. Er...she's not quite as bright as her sister and I think that makes her feel a bit inferior really. Well, you know, she sulks a bit when she gets things wrong or if she misunderstands you. But on the whole, very sensible girl.
Chris: OK.
Barbara: Then there's, oh, Helen. Er...
Chris: Er...Helen, Helen, Helen, Helen.
Barbara: Yes, she's very very pretty with a...with a nice smile and she's...but she...she's quite ...quite shy and quiet, so you have to sort of ...encourage her a bit. And she's very bright. Er...does tend to seem...well, she seems a bit wrapped up in her own little world but the...er ...written work she does shows that she's learning a lot. Oh, she laughs at my jokes, too.
Chris: Oh, hope she laughs at mine!
Barbara: Yes. And then there's Peter, who's older than the others. He's sort of...um...a bit more distinguished, he's got sort of moustache and spectacles and wavy dark brown hair. And he usually wears a jacket and sometimes a suit. Very smart and very...takes notes all the time and very serious and determined to learn as much as possible. He also...
Chris: Oh, soon put a stop to that!
Barbara: Ah, but he asks quite difficult questions. He doesn't...doesn't mean to be nasty but if you're not careful, he can catch you out.

Chris: Well, thanks, Barbara. It's all up to me now, isn't it? Have a good holiday, won't you?
Barbara: Thanks.
Chris: Bye.

(Time: 2 minutes 30 seconds)

C Look at the photo in Activity 38 and record a description of the people there. Listen to your recording. Then look at Activity 49 and perhaps do the same!

13.10 Describing people *Composition*

A Although the first paragraph is probably the most interesting to read, perhaps the second is more the kind of paragraph that you should write in the exam – writing long complex sentences often leads to errors.

Instead of repeating 'He' so much, giving the person a name would reduce the dullness of the second and even the third paragraphs.

B *Model paragraphs*

(Many variations are possible.)

```
He is a slightly overweight man in his
mid-thirties. He is terribly selfish
and even dishonest but his worst
feature is that he loses his temper
whenever people disagree with him.

She is a very thin lady in her late
fifties. She does tend to be rather
absent-minded but she has a delightful
sense of humour and is always ready to
help other people with their problems.

He is 18 years old and very athletic.
He really loves sport and his
favourite game is football. In his
spare time he enjoys going out with
his friends and particularly going to
the cinema.

She is 16 years old and a very
studious young woman, who enjoys
reading. She has four brothers and two
sisters. When she leaves school, she
hopes to go to university, where she
wants to study engineering.
```

C There are model compositions for the first three topics only, as the details of the fourth depend on a particular book.

Model compositions

I remember the first time I met Tim. He was sitting on a bench in the park, looking very depressed and cold. He hadn't got a coat on and it had started to rain. Normally, I don't think I'd have stopped to speak to a complete stranger who looked like that - not that he looked like a tramp or anything: his shoes were well polished and his clothes were quite smart. But on an impulse I stopped walking and said to him, 'Are you OK?' in a sympathetic voice. He said he was but I sat down beside him and he started telling me how his wife had just locked him out of the house after a row and so he was sitting in the rain waiting for her to calm down and let him in again. I suggested that we went somewhere warm and dry, so we found a nearby café and continued our conversation. And that was how I met Tim - the man who was later to become my worst enemy.

48 West Green Lane
Brompton
Herts   England

17 May 19##

Dear Maria,

As this is my first letter to you, let me begin by introducing myself: my name's Susan Underwood and I live with my parents in a detached house in Brompton, which is a little town about 40 km north of London.

I have curly fair hair, blue eyes and a round freckled face. I'm quite tall and a bit overweight at the moment! I enjoy listening to classical music and going to the cinema. Of course I also watch TV - especially the old movies they have on.

I'm still at college and I'm studying for a diploma in hotel management at Brompton Technical College. If I pass my final exams next summer, I hope to get a job somewhere abroad for a year to get experience of foreign hotels and learn a useful foreign language. I'm really looking forward to starting work, even though the course I'm doing is excellent.

That's about all I can think of to tell you about myself. Do write back and tell me all about yourself. I'll write again soon.

Yours truly,

The two people I admire most are my aunt and uncle. They are my mother's sister and her husband and they have a small farm in the country about 200 km from where I live.

My aunt is quite tall, she has wavy black hair and wears glasses. She has a round, friendly face and smiles quietly to herself while she's working - even when she's cooking or washing up! She has two children, who are two and four years old. Amazingly, she is able to look after them and do all her work in the home and on the farm and she never, never loses patience or gets cross. That's what I admire in her.

Her husband is quite a short man with attractive brown eyes who always behaves charmingly even when people are not pleasant to him. He's busy every day of the week from morning till evening. Whenever I go to visit them he encourages me to help with the work, and with him even routine jobs seem fun. That's what I admire about him - he makes work seem a pleasure.

13.11 That's a problem! *Interview exercises*

B Look at Activity 31 and record what you would say to someone who had this problem. Then do the same with the problems in Activities 36 and 50.

13.12 Grammar revision *Exam practice*

A Question 4 is particularly tricky – in the exam there are often one or two questions in this kind of exercise which are difficult or where there are hidden difficulties.

1 It's important/essential/necessary to be more polite to people.
2 The letter (that) she wrote (to) me said (that) she never wanted to see me again.
3 He's such a dull person that people fall asleep while he's talking.
4 In spite of her father's wealth he doesn't want to marry her. / In spite of her being the daughter of a rich man, he doesn't want to marry her.
5 If you don't write to him you'll lose touch with him.

6 She told me (that) she was leaving and (that she was) never coming back.
7 Her brother is much less amusing than her. / Her brother isn't anything like as amusing as she is.
8 They have known each other for ten years.
9 While her husband was away, she was very lonely.
10 Everyone still seems to like him although he's a liar and a cheat.

B *Suggested answers*

1 you feeling all right?
2 do you feel / are you depressed?
3 is the problem with him?
4 you persuade them to stop arguing / to make up their differences?
5 does that make matters worse / do you find that so annoying?
6 long has he been staying with you?
7 long is he going to stay?
8 does he do / do you mean?
9 put up with it!
10 come round to my place / share my room / spend the evenings with me while your uncle is staying.

14 The past

▶ If you are doing Papers 4 and/or 5 some time before you do the written papers, make sure you are prepared for these by starting this unit at 14.10 or 14.13.

14.1 Vocabulary and grammar — *Reading comprehension*

▶ The first part of Paper 1 in the exam consists of 25 questions on vocabulary, grammar and usage.

1 C 2 A 3 B 4 B 5 B 6 A 7 C
8 B 9 A 10 D 11 A 12 A 13 B
14 D 15 B 16 C 17 A 18 D 19 A
20 B 21 A 22 A 23 D 24 B 25 B

▶ In the exam, you should spend about 25 minutes on this exercise. Each question is worth one mark (total 25 marks), but the questions based on the passages are worth two marks each (total 30 marks).

14.2 1900 — *Reading comprehension*

1 B 2 D 3 B 4 C 5 A

14.3 The Lost Viking Capital — *Reading comprehension*

1 D 2 A 3 C 4 A 5 C 6 A 7 A
8 D 9 D 10 D

14.4 Under exam conditions — *Composition – 1½ hours*

B Ask someone to mark your compositions. Ask them to point out what particular points you should be careful about in the exam.
- What are your typical 'careless mistakes' of spelling and grammar that you should notice when checking your work?
- Decide now what types of questions you feel more confident about (e.g. writing an informal letter or a narrative) and which you feel less confident about.

14.5 Fill the gaps — *Use of English*

1 less; 2 spend; 3 sister; 4 mention;
5 myself; 6 provided/providing;

7 company/protection; 8 distance;
9 scared/frightened; 10 behind; 11 seen/observed; 12 another; 13 upside;
14 down/along; 15 through; 16 barking;
17 trying/managing; 18 share; 19 promise;
20 case.

14.6 Grammar revision *Use of English*

A The advice about checking for mistakes is equally valid for the Directed Writing exercise – and the other exercises in Paper 3.

Mistakes corrected

1 **Careless mistakes and slips of the pen:**
   A The castle contain**s** many treasures and paintings.
   B I wonder **which** of the **mistakes** is most **serious**.
   C My brother and sister **have** brown eyes but my eyes **are** blue.
   D Could you tell me what time **it opens**?
   E Who **paid** for the ticket?

2 **Mistakes that are harder to notice:**
   A After visiting the museum he **didn't/did not have** very much time left.
   B His hair is very long, it's time for him to **have it cut**.
   C I **have been** waiting for you **for** four hours.
   D They **had** never visited Rome before their first visit in 1987.
   E She **has never written** a letter by hand since she **bought** a word processor.
   F I **have been** learning English **for** five years.
   G A **suspicious person / suspect** is **being questioned** by the police.
   H Before they **went** out they had been **watching** the news on TV.

B
1 During your holiday I'll be busy working.
2 It's ages since I saw my old school friend.
3 I hadn't been to / visited North America before.
4 The Pyramids were built by the ancient Egyptians.
5 Soon she'll have to give up her job.
6 We found out that the office was closed due to illness.
7 We managed to reach the top of the hill in spite of the heat / although it was hot.
8 By the time you arrive, I'll be ready.
9 You shouldn't / oughtn't to have put so much salt in the soup.
10 It's so salty (that) I can't eat it now.

14.7 Word-building revision *Use of English*

A 1 impatience; 2 unselfishness/selflessness; 3 replacement;
4 irresponsibly; 5 unemployment;
6 encouraged; 7 disagreeing;
8 sharpening.

B 1 unpredictable; 2 unforgettable;
3 daily; 4 photographic; 5 probability;
6 certainty; 7 likelihood; 8 memorable;
9 unfashionable; 10 difficulty.

14.8 Unusual exercises *Use of English*

A 1 made it up; 2 make do with;
3 done up; 4 made off with; 5 done;
6 making for.

B 1 title; 2 margin; 3 index;
4 columns; 5 volumes; 6 bookmark.

C 1 fortnight; 2 dozens; 3 doubled;
4 fifth; 5 quarter; 6 century.

14.9 Problem solving / Directed writing *Use of English*

A and B Under exam conditions, this exercise should take 35 minutes or so, including time for planning and checking.
  In this kind of Directed Writing exercise, there is not necessarily a 'best solution'. In this case, there are certainly equally valid reasons why the Meiers should go to York or to Cambridge. The model answer below is 130

words long, rather longer than required according to the instructions in **B**.

Model answer

```
I think the Meiers would enjoy
spending Sunday in Cambridge, because
the two-hour journey to York would
take four hours out of their day. I
know this would disappoint Richard,
but never mind.
     Once in Cambridge Helen would
enjoy seeing the paintings in the
Fitzwilliam Museum and Kettle's Yard,
but this would not appeal to her
father. I think Helen and her mother,
who isn't a keen walker, should
concentrate on the museums before
lunch, while Richard and his father go
for a walk beside the river and walk
through the old colleges. They could
meet for lunch, perhaps in a pub by
the river, and after lunch hire a boat
on the river before going together to
admire King's College Chapel and then
catching the train back to London.
```

14.10　I remember … *Listening comprehension*

Follow this procedure for the listening exercises in this unit:
1 Read the questions.
2 Listen to the recording for the first time, answering the questions you can manage.
3 Listen to the recording again for the answers you missed out.
4 Check your answers carefully.

1 C 2 C 3 C 4 A 5 B 6 D 7 A
8 B 9 D 10 C

Tapescript

Liz: I remember when I was very little, about three or four, my brother used to take me to the local playground. He was a bit older than me. And he used to look after me while I went on the swings and, you know, the slide and things. Well, one afternoon I went out with him after tea and I was sitting on one of the swings with my teddy bear and I was swinging away and talking to Teddy, you see, when it gradually dawned on me that I was all alone and that my brother had left me by myself and there was no one else in the playground at all. And it was starting to get dark. Then – ooh, I can remember it, it sends shivers down my spine even now – I saw this big fierce dog sniffing around the swings a...and as I was going backwards and forwards it started to bark at me. Well, first I sort of, you know, tried to be terribly brave and I wanted to make it go away so I shouted at it and it took no notice and started, you know, jumping up at me and trying to bite, well not me, but I think it was my teddy bear. Well, I started to cry and scream and got in a terrible state sort of trying to climb up the swing and...and no one came and it was getting darker and darker. And...er...oh, I was in such a state. Well, eventually I saw my Dad running towards me waving a big stick and shouting at the dog and he chased the dog away and took me in his arms and I...I clung onto him and he held...held me and I cried and cried and cried until eventually I suppose I stopped. Well, I never saw the dog again but I always made sure that, you know, after that there were other people in the playground when I went. And well, of course, later I realised that my brother hadn't abandoned me to be eaten by this dog. I suppose he must have run back home to fetch my father and...and er...I suppose he must have been very frightened too. But he obviously felt very responsible for me and he ran home to get help. But since then...whew...I've always been so careful with dogs and I've never trusted them.

(Time: 1 minute 50 seconds)

14.11　The slave trade *Listening comprehension*

TRUE: 2, 4, 5, 6, 7, 9, 10, 12, 13, 16, 17, 18; FALSE: 1, 3, 8, 11, 14, 15.

Tapescript

Presenter: Good afternoon. We have with us Professor Nicholson, who is the author of a new book on the slave trade and he's going to tell us something about it. Professor Nicholson.

Professor: Thank you. Well, first of all I think I ought to clear up a bit of a misunderstanding. People normally mean when they talk about the slave trade the buying of Africans from other Africans by Europeans for sale to other Europeans. But of course, there are much wider implications. You see, slavery seems to have existed in many societies at all times in history – perhaps it always will. You see, even today there are people in some countries, who can't officially be described as slaves but who are still slaves in all but name.

324

Presenter: Can you tell us a little bit about the origins of the first African slaves?

Professor: Yes, indeed. The...the first African slaves were brought to Portugal by the Portuguese in 1434 and the Portuguese in fact dominated the slave trade right up until the...er...18th century. After the establishment of colonies in Brazil, slaves were shipped over there to work in the plantations, particularly in the 17th century. And also, of course, the English needed slaves for their plantations in the West Indies. And by 1700 the trade was dominated by England and, of course, by France. Then, in the 18th century six million slaves were shipped across the Atlantic because the...the colonies in North America depen... depended on slave labour to produce the sugar crops and tobacco and cotton and so forth for the...for the European market. Altogether...er... the...the estimate is that about ten million people were sent from Africa, but of course, not all arrived and certainly not all survived for very long even if they did arrive safely.

Presenter: What were the conditions like?

Professor: Well, aboard ship, of course, the conditions were absolutely unspeakable, absolutely unspeakable. You see, on some ships only a handful of people arrived alive.

Presenter: Mm, and in the plantations?

Professor: Well, the conditions there were equally horrible. In fact they were so bad that many of the slaves only survived for a few years. Gradually, of course there...there grew up a movement in Europe – Wilberforce and so on – a...a...against the slave trade but it...it wasn't until 1809 that English ships finally stopped taking slaves from Africa to North America and the West Indies.

Presenter: And when were they actually set free?

Professor: Well in the...in the Americas they weren't set free until...er...quite a bit later on. 1833 in the British colonies and then 1865 in the USA. But of course, before that many slave owners did set their own slaves free of their own accord. In fact...in fact it's interesting, in 1822 in West Africa a state was...um...was set up for slaves who were in fact freed and sent back there and of course the...er...the state has the name Liberia, which is quite apt, isn't it?

Presenter: Yes, indeed. Professor, I'm sorry, I'll have to stop you there because we're out of time. But thank you very much for talking to us.

Professor: Thank you.

(Time: 3 minutes 5 seconds)

14.12 Gipsy signs *Listening comprehension*

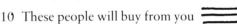

1 Beware of the dog
2 Fierce dog
3 Friendly people
4 Friendly, generous people
5 Very friendly, generous people
6 Work to be had here
7 Gipsies not liked
8 Nothing to be had
9 Work available with good pay
10 These people will buy from you
11 This place has been robbed

Tapescript

Guide: ...and the gipsies also had a whole system of communications of...of...way of communicating with each other as well. When they went from house to house around the country they left behind chalk marks on the wall...um...and these were messages for any other gipsies who came along later. Now, these signs were useful because, for one thing, many gipsies were illiterate in those days but also the signs couldn't be understood by the country people, they were only intelligible to the gipsies themselves.

Now, I'll show you some of the signs, I'll draw them on this board. Now, if there was a dog at the house then they used this sign, see: a triangle. If it was a fierce dog then they put a horizontal line through the triangle like this. If the people in the house were friendly, then they'd draw a circle, like so.

Now, what do you think this one meant? This is a circle with a dot in the middle. Now, I wonder what that meant?

Man: Angry? Angry neighbours?

Guide: No, no, no. It meant 'friendly and generous people'. Now, what about this? This is a circle with a dot in the middle and a line underneath and this meant 'very friendly and very generous people'. Now, this one, this is a circle with a horizontal line through it and this meant 'work to be had here'.

Now, if a house was known to be unfriendly, then they would leave a sign like this, this is a vertical line with two horizontal lines and that meant 'gipsies not liked', so they could steer clear of that one. Now, I wonder what you think about this one? This is a very common one: it's a cross made with one vertical line and one horizontal line. What... what do you think that might have meant?

Woman: No idea.

Guide: Any ideas? It meant 'nothing to be had' at this house, so again they could...er...they could go on by and not waste their time knocking on the door. Um...here's another one. This is a circle with two horizontal lines and...er...probably fairly uncommon in those days, this one meant 'work available and good pay'. So they'd obviously stop there. Er, now, three horizontal lines – any ideas what that might be? No? Now, this was a very hopeful sign for a gipsy because this meant 'these people will buy from you' so it would be well worth your time stopping by here. Now, here's the last one: three slanting lines, like this. Anyone care to guess? This was a very important one for the gipsies. Three slanting lines means 'don't stop here because this place has been robbed'...

(Time: 3 minutes 15 seconds)

14.13 A long time ago ... *Interview exercises*

▶ If possible, ask someone else (preferably an English-speaking person) to play the role of 'examiner' in **A**, **B** and **C**. If you are working on your own, record your answers to the questions.

B In the exam, you won't be asked 'comprehension questions' during the Interview, but may be asked to react to the content of the text.

C In the exam, the examiner might ask questions like these to 'get you talking' – they aren't intended to test your knowledge about the particular subject.

(1066 – Norman Conquest and Battle of Hastings; 1588 – Spanish Armada)

14.14 Last minute advice

Before the exam takes place, go through the exercises you have done in *Progress to First Certificate* and try the more difficult ones again.

To get more practice in doing exam-style questions, use *Cambridge First Certificate Examination Practice 3*.

In the exam ...
 DON'T spend too long on any one question.
 DON'T worry when there are any words or questions you don't understand.
 DON'T panic if time seems to be short.
And ...
 DO read all the instructions carefully.
 DO make notes.
 DO check all your written work for mistakes.

Good luck!

Leo Jones

Notes

Notes

Notes